HARDEN'S

Hotel Guide
2004

Other Harden's titles

UK Restaurants
London Restaurants
Good Cheap Eats in London
London Bars & Pubs
London Food Shops
London for Free
London Baby Book
London Party Guide

The ideal corporate gift

Harden's Hotel Guide, *Harden's London Restaurants*, *Harden's UK Restaurants* and *Harden's London Bars & Pubs* are available in a range of specially customised corporate gift formats.

For further information on any of the above, please call (020) 7839 4763 or visit www.hardens.com.

© Harden's Limited 2003

ISBN 1-873721-55-2

British Library Cataloguing-in-Publication data:
a catalogue record for this book is available from
the British Library.

Printed and bound in Italy by
Legoprint

Production Manager: Elizabeth Warman

Harden's Limited
14 Buckingham Street
London WC2N 6DF

CONTENTS

PRICES

The General Rule

Prices given in this guide are the best indication we can obtain of the tariff for the least expensive **double room** in mid-season, on a room-only (or room and breakfast) basis, inclusive of VAT and any service charge.

* An asterisk next to the price indicates some qualification to this general rule, usually that the price is on a Dinner, Bed and Breakfast (DB&B) basis – see the text of the entry concerned for details.

Why prices must be treated with caution

We think it is helpful to include prices, but we do so with the following reservations:

• Even published tariff prices can sometimes change both by the day of the week and the season.

• You can often spend much more than our basic price (and may have to do so if basic accommodation happens not to be available).

• Leisure (and weekend) travellers should always enquire about special rates/packages. Savvy travellers (especially in cities) often pay less, and sometimes very much less, than the published tariff.

• In current market conditions, a few hotels (especially in New York) have abandoned published tariffs altogether.

In these circumstances, the prices we quote can only be a general indication. If you have time, you should always check out the tariff of the hotel concerned (often available on the web) before booking. Depending on your skills as a negotiator, you may – subject to market forces at the time – be able to get a better deal than our figures would suggest.

VAT

Some superior hotels, especially in London, quote prices ex-VAT, and sometimes don't point this out to telephone enquirers. This practice appears to us to be thoroughly misleading. The cautious traveller will clearly wish to check that VAT is included in prices quoted. If, however, an establishment seeks to 'spring' a previously unmentioned VAT charge on top of a previously quoted price, it would appear to us that you would be well within your rights to refuse to pay it: if the hotelier fails to mention that he intends to charge you 17.5% more than he said, that is his problem, not yours.

RATINGS

Our rating system is unlike those found in other guides (which generally tell you nothing more helpful that that expensive establishments are, as a general rule, better than cheap ones).

Our system indicates the overall level of satisfaction noted by reporters. A modest inn which does what it does well may be rated just as highly as the grandest 'five-star' establishment.

Satisfaction ratings

☺☺☺ **Exceptional**
Almost all reports very positive

☺☺ **Very good**
Most reports notably positive

☺ **Good**
Most reports mainly positive

☺ **Variable**
A perceptible proportion of reports (often around a quarter) less than satisfactory

☹ **Poor**
At least one report in three is less than satisfactory.

T **A 'tip'**
An establishment strongly recommended, but only on limited feedback –
we especially invite further reports on such establishments.

N **A newcomer**
An establishment which opened too late to figure in the survey (or which has moved into new ownership since the survey).

SMALL PRINT

Rooms: the number of rooms is given for all establishments. If non-smoking rooms or family/inter-connecting rooms are available, further details are provided.

Facilities: the following are noted if they are available at the property itself – indoor pool; outdoor pool; gym; spa; golf; tennis.

Other details (noted as applicable): Seasonal closures; Major restrictions on times of food service not evident from text; Restrictions on the use of credit cards (if nothing is mentioned, you can assume an establishment takes Visa, Mastercard, American Express and Switch); Minimum age for children.

HOW THIS BOOK IS ORGANISED

This directory is divided into the following sections:

- Great Britain (except London) & Ireland

- London

- New York

- Paris

The Great Britain & Ireland section is organised alphabetically by place name, without any divisions between England, Wales, Scotland, Northern Ireland and the Republic of Ireland. In country areas, you will generally find it easiest to start with the map of the relevant region at the back of the book, which will guide you to the appropriate place names.

PHOTOGRAPHS

We have included photographs of certain establishments which were able to supply us with suitable material for publication. *We have made no charge for including these photographs.*

WHY THIS GUIDE IS DIFFERENT

This book is the result of a unique co-operative research effort involving nearly 2,500 'reporters'. These are 'ordinary' travellers who have shared with us some 10,000 reports of the best (and the worst) of their recent accommodation experiences. This range of information enables us to identify key places to stay and to assess how good they are in a way which no guide has previously attempted.

The reports submitted to us together named some 2000 establishments, but coverage in this guide has been whittled down to a little less than half of that – see further opposite.

In analysing feedback, we have adopted an essentially statistical approach broadly similar to our restaurant guides, but paying particular regard to the proportion of reporters expressing dissatisfaction about each establishment.

HOW YOU CAN JOIN THE SURVEY

Register – at www.hardens.com or by writing to us – and you will be invited to participate in our next survey. **If you take part you will, on publication, receive a complimentary copy of *Harden's Hotel Guide 2005*.**

FROM THE EDITORS

Over a dozen years, Harden's has gained considerable experience in producing independent survey-driven guides to restaurants – initially in London, and for the last five years also across the UK.

The backbone of our approach is the rigorous analysis of reports from interested consumers rather than reliance on so-called expert inspectors. Its key strength is that it produces an unbiased overview of the practical issues of concern to 'real' consumers.

This is our first foray into the world of hotels. It is, we believe, the first new hotel guide in the UK to have been published in recent times which is both independent of the hotels and comprehensive.

The importance of independence cannot be emphasised too strongly. Most hotel guides, including those published by the motoring organisations, are – to an extent which might well surprise the uninformed reader – little more than 'advertorial'. Their content is often more notable not for what is included but for what is left out (which is pretty much anything in the way of criticism). The business reality of the paid-for inspections approach is that such guides just can't afford to say that an hotel is bad, or even mediocre. (This presumably explains the long-standing popularity of 'star' systems, based on facilities *not* quality.)

Adopting the same 'warts and all' approach as our restaurant guides, our write-ups tend to include the drawbacks noted in reports as well as praise for the good points. What's more, we have included some much commented-on establishments upon which reporters' overall views were not especially positive. People sometimes wonder why we do so. There are three answers. The first is that a guide should be as comprehensive as possible – you may well want to visit a particular town, whether its hotels are any good or not. The second is that some bad hotels have 'big' names – a warning can sometimes be much more valuable than a recommendation. And the third is that it means that when we write our reviews we are under no pressure, even subliminally, to suggest that everything in every garden is rosy – when we all know life just isn't like that!

This book, too, will no doubt have its faults and – as the first edition of a new guide – perhaps especially so. Would you like to help us improve it? **Take part in our next survey, and you will earn yourself a free copy of the next edition.** Details of how to sign-up are given opposite.

Richard Harden   **Peter Harden**

A WORD ON GROUPS

This guide started with no 'view' on the virtues of chain establishments (as opposed to those individually owned and run). We simply asked reporters, without any preconceptions, to tell them about hotels which had pleased them (and those which hadn't).

Patterns do, of course, emerge, and it will not surprise many people to know that hotels forming part of the bigger chains did not for the most part emerge especially favourably from the survey. Even such brands usually turn out to have the occasional 'star', though, and in many under-served towns and cities they provide the only hotel(s) of any note.

It does seem to be true – at the most general level – that group size and quality are inversely related. Such names as Crowne Plaza, De Vere, Hilton, Meridien and Thistle are rarely associated by reporters with particular quality (particularly when such groups purport to run 'character' properties).

Some large groups emerged not entirely without credit. Marriott hotels, for example, often seem – other things being equal – to be a better bet than the other chains, but the name still falls far short of being the guarantee of consistent quality one might hope for from, say, a branded consumer product.

The chain most represented in this guide is the 'hidden giant', Macdonald Hotels which owns many historic properties which trade under their individual names. Sadly, the burden of much of reporters' commentary was to the effect that the group's method of operation often robs its hotels of much of their instrinsic appeal. Even here, though, there are some worthwhile properties.

Smaller groups are making a major contribution in the transformation – for the better – of hotels in UK and Ireland. Groups which include some commendable properties – some of which are growing fast – include Alias (and the related Luxury Family Hotels), Arcadian, Brend (a West Country chain), City Inn, Hotels du Vin, Malmaison, Marston, Rocco Forte Hotels and Von Essen (which is snapping up many top-end country houses).

It is particularly at what – to use a restaurant analogy – one might call the PizzaExpress end of the market that chains should have much to offer. The survey's conclusions about the major budget groups are summarised opposite.

THE 'BUDGET' GROUPS

Britons have long complained about the absence of clean and inexpensive places simply to lay their heads for the night when travelling. The arrival of the budget chains, which has gathered pace over the past decade, has therefore been a welcome development.

The four main chains, in descending order of size, are Travel Inn, Travelodge, Premier Lodge and Holiday Inn Express. In descending order of quality – and there is a pretty clear 'pecking order' – reporters rate them as follows:

Premier Lodge

(08702) 010203, www.premierlodge.co.uk
Amazingly, "Premier Lodge" really does seem to mean roughly what it says! Reporters were very complimentary about this 130-strong chain (which is owned by Scottish & Newcastle), often using such words as "nice", "excellent" and "friendly". If you're looking for "exceptional value" in this sector, this is the first group to turn to.

Travel Inn

(0870) 242 8000, www.travelinn.co.uk
This Whitbread-owned chain is by far the largest in terms of the number of rooms (over 15,000). It gave rise to somewhat polarised, but overall reasonably favourable, commentary as a provider of "good", if "basic", accommodation. Some properties have particularly useful city-centre locations.

Holiday Inn Express

(0800) 434040, www.holidayinnexpress.co.uk
Though not quite as good overall, commentary was broadly similar to that on Travel Inn. Quite a proportion of reporters seem to think that staying here is at least a "predictable" proposition.

Travelodge

(0870) 085 0950, www.travelodge.co.uk
The successor to an organisation originally founded by Forte in 1985 (acquired in 2003 by an investment fund) suffers from some ageing properties. Though some reporters are content with the "good-value basic accommodation", the proportion finding staying at this chain an "awful" – and, in particular, "sterile" – experience was notably higher than its competitors.

Note: we occasionally list individual branches of the above groups, where the property concerned attracts a notable volume of support in its own right.

GREAT BRITAIN & IRELAND

Comments in "double quotation-marks" were made by reporters

RECOMMENDATIONS & SURVEY RESULTS

The very best places to stay in Great Britain & Ireland

Up to £100

The Fox Inn *(Lower Oddington)*
The Griffin Inn *(Fletching)*
Inn at Whitewell *(Clitheroe)*
Lavenham Priory *(Lavenham)*
Monachyle Mhor *(Balquhidder)*
Pen y Dyffryn *(Oswestry)*
Plas Bodegroes *(Pwllheli)*
Raemoir House *(Banchory)*
Star Inn *(Harome)*

Over £100

Calcot Manor *(Tetbury)*
Castell Deudraeth *(Portmeirion)*
Chewton Glen *(New Milton)*
Dromoland Castle *(Newmarket-on-Fergus, ROI)*
Hotel du Vin and Bistro *(Bristol)*
Fairyhill *(Reynoldston)*
Four Seasons *(Dublin, ROI)*
Parknasilla *(Sneem, ROI)*
Holbeck Ghyll *(Windermere)*
Kinnaird *(Dunkeld)*
Manoir aux Quat' Saisons *(Great Milton)*
The Nare *(Veryan)*
Portmeirion *(Portmeirion)*
Samling *(Windermere)*
Sharrow Bay *(Ullswater)*
The Witchery by the Castle *(Edinburgh)*

Note: For London, see separate section starting on p. 276

Good places to stay – £100 or less

Apex City *(Edinburgh)*	☺☺
Ardanaiseig Hotel *(Taynuilt)*	☺☺
The Beeches *(Norwich)*	☺☺
Beechleas *(Wimborne Minster)*	☺☺
Beechwood Country House *(Moffat)*	☺☺
Borough *(Edinburgh)*	☺☺
Bryn Derwen *(Llangollen)*	☺☺
By Appointment *(Norwich)*	☺☺
Cally Palace *(Gatehouse of Fleet)*	☺☺
Castleman *(Blandford Forum)*	☺☺
Churchill Arms *(Paxford)*	☺☺
City Inn *(Glasgow)*	☺☺
Clytha Arms *(Abergavenny)*	☺☺
Crossways *(Polegate)*	☺☺
Cubley Hall *(Penistone)*	☺☺
Falkland Arms *(Great Tew)*	☺☺
Feathers *(Ledbury)*	☺☺
Felin Fach Griffin *(Brecon)*	☺☺
The Fox Inn *(Lower Oddington)*	☺☺☺
The George *(Inveraray)*	☺☺
Glen Rothay *(Ambleside)*	☺☺
Glenfield House *(Edinburgh)*	☺☺
Grand *(Tynemouth)*	☺☺
Great House *(Lavenham)*	☺☺
The Griffin Inn *(Fletching)*	☺☺☺
Hallgarth Manor *(Durham)*	☺☺
Hassop Hall *(Bakewell)*	☺☺
Barcelona *(Exeter)*	☺☺
Hotel du Vin et Bistro *(Tunbridge Wells)*	☺☺
La Place *(Jersey)*	☺☺
Hougue du Pommier *(Guernsey)*	☺☺
Ibis *(Edinburgh)*	☺☺
11 Didsbury Park *(Manchester)*	☺☺
Inn at Whitewell *(Clitheroe)*	☺☺☺
Ivy House Farm *(Lowestoft)*	☺☺
Kandinsky *(Cheltenham)*	☺☺
Kings Arms *(Berwick-upon-Tweed)*	☺☺
Kirkstone Pass Inn *(Ambleside)*	☺☺
The Lamb Inn *(Burford)*	☺☺
Lavenham Priory *(Lavenham)*	☺☺☺
Leeming House *(Penrith)*	☺☺
Little Barwick House *(Barwick)*	☺☺

Loch Melfort *(Arduaine)* ☺☺
Lord Nelsons House *(Oakham)* ☺☺
Lugger *(Truro)* ☺☺
Malmaison *(Glasgow)* ☺☺
The Malt House *(Chipping Campden)* ☺☺
Manor House *(Fishguard)* ☺☺
McCoys *(Staddlebridge)* ☺☺
Milestone House *(Broadway)* ☺☺
Mill and Old Swan *(Minster Lovell)* ☺☺
Monachyle Mhor *(Balquhidder)* ☺☺☺
Norfolk Mead *(Coltishall)* ☺☺
Old Black Lion *(Hay on Wye)* ☺☺
Old Trout *(Thame)* ☺☺
Ye Olde Bulls Head Inn *(Beaumaris)* ☺☺
Paskins *(Brighton)* ☺☺
Pen y Dyffryn *(Oswestry)* ☺☺☺
Plas Bodegroes *(Pwllheli)* ☺☺☺
Plockton Inn *(Plockton)* ☺☺
Powder Mills *(Battle)* ☺☺
Raemoir House *(Banchory)* ☺☺☺
Riverdale Hall *(Bellingham)* ☺☺
Rowton Castle *(Shrewsbury)* ☺☺
Royal Oak *(Luxborough)* ☺☺
The Royal Oak *(Betws-y-Coed)* ☺☺
Sportsman's Arms *(Wath-in-Nidderdale)* ☺☺
St Michaels *(Falmouth)* ☺☺
Star Inn *(Harome)* ☺☺☺
Stone House *(Hawes)* ☺☺
Stratford Victoria *(Stratford upon Avon)* ☺☺
Stratton's *(Swaffham)* ☺☺
Three Ways *(Chipping Campden)* ☺☺
Tormaukin Inn *(Glendevon)* ☺☺
Tregea *(Padstow)* ☺☺
Waltzing Weasel *(Birch Vale)* ☺☺
Weavers Shed *(Golcar)* ☺☺
Wesley House *(Winchcombe)* ☺☺
White Hart Inn *(Dorchester)* ☺☺
The White Horse *(Blakeney)* ☺☺
Willerby Manor *(Hull)* ☺☺
Wykeham Arms *(Winchester)* ☺☺

Top country house hotels

Up to £100

Ardanaiseig *(Taynuilt)*	☺☺
Beechwood Country *(Moffat)*	☺☺
Cally Palace *(Gatehouse of Fleet)*	☺☺
Castleman *(Blandford Forum)*	☺☺
Chilston Park *(Ashford)*	☺☺
Crossways *(Polegate)*	☺☺
Hallgarth Manor *(Durham)*	☺☺
Hassop Hall *(Bakewell)*	☺☺
Ivy House Farm *(Lowestoft)*	☺☺
La Place *(Jersey)*	☺☺
Lancrigg Country *(Grasmere)*	☺☺
Leeming House *(Penrith)*	☺☺
Linthwaite *(Bowness)*	☺☺
Little Barwick House *(Barwick)*	☺☺
Monachyle Mhor *(Balquhidder)*	☺☺☺
Norfolk Mead *(Coltishall)*	☺☺
Pen y Dyffryn *(Oswestry)*	☺☺☺
Plas Bodegroes *(Pwllheli)*	☺☺☺
Powder Mills *(Battle)*	☺☺
Raemoir House *(Banchory)*	☺☺☺
Riverdale Hall *(Bellingham)*	☺☺
Rowton Castle *(Shrewsbury)*	☺☺
Stone House *(Hawes)*	☺☺
Willerby Manor *(Hull)*	☺☺

Over £100

Amberley Castle *(Amberley)*	☺☺
Amerdale House *(Arncliffe)*	☺☺
Ashford Castle *(Cong, ROI)*	☺☺
Aynsome Manor *(Cartmel)*	☺☺
Babington House *(Babington)*	☺☺
Bailiffscourt *(Climping)*	☺☺
Balbirinie House *(Markinch)*	☺☺
Barberstown Castle *(Straffan, ROI)*	☺☺
Baslow Hall *(Baslow)*	☺☺
Bath Priory *(Bath)*	☺☺
Billesley Manor *(Alcester)*	☺☺
Bindon Country House *(Langford Budville)*	☺☺
Bodsgallen Hall *(Llandudno)*	☺☺
Brockencote Hall *(Chaddesley Corbett)*	☺☺
Buckland Manor *(Buckland)*	☺☺
Calcot Manor *(Tetbury)*	☺☺☺

TOP COUNTRY HOUSE HOTELS

Callow Hall *(Ashbourne)* ☺☺
Castlegrove Country House *(Letterkenny, ROI)* ☺☺
Charlton House *(Shepton Mallet)* ☺☺
Chewton Glen *(New Milton)* ☺☺☺
Cliveden House *(Taplow)* ☺☺
Combe House *(Exeter)* ☺☺
Cowley Manor *(Cowley)* ☺☺
The Chester Crabwall Manor *(Chester)* ☺☺
Crathorne Hall *(Yarm)* ☺☺
Craxton Wood *(Chester)* ☺☺
Dormy House *(Broadway)* ☺☺
Dromoland Castle *(Newmarket-on-Fergus, ROI)* ☺☺☺
East Lodge Country House *(Matlock)* ☺☺
Fairyhill *(Reynoldston)* ☺☺☺
Fawsley Hall *(Daventry)* ☺☺
Gibbon Bridge *(Chipping)* ☺☺
Gidleigh Park *(Chagford)* ☺☺
Gilpin Lodge *(Windermere)* ☺☺
Glenapp Castle *(Ballantrae)* ☺☺
Glenmorangie House *(Tain)* ☺☺
Gravetye Manor *(East Grinstead)* ☺☺
Great Fosters *(Egham)* ☺☺
The Greenway *(Shurdington)* ☺☺
Greywalls *(Gullane)* ☺☺
Hambleton Hall *(Hambleton)* ☺☺
Hartwell House *(Aylesbury)* ☺☺
Hayfield Manor *(Cork, ROI)* ☺☺
Hintlesham Hall *(Hintlesham)* ☺☺
Holbeck Ghyll *(Windermere)* ☺☺☺
Inverlochy Castle *(Fort William)* ☺☺
K Club *(Straffan, ROI)* ☺☺
Kinnaird *(Dunkeld)* ☺☺☺
Knockendarroch House *(Pitlochry)* ☺☺
Lake Vyrnwy *(Llanwddyn)* ☺☺
Langar Hall *(Langar)* ☺☺
Longueville Manor *(Jersey)* ☺☺
Lucknam Park *(Colerne)* ☺☺
Lumley Castle *(Chester-le-Street)* ☺☺
Maes Y Neuadd *(Harlech)* ☺☺
Maison Talbooth *(Dedham)* ☺☺
Manoir aux Quat' Saisons *(Gt Milton)* ☺☺☺
Marcliffe *(Aberdeen)* ☺☺
Morston Hall *(Morston)* ☺☺
Nailcote Hall *(Berkswell)* ☺☺
Newick Park *(Lewes)* ☺☺

Nidd Hall *(Harrogate)* ☺☺

Northcote Manor *(Blackburn)* ☺☺

Nuthurst Grange *(Hockley Heath)* ☺☺

Ockenden Manor *(Cuckfield)* ☺☺

Peterstone Court *(Brecon)* ☺☺

Rothay Manor *(Ambleside)* ☺☺

Samling *(Windermere)* ☺☺☺

Seaham Hall *(Seaham)* ☺☺

Sharrow Bay *(Ullswater)* ☺☺☺

Sheen Falls *(Kenmare, ROI)* ☺☺

South Lodge *(Lower Beeding)* ☺☺

Stapleford Park *(Stapleford)* ☺☺

Ston Easton Park *(Ston Easton)* ☺☺

The Well House *(St Keyne)* ☺☺

Underscar Manor *(Applethwaite)* ☺☺

Waterton Park *(Wakefield)* ☺☺

West Lodge Park *(Hadley Wood)* ☺☺

Westover Hall *(Milford-on-Sea)* ☺☺

Ynyshir Hall *(Eglwysfach)* ☺☺

Top foodie destinations

Albananch *(Baddidarroch)*	☺☺
Amberley Castle *(Amberley)*	☺☺
Amerdale House *(Arncliffe)*	☺☺
Balbirinie House *(Markinch)*	☺☺
Ballathie House *(Stanley)*	☺☺
Barberstown Castle *(Straffan, ROI)*	☺☺
Baslow Hall *(Baslow)*	☺☺
Bath Priory *(Bath)*	☺☺
Beechleas *(Wimborne Minster)*	☺☺
Beechwood Country *(Moffat)*	☺☺
Bindon House *(Langford Budville)*	☺☺
Bridge House *(Beaminster)*	☺☺
Brockencote Hall *(Chaddesley Corbett)*	☺☺
By Appointment *(Norwich)*	☺☺
Callow Hall *(Ashbourne)*	☺☺
Cally Palace *(Gatehouse of Fleet)*	☺☺
Carlton House *(Llanwrtyd Wells)*	☺
Caseys of Baltimore *(Cork, ROI)*	☺☺
Castell Deudraeth *(Portmeirion)*	☺☺☺
Castle House *(Hereford)*	☺☺
Castlegrove House *(Letterkenny, ROI)*	☺☺
Castleman *(Blandford Forum)*	☺☺
Cavendish *(Baslow)*	☺☺
Charlton House *(Shepton Mallet)*	☺☺
The Chester Crabwall Manor *(Chester)*	☺☺
Chewton Glen *(New Milton)*	☺☺☺
Churchill Arms *(Paxford)*	☺☺
Cornwallis Country *(Brome)*	☺☺
Crab Manor *(Thirsk)*	☺
Craxton Wood *(Chester)*	☺☺
The Crown *(Southwold)*	☺☺
Dering Arms *(Pluckley)*	☺
Devonshire Arms *(Bolton Abbey)*	☺☺
Dormy House *(Broadway)*	☺☺
Driftwood *(Rosevine)*	☺☺
Drunken Duck *(Ambleside)*	☺
Evesham *(Evesham)*	☺☺
Fairyhill *(Reynoldston)*	☺☺☺
The Fox Inn *(Lower Oddington)*	☺☺☺
General Tarleton Inn *(Ferrensby)*	☺
Gidleigh Park *(Chagford)*	☺☺
Gilpin Lodge *(Windermere)*	☺☺
Gleneagles *(Auchterarder)*	☺☺

Glenmorangie House *(Tain)* ☺☺
Gravetye Manor *(East Grinstead)* ☺☺
Great House *(Lavenham)* ☺☺
The Griffin Inn *(Fletching)* ☺☺☺
Hartwell House *(Aylesbury)* ☺☺
Hintlesham Hall *(Hintlesham)* ☺☺
Holbeck Ghyll *(Windermere)* ☺☺☺
L' Horizon *(Jersey)* ☺☺
Hotel des Clos *(Nottingham)* ☺☺
Hougue du Pommier *(Guernsey)* ☺☺
Howards House *(Teffont Evias)* ☺☺
Ickworth *(Bury St Edmunds)* ☺☺
Idle Rocks *(St Mawes)* ☺☺
Inn at Whitewell *(Clitheroe)* ☺☺☺
Inverlochy Castle *(Fort William)* ☺☺
K Club *(Straffan, ROI)* ☺☺
Kinloch Lodge *(Sleat)* ☺
Kinnaird *(Dunkeld)* ☺☺☺
Lake Vyrnwy *(Llanwddyn)* ☺☺
Lancrigg Country House *(Grasmere)* ☺☺
Langar Hall *(Langar)* ☺☺
Leeming House *(Penrith)* ☺☺
Linthwaite *(Bowness)* ☺☺
Little Barwick House *(Barwick)* ☺☺
Longueville Manor *(Jersey)* ☺☺
Lord Nelsons House *(Oakham)* ☺☺
Lugger *(Truro)* ☺☺
Maes Y Neuadd *(Harlech)* ☺☺
The Malt House *(Chipping Campden)* ☺☺
Manoir aux Quat' Saisons *(Gt Milton)* ☺☺☺
McCoys *(Staddlebridge)* ☺☺
Monachyle Mhor *(Balquhidder)* ☺☺☺
Morston Hall *(Morston)* ☺☺
Mount Juliet Conrad *(Kilkenny, ROI)* ☺☺
New Inn At Coln *(Coln St Aldwyns)* ☺☺
Nobody Inn *(Doddiscombsleigh)* ☺
Norfolk Mead *(Coltishall)* ☺☺
Northcote Manor *(Blackburn)* ☺☺
Nuthurst Grange *(Hockley Heath)* ☺☺
Ockenden Manor *(Cuckfield)* ☺☺
Old Bridge *(Huntingdon)* ☺
Old Course *(St Andrews)* ☺☺
Old Trout *(Thame)* ☺☺
Ye Olde Bulls Head Inn *(Beaumaris)* ☺☺
1 Devonshire Gardens *(Glasgow)* ☺☺

TOP FOODIE DESTINATIONS

Parknasilla *(Sneem, ROI)*	☺☺☺
Penhelig Arms *(Aberdyfi)*	☺☺
Percy's Country Hotel *(Virginstow)*	☺
Plas Bodegroes *(Pwllheli)*	☺☺☺
Porth Tocyn *(Abersoch)*	☺
Portmeirion *(Portmeirion)*	☺☺☺
Powder Mills *(Battle)*	☺☺
The Punch Bowl Inn *(Crosthwaite)*	☺
Riverside *(Evesham)*	☺
The Rose and Crown *(Romaldkirk)*	☺
Royal *(Ventnor)*	☺☺
Samling *(Windermere)*	☺☺☺
The Seafood Restaurant *(Padstow)*	☺☺
Seaham Hall *(Seaham)*	☺☺
Sharrow Bay *(Ullswater)*	☺☺☺
St Edmund House *(Padstow)*	☺☺
St Enedoc *(Rock)*	☺☺
St Petroc's Hotel & Bistro *(Padstow)*	☺
St Tudno *(Llandudno)*	☺☺
Star Inn *(Harome)*	☺☺☺
Stratton's *(Swaffham)*	☺☺
Studley Priory *(Horton-Cum-Studley)*	☺
Summer Isles *(Achiltibuie)*	☺☺
The Swan *(Bibury)*	☺☺
Three Acres *(Shelley)*	☺
Three Chimneys *(Dunvegan)*	☺☺
Tormaukin Inn *(Glendevon)*	☺☺
Ty'n Rhos *(Llanddeiniolen)*	☺
Tylney Hall *(Hook)*	☺
Underscar Manor *(Applethwaite)*	☺☺
Waltzing Weasel *(Birch Vale)*	☺☺
Waterside Inn *(Bray)*	☺☺
Weavers Shed *(Golcar)*	☺☺
The Well House *(St Keyne)*	☺☺
Westin Turnberry Resort *(Turnberry)*	☺☺
The White Hart Inn *(Nayland)*	☺☺
Winteringham Fields *(Winteringham)*	☺☺
Wykeham Arms *(Winchester)*	☺☺
Ynyshir Hall *(Eglwysfach)*	☺☺
Yorke Arms *(Ramsgill-in-Nidderdale)*	☺

Hotels with views

Adare Manor *(Adare, ROI)*	☺
Aghadoe Heights *(Killarney, ROI)*	☺☺
Apex European hotel *(Edinburgh)*	☺
Apex International *(Edinburgh)*	☺
Armanthwaite Hall *(Keswick)*	☺
Aynsome Manor *(Cartmel)*	☺☺
Bay Horse *(Ulverston)*	☺
Bodsgallen Hall *(Llandudno)*	☺☺
Caledonian Hilton *(Edinburgh)*	☻
De Vere Cameron House *(Loch Lomond)*	☻
Carnoustie Gold *(Carnoustie)*	⊤
Caseys of Baltimore *(Cork, ROI)*	☺☺
Royal Castle *(Dartmouth)*	☺
Cavendish *(Baslow)*	☺☺
Cottage in the Wood *(Malvern Wells)*	☹
County *(Bath)*	☺
Dinham Hall *(Ludlow)*	☻
Driftwood *(Rosevine)*	☺☺
Ees Wyke *(Ambleside)*	☺
The George *(Inveraray)*	☺☺
Glenfinnan House *(Glenfinnan)*	⊤
Graythwaite Manor *(Grange-over-Sands)*	⊤
Grand *(Tynemouth)*	☺☺
Greenbank *(Falmouth)*	☺
Hatton Court *(Upton St Leonards)*	☺
Highgrove House *(Troon)*	⊤
Holbeck Ghyll *(Windermere)*	☺☺☺
Holiday Inn Express *(Liverpool)*	☺
Continental *(Whitstable)*	☺
Imperial *(Torquay)*	☺
Inn on the Lake *(Ullswater)*	☻
Inverlochy Castle *(Fort William)*	☺☺
Lake Vyrnwy *(Llanwddyn)*	☺☺
Loch Melfort *(Arduaine)*	☺☺
Lodge on Loch Lomond *(Loch Lomond)*	☻
Maes Y Neuadd *(Harlech)*	☺☺
Malmaison *(Newcastle Upon Tyne)*	☻
Manor House *(Fishguard)*	☺☺
Manor House *(Oban)*	☺
Marina *(Fowey)*	☺
Maypool Park *(Galmpton)*	☺
Miller Howe *(Bowness)*	☺
Mr Underhills *(Ludlow)*	☺
The Nare *(Veryan)*	☺☺☺

HOTELS WITH VIEWS

Porthminster *(St Ives)*	☺☺
Rose and Crown *(Salisbury)*	☺
Rushpool Hall *(Saltburn-by-the-Sea)*	☺
Sheen Falls *(Kenmare, ROI)*	☺☺
Sheraton Grand *(Edinburgh)*	☺
St David's *(Cardiff)*	☺☺
St Enedoc *(Rock)*	☺☺
St Michaels *(Falmouth)*	☺☺
Talland Bay *(Looe)*	☺
The Leathes Head *(Keswick)*	T
Thistle *(Liverpool)*	☹
Three Choirs Vineyard *(Newent)*	☺
Travel Inn *(Edinburgh)*	☺
Westin Turnberry Resort *(Turnberry)*	☺☺
Ty'n Rhos *(Llanddeiniolen)*	☺
Underscar Manor *(Applethwaite)*	☺☺
Victoria *(Sidmouth)*	☺☺
Warpool Court *(St David's)*	☺

Recommended romantic hotels

Amberley Castle (Amberley)	☺☺
Angel (Midhurst)	☺☺
At the Sign of the Angel (Lacock)	☺☺
Bailiffscourt (Climping)	☺☺
The Bear (Crickhowell)	☺
Beetle and Wedge (Moulsford)	☺☺
Bodsgallen Hall (Llandudno)	☺☺
Brockencote Hall (Chaddesley Corbett)	☺☺
Castlegrove House (Letterkenny, ROI)	☺☺
Charlton House (Shepton Mallet)	☺☺
Chilston Park (Ashford)	☺☺
Combe House (Exeter)	☺☺
Cornwallis Country Hotel (Brome)	☺☺
Driftwood (Rosevine)	☺☺
Falkland Arms (Great Tew)	☺☺
Fawsley Hall (Daventry)	☺☺
Feathers (Ledbury)	☺☺
The George (Inveraray)	☺☺
Gibbon Bridge (Chipping)	☺☺
Glenapp Castle (Ballantrae)	☺☺
Grand (Tynemouth)	☺☺
Great House (Lavenham)	☺☺
The Greenway (Shurdington)	☺☺
Holbeck Ghyll (Windermere)	☺☺☺
The Lamb Inn (Burford)	☺☺
Lord Nelsons House (Oakham)	☺☺
Lords of the Manor (Upper Slaughter)	☺
Maes Y Neuadd (Harlech)	☺☺
Manoir aux Quat' Saisons (Gt Milton)	☺☺☺
Monachyle Mhor (Balquhidder)	☺☺☺
Nailcote Hall (Berkswell)	☺☺
Norfolk Arms (Arundel)	☺☺
Norfolk Mead (Coltishall)	☺☺
Northcote Manor (Blackburn)	☺☺
Old Black Lion (Hay on Wye)	☺☺
Ye Olde Bell (Maidenhead)	☺☺
Ye Olde Bulls Head Inn (Beaumaris)	☺☺
Plas Bodegroes (Pwllheli)	☺☺☺
Powder Mills (Battle)	☺☺
Priory (Wareham)	☺☺
Raemoir House (Banchory)	☺☺☺
Sir Christopher Wren's (Windsor)	☺
Slipway (Port Isaac)	☺

sign up for our next survey at www.hardens.com   25

RECOMMENDED ROMANTIC HOTELS

Snooty Fox *(Tetbury)*   ☺
Stoke Park *(Stoke Poges)*   ☺☺
Stratton's *(Swaffham)*   ☺☺
Thornbury Castle *(Thornbury)*   ☺
Three Lions *(Stuckton)*   ☺
Tormaukin Inn *(Glendevon)*   ☺☺
Upper Reaches *(Abingdon)*   ☺
Victoria *(Holkham)*   ☺☺
Waterside Inn *(Bray)*   ☺☺
Waterton Park *(Wakefield)*   ☺☺
Witchery by the Castle *(Edinburgh)*   ☺☺☺

Recommended spa hotels

Adare Manor *(Adare, ROI)* ☺
Aghadoe Heights *(Killarney, ROI)* ☺☺
Aldwark Manor *(Alne)* ☺
Ashford Castle *(Cong, ROI)* ☺☺
Babington House *(Babington)* ☺☺
Bailiffscourt *(Climping)* ☺☺
Billesley Manor *(Alcester)* ☺☺
Bishopstrow House *(Warminster)* ☺
Bodsgallen Hall *(Llandudno)* ☺☺
Calcot Manor *(Tetbury)* ☺☺☺
Cally Palace *(Gatehouse of Fleet)* ☺☺
Charlton House *(Shepton Mallet)* ☺☺
The Chester Crabwall Manor *(Chester)* ☺☺
Chester Grosvenor *(Chester)* ☺☺
Chewton Glen *(New Milton)* ☺☺☺
Cliveden House *(Taplow)* ☺☺
Cowley Manor *(Cowley)* ☺☺
Crieff Hydro *(Crieff)* ☺
Danesfield House *(Marlow)* ☺
De Vere Dunston Hall *(Norwich)* ☺
Devonshire Arms *(Bolton Abbey)* ☺☺
Dromoland Castle *(Newmarket-on-Fergus, ROI)* ☺☺☺
Eastwell Manor *(Boughton Lees)* ☺
Fawsley Hall *(Daventry)* ☺☺
Four Seasons *(Dublin, ROI)* ☺☺☺
Gleneagles *(Auchterarder)* ☺☺
The Grand *(Eastbourne)* ☺☺
Hartwell House *(Aylesbury)* ☺☺
Haven *(Poole)* ☺☺
Hayfield Manor *(Cork, ROI)* ☺☺
Hintlesham Hall *(Hintlesham)* ☺☺
Holbeck Ghyll *(Windermere)* ☺☺☺
Holbrook House *(Wincanton)* ☺
L' Horizon *(Jersey)* ☺☺
Ickworth *(Bury St Edmunds)* ☺☺
Linden Hall *(Morpeth)* ☺
The Lowry *(Manchester)* ☺
Lucknam Park *(Colerne)* ☺☺
Marriott *(Newcastle Upon Tyne)* ☺
Merrion *(Dublin, ROI)* ☺☺
Millennium Madejski *(Reading)* ☺☺
Mount Juliet Conrad *(Kilkenny, ROI)* ☺☺
Nailcote Hall *(Berkswell)* ☺☺

The Nare *(Veryan)*	☺☺☺
New Hall *(Sutton Coldfield)*	☺
Nidd Hall *(Harrogate)*	☺☺
Old Course *(St Andrews)*	☺☺
Parknasilla *(Sneem, ROI)*	☺☺☺
Peebles Hydro *(Peebles)*	☺
Rowhill Grange *(Wilmington)*	☺
Royal Crescent *(Bath)*	☺☺
Runnymede *(Egham)*	☺
Scotsman *(Edinburgh)*	☺☺
Seaham Hall *(Seaham)*	☺☺
Sheen Falls *(Kenmare, ROI)*	☺☺
Sheraton Grand *(Edinburgh)*	☺
Spread Eagle *(Midhurst)*	☺
St Andrews Bay *(St Andrews)*	☺
St David's *(Cardiff)*	☺☺
Stapleford Park *(Stapleford)*	☺☺
Stoke Park *(Stoke Poges)*	☺☺
Underscar Manor *(Applethwaite)*	☺☺
Victoria *(Sidmouth)*	☺☺
Wallett's Court *(St Margaret's at Cliffe)*	☺
Waterton Park *(Wakefield)*	☺☺
Westin Turnberry Resort *(Turnberry)*	☺☺
Willerby Manor *(Hull)*	☺☺

Best hotels for kids (other than seaside)

Babington House *(Babington)*	☺☺
Calcot Manor *(Tetbury)*	☺☺☺
Crieff Hydro *(Crieff)*	☺
The Crown *(Southwold)*	☺☺
Evesham *(Evesham)*	☺☺
Fowey Hall *(Fowey)*	☺
Ickworth *(Bury St Edmunds)*	☺☺
Kandinsky *(Cheltenham)*	☺☺
The Well House *(St Keyne)*	☺☺
Woolley Grange *(Bradford On Avon)*	☺☺

Hotels most mentioned in survey

For your interest only, here is a list of the British and Irish hotels that were most mentioned in the survey.

1	Manoir aux Quat' Saisons *(Great Milton)*
2	Chewton Glen *(New Milton)*
3	Babington House *(Babington)*
4	Malmaison *(Manchester)*
5	Tresanton *(St Mawes)*
6=	Hotel du Vin et Bistro *(Bristol)*
6=	Lygon Arms *(Broadway)*
8	Malmaison *(Newcastle Upon Tyne)*
10=	42 The Calls *(Leeds)*
10=	Malmaison *(Glasgow)*
12	Hotel du Vin and Bistro *(Winchester)*
13=	Bath Spa *(Bath)*
15	Malmaison *(Leeds)*
16=	Malmaison *(Edinburgh)*
18=	The Lowry *(Manchester)*
20=	Merrion *(Dublin, ROI)*
20=	Sharrow Bay *(Ullswater)*
22=	Gidleigh Park *(Chagford)*

Ardoe House   £106

South Deeside Rd, Blairs AB12 5YP
🖰 www.macdonaldhotels.co.uk
☎ (01224) 860600   🖷 (01224) 861283

*Opinions differ on this 19th-century Baronial pile (inspired by
nearby Balmoral, apparently), set in 30 acres. Some reporters find
it an "unstuffy" place that's "full of charm", whereas doubters say
this Macdonald hotel "suffers from the chain mentality, and
overdoes the chintz".* / **Rooms:** 117 (of which 78 non smoking and some
family rooms). **Facilities:** indoor pool; gym.

Marcliffe   £130

North Deeside Rd, Pitfodels AB15 9YA
🖰 www.marcliffe.com   🖃 info@marcliffe.com
☎ (01224) 861000   🖷 (01224) 868860

*It may be "an expensive place by Aberdeen standards", but this
"peaceful" villa in eight acres of grounds, just outside the city –
part of the Small Luxury Hotels of the World consortium – seems
to be worth the premium, and it's roundly praised for its "very
well-furnished rooms", and its "good service and food".* / **Rooms:** 40
(of which 20 non smoking and 4 family rooms).

The Thistle Aberdeen
Caledonian   £77

10-14 Union Terrace AB10 1WE
🖰 www.thistlehotels.com
🖃 Reservations.AberdeenCaledonian@thistle.co.uk
☎ 0870 333 9151   🖷 0870 333 9251

*"More personal than many chain outlets", this city-centre hotel –
in a Victorian building – attracts generally positive reports.*
/ **Rooms:** 77 (of which 16 non smoking and 4 family rooms). **Details:** meals
unavailable: L; min age for children: 14.

sign up for our next survey at www.hardens.com   30

ABERDYFI, GWYNEDD   4–3C

Penhelig Arms   £112*
LL35 0LT
🖱 www.penheligarms.com   ✉ info@penheligarms.com
☎ (01654) 767215   🖨 (01654) 767690
A great location on the seafront and overlooking the Dyfi estuary
is not the least of the attractions of this "lovely" inn, parts of
which are 18th-century. It provides "fine food" – the restaurant
has quite a name in its own right – and staff for whom "nothing is
too much trouble". *Prices are quoted on a DB&B basis.
/ **Rooms:** 14 (of which all non smoking and 4 family rooms). **Details:** no Amex.

ABERGAVENNY, MONMOUTHSHIRE   2–1A

Clytha Arms   £70
Clytha NP7 9BW
🖱 www.clytha-arms.com   ✉ clytharms@piscali.co.uk
☎ (01873) 840206   🖨 (01873) 840209

"Very good food and A1 wines" are the particular draw to this
"country pub with a few rooms". It's in "good walking country",
too. / **Rooms:** 4 (of which all non smoking). **Details:** meals unavailable: Sun D,
Mon.

ABERSOCH, GWYNEDD   4–2C

Porth Tocyn   £78
Bwlchtocyn LL53 7BU
🖱 www.porth-tocyn-hotel.co.uk
✉ porthtocyn.hotel@virgin.net
☎ (01758) 713303   🖨 (01758) 713538
The Fletcher-Brewers have run this seaside hotel – some little way
outside the village – since just after the war. "Great food" has
always been part of the package (and the hotel is one of the two
longest-serving non-metropolitan entries in the 'Good Food Guide')
– otherwise its appeal can seem a bit "threadbare", nowadays, if
in a thoroughly genteel way. / **Rooms:** 17 (of which all non smoking and 3
family rooms). **Facilities:** outdoor pool; tennis. **Details:** closed mid Nov-mid Mar;
no Amex.

ABINGDON, OXFORDSHIRE 2–2D

Upper Reaches £100
Thames St OX14 3JA
🖰 www.macdonaldhotels.co.uk
✉ upperreaches@macdonald-hotels.co.uk
☎ 0870 400 8101 🖨 (01235) 555182
A sibling to Marlow's famous Compleat Angler (also a Macdonald hotel), this former cornmill (whose restaurant boasts a working wheel) is in some ways rather similar. It has a "lovely riverside location" and is sometimes "billed as a romantic hideaway", but reporters find standards rather variable. / **Rooms:** 31 (of which 15 non smoking and 16 family rooms). **Details:** meals unavailable: Mon-Fri L.

ACHILTIBUIE, HIGHLAND 9–1B

Summer Isles £112
IV26 2YG
🖰 www.summerisleshotel.co.uk
✉ summerislehotel@aol.com
☎ (01854) 622282 🖨 (01854) 622251

It is, to put it mildly, rather off the beaten track, but "one of the best locations in the British Isles" has helped to win a big name for this "lovely", "comfortable" and "relaxing" hotel, whose "seriously good restaurant" has a big (and deserved) name in its own right. There is the occasional report of "slightly disappointing" accommodation. / **Rooms:** 12 (of which all non smoking). **Details:** closed Oct; no Amex; min age for children: 8.

Adare Manor   €175

🖰 www.adaremanor.com   ✉ info@adaremanor.ie
☎ +353-61 396566   🖳 +353-61 396124

"A beautiful Victorian pile" where some rooms are *"huge"*, and many offer *"views over the stunning golf course and river"*. Further plus-points of this 2002 Condé Naste Traveller No 1 European Resort winner include *"great facilities"* (equestrian centre, fishing, …), and the fact that it's *"within very easy reach of Shannon Airport"*. / **Rooms:** 138 (of which 25 family rooms). **Facilities:** indoor pool; gym; spa; golf. **Details:** no Switch.

Albrighton Hall   £112

Ellesmere Rd SY4 3AG
🖰 www.macdonaldhotels.co.uk
✉ albrighton@macdonald-hotels.co.uk
☎ (01939) 291000   🖳 (01939) 291123

A *"peaceful"* and *"spacious"* Tudor manor house (*"with oak panelling throughout"*) provides the *"dramatic"* setting for an establishment which – almost all reporters agree – has *"loads of character"*. Characteristically for a Macdonald hotel, though, reports – especially on the catering – are mixed. / **Rooms:** 71 (of which 32 non smoking and 10 family rooms). **Facilities:** indoor pool; gym; spa. **Details:** meals unavailable: Sat L; min age for children: 14.

ALCESTER, WARWICKSHIRE   2–1C

Billesley Manor   £170
Billesley B49 6NF
🖰 www.billesleymanor.co.uk
✉ bookings@billesleymanor.co.uk
☎ (01789) 279955   🖷 (01789) 764145

This "beautiful manor house" has "lots of history" (from the 16th
century onwards), plus "great gardens" and "excellent" facilities
(of a traditional type). Service is praised as "accommodating", too.
Even a reporter who thought the rooms in the main house
"needed updating" praised those in the annexe as "modern and
stylish", and further investment in the property is ongoing (with
additional bedrooms, a bistro and spa opening in late-2003).
/ Rooms: 62. Facilities: spa; tennis.

ALDEBURGH, SUFFOLK   3–1D

Brudenell   £96
The Parade IP15 5BU
🖰 www.brudenellhotel.co.uk   ✉ info@brudenellhotel.co.uk
☎ (01728) 452071   🖷 (01728) 454082
In the period leading up to its relaunch in mid-2003, this Victorian
seaside hotel attracted a reasonable volume of reviews, but they
were rather mixed – let's hope the refurb puts it all to rights.
/ Rooms: 42 (of which all non smoking and 3 family rooms).

Wentworth   £120
Wentworth Rd IP15 5BD
🖰 www.wentworth-aldeburgh.com
✉ stay@wentworth-aldeburgh.co.uk
☎ (01728) 452312   🖷 (01728) 454343
"Loads of space to sit" and a "genuinely warm welcome" are the
sort of features which make this "old-established hotel" (in the
same family since the '20s) a "lovely", atmospheric destination.
It impresses with the sheer consistency of commentary it attracts,
with the only criticism being of sometimes "compact"
accommodation – "the comfortable annex rooms are larger than
those in the main building". / Rooms: 38 (of which all non smoking).
Details: closed Christmas.

ALMONDSBURY, CITY OF BRISTOL 2–2B

Aztec £155
Aztec West BS32 4TS
🖰 www.shirehotels.co.uk ✉ aztec@shirehotels.co.uk
☎ (01454) 201090 🖨 (01454) 201593
A location "on a business park" may not sound promising, but "good facilities" and "charming service" come together to make a reasonably desirable package at this modern hotel (which is voted by some as "Bristol's best for business"). That said, although "some attempts at character" have been made, particularly in the restaurant, most find the overall impression as "anonymous" as you might expect. / **Rooms:** *128 (of which some family rooms).* **Facilities:** *spa.*

ALNE, NORTH YORKSHIRE 8–4C

Aldwark Manor £125
YO61 2NF
🖰 www.marstonhotels.com
✉ aldwarkmanor@marstonhotels.com
☎ (01347) 838146 🖨 (01347) 838867
"Excellent facilities" – especially a "fantastic new spa and swimming pool", and an 18-hole golf course – and "great food" commend this originally Victorian (but much extended) Marston hotel to all who comment on it. The new wing, however, "lacks character". / **Rooms:** *56 (of which 15 non smoking and some family rooms).* **Facilities:** *indoor pool; spa; golf.*

AMBERLEY, WEST SUSSEX 3–4A

Amberley Castle £170
BN18 9ND
🖰 www.amberleycastle.co.uk ✉ info@amberleycastle.co.uk
☎ (01798) 831992
A "dramatic-looking" medieval castle, "beautifully restored in unspoilt countryside" (on the South Downs Way) sounds a pretty "romantic" proposition, and most reporters proclaim a stay at this family-owned establishment a "fairytale" experience – "very expensive, but worth it". The well-equipped rooms are extremely highly rated, and the restaurant – though less so – is still seen as an attraction by many. Beware though: "they get a bit busy with weddings". / **Rooms:** *19 (of which all non smoking).* **Facilities:** *golf; tennis.* **Details:** *min age for children: 12.*

Drunken Duck £85

Barngates LA22 0NG
🔗 www.drunkenduckinn.co.uk
✉ info@drunkenduckinn.co.uk
☎ (01539) 436347

"Open fires, home-made cakes, a cosy bar, an excellent restaurant" – if that's your idea of Lakeland heaven, this *"interesting"* restaurant-with-rooms and micro-brewery may be just the place. / **Rooms:** 16 (of which all non smoking). **Details:** closed 24-25 Dec.

Ees Wyke £136*

Nr Sawrey LA22 0JZ
🔗 www.eeswyke.co.uk ✉ mail@eeswyke.co.uk
☎ (01539) 436393 🖨 (01539) 436393

"Thoughtfully run by charming man-and-wife team", this Georgian house – once the home of Beatrix Potter – offers *"beautiful"* views over Esthwaite. It's a comfortable" and *"relaxed"* place, and the food – *dinner is included in the price given – is *"good"*, too. / **Rooms:** 8 (of which all non smoking). **Details:** meals unavailable: L; no Amex; min age for children: 10.

Glen Rothay £60

Rydal LA22 9LR
🔗 www.theglenrothay.co.uk
☎ (01539) 434500

"Very large" (and tasteful) rooms are to be had at very *"reasonable prices"* at this *"cosy"* 17th-century coaching inn, which enjoys a *"superb"* position beside Rydal Water. / **Rooms:** 9.

Kirkstone Pass Inn £50

Kirkstone Pass LA22 9LQ
🔗 www.geocities.com/kirkstonepassinn
✉ kirkstonepassinn@ukonline.co.uk
☎ (01539) 433624 🖨 (01539) 431214

The highest pub in the Lakes (at 1481 feet above sea level) is a get-away-from-it-all destination par excellence, detached even from the National Grid (though they do have a generator). The small number of reporters who comment are unanimous that it's *"just how such a place should be"* – *"warm and welcoming"* and *"just lovely in every way"*. / **Rooms:** 5 (of which all non smoking and some family rooms). **Details:** meals unavailable: Sat & Sun.

Rothay Manor £130

Rothay Bridge LA22 0EH
🖰 www.rothaymanor.co.uk 📧 hotel@rothaymanor.co.uk
☎ (01539) 433605 📠 (01539) 433607

"Lovely personal attention" is something of a defining feature of this "comfortable" Regency country house hotel, run by the Nixon family for over 35 years. Unusually for an hotel of this type, family suites are available, and they are well geared up to deal with little 'uns. / **Rooms:** 17 (of which all non smoking and 5 family rooms). **Details:** closed 3 Jan-6 Feb.

AMERSHAM, BUCKINGHAMSHIRE 3–2A

The Crown £139

16 High Street HP7 0DH
🖰 www.macdonaldhotels.co.uk
📧 crown@macdonald-hotels.co.uk
☎ 0870 400 8103 📠 (01949) 431283

"It featured in 'Four Weddings', but don't let that put you off" – this "quaint" inn (run by Macdonald Hotels) is generally applauded as an "atmospheric" destination. The restaurant, though, is rather "average". / **Rooms:** 37 (of which 21 non smoking and 5 family rooms).

ANSTY, WARWICKSHIRE 5–4C

Ansty Hall £100

Main Rd CV7 9HZ
🖰 www.macdonaldhotels.co.uk
📧 sales.ansty@macdonald-hotels.co.uk
☎ (02476) 612222 📠 (02476) 605 122

Perhaps inevitably given its proximity to a major conurbation (and its ownership by Macdonald Hotels), this Victorian country house hotel strikes some reporters as rather "too function-orientated" and "lacking in character" – that's a shame as both the accommodation (especially in the "smart new wing") and service ("superb") win general praise. / **Rooms:** 62 (of which 15 non smoking and 4 family rooms).

APPLETHWAITE, CUMBRIA 7–3C

Underscar Manor £180*

CA12 4PH
☎ (01768) 775000 📠 (01768) 774904

*"Wonderful views, superb food and, nowadays, a good leisure centre" – guests want for very little at this rather "theatrical" country house hotel, set in 40 acres of grounds and overlooking Derwentwater. If there is a reservation, it is that some find its style just a fraction "over the top". *Prices are quoted on a DB&B basis.* / **Rooms:** 11. **Facilities:** indoor pool; gym; spa. **Details:** closed 1-3 Jan; min age for children: 12.

ARDUAINE, ARGYLL & BUTE   9–3B

Loch Melfort   £59

PA34 4XG

🖰 www.lochmelfort.co.uk   ✉ reception@lochmelfort.co.uk

☎ (01852) 200233   🖷 (01852) 200214

*"Outstanding" views, "excellent" service and "delicious" cooking –
reporters can find nothing to criticise at this family-owned hotel,
which claims, apparently with some justification, to have 'the
finest location on the West Coast'.* / **Rooms:** 23. **Details:** no Switch.

ARNCLIFFE, NORTH YORKSHIRE   5–1C

Amerdale House   £156*

BD23 5QE

☎ (01756) 770250   🖷 (01756) 770266

*This "fabulous" country house hotel is "a welcome retreat in a
lovely part of the Yorkshire Dales". It's "handy for walking", and
offers "very helpful" service. The food can be "great", too. *Prices
are quoted on a DB&B basis.* / **Rooms:** 11 (of which some family rooms).
Details: closed Nov-Mar; meals unavailable: L; no Amex.

ARNOLD, NOTTINGHAMSHIRE   5–3D

Cockcliffe Country House £105   🛆

Burnt Stump Hill NG5 8PQ

🖰 www.cockcliffehouse.co.uk

✉ enquiries@cockcliffehouse.co.uk

☎ (0115) 968 0179   🖷 (0115) 968 0623

*An hotel (some ten miles from Nottingham) converted in the late-
'90s from a 17th-century manor house. It's tipped for its "quirky
rooms" and "personal service".* / **Rooms:** 10 (of which 5 family rooms).

ARUNDEL, WEST SUSSEX   3–4A

Norfolk Arms   £115

High Street BN18 9AD

🖰 www.norfolkarmshotel.com

✉ norfolk.arms@forestdale.com

☎ (01903) 882101   🖷 (01903) 884275

*Under the battlements of Arundel Castle, this Georgian coaching
inn, with its "roaring fires", makes something of a picturebook-
perfect "charming" destination. Group-owned (Forestdale), it
retains an "individual" feel.* / **Rooms:** 34 (of which 7 non smoking and some
family rooms).

ASHBOURNE, DERBYSHIRE   5–3C

Callow Hall   £130

DE6 2AA

⌂ www.callowhall.co.uk   ✉ reservations@callowhall.co.uk

☎ (01335) 343403   🖨 (01335) 343624

"You feel like you're family", when you stay at this small country house – a creeper-clad Victorian building, in an estate of 40 acres, with its own fishing. "Wonderful food" is a highlight.
/ **Rooms:** 16 (of which some non smoking and some family rooms). **Details:** closed Christmas; meals unavailable: Mon-Sat L.

ASHBURTON, DEVON   1–3D

Holne Chase   £140

TQ13 7NS

⌂ www.dartmoor.co.uk/holnechase

✉ info@holne-chase.co.uk

☎ (01364) 631471   🖨 (01364) 631453

The "homely" and "friendly" charms of this "nice country house hotel" – in use as such for half a century – are sufficiently attractive that most reporters can overlook the occasional incident of "dismissive" attention from the management. There are some "lovely walks" nearby. / **Rooms:** 17 (of which 4 family rooms). **Details:** no Amex.

ASHFORD, KENT   3–3C

Ashford International   £110

Simone Weil Av TN24 8UX

⌂ www.ashfordinthotel.co.uk

✉ sales@ashfordinthotel.com

☎ (01233) 219988   🖨 (01233) 647743

"A good place to stop off en route to the Continent". This large, "modern" establishment is included purely for its practical appeal – even fans make few claims for its ambience or amenities.
/ **Rooms:** 201 (of which 150 non smoking and 58 family rooms). **Facilities:** indoor pool; gym; spa. **Details:** closed 24-29 Dec; meals unavailable: Mon L.

Chilston Park   £100

Sandway, Lenham ME17 2BE

⌂ www.handpicked.co.uk/chilstonpark

✉ chilstonpark@handpicked.co.uk

☎ (01622) 859803   🖨 (01622) 858588

"The 'house' dogs, lounging in reception" set the countrified tone at this "enchanting, picturesque hotel, set in the woods in Lenham". With its "exquisite antiques", its "candles" and its "fires", it's proclaimed a "romantic" sort of place by many reporters (oddly really, considering its corporate, Arcadian, ownership and its extensive conference facilities). "The food is good", too. / **Rooms:** 53 (of which 2 family rooms). **Facilities:** tennis. **Details:** meals unavailable: Sat L.

AUCHTERARDER, PERTH & KINROSS   9–3C

Gleneagles   £320
PH3 1NF

🖰 www.gleneagles.com   ✉ resort.sales@gleneagles.com
☎ (01764) 662231   🖷 (01764) 662134

"High expectations are met", according to most reports on this *"stunning"* and *"really luxurious"* hotel, which has *"a magnificent location, and wonderful outdoor and indoor leisure activities"* (not least the golf for which it is renowned). Almost everyone speaks very highly of all aspects of the operation, including Andrew Fairlie's restaurant, and the only repeated gripes are the expense (of course) and some *"small"* rooms. Price includes full use of the leisure and sports facilities (but not the course fees). / **Rooms:** 273 (of which some non smoking and some family rooms). **Facilities:** indoor pool; outdoor pool; gym; spa; golf; tennis.

AUGHTON, LANCASHIRE   5–2A

West Tower Country House   £106
Mill Ln, Aughton L39 7HJ

🖰 www.westtower.com   ✉ weddings@west-tower.com
☎ (01695) 423328   🖷 (01695) 420704

Recently refurbished at considerable expense – and now boasting facilities for conferences, as well as weddings – this hotel in an 18th-century country house is tipped as "very good indeed". / **Rooms:** 12 (of which 5 non smoking). **Details:** meals unavailable: Sat L & Sun D.

AYLESBURY, BUCKINGHAMSHIRE   3–2A

Hartwell House   £240
Oxford Rd HP17 8NL

🖰 www.hartwell-house.com   ✉ info@hartwell-house.com
☎ (01296) 747444   🖷 (01296) 747450

This "beautifully restored" part-Jacobean country house is now "a magnificently appointed hotel". Easy access from the capital makes it "perfect for a weekend getaway". The "exceptional and wonderful spa" is a further attraction, as, for many, is the "fine restaurant" (though opinions here differ). / **Rooms:** 49 (of which some non smoking). **Facilities:** indoor pool; gym; spa; tennis. **Details:** min age for children: 8.

sign up for our next survey at www.hardens.com   40

Babington House £195
BA11 3RW

🖰 www.babingtonhouse.co.uk
✉ enquiries@babingtonhouse.co.uk
☎ (01373) 812266   🖷 (01373) 812112

*By providing "lap-of-London luxury in deepest Somerset", this
"chic", "chintz-free" Georgian country house hotel (linked to the
Soho House club) has achieved cult status amongst stylish
urbanites. Rooms that are "beautiful", and such 'rural' delights as
a spa ("excellent"), a private cinema, a contemporary restaurant,
and so on have made it a No 1 destination for a "fun and lively
break from the Smoke" (and "brilliant for kids"). There is a small
minority, though, which just doesn't "get it", often citing "haughty"
and "inattentive" staff as their underlying complaint. / **Rooms:** 28 (of
which 5 family rooms).* **Facilities:** *indoor pool; outdoor pool; gym; spa; golf; tennis.*

Albananch £190
IV27 4LP

🖰 www.thealbannach.co.uk/yourhosts.htm
✉ info@thealbannach.co.uk
☎ (01571) 844407

*"A charming host, and excellent food to match" – reporters speak
in the highest terms of this modestly-scaled but "exceptional"
Victorian country house hotel. "Small rooms" are not seen as
being of any great consequence – "you go here to eat". / **Rooms:** 5
(of which all non smoking).* **Details:** *closed 15 Nov-15 Mar; meals unavailable: L; no
Amex; min age for children: 12.*

BAGSHOT, SURREY   3–3A

Pennyhill Park   £205
London Rd GU19 5EU
🖰 www.exclusivehotels.co.uk
✉ enquiries@pennyhillpark.co.uk
☎ (01276) 471774   🖷 (01276) 473217
*With its handy-for-the-capital location, this Victorian country
house hotel was the 'AA hotel of the Year 2002' – a fact which
may say more about the AA than it does for the establishment
concerned. There are admittedly many reporters who say the
place (owned by 'Exclusive Hotels'), is "lovely, with lots of modern
facilities" (including a very extensive spa and high-tech gym) and
"great for a special occasion", but there is also a voluble minority,
which think it a "big curate's egg of a place" – "overpriced" and
"pretentious".* / **Rooms:** 123 (of which 6 family rooms). **Facilities:** gym; spa;
golf; tennis. **Details:** no Amex.

BAKEWELL, DERBYSHIRE   5–2C

Hassop Hall   £79
Hassop DE45 1NS
✉ hassophallhotel@btinternet.com
☎ (01629) 640488   🖷 (01629) 640577
*"Personal" touches impart a "homely" feel to this imposing
country house hotel, which has a history stretching back to the
Domesday book. Even those who find the accommodation a touch
"tired" admit the place is very "comfortable" (and our rating gives
a certain amount of credit for the very reasonable prices).*
/ **Rooms:** 13. **Facilities:** tennis. **Details:** closed every Sun pm; meals unavailable:
Mon L.

BALCARY BAY, DUMFRIES & GALLOWAY   7–3B

Balcary Bay   £110*
Shore Rd DG7 1QZ
🖰 www.balcary-bay-hotel.co.uk
✉ info@balcary-bay-hotel.co.uk
☎ (01556) 640217   🖷 (01556) 640272
*A country house hotel, that's tipped in particular for its "delightful
peaceful location, overlooking the sea and surrounded by gentle
walks". *Prices are quoted on a DB&B basis.* / **Rooms:** 20 (of which all
non smoking and 3 family rooms). **Details:** closed Nov-Feb; meals unavailable: L.

sign up for our next survey at www.hardens.com

BALLANTRAE, AYRSHIRE 7–2A

Glenapp Castle £440*
KA26 0NZ
🖰 www.glenappcastle.com ✉ info@glenappcastle.com
☎ (01465) 831212 🖨 (01465) 831000

Reporters speak in very high terms of all aspects of this "fantastic" and "romantic" Baronial retreat, which appears to live up to everything anyone (well at least anyone looking for Relais & Châteaux style) could ever want. *The prices are, in fact, a little less terrifying than they look, as they are (seriously) all-inclusive! / **Rooms:** 17 (of which all non smoking and some family rooms). **Details:** closed Nov-Mar.

BALQUHIDDER, PERTH & KINROSS 9–3C

Monachyle Mhor £95
FK19 8PQ
🖰 www.monachylemhor.com ✉ info@monachylemhor.com
☎ (01877) 384622 🖨 (01877) 384305

'A small family-run farmhouse hotel in the heart of the Trossachs', says the management. Reporters tend to be more upbeat, speaking of a "fabulous" and "outstandingly romantic" lochside setting, the "superb" accommodation", "amazing" service and the "top-notch" food. The empire is growing – self-catering accommodation is available in the coach house, and Airlie House, in nearby Strathyre, has been acquired to provide 'overspill' accommodation. / **Rooms:** 10 (of which all non smoking and 2 family rooms). **Details:** closed Jan-mid Feb; no Amex; min age for children: 12.

BAMBURGH, NORTHUMBERLAND 8–1B

Waren House £120
Waren Mill, Belford NE70 7EE
🖰 www.warenhousehotel.co.uk
✉ enquiries@warenhousehotel.co.uk
☎ (01668) 214581 🖨 (01668) 214484

Accommodation at this attractive country house hotel come in a variety of themes and styles (see the website for details). In this "fantastic area for sightseeing", it's tipped for its "relaxing" ambience and its "marvellous" food. / **Rooms:** 12 (of which all non smoking and no family rooms). **Details:** meals unavailable: L; min age for children: 14.

BANCHORY, ABERDEEN 9–2D

Raemoir House £90

Raemoir AB31 4BD

🖰 www.raemoir.com ✉ enquiries@raemoir.com
☎ (01330) 824884 🖷 (01330) 822171

This "excellent country house hotel" occupies an impressive Georgian building and offers a true "stately home" experience at relatively modest cost. It has a "very romantic" location, too – part of an overall package with which reporters find simply no fault. / **Rooms:** 21 (of which 1 family room). **Facilities:** golf; tennis. **Details:** closed Christmas; no Amex.

BARNHAM BROOM, NORFOLK 6–4C

Barnham Broom £120

Honingham Rd NR9 4DD

🖰 www.barnham-broom.co.uk
✉ enquiry@barnhambroomhotel.co.uk
☎ (01603) 759393 🖷 (01603) 758224

This "good golfing and touring hotel" (some ten miles from Norwich) markets itself as a 'complete resort destination', and – for example – boasts no fewer than two 18-hole courses in its 250 acres. Even some who recognise its objective attractions, however, can find its style "a bit impersonal". / **Rooms:** 52 (of which 34 non smoking and 15 family rooms). **Facilities:** indoor pool; gym; spa; golf; tennis.

BARNSTAPLE, DEVON 1–2C

Huxtable Farm £50

West Buckland EX32 0SR

🖰 www.huxtablefarm.co.uk ✉ h@huxtablefarm.co.uk
☎ (01598) 760254 🖷 (01598) 760254

A top B&B (where you can also dine), which occupies a farmhouse dating back to 1520. It's tipped as a "wonderful place" with "excellent" food – "make sure you get a room in the main house". / **Rooms:** 6 (of which all non smoking and 2 family rooms). **Facilities:** gym; tennis. **Details:** closed Nov-Jan; meals unavailable: L; no Amex or Switch.

BARROW-IN-FURNESS, CUMBRIA 7–4C

The Chetwynde £65
Abbey Rd LA13 9JS
🖰 www.chetwyndehotel.activehotels.com
✉ enquiries@chetwyndehotel.co.uk
☎ (01229) 811011   🖷 (01229) 835997

Tipped by one reporter as "full of charm and hospitality", this small hotel is one of the survey's few recommendations in this thinly reported-on area. / Rooms: 10 (of which 2 family rooms). Details: meals unavailable: L.

BARWICK VILLAGE, SOMERSET 2–3B

Little Barwick House £94
BA22 9TD
🖰 www.littlebarwick.co.uk
✉ reservations@littlebarwickhouse.co.uk
☎ (01935) 423902

"Great food and service" is the tenor of all reports on this "charming" and "secluded" small establishment (in a Georgian dower house), where the restaurant is a key part of the appeal. It draws a fairly "mature" crowd, who say it's "great for a weekend break", and that "the village and church are friendly too". / Rooms: 6. Details: closed 2 wks in Jan; meals unavailable: Sun D, Mon & Tue L.

BASINGSTOKE, HAMPSHIRE 2–3D

Audleys Wood £105 ☺
Audleys Wood, Alton Rd RG25 2JT
🖰 www.thistlehotels.com/audleyswood
✉ AudleysWood@Thistle.co.uk
☎ 0870 333 9125   🖷 0870 333 9225

The "pleasant setting and grounds" are almost invariably a point of comment for reporters on this "lovely" Victorian country house. There's also a fair degree of consensus about the "good service" and the "excellent restaurant" – in short, you'd never know it was a Thistle hotel at all! / Rooms: 72.

BASLOW, DERBYSHIRE 5–2C

Baslow Hall £120 ☺☺
Calver Rd DE45 1RR
🖰 www.fischers-baslowhall.co.uk
✉ m.s@fischers-baslowhall.co.uk
☎ (01246) 583259   🖷 (01246) 583818

The "fantastic new rooms" at this country house hotel – "peacefully situated" on the borders of the Chatsworth Estate, and with "a great location for exploring the Peak District" – are particularly praised by reporters. The restaurant's reputation for "fantastic" cooking is generally upheld, too. / Rooms: 11 (of which all non smoking). Details: closed 25-26 Dec.

Cavendish £130
DE45 ISP
 www.cavendish-hotel.net ✉ info@cavendish-hotel.net
☎ (01246) 582311 🖷 (01246) 582312
"Beautiful rooms and excellent views" commend this ancient, ducally-owned Chatsworth Estate inn (with interior design by her grace) to all of the small number of reporters who have sampled it. The food is "great", too – for a slightly 'different' dinner-date, "try the table in the kitchen". / **Rooms:** 24 (of which 2 non smoking and 3 family rooms).

BATH, BATH & NE SOMERSET 2–2B

For those for whom budget is not a particular consideration, there are some 'destination' establishments in or near this beautiful city which clearly merit their fame. Good mid-range accommodation is relatively difficult to find, however, but the survey did unearth some useful suggestions.

Bath Priory £260
Weston Rd BA1 2XT
 www.thebathpriory.co.uk
☎ (01225) 331922 🖷 (01225) 448276
For sheer consistency of positive feedback, few places match this small, "understatedly luxurious" hotel – a 19th-century manor house built in Bath stone and set in "lovely" gardens, "about 15 minutes walk from the centre". All aspects of the operation show "fantastic attention to detail", with the "outstanding" restaurant singled out for particular praise. / **Rooms:** 28 (of which 6 family rooms).
Facilities: indoor pool; outdoor pool; gym.

Bath Spa £220
Sydney Rd BA2 6JF
 www.bathspahotel.com
✉ sales.bathspa@macdonald-hotels.co.uk
☎ (01225) 444424 🖷 (01225) 444006
Perhaps Condé Nast's 2001 nomination of this grand city-fringe Macdonald hotel as 'the UK's best spa-hotel' (which must have created a lot of business, and helped generate many survey reports) went to the place's head. It does indeed have many fans, who proclaim it "very relaxing, and great for a romantic weekend", but more striking is the proportion of critics who found it "a bit of anticlimax", complaining of "cramped" bedrooms, "pathetic" service, "minimal" food portions and overall "bad value for money". / **Rooms:** 102 (of which 40 non smoking and 20 family rooms).
Facilities: indoor pool; gym; tennis.

County £100
18-19 Pulteney St BA2 4EZ
🖰 www.county-hotel.co.uk
✉ reservations@county-hotel.co.uk
☎ (01225) 425003 🖷 (01225) 466493
"Classy without being snotty", this small hotel (where some rooms have "very good views") achieved only a modest level of commentary, but it was very consistent. Rooms may be "a bit small", but breakfasts are "superb". / **Rooms:** 22. **Details:** min age for children: 13.

Dukes £135
Great Pulteney St BA2 4DN
🖰 www.dukesbath.co.uk/business_serv.html
✉ info@dukesbath.co.uk
☎ (01225) 787960 🖷 (01225) 787961
For its supporters this is "nearly a perfect townhouse hotel", offering "real value for money" and in a "good location", too. Not all reporters were equally impressed, however, and at press time the hotel was up for sale. / **Rooms:** 18 (of which some family rooms).

Francis £138
Queen Sq BA1 2HH
🖰 www.macdonaldhotels.co.uk
✉ francis@macdonald-hotels.co.uk
☎ 0870 400 8223 🖷 (01225) 319715
There were a fair number of reports on this "well-located" Macdonald hotel converted from a series of Georgian townhouses. No major failings were highlighted, but the overall consensus was of an experience "below the standard expected". / **Rooms:** 95 (of which 45 non smoking and 4 family rooms).

Kennard £118
11 Henrietta St BA2 6LL
🖰 www.kennard.co.uk ✉ reception@kennard.co.uk
☎ (01225) 310472 🖷 (01225) 460054
Pity this central Georgian townhouse generated so little feedback – it was tipped as a "fabulous" place, offering the "highest quality of everything". / **Rooms:** 13 (of which all non smoking). **Details:** meals unavailable: no restaurant; min age for children: 14.

Queensberry £120
Russel St BA1 2QF
🖰 www.bathqueensberry.com
✉ enquiries@batholivetree.com
☎ (01225) 447928 🖷 (01225) 446065
New owners took over at this "tasteful", "rambling" and "characterful" hotel in the spring of 2003 – let's hope they maintain standards at an establishment which reporters commented favourably on across the board. / **Rooms:** 29 (of which all non smoking). **Details:** meals unavailable: Mon L; no Amex.

Royal Crescent £170

16 Royal Crescent BA1 2LS
🔗 www.royalcrescent.co.uk
✉ reservations@royalcrescent.co.uk
☎ (01225) 823333   📠 (01225) 339401

An "exceptional setting" in the heart of one of the architectural glories of Bath ensures a high profile for this townhouse-hotel (now part of the swanky Von Essen group), and most reporters find a visit "a fabulous treat". Staff are "obliging" and "the garden is lovely in summer". The "beautiful" spa is a key attraction.
/ **Rooms:** 45 (of which 8 non smoking and 14 family rooms). **Facilities:** indoor pool; gym; spa.

BATTLE, EAST SUSSEX 3–4C

Powder Mills £100

Powdermill Ln TN33 0SP
✉ powdc@aol.com
☎ (01424) 775511   📠 (01424) 774540

"This fabulous, romantic hotel" – in an 18th-century country house set in 150 acres – receives nothing but praise from reporters for its "great location and charm". "Very good food" is among the attractions which make it "ideal for a quiet break".
/ **Rooms:** 40 (of which some non smoking). **Facilities:** outdoor pool.
Details: meals unavailable: Sun in winter; not suitable for children.

BEAMINSTER, DORSET 2–4B

Bridge House £122

3 Prout Bridge DT8 3AY
🔗 www.bridge-house.co.uk
✉ enquiries@bridge-house.co.uk
☎ (01308) 862200   📠 (01308) 863700

"Delightfully olde worlde, but still offering highly modern comfort and excellent service and food" – reporters all speak in the highest terms of this "small, privately-owned hotel", with its "individually-furnished (if small) bedrooms" and its "well-kept terrace and gardens". / **Rooms:** 14. **Details:** no Switch.

BEAULIEU, HAMPSHIRE   2–4D

Montagu Arms   £145

Palace Ln SO42 7ZL
⌂ www.montaguarmshotel.co.uk
✉ reservations@montaguarmshotel.co.uk
☎ (01590) 612324   📠 (01590) 612188

This "old-style country hotel" (in the same family since the '60s, and whose premises date from Georgian times) enjoys a "lovely" New Forest location. Its "tasteful, traditionally-furnished rooms" and its "caring" service combine to create a "cosseting" atmosphere. / **Rooms:** 23 (of which some family rooms). **Facilities:** golf.

BEAUMARIS, ISLE OF ANGLESEY   4–1C

Ye Olde Bulls Head Inn   £92

Castle St LL58 8AP
⌂ www.bullsheadinn.co.uk   ✉ info@bullsheadinn.co.uk
☎ (01248) 810329   📠 (01248) 811294

Claimed by some as "the best pub hotel in Wales", this "charming" ancient coaching inn near the castle (which has in its time numbered both Dickens and Dr Johnson amongst its guests) is warmly commented on by most reporters. "Friendly" service and "fabulous" food are among the highlights. / **Rooms:** 13 (of which all non smoking).

BELFAST, COUNTY ANTRIM   10–1D

Belfast remains a destination perhaps rather under-appreciated by leisure visitors. On the downside, this means that it offers little – with the possible exception of the recent McCausland – which could be said to rise to 'destination' status. In compensation, though, there are a number of reasonably-priced and quite attractive small hotels, in locations which are both pleasant and handy for the city-centre.

Benedict's of Belfast   £75

7-21 Bradbury Pl, Shaftesbury Sq BT7 1RQ

🖰 www.benedictshotel.co.uk   ✉ info@benedictshotel.co.uk

☎ (028) 9059 9199   🖨 (028) 9059 1990

If you don't mind the fact that it's attached to "an incredibly noisy bar", this "very friendly" boutique-hotel – in the heart of the South Belfast 'action' – is a "friendly" place, offering "good value for money". / **Rooms:** 32 (of which 10 family rooms). **Details:** closed 12 July.

Culloden   £200

Bangor Rd BT18 0EX

🖰 www.slh.com/culloden   ✉ culloden@slh.com

☎ (028) 9042 5223   🖨 (028) 9042 6777

This former bishop's palace has a "fantastically beautiful" location (if one that's "very inconvenient for meeting in the city"). Most reporters find its ambience "very nice" too, but even fans may find the clientèle "middle-aged" (and one reporter bemoaned a notably "child-unfriendly approach"). / **Rooms:** 79 (of which 28 non smoking and 12 family rooms). **Facilities:** indoor pool; gym; spa.

De Vere Europa   £160

Great Victoria St BT2 7AP

🖰 www.devereonline.co.uk   ✉ res@eur.hastingshotels.com

☎ (028) 9027 1066   🖨 (028) 9032 7800

With its "great location", right in the heart of the city, Belfast's classic modern business hotel is certainly an extremely "convenient" place to stay. Otherwise commentary is very up-and-down. / **Rooms:** 240 (of which 90 non smoking and some family rooms).

Hilton Belfast   £145

4 Lanyon Pl BT1 3LP

🖰 www.hilton.co.uk

☎ (028) 9027 7000   🖨 (028) 9027 7277

A "welcoming" city-centre hotel which makes "a smart and efficient place to stay on business". It may not be saying much, but the place does appear to be one of the UK's very best Hiltons! / **Rooms:** 195 (of which some non smoking and some family rooms). **Facilities:** indoor pool; gym; spa.

Holiday Inn £140

22-26 Ormeau Av BT2 8HS
🖰 www.belfast.holiday-inn.com
✉ belfast@ichotelsgroup.com
☎ 0870 400 9005   📠 (028) 9062 6546

*This modern, stylish and very central destination comes as "a big surprise" – and a pleasant one, too – for some people. Its "excellent facilities" are particularly praised. / **Rooms:** 170 (of which 102 non smoking and 40 family rooms). **Facilities:** indoor pool; gym; spa.*

Madison's £65

59-63 Botanic Ave BT7 IJL
🖰 www.madisonshotel.com   ✉ madisons@unite.co.uk
☎ (028) 9050 9800   📠 (028) 9050 9808

*This modestly-priced modern hotel – above a bar/restaurant/nightclub – has "a great location for a city break or business travel", in the heart of the trendy Botanic Gardens area and only a ten-minute walk from the city-centre. It's tipped as a "stylish" place with "helpful" staff. / **Rooms:** 35 (of which some non smoking and some family rooms).*

McCausland £140

34-38 Victoria St BTI 3GH
🖰 www.mccauslandhotel.com   ✉ mccausland@slh.com
☎ (028) 9022 0200   📠 (028) 9022 0220

*"Imaginatively converted" (in 1998) from a Victorian warehouse, this impressive hotel offers a "good location", and a "high level of personal service". Prices are quite high by local standards, though, and one reporter found some rooms "rather small". / **Rooms:** 60 (of which some non smoking and some family rooms). **Facilities:** gym; spa.*

Riverdale Hall £88

NE48 2JT
🖱 www.riverdalehall.demon.co.uk
✉ sales@riverdalehallhotel.co.uk
☎ (01434) 220254 📠 (01434) 220457

"A wonderful site looking across a cricket pitch to the River Tyne", "good food" and a location in the Northumberland National Park together providing "everything one could want for an outdoor holiday" – these are the themes which recur in commentary on this family-owned hotel. Even those who find some of the décor "tired" were mollified by the place's other attractions (and its reasonable prices). / **Rooms:** 23 (of which 12 family rooms). **Facilities:** indoor pool; golf.

Nailcote Hall £165

Nailcote Ln CV7 7DE
🖱 www.nailcotehall.co.uk ✉ info@nailcotehall.co.uk
☎ (02476) 466174 📠 (02476) 470720
Don't be too put off by the garish website – reporters speak only well of this hotel and country club organized around a "beautiful" half-timbered house, with its "large" rooms and "fantastic" pool and sports facilities. You can dine at 'Rick's' – within the leisure and conference centre, and promising 'a Mediterranean holiday atmosphere, with music and food to match' – or there's the more "romantic" Oak Room. / **Rooms:** 40 (of which 2 family rooms). **Facilities:** indoor pool; gym; spa; golf; tennis.

Kings Arms £99

Hide Hill TD15 1EJ
🖱 www.kings-arms-hotel.com
✉ king-s_arms.hotel@virgin.net
☎ (01289) 307454 📠 (01289) 308867
"A trendy oasis, behind a traditional exterior" – this "historic" inn has recently been refurbished, and attracts little but praise, not least for its "very good" dining facilities. / **Rooms:** 36 (of which some non smoking and 3 family rooms). **Details:** closed Christmas.

Marshall Meadows £105
TD15 IUT
🖰 www.marshallmeadows.co.uk
✉ admin@marshallmeadows.co.uk
☎ (01289) 331133 📠 (01289) 331438

There weren't many reports on 'England's most northerly hotel', in an 18th-century country house hotel that's both "near the sea" and "handy for many of the attractions of Northumbria". They make quite an effort on the cuisine front, but verdicts on the level of achievement were mixed. / **Rooms:** 19. **Details:** no Amex.

BETWS-Y-COED, CONWY 4–1D

The Royal Oak £70
Snowdonia National Park LL24 OAS
🖰 www.royaloakhotel.net
✉ royaloakmail@btopenworld.com
☎ (01690) 710219

"A fine hotel at a reasonable price" – limited reports speak only well of this "fine" and "comfortable" former coaching inn, which has a "beautiful location" in the town which marks the crossroads of North Wales. / **Rooms:** 45 (of which 5 non smoking and 4 family rooms).

BIBURY, GLOUCESTERSHIRE 2–2C

The Swan £130
GL7 5NW
🖰 www.swanhotel.co.uk ✉ info@swanhotel.co.uk
☎ (01285) 740695 📠 (01285) 740473

This 17th-century coaching inn is "a lovely place, overlooking a trout stream" and – though quite "expensive" – is "seriously comfortable", and offers "great" service. The food was well rated, too – there's quite a grand traditional restaurant, as well as a brasserie. / **Rooms:** 23 (of which all non smoking and 1 family room).

BIGBURY ON SEA, DEVON   1–4D

Burgh Island   £160*

TQ7 4BG

🏠 www.burghisland.com   ✉ reception@burghisland.com

☎ (01548) 810514   🖷 (01548) 810243

*Built in 1929, this famous, Agatha Christie-esque Art Deco hotel
(set on its own island, that's reachable at high tide only by a 'sea
tractor') has, under new management, been going through an 18
month make-over. Reports have naturally been unsettled, but they
suggest that now the work is over the place "could really be very
good". *Prices are quoted on a DB&B basis. / **Rooms:** 21 (of which all
non smoking and 4 family rooms). **Facilities:** tennis. **Details:** closed 3 wks in Jan.*

BIRCH VALE, DERBYSHIRE   5–2B

Waltzing Weasel   £78

New Mills Rd SK22 1BT

🏠 www.w-weasel.co.uk   ✉ w-weasel@zen.co.uk

☎ (01663) 743402   🖷 (01663) 743402

*This "charming gastropub near the Peaks" – newly built, but in
traditional style – enjoys a "lovely" setting. It wins praise for its
"friendly" service and "excellent" food. / **Rooms:** 8.*

BIRMINGHAM, WEST MIDLANDS   5–4C

It may famously be a city in the throes of total renovation,
but Birmingham still boasts a good complement of utterly
undistinguished chain hotels – those is search of a
'traditional' hotel experience will probably do best at the
commendable Burlington. The recent arrival of both an
Hotel du Vin and a Malmaison may presage better for the
future.

Burlington   £155

Burlington Arcade, 126 New St B2 4JQ

🏠 www.burlingtonhotel.com   ✉ mail@burlingtonhotel.com

☎ (0121) 643 9191   🖷 (0121) 643 5075

*"Large and well-equipped rooms" and "extremely obliging service"
are among the plus-points that generally win support for this
traditionally-styled hotel, near the railway station. / **Rooms:** 112 (of
which 50 non smoking and some family rooms). **Facilities:** gym. **Details:** closed 25
Dec, 1 Jan.*

Campanile   £47

Chester St B6 4BE

🏠 www.necgroup.co.ukhotelscampanilebham

✉ birmingham@envergura.co.uk

☎ (0121) 359 3330   🖷 (0121) 359 1223

*If you're looking for a "no-frills" establishment, this shed-like
canalside establishment near the city-centre is tipped as being
"as cheap as chips", and for offering "fantastic service", too.
/ **Rooms:** 111 (of which some non smoking and some family rooms). **Details:** no
Amex or Switch.*

City Inn £109

1 Brunswick Sq, Brindley Pl B1 2HW

🖰 www.cityinn.com

✉ birmingham.reservations@cityinn.com

☎ (0121) 643 1003   🖨 (0121) 643 1005

"Furniture straight from IKEA, but the attention to detail is what impresses". "Good modern bedrooms" and a "good" central location make this modern hotel a useful destination. / **Rooms:** 238 (of which 138 non smoking). **Facilities:** gym. **Details:** meals unavailable: L.

Crowne Plaza £130

Pendigo Way, NEC B40 1PS

🖰 www.birminghamnec.crowneplaza.com

✉ necroomsales@ichotelsgroup.com

☎ (0121) 781 4000   🖨 (0121) 781 4321

"Convenience for the NEC" puts this new establishment a cut above your standard chain-outlet for some reporters. For others it represents "all that is wrong with plc hotels", but even one who dismissed the overall experience as "dire" rated the actual rooms very highly! / **Rooms:** 242 (of which some non smoking and 12 family rooms). **Facilities:** gym. **Details:** closed Christmas.

Hilton Birmingham Metropole £125

National Exhibition Centre B40 1PP

🖰 www.hilton.co.uk

☎ (0121) 780 4242   🖨 (0121) 780 3923

Proximity to the NEC plus sheer "massive" scale ensures many reports on this "faceless", "formulaic" and "frustrating" conference hotel (which some feel has all the ambience of "a tube station"). It does have "good leisure facilities", but even these can be "overcrowded". / **Rooms:** 802 (of which some non smoking and some family rooms). **Facilities:** indoor pool; gym; spa.

Hotel du Vin et Bistro £110

Church St B3 2NR

🖰 www.hotelduvin.com

✉ info@birmingham.hotelduvin.com

☎ (0121) 200 0600   🖨 (0121) 236 0889

"Comfortable and homely, despite the large number of business guests", this "tasteful" new branch of the popular chain – a "superb refurbishment" of a former hospital in the city-centre – has been a resounding success. Being larger-than-average, it has "not quite so much charm" as its siblings, but its range of other attractions – including "bistro food at its best", "two cool bars" and a "good gym" – make it a good all-purpose destination. / **Rooms:** 66 (of which 1 family room). **Facilities:** gym; spa.

Hyatt Regency £165

2 Bridge St B1 2JZ

🖰 www.birmingham.regency.hyatt.com

✉ Birmingham@hyattintl.com

☎ (0121) 643 1234 🖨 (0121) 616 2323

'The celebrated Hyatt Touch' – well, that's what they say – has helped make this "efficient business hotel" popular with executive types, and its attractions include a covered link to the Conference Centre and "great views" from the (pricier) top-floor rooms. Commentary, though, is rather mixed. / **Rooms:** 319. **Facilities:** indoor pool; gym; spa.

Jonathans £125 ☺

16-24 Wolverhampton Rd B68 0LH

🖰 www.jonathans.co.uk ✉ bookings@jonathans.co.uk

☎ (0121) 429 3757

"Individual, chaotic and great fun" – "every room is themed and called after a town in the Black Country", at this bric-a-brac filled, Victorian-styled restaurant-with-rooms, which has long been a celebrated local destination. / **Rooms:** 46 (of which some non smoking and some family rooms). **Details:** closed 1 Jan.

Jurys Inn £59

245 Broad St B12 HQ

🖰 www.jurysdoyle.com

☎ (0121) 606 9000 🖨 (0121) 606 9001

"A good location for the city-centre" distinguishes this modern chain-hotel, which otherwise offers a pretty "basic" experience. / **Rooms:** 445 (of which some non smoking and some family rooms). **Details:** closed Christmas.

Malmaison £125

Mailbox, Royal Mail St B1 1XL

🖰 www.malmaison.com ✉ malmaison@birmingham.com

☎ (0121) 246 5000 🖨 (0121) 246 5002

Early reports of the "smart" new outlet of this popular boutique-hotel chain – a former Royal Mail sorting office, now part of the Mailbox development – are of necessity few, but they suggest that it is one of the best. Even in the early days, staff won praise for being "exceptionally well-trained and efficient", and reporters thought the overall package "very good value". / **Rooms:** 189. **Facilities:** spa.

Marriott £118

12 Hagley Rd, Fiveways B16 8SJ

🖰 www.marriott.com ✉ claire.lawson@whitbread.com

☎ (0121) 452 1144 🖨 (0121) 456 3442

"For a long time, Birmingham lacked hotels, which may explain why this one gets away with such small rooms." It has its fans ("a typical Marriott, but the best place in Brum"), but some reporters just say it's "dreadful". / **Rooms:** 104 (of which some non smoking and 5 family rooms). **Facilities:** indoor pool; gym; spa.

Marriott -
Forest of Arden   £149

Maxstoke Ln, Meriden CV7 7HR
🏠 www.marriott.com
☎ (01676) 522335   🖷 (01676) 523711

"Large and modern, but not soulless", this *"friendly"*
establishment set in 10,000 acres – but only four miles from the
NEC – makes a good choice for those combining business and
pleasure. Leisure facilities include a golf course (which is
"decentish" or *"superb"*, depending on your standards).
/ **Rooms:** 214 (of which 90 non smoking and 20 family rooms). **Facilities:** indoor
pool; gym; spa; golf; tennis.

BISHOPS TACHBROOK, WARWICKSHIRE   5–4C

Mallory Court   £185   N

Harbury Ln CV33 9QB
🏠 www.mallory.co.uk   ✉ reception@mallory.co.uk
☎ (01926) 330214   🖷 (01926) 451714

"One feels cosseted, but not fussed over" – this *"sumptuously
comfortable"* inter-war country house (a member of Relais &
Châteaux) attracts almost unanimous praise as a *"great weekend
hide-away"*, with *"excellent"* food a particular attraction. It
changed hands in late-2002, and the new owners propose an
extension, including conference facilities and more
accommodation. / **Rooms:** 18 (of which 1 family room). **Facilities:** outdoor
pool; tennis. **Details:** min age for children: 9.

BLACKBURN, LANCASHIRE   5–1B

Northcote Manor   £130

Northcote Road, Langho BB6 8BE
🏠 www.northcotemanor.com
✉ admin@northcotemanor.com
☎ (01254) 240555   🖷 (01254) 246568

A *"fantastically elegant restaurant"* is the star attraction at this
"lovely, traditional hotel, near the Ribble Valley". Facilities are
otherwise few, but those in search of a place that's just *"luxurious,
spacious and relaxing"* really won't do much better – *"awful
Lancashire weather"* contributes much to the place's attractions
for a *"romantic escape"*. / **Rooms:** 14 (of which some family rooms).

De Vere Herons' Reach £110*
East Park Drive FY3 8LL
🖱 www.devereonline.co.uk
✉ reservations.herons@devere-hotels.com
☎ (01253) 838866 🖷 (01253) 798800

*For once, the hype is not mere puffery: De Vere's claim that this modern establishment is 'Blackpool's most stylish and comfortable hotel' is almost certainly true. On the downside, it is a couple of miles from the Golden Mile, but the reporter who tips it finds more than sufficient consolation in "great sports facilities" (including "a good golf course") and "nice public areas". *Prices are quoted on a DB&B basis. / **Rooms:** 172. **Facilities:** indoor pool; gym; golf; tennis.*

Hilton Blackpool £106
North Promenade FY1 2JQ
🖱 www.hilton.co.uk
☎ (01253) 623434 🖷 (01253) 294371

*This modern hotel which has been through many changes of ownership over the years "allegedly has the best location in Blackpool". It really is "third-rate", though, — it very nearly managed to get the lowest possible survey rating for charm from every single reporter who commented on it! **Rooms:** 247 (of which some non smoking and some family rooms). **Facilities:** indoor pool; gym; spa.*

Imperial £110
North Promenade FY1 2HB
🖱 www.paramount-hotels.co.uk
✉ imperialblackpool@paramount-hotels.co.uk
☎ (01253) 623971 🖷 (01253) 751784

*"Faded elegance and a great sea view, but you wouldn't want to stay longer than a night" — all of the (fair number of reports) on this famous seaside hotel, run by Paramount, tend to the view that it's "disappointing, particularly the restaurant". / **Rooms:** 181. **Facilities:** indoor pool; gym; spa.*

Kinloch House £220*
PH10 6SG
🖱 www.kinlochhouse.com ✉ kinloch@kinlochhouse.com
☎ (01250) 884237 🖷 (01250) 884333

*"The best" Scottish cooking — *prices are DB&B — is a particular strength of this luxurious country house hotel, set in 35 acres and now owned by the family which made its name at the famous Airds Hotel. (The take-over was too recent to make a rating here appropriate.) The building is Victorian in origin, but comes complete with many modern facilities. / **Rooms:** 19 (of which 6 non smoking and 1 family room). **Facilities:** indoor pool; gym; spa. **Details:** closed 14-28 Dec; no Amex; min age for children: 12 & babies.*

BLAKENEY, NORFOLK 6–3C

The White Horse £60
4 High St NR25 7AL

🕙 www.blakeneywhitehorse.co.uk

📠 enquiries@blakeneywhitehorse.co.uk

☎ (01263) 740574 🖨 (01263) 741303

"A great pub in a marvellous location" (near the quayside) – this "relaxing" establishment is unanimously hailed as "a value-for-money small hotel". It has a "good restaurant", too. / **Rooms:** 10 (of which some family rooms). **Details:** no Switch.

BLANCHLAND, COUNTY DURHAM 8–2A

Lord Crewe £110
DH8 9SP

🕙 www.lordcrewehotel.com

📠 lord@crewearms.freeserve.co.uk

☎ (01434) 675251 🖨 (01434) 675 337

The "lovely little village" in which it is situated provides a large part of the appeal of this "unspoilt" and very "atmospheric" inn (dating from the 12th and 17th centuries). Its accommodation is "spacious" and "tastefully decorated", and service is notably "friendly", too. / **Rooms:** 21 (of which some non smoking and 2 family rooms). **Details:** meals unavailable: Mon-Sat L.

BLANDFORD FORUM, DORSET 2–4B

Castleman £70
Chettle DT11 8DB

🕙 www.castlemanhotel.co.uk

📠 enquiry@castlemanhotel.co.uk

☎ (01258) 830096 🖨 (01258) 830051

This "pretty" rural restaurant-with-rooms avowedly does not seek to offer a 'full-on country house hotel experience'. As a place to stay, however, the few reporters unanimously think it "friendly and good value" – a "caring" establishment, offering "good hospitality and super food". / **Rooms:** 8 (of which 1 family room). **Details:** closed 25-26 Dec, Feb; meals unavailable: Mon-Sat L; no Amex.

BLESSINGTON LAKES, CO. WICKLOW, *ROI* 10–3D

Tulfarris €150
🕙 www.tulfarris.com 📠 info@tulfarris.com

☎ +353-45 867600 🖨 +353-45 867565

A "picturesque" setting – in the shadow of the Wicklow Mountains – and "very friendly" service are the distinguishing features of this golf-and-leisure hotel, centred on a Georgian house in a 200-acre estate. There is also a 'walled holiday village'. Weekday prices are considerably lower. / **Rooms:** 70 (of which 5 family rooms). **Facilities:** indoor pool; gym; golf; tennis. **Details:** no Switch.

BOLTON ABBEY, NORTH YORKSHIRE   8–4B

Devonshire Arms   £210

Grassington Rd BD23 6AJ
🖰 www.devonshirehotels.co.uk
🖂 reservations@thedevonshirearms.co.uk
☎ (01756) 710441   🖷 (01756) 710564

Country inns don't come any grander than this "truly luxurious" hotel (owned by the Devonshires for over 250 years), from where almost all reports are along the lines of "supreme surroundings and excellent attention to detail" (even if some do find the style, perhaps unsurprisingly, a touch "duchessy"). There is both a restaurant and a brasserie, but reports on the cuisine are broadly complimentary throughout. / **Rooms:** *41 (of which 15 non smoking and 3 family rooms).* **Facilities:** *indoor pool; gym; spa; tennis.*

BOLTON, LANCASHIRE   5–2B

Last Drop   £80

Bromley Cross BL7 9PZ
🖰 www.macdonaldhotels.co.uk
🖂 lastdrop@macdonald-hotels.co.uk
☎ (01204) 591131   🖷 (01204) 304122

"A lovely location" and "generally good value" combine to make this a "quaint, if rather touristy" old hotel. New leisure facilities are due to open in 2004. / **Rooms:** *128 (of which 64 non smoking).*

BOSHAM, WEST SUSSEX   3–4A

Millstream   £129

Bosham Ln PO18 8HL
🖰 www.millstream-hotel.co.uk
🖂 info@millstream-hotel.co.uk
☎ (01243) 573234   🖷 (01243) 573459

"A hands-on manager with an excellent staff and chef" helps win nothing but praise from a small fan club for this "pretty" hotel, whose gardens back on to a stream. Nearby, there are some "fabulous" walks. / **Rooms:** *35 (of which all non smoking and 2 family rooms).* **Details:** *no Amex.*

BOUGHTON LEES, KENT   3–3C

Eastwell Manor   £200
Eastwell Park TN25 4HR
🖰 www.eastwellmanor.co.uk ✉ eastwell@btinternet.com
☎ (01233) 213000 🖨 (01233) 635530

This grand Victorian country house hotel, now run by Marston Hotels, is set in manicured formal gardens, and offers a good range of leisure facilities, including an impressive spa (and it's also well geared up for conferences). Reports were all satisfactory, but there were no 'raves'. / **Rooms:** 62 (of which some family rooms). **Facilities:** indoor pool; outdoor pool; gym; spa; tennis.

BOURNEMOUTH, DORSET   2–4C

Bournemouth Highcliff Marriott   £99
St Michaels Rd, West Cliff BH2 5DU
🖰 www.marriott.com
✉ reservations.bournemouth@marriothotels.co.uk
☎ (01202) 557702 🖨 (01202) 292734

A funicular railway joins this imposing, and appropriately-named, hotel – "very well placed for access to town centre and shops" – to the beach. "Plentiful supplies" of grub ("enough at breakfast to feed a regiment") were a highlight of reports. / **Rooms:** 157 (of which some non smoking and some family rooms). **Facilities:** indoor pool; outdoor pool; gym; spa.

Carlton   £140
Meyrick Rd, East Overcliff BH1 3DN
🖰 www.menzies-hotels.com
☎ (01202) 552011 🖨 (01202) 299573

"A luxury hotel slowly rediscovering its past glory" or a "faded institution trading on a soon-to-be-lost reputation"? Views diverge on this grand seaside pile, run by Menzies Hotels, which attracted quite a lot of survey commentary. / **Rooms:** 73 (of which 20 non smoking and 6 family rooms). **Facilities:** indoor pool; outdoor pool; gym; spa.

sign up for our next survey at www.hardens.com   61

De Vere Royal Bath £170

Bath Rd BH1 2EW

🖳 www.devereonline.co.uk

✉ royalbath@devere-hotels.com

☎ (01202) 555555   📠 (01202) 292421

*At least a couple of reporters noted that this 'grande dame' of a large Victorian establishment is "in need of updating". It has its merits, though, not least an "excellent location" and "courteous" service. / **Rooms:** 140 (of which some family rooms). **Facilities:** indoor pool; gym; spa.*

Miramar £119

East Overcliff Drive, East Cliff BH1 3AL

🖳 www.miramar-bournemouth.com

✉ sales@miramar-bournemouth.com

☎ (01202) 716352556581   📠 (01202) 291242

*A "good position on a cliff" and "well modernised" accommodation combine to make this Edwardian establishment a "very good seaside hotel". / **Rooms:** 43 (of which some family rooms).*

Norfolk Royal £150

Richmond Hill BH2 6EN

🖳 www.englishrosehotels.co.uk/hotels/norfolk

✉ norfolkroyal@englishrosehotels.co.uk

☎ (01202) 551521   📠 (01202) 299729

*The rooms may "vary considerably" (and service can be "inexperienced"), but this large Edwardian establishment in the town centre is hailed by some reporters as a "good weekend break hotel". / **Rooms:** 95 (of which some non smoking and some family rooms). **Facilities:** indoor pool; spa.*

Linthwaite £99

Crook Rd LA23 3JA
🖰 www.linthwaite.com ✉ admin@linthwaite.com
☎ (01539) 488600 📠 (01539) 488601

A "cosy 'family' feeling" pervades this "first-class country house hotel", which is decorated in a more contemporary style than most such places, and set in "beautiful gardens" at the top of a hill, overlooking Lake Windermere. The food is "very good", too, and service "attentive, without being intrusive". / **Rooms:** 26 (of which 1 family room). **Facilities:** golf.

Miller Howe £170* 🙂

Rayrigg Rd LA23 1EY
🖰 www.millerhowe.com ✉ lakeview@millerhowe.com
☎ (01539) 442536 📠 (01539) 445664

For fans, John Tovey's successor, Charles Garside "has succeeded in carrying on the tradition" of this famous and "opulent" Lakeland hotel, famed for its "fine views" over Windermere (especially from the dining room). For others, though, the style of the place seems just too "chintzy" nowadays. *Prices are quoted on a DB&B basis. / **Rooms:** 15 (of which some non smoking and some family rooms). **Details:** min age for children: 8.

Cromleach Lodge €264

Castlebaldwin
🖰 www.cromleach.com ✉ info@cromleach.com
☎ +353-71 916 5155 📠 +353-71 916 5455

A striking modern building on a hillside looking down on Lough Arrow provides the setting for this "quiet" and luxurious family-owned establishment, tipped in particular for its "wonderful" food. / **Rooms:** 11 (of which 6 non smoking and some family rooms). **Details:** closed Nov-Jan; meals unavailable: L.

BRACKNELL, BERKSHIRE   3–3A

Coppid Beech   £89

John Nike Way RG12 8TF
🖰 www.coppidbeech.com
✉ sales@coppid-beach-hotel.co.uk
☎ (01344) 303333   🖷 (01344) 301200

This modern hotel just off the M4, is "near Legoland" and its idiosyncratic, chalet-styled design looks a bit like a giant model that's escaped. An extensive leisure complex (including a dry ski slope) and its "friendly" staff are particularly praised by reporters. / **Rooms:** 105 (of which 55 non smoking and 17 family rooms). **Facilities:** indoor pool; gym.

BRADFORD ON AVON, WILTSHIRE   2–3B

Woolley Grange   £135

Woolley Gn BA15 1TX
🖰 www.luxury-family-hotels.co.uk
✉ info@woolleygrange.com
☎ (01225) 864705

"Excellent for children, and their parents", the founder member of the Luxury Family Hotels group is "one of the best family hotels in the UK". The large amount of feedback was uniformly complimentary about the "great facilities" for juniors, the "relaxation" for adults and the "good food" for all. It can, though, seem "very expensive". / **Rooms:** 26 (of which 25 family rooms). **Facilities:** outdoor pool.

BRAMPTON, CUMBRIA   8–2A

Farlam Hall   £235*

CA8 2NG
🖰 www.farlamhall.co.uk   ✉ farlamhall@dial.pipex.com
☎ (01697) 746234   🖷 (01697) 746683

*This small but quite grand (Relais & Châteaux) family-owned country house, set in a dozen acres, is run by "very nice people". It attracted few, but consistently positive, reports. *Prices are quoted on a DB&B basis.* / **Rooms:** 12 (of which all non smoking). **Details:** closed 24-30 Dec; meals unavailable: L; no Amex; min age for children: 5.

sign up for our next survey at www.hardens.com

BRAY, WINDSOR & MAIDENHEAD   3–3A

Waterside Inn   £165

Ferry Rd SL6 2AT

🖰 www.waterside-inn.co.uk

✉ reservations@watersideinn.co.uk

☎ (01628) 620691   🖷 (01628) 784710

The UK's longest-established grand restaurant near (as opposed to in) the capital – with a "charming location" in a smart Thames-side village – boasts "limited facilities" and "only a few rooms". The latter, however, are "so tastefully beautiful and comfortable that you wouldn't want to leave them anyway" – except perhaps for Michel Roux's cooking, which maintains an impressive following. / **Rooms:** 9 (of which all non smoking). **Details:** closed 4 wks over Christmas; meals unavailable: Mon & Tues L; min age for children: 12.

BRECON, POWYS   2–1A

Felin Fach Griffin   £82

Felin Fach LD3 0UB

🖰 www.eatdrinksleep.ltd.uk

✉ enquiries@eatdrinksleep.ltd.uk

☎ (01874) 620111   🖷 (01874) 620120

"A jewel in this part of Wales where there are so few good hotel and restaurants." This "trendy, welcoming gastropub" wins praise for its "stylish" decor, "notable accommodation" and "superb restaurant". Communal breakfasts ("DIY toast on the Aga") are one of the features that make it ideal "for a friends' rendezvous". The only recurrent gripe: "it's a little close to a main road". / **Rooms:** 7. **Details:** no Amex.

Peterstone Court   £109

Llanhamlach LD3 7YB

🖰 www.peterstone-court.com

✉ info@peterstone-court.com

☎ (01874) 665387   🖷 (01874) 665376

This "delightful, small hotel", once a Georgian manor house, has a "beautiful setting" on the edge of the Brecon Beacons, and offers some "stunning" accommodation. Reports are not especially numerous, but are notable for their enthusiasm. / **Rooms:** 12 (of which 2 family rooms). **Facilities:** outdoor pool; gym; spa.

BRIGHTON, EAST SUSSEX   3–4B

We do not know whether Brighton's hoteliers have become fat in the two centuries that the city has been a more-or-less fashionable destination, but they have certainly become complacent. The large hotels, all run by major groups, incited a shamefully high proportion of negative commentary in the (significant) number of reports they generated. A new wave of boutique hotels brings the hope of some relief, but – the accommodation they offer being but a small proportion of the total available – you really must book well ahead if you want to guarantee escaping the tired clutches of the old guard.

Alias Hotel Seattle £95

The Strand, Brighton Marina BN2 5WA
🖰 www.aliasseattle.com   ✉ info@aliasseattle.com
☎ (01273) 679799

It opened too late for survey commentary, but it's difficult to imagine that this funky new waterside hotel – a sibling to Cheltenham's Kandinsky and Exeter's Barcelona – is not going to be a much talked-about addition to Brighton's accommodation possibilities. The obvious downside is that it's located a little way from the city itself, in a marina that's undergoing a major revamp.
/ **Rooms:** 71 *(of which 8 family rooms).*

Blanch House £125

17 Atlingworth St BN2 1PL
🖰 www.blanchhouse.co.uk   ✉ info@blanchhouse.co.uk
☎ (01273) 603504   🖨 (01273) 645755
"Trendy and sophisticated", this boutique hotel "tucked away in Kemptown" is hailed by most reporters as a "stylish" and "quirky" destination. In its early days, however, quite a number of reports expressed disappointment, in particular regarding staff attitude.
/ **Rooms:** 12. **Details:** *closed 25-31 Dec; meals unavailable: Sun & Mon.*

Brighton Metropole £128

Kings Road BN1 2FU
🖰 www.hilton.com
✉ reservation@brightonmet.stackis.co.uk
☎ (01273) 775432   🖨 (01273) 207764
"Distinctly faded, but without the charm" – thanks to the "best location in Brighton", this grand old establishment (now a Hilton) attracted much survey comment, but most of it negative with "tatty" rooms and "disorganised" service major causes of complaint. If you must stay here, some tip the "higher-floor seaview rooms" as affording "plenty of comfort and luxury".
/ **Rooms:** 335 *(of which some non smoking and some family rooms).* **Facilities:** *indoor pool; gym; spa.*

De Vere Grand £240
97-99 Kings Rd BN1 2FW
⌂ www.devereonline.co.uk
✉ general@grandbrighton.co.uk
☎ (01273) 224300   🖨 (01273) 224321

Some of those lucky enough to secure "a big room on the seafront" speak only well of this famous "Belle Epoque" landmark (which nowadays benefits from "very good business facilities"). Overall, however, reports included an unacceptably high level of negatives – "tired", "characterless", "complacent" and "way too expensive" are typical. / **Rooms:** 200. **Facilities:** *indoor pool; gym; spa.*

The Granville £75
124 Kings Rd BN1 2FA
⌂ www.granvillehotel.co.uk   ✉ granville@brighton.co.uk
☎ (01273) 326302   🖨 (01273) 728294

Though it gets few and slightly uneven reports, this "friendly" and "stylish" hotel is certainly worth considering in this under-served city. The Noel Coward suite comes especially recommended. / **Rooms:** 24 (of which all non smoking and 2 family rooms). **Facilities:** *golf; tennis.*

Hotel du Vin and Bistro £115
Ship St BN1 1AD
⌂ www.hotelduvin.com   ✉ info@brighton.hotelduvin.com
☎ (01273) 718588   🖨 (01273) 718599

Hailed by early reporters as "just superb", this "clever" and "imaginative" late-2002 addition to the most popular of the boutique-hotel chains looks quite likely to become THE place to stay in Brighton. As usual, it offers accommodation "of character", and enjoys a "great location", too (just behind the seafront). / **Rooms:** 37 (of which some non smoking and some family rooms).

Old Ship £118
Kings Rd BN1 1NR
⌂ www.paramount-hotels.co.uk
☎ (01273) 329001

Though it's been partially modernised (and boasts some "attractive" public areas), this prominently-located, old-fashioned seaside hotel (owned by Paramount) still gets a lot of flak for 'traditional' English hotel problems – "dull" décor, "stuffy" bedrooms and sometimes "burdened" service are the sorts of themes cropping up in nearly half of the reports. / **Rooms:** 152.

Paskins £70

18-19 Charlotte St BN2 1AG

🖰 www.paskins.co.uk ✉ welcome@paskins.co.uk

☎ (01273) 601203

*"Very friendly and clean", this charmingly-located townhouse-hotel is praised for its "beautiful" accommodation ("all rooms are different") and its "lovely organic breakfasts". / **Rooms:** 19 (of which 1 family room).*

Pelirocco £85

10 Regency Sq BN1 2FG

🖰 www.hotelpelirocco.co.uk ✉ info@hotelpelirocco.co.uk

☎ (01273) 327055 📠 (01273) 733845

*"Wild, eccentric, funky and friendly" (and in a "very central location", too); reporters speak well of this "rock-star" establishment – "a trendified hotel in a Regency square", where each room is designed around "a different bizarre theme", and where a stay is usually "good fun". / **Rooms:** 19. **Details:** meals unavailable: no restaurant.*

Thistle £147

Kings Rd BN1 2GS

🖰 www.thistlehotels.com ✉ brighton@Thistle.co.uk

☎ 0870 333 9129 📠 (01273) 820692

*This vast and hideous "blot on the landscape/seascape" – a concrete box, complete with internal atrium – would not be recommendable in most places. In this under-served city, however, it's worth knowing about, despite its sometimes below-par housekeeping, and too-often "horrid" food. / **Rooms:** 208 (of which 156 non smoking and 12 family rooms). **Details:** meals unavailable: L.*

Topps £80

17 Regency Sq BN1 2FG

🖰 www.brighton.co.ukhotelstopps ✉ toppshotel@aol.com

☎ (01273) 729334 📠 (01273) 203679

*A "very friendly welcome and atmosphere" characterise this superior B&B of long standing, in a "quiet square" just off the seafront. "Very good breakfast", too. / **Rooms:** 5 (of which 2 non smoking). **Details:** meals unavailable: no restaurant.*

BRISTOL, CITY OF BRISTOL 2–2B

Bristol is something of a 'chain-hell'. It is relieved, however, by the presence of the best outlet of one of the country's best up-and-coming small groups, the Hotels du Vin et Bistro.

Brigstow £140

5-7 Welsh Back BS1 4SP

🖰 www.brigstowhotel.com ✉ brigstow@fullers.co.uk
☎ (0117) 929 1030 🖷 (0117) 929 2030

*As a place to lay your head, this "modern, minimalist and
unusual" waterfront city-centre hotel has its charms. This Fullers
establishment is otherwise of no particular note, however, and the
cooking is "uninspiring" – it "tries far too hard, and ends up at
pub standard", says one reporter.* / **Rooms:** 116 (of which 99 non
smoking and 7 family rooms).

City Inn £99

Temple Way BS1 6BF

🖰 www.cityinn.com ✉ bristol.reservations@cityinn.com
☎ (0117) 925 1001 🖷 (0117) 907 4116

*"Despite being a formula hotel" this establishment near the
railway station offers "clean" and "comfortable" accommodation
that's hailed for its "exceptional value for money". The restaurant,
too, attracts surprisingly favourable comments.* / **Rooms:** 167 (of
which 136 non smoking). **Facilities:** gym. **Details:** meals unavailable: L.

Hilton Bristol £129

Woodlands Ln, Bradley Stoke BS32 4JF

🖰 www.hilton.co.uk
☎ (01454) 201144 🖷 (01454) 612022

*"Busy" and generally "efficient", this modern hotel some eight
miles from the city (by J16 of the M5) is judged "very adequate
for its purpose".* / **Rooms:** 141 (of which some non smoking and some family
rooms). **Facilities:** indoor pool; gym; spa.

Holiday Inn £161

Filton Rd BS16 1QX

🖰 www.holiday-inn.co.uk
☎ (0117) 956 4243 🖷 (0117) 956 9735

*There is also a city-centre Holiday Inn (tel 956 4243, not to
mention two Expresses), but it's this one, at Filton, which attracts
most interest from reporters. "An excellent pool" and a location
that's "handy for both Bath and Bristol" are among features
recommending it.* / **Rooms:** 222 (of which some non smoking and some family
rooms). **Facilities:** indoor pool; gym; golf.

Hotel du Vin et Bistro £125

The Sugar House, Narrow Lewins Mead BS1 2NU
🖰 www.hotelduvin.com ✉ info@bristol.hotelduvin.com
☎ (0117) 925 5577 🖷 (0117) 925 1199

*"Charming and individual" accommodation " – "quality, from
sheets to showers" – is just part of the formula which makes this
"idiosyncratic" and "welcoming" warehouse-conversion a "10/10
location" (and the most popular member of the justly celebrated
boutique-hotel chain). It has an "excellent" city-centre location,
too, where the restaurant has established itself as a very popular
destination in its own right.* / **Rooms:** 40 (of which 3 family rooms).

Jurys £140 ☹

Prince St BS1 4QF
🖰 www.jurysdoyle.com ✉ bristol@jurysdoyle.com
☎ (0117) 923 0333 🖷 (0117) 923 0300
*This "large", "modern" waterfront hotel is "hard to beat for
location", and supporters praise its "child-friendliness", too.
It "looks like a car park", though, and with its "indifferent"
bedrooms and "plastic" ambience, it's dismissed as an "overpriced
bed factory" by too many reporters.* / **Rooms:** 191 (of which some non
smoking and some family rooms). **Details:** no Switch.

Marriott £149 ☺

College Gn BS1 5TA
🖰 www.marriott.com
✉ bristol.royal@marriott.hotels.co.uk
☎ (0117) 925 5100 🖷 (0117) 925 1515
*Bristol's grand (and very large) traditional city-centre hotel, by the
cathedral, was taken over by Marriott in 2000, and refurbishment
work was still under way in summer 2003 (which also saw the
opening of a new restaurant overseen by Michael Caines,
celebrated chef of Gidleigh Park). In this period of transition,
reports have been notably inconsistent, but the more enthusiastic
ones have spoken in terms of "top quality, both for business and
leisure". (NB Bristol also has another Marriott, which one reporter
characterises as "a charmless business hotel".)* / **Rooms:** 242 (of
which 133 non smoking and 11 family room). **Facilities:** indoor pool; gym; spa.

BROADWAY, WORCESTERSHIRE 2–1C

Dormy House £165
Willersey Hill WR12 7LF
🖰 www.dormyhouse.co.uk
✉ reservations@dormyhouse.co.uk
☎ (01386) 852711 📠 (01386) 858636

"A beautifully appointed hotel run by attentive staff" in a 17th-century farmhouse building, in the heart of the Cotswolds. The staff *"try hard"*, and the *"lovely atmosphere"* is praised by all reporters. There are two restaurants serving *"very good food"* – the bistro is especially praised for those trying to keep budgets in check. / **Rooms:** 48 (of which 1 non smoking and 5 family rooms). **Facilities:** gym. **Details:** closed Christmas.

Lygon Arms £179
High St WR12 7DU
🖰 www.the-lygon-arms.co.uk ✉ info@the-lygon.co.uk
☎ (01386) 852255 📠 (01386) 858611

In the dying days of the Savoy régime (which ended in the summer of 2003), *"trading on former glories"* was the gist of far too many reports on this famously *"olde worlde"* Baronial Cotswold bastion, in the heart of a picture-postcard-pretty town. New owners Furlong Hotels apparently intend to spend a lot of money on the place – just as well, as the former owners had neglected it appallingly. / **Rooms:** 69 (of which 5 family rooms). **Facilities:** indoor pool; gym; spa; tennis.

Milestone House £55
122 High St WR12 7AJ
🖰 www.milestone-broadway.co.uk
✉ enquiries@milestone-broadway.co.uk
☎ (01386) 853432

Mr and Mrs Norman run this 17th-century house in a pretty Cotswold town – it's a smart establishment, hailed by reporters as offering *"everything one could wish for in a B&B"*. / **Rooms:** 4 (of which all non smoking). **Details:** no Amex.

BROCKENHURST, HAMPSHIRE 2–4C

Rhinefield £115
Rhinefield Rd SO42 7QB
🖰 www.rhinefieldhousehotel.co.uk
✉ rhinefield-house@arcadianhotels.co.uk
☎ (01590) 622922 📠 (01590) 622800

This *"fairytale hotel"* (an impressive Victorian house now owned by the Arcadian group) sits *"in outstanding grounds in the depth of New Forest"*. As such, it's surprising that it didn't generate rather more feedback – such as there was positive but a little uneven (especially regarding the restaurant). / **Rooms:** 34 (of which 6 non smoking). **Facilities:** outdoor pool; tennis. **Details:** meals unavailable: Sat L & Mon L; no Switch.

Cornwallis Country Hotel £110

Rectory Rd IP23 8AJ

🏠 www.thecornwallis.com ✉ info@thecornwallis.com

☎ (01379) 870326 📠 (01379) 870051

This "charming" small hotel – in a dower house whose origins go back to the 16th century – boasts "beautiful" grounds, and attracts nothing but positive reports. On the food front, there's not only a restaurant, but also a pub-like Tudor Bar, which serves "good food". / **Rooms:** *16 (of which 1 family room).* **Details:** *no Amex.*

Bryn Garw House £65

Bryn Garw Country Park CF32 8UU

🏠 www.bryngarwhouse.co.uk

✉ bryngarwhouse@bridgend.gov.uk

☎ (01656) 729009 📠 (01656) 729007

If you should find yourself in these parts, this Tudorbethan house (renovated by the council in the early '90s into a country house hotel and conference centre, and set in 113 acres of parkland) is tipped as an all-round satisfactory destination. / **Rooms:** *19 (of which 15 non smoking and 2 family rooms).* **Details:** *no Amex or Switch.*

Buckland Manor £225

WR12 7LY

🏠 www.bucklandmanor.com

✉ enquire@bucklandmanor.com

☎ (01386) 852626 📠 (01386) 853557

"An overall wonderful experience" is the tenor of all reports of this grand (Relais & Châteaux) country house (whose existence was recorded in the Domesday Book) – a "wonderful location" with "fabulous gardens". Rooms are decked out in chintzy style, some with four-posters. / **Rooms:** *14 (of which 1 family room).* **Facilities:** *outdoor pool; tennis.* **Details:** *min age for children: 12.*

BURFORD, OXFORDSHIRE 2–2C

The Bay Tree £155
Sheep St OX18 4LW
⌂ www.cotswold-inns-hotels.co.uk
✉ bookings@cotswold-inns-hotels.co.uk
☎ (01993) 822791 📠 (01993) 823008

"A lovely location and great character" are the dominant themes
of the (almost) uniformly positive feedback on this ancient (16th-
century) inn, with its flagstone floors and its antique tapestries
and furniture. / **Rooms:** 21 (of which 4 family rooms).

Burford House £105
99 High Street OX18 4QA
⌂ www.burford-house.co.uk ✉ stay@burfordhouse.co.uk
☎ (01993) 823151 📠 (01993) 823240

*A small, family-run Cotswold hotel, tipped as a "wonderfully
quiet", "no-hassle" destination, with "fantastic" accommodation.
/ **Rooms:** 8 (of which all non smoking and 1 family room). **Details:** meals
unavailable: D.*

Inn for All Seasons £93
The Barringtons OX18 4TN
⌂ www.innforallseasons.demon.co.uk
✉ sharp@innforallseasons.com
☎ (01451) 844324 📠 (01451) 844375

*For a true "Cotswold experience", this "very good family-run hotel,
with a busy bar and restaurant" is hailed by all reporters as a
"beautiful" place with a "cosy" atmosphere. Even a self-avowed
fan, though, believes that "the rooms could be brought into the
21st century without any loss of charm".* / **Rooms:** 10 (of which some
non smoking and 2 family rooms).

The Lamb Inn £99
Sheep St OX18 4LR
⌂ www.traditionalvillageinns.co.uk
☎ (01993) 830465

*"Where better for a weekend break than a gateway to the
Cotswolds?"* This *"lovely family-run coaching inn"* – with its
"ancient flagstones", *"beams"* and *"roaring fires"* – *"fits like an
old suit"*. It offers *"genuine charm"*, *"good, if unmemorable,
cooking"* and an *"uncomplacent attitude"*. / **Rooms:** 5. **Details:** meals
unavailable: Mon & Sun D; no Amex.

BURNHAM MARKET, NORFOLK | 6–3B

Hoste Arms £92

The Green PE31 8HD
⌂ www.hostearms.co.uk ✉ reception@hostearms.co.uk
☎ (01328) 738777 📠 (01328) 730103

"A good reputation" precedes Paul Whittome's "upmarket pub" in a "pretty" village – it's long been "an 'in'-destination" for jaded townies and, at weekends in particular, can be "very busy". Given the "friendly" and "buzzing" bar scene, the "excellent food" and the "staff who try hard", most reports are of "a warm feeling of wellbeing", but there are former fans who say "they've over-extended, and ruined the former ambience". / **Rooms:** 36 (of which 1 family room). **Details:** no Amex.

BURY ST EDMUNDS, SUFFOLK | 3–1C

Angel £119

3 Angel Hill IP33 1LT
⌂ www.theangel.co.uk ✉ reservations@theangel.co.uk
☎ (01284) 753926

There's some disagreement between reporters as to whether they prefer the "quiet" (if slightly "soulless") modern accommodation to the more characterful old rooms at this imposing hotel, whose origins are 15th-century (and which Dickens mentioned in the Pickwick Papers). It makes "an ideal base for exploring East Anglia". / **Rooms:** 66 (of which 20 non smoking and some family rooms).

Ickworth £160*

Horringer IP29 5QE
⌂ www.ickworthhotel.com ✉ info@ickworthhotel.com
☎ (01284) 735350 📠 (01284) 736300

*This "upmarket family hotel" (part of the Luxury Family Hotels group and with their customary focus on crêches and other kids' facilities) has a "wonderful location" in a "superb conversion of the east wing of Ickworth House". It's a "stylish" and "luxurious" place amidst "beautiful" and "peaceful" grounds (1800 acres including horse and bike riding), and the food is "very good" too. *Prices are quoted on a DB&B basis.* / **Rooms:** 27 (of which all non smoking and 15 family rooms). **Facilities:** indoor pool; spa; tennis. **Details:** meals unavailable: Mon-Sat L, Sun D.

Fishes
01328 738589

BUXTON, DERBYSHIRE

Palace
£98

Palace Rd SK17 6AG
🖰 www.paramount-hotels.co.uk
☎ (01298) 22001
This "magnificent old building" (run by Paramount) boasts "the most stunning staircase, and views over Buxton". Many reporters judge it "very much in need of refurbishment", though, and there are too many reports to the effect that Basil Fawlty is alive and well here – he seems to be most in evidence in the dining room.
/ **Rooms:** 118. **Facilities:** indoor pool; gym.

CAMBRIDGE, CAMBRIDGESHIRE

A more dreary and depressing collection of hotels than Cambridge's is really hard to imagine. We have, however, managed to identify a couple of places to stay which are at least acceptable.

Cambridge Garden House Moat House
£172

Granta Pl, Mill Ln CB2 1RT
🖰 www.moat-gardenhouse.activehotels.com
✉ reservations.cambridgegarden@moathousehotels.com
☎ (01223) 259988 🖨 (01223) 316605
A "beautiful riverside setting" plus "a good location for exploring the city make this modern hotel a potentially wonderful destination (and it's also "one of the few central places with a car park"). It's a shame, then, that the restaurant is well below par and that the rooms are decidedly indifferent (with one reporter dismissing the furnishings for giving an "overall flat-pack impression"). / **Rooms:** 121 (of which 60 non smoking). **Facilities:** indoor pool; gym; spa.

Crowne Plaza
£180

Downing St CB2 3DT
🖰 www.crowneplaza.com
✉ reservations-cambridgecp@6c.com
☎ (01223) 464466 🖨 (01223) 464440
"Charmless but comfortable", this "modern and functional" establishment is worth knowing about for two reasons (only). Firstly, it is "very convenient for the city-centre", and secondly because it offers "good value at weekends". / **Rooms:** 198 (of which some non smoking and 4 family rooms). **Facilities:** gym.

sign up for our next survey at www.hardens.com

De Vere University Arms £180

Regent St CB2 1AD
🖰 www.devereonline.co.uk
✉ dua.sales@devere-hotels.com
☎ (01223) 351241   🖷 (01223) 461319

Victorian architecture with much "old charm", a pleasant setting (overlooking a large common) and "a very central location" are the lingering attractions of this "typical" hotel of the old school. "There's a very mixed quality in both rooms and service", though – the former can be of "poor quality", and the latter "careless". / **Rooms:** *120 (of which 80 non smoking and 4 family rooms).*

Holiday Inn £139

Bridge Rd, Histon CB4 9PH
🖰 www.holiday-inn.co.uk
✉ reservations-cambridge@6c.com
☎ 0870 400 9015   🖷 (01223) 233426

It may lack any particular charm, but this "friendly" hotel displays "surprisingly good attention to detail". "Comfortable" accommodation and "an excellent swimming pool" are among aspects reporters particularly praise. You think there might be a catch? – indeed, the location is some three miles from the city-centre. / **Rooms:** *161 (of which 80 non smoking and some family rooms).* **Facilities:** *indoor pool; gym.*

Regent £99

41 Regent St CB2 1AB
🖰 www.regenthotel.co.uk
✉ reservations@regenthotel.co.uk
☎ (01223) 351470   🖷 (01223) 566562

Even pre-refurbishment (it's closed as we go to press) this hotel in the very "heart" of the city was considered "the best of the medium-price hotels" by at least one reporter (if "noisy, at the front"). The omens therefore seem set for its standards after its scheduled 2004 re-opening. / **Rooms:** *25 (of which some non smoking and some family rooms).* **Details:** *closed Christmas.*

Old Rectory £75

Station Rd IP13 0PU
🖰 www.theoldrectorysuffolk.com
✉ mail@theoldrectorysuffolk.com
☎ (01728) 746524   🖷 (01728) 746524

The "eccentric" former régime which made a name for this "delightful" and "very individual" hotel – in a Georgian rectory – drew to a close in the summer of 2002. We've not therefore included a rating, but the new owners tell us they very much aim to take over where the old guard left off. / **Rooms:** *8 (of which all non smoking and some family rooms).* **Details:** *closed Dec-Jan; meals unavailable: no restaurant; no Amex or Switch.*

CANTERBURY, KENT   3–3D

Chaucer   £120

Ivy Ln CT1 1TU
⌂ www.macdonaldhotels.co.uk
✉ chaucer@macdonald-hotels.co.uk
☎ (01227) 464427   ▤ (01227) 450397

Despite some reservations, this "comfortable"-enough old Macdonald Hotels establishment "in the heart of the city" is rated "good, on the whole" by most reporters. / **Rooms:** 42 (of which some non smoking and 4 family rooms). **Details:** meals unavailable: L.

Ebury   £70

65 New Dover Rd CT1 3DX
⌂ www.ebury-hotel.co.uk   ✉ info@ebury-hotel.co.uk
☎ (01227) 768433   ▤ (01227) 459187

In this city "strangely lacking in nice hotels", this "old-fashioned" (and quite modestly-priced) Victorian establishment has its fans. "A great swimming pool" is a particular plus. / **Rooms:** 15 (of which some non smoking and some family rooms). **Facilities:** indoor pool. **Details:** closed Christmas; meals unavailable: L.

CARDIFF, CARDIFF   2–2A

The Welsh capital is about as well blessed with decent hotels as it is with decent restaurants, which is to say hardly at all. If money is no object, *St David's* is clearly the place to stay.

Angel   £108

Castle St CF10 1SZ
⌂ www.paramounthotels.co.uk
✉ angelevents@paramount-hotels.co.uk
☎ (02920) 649200

Some feedback speaks of "slightly tired" rooms, but, even so, reporters seem to have a soft spot for this restored Victorian hotel, near the Castle. A "nice entrance and lobby" and "helpful staff" ("they accommodated my dog happily, and even volunteered to walk it") are among the plus-points. The restaurant is considered to be an "under-used" facility, especially given the lack of city centre competition. / **Rooms:** 102 (of which 15 non smoking and some family rooms).

Hilton Cardiff   £145

Kingsway CF10 3HH
⌂ www.hilton.co.uk
☎ (02920) 646300   ▤ (02920) 646333

A "very central" location adds lustre to this "modern" and "spacious" hotel, which is a recent addition to the chain, and "very good for business". The "complete range of facilities" (which include "an interesting stainless steel swimming pool") is much praised, but the restaurant is "overpriced", and the ambience very "corporate". / **Rooms:** 197 (of which some non smoking and some family rooms). **Facilities:** indoor pool; gym; spa.

Marriott £114
Mill Ln CF1 1EZ
🖰 www.marriott.com
☎ (02920) 399944   🖷 (02920) 395578
An "excellent location for the city-centre" and "a good swimming pool and sauna" are seen by some reporters as the saving grace of this "busy and noisy" chain hotel. / **Rooms:** 182 (of which 100 non smoking and 40 family rooms). **Facilities:** indoor pool; gym.

St David's £200 ☺☺
Havannah St CF10 5SD
🖰 www.roccofortehotels.com
☎ (02920) 454045   🖷 (02920) 313075

With its "wonderful views over Cardiff Bay" and some "stunning" modern design, Rocco Forte has created a "first-class modern hotel". "Fantastic-quality rooms and facilities" and "friendly and helpful service" are most highly rated and "one of the best spas of the country" is a particular attraction". The only notably "average" part of the package is the restaurant (Tides). / **Rooms:** 132 (of which 24 non smoking and some family rooms). **Facilities:** indoor pool; gym; spa.

Carnoustie Gold £190
The Links DD7 7JE
🖰 www.carnoustie-hotel.com
📧 enquiries@carnoustie-hotel.com
☎ (01241) 411999   🖷 (01241) 411998
Adjacent to the golf course which they claim is 'the most challenging in the world', this privately-owned modern hotel is tipped for its "exceptional views", and also for having "the friendliest staff". / **Rooms:** 75 (of which 4 family rooms). **Facilities:** indoor pool; gym; spa; golf.

CARTMEL, CUMBRIA 7–4D

Aynsome Manor £122*

LA11 6HH
⌂ www.aynsomemanorhotel.co.uk
✉ info@aynsomemanorhotel.co.uk
☎ (01539) 536653   ᠍ (01539) 536016

"Excellent catering and a wonderful atmosphere" – these are the key strengths of this *"welcoming"* country house hotel, which offers some *"wonderful views"*. It's reasonably priced, too, especially as prices are quoted on a *DB&B basis. / **Rooms:** 12 (of which all non smoking). **Details:** closed Jan; meals unavailable: Mon-Sat L; min age for children: 5.

CASHEL, CO. TIPPERARY, *ROI* 10–3C

Cashel Palace €185

Main St
⌂ www.cashel-palace.ie   ✉ reception@cashel-palace.ie
☎ +353-62 62707   ᠍ +353-62 61521

"In the touristy town of Cashel", this former bishop's palace in a Queen Anne-style building (set in 30 acres of grounds) is widely tipped as *"an idyllic country house hotel"*. And for anglers, there are fishing rights to five miles of the nearby River Suir. Some reporters say the dining is *"great"*, but reports are rather up-and-down. / **Rooms:** 23 (of which some family rooms). **Details:** closed Christmas.

CASTLE COMBE, WILTSHIRE 2–2B

Castle Inn £95

SN14 7HN
⌂ www.castle-inn.co.uk   ✉ res@castle-inn.co.uk
☎ (01249) 783030   ᠍ (01249) 782315

Fans of *"the quaint English country look"* will be pleased by this *"beautiful"*, *"higgledy-piggledy"* inn, which can trace its origins back to the 12th century. Changes are afoot, though, here – refurbishment by a new owner is under way as we go to press. / **Rooms:** 10 (of which all non smoking). **Details:** meals unavailable: L.

CHADDESLEY CORBETT, WORCESTERSHIRE 5–4B

Brockencote Hall £116

DY10 4PY
⌂ www.brockencotehall.com   ✉ info@brockencotehall.com
☎ (01562) 777876   ᠍ (01562) 777872

A *"beautiful"* location, *"fabulous"* accommodation, *"charming"* service and *"really lovely Gallic cooking"* – reporters can find little to criticise at this charming, family-owned, château-like country house hotel. The main building is late-Victorian, but the estate is of greater antiquity. / **Rooms:** 17 (of which 1 family room). **Facilities:** tennis. **Details:** meals unavailable: Sat L.

CHAGFORD, DEVON   1–3D

Gidleigh Park   £420*   😊😊
TQ13 8HH

🖰 www.gidleigh.com   ✉ gidleighpark@gidleigh.co.uk
☎ (01647) 432367   🖨 (01647) 432574

"A perfect weekend retreat." Paul and Kay Henderson's "tucked
away idyll" – a "very comfortable", 'Stockbroker Tudor' house in
"magical gardens" on the fringe of Dartmoor – was one of
reporters' most-visited country destinations. "It does not have
many facilities", but with its "stunning location", "fabulous dining"
(with a "great wine list") and "service to dream about" it was
generally thought "outstanding all round". "Very significant prices"
– quoted, mercifully, on a *DB&B basis – were the only real
complaint. / **Rooms:** 14. **Facilities:** tennis.

22 Mill Street   £55   T
22 Mill St TQ13 8AW

🖰 www.22millstreet.co.uk   ✉ walkermarra@aol.com
☎ (01647) 432244   🖨 (01647) 433101

"Really a restaurant, and with just two rooms, but surpassing
most hotels"; this "quiet, comfortable and individual"
establishment is run by chef Duncan Walker (formerly at Gidleigh
Park, which is just down the lane) and is tipped for its "very
personal service", plus, naturally, some "superb" cooking.
/ **Rooms:** 2 (of which some non smoking). **Details:** closed 1 wk in Jun, 2 wks in
Jan; meals unavailable: Sun-Tue; no Amex.

CHANDLER'S CROSS, HERTFORDSHIRE   3–2A

The Grove   £240   N
WD3 4TG

🖰 www.thegrove.co.uk   ✉ info@thegrove.co.uk
☎ (01923) 807807   🖨 (01923) 221008

'London's cosmopolitan country estate' – that's the theme of this
major new 'groovy grand' venture, built around an impressive
18th-century house, scheduled to open its gates in the autumn of
2003. In addition to a whole range of restaurants and bars, it
promises a huge range of leisure facilities, including an 18-hole
golf course and a 'state-of-the-art' spa, complete with swimming
pools indoor and out. / **Rooms:** 227 (of which some family rooms).
Facilities: indoor pool; outdoor pool; gym; spa; golf; tennis.

CHELTENHAM, GLOUCESTERSHIRE   2–1C

Georgian House   £70   T
77 Montpellier Terrace GL50 1XA

🖰 www.georgianhouse.net   ✉ georgian_house@yahoo.com
☎ (01242) 515577   🖨 (01242) 545929

An elegant Georgian townhouse B&B, that's tipped as an
"absolutely delightful" place, with "wonderful" service. / **Rooms:** 3.
Details: closed Christmas; min age for children: 16.

Kandinsky £90

Bayshill Rd, Montpellier GL50 3AS
www.aliashotels.com info@hotelkandinsky.com
☎ (01242) 527788

This "very modern", "very original" boutique hotel (occupying a Regency townhouse) gets a unanimous thumbs up from reporters and wins recommendations for business as well as weekending. All aspects of the operation are highly rated – the "fun" and "comfortable" décor, "great food" and "good way with kids" – with the "brilliant" club/bar in particular a "real plus". / **Rooms:** 48.

Queens £110

The Promenade GL50 1NN
www.macdonaldhotels.co.uk
☎ 0870 400 8107   📠 (01242) 224145
"Cheltenham's grand old hotel" (which moved into the Macdonald Hotels stable in 2002) still strikes a fair proportion of reporters as a "lovely" place. In this transitional period, a rating hardly seems appropriate. / **Rooms:** 79 (of which 28 non smoking).

CHEPSTOW, GWENT 2–2B

Marriott Chepstow £110

St Pierre Pk NP16 6YA
www.marriott.com
☎ (01291) 625261   📠 (01291) 629975
"A good location set in two good golf courses, but otherwise a standard Marriott" – one reporter neatly summarises the views of all on this "friendly" establishment, built around a 14th-century manor house. / **Rooms:** 148 (of which 100 non smoking and 15 family rooms). **Facilities:** indoor pool; gym; spa; golf.

The Chester Crabwall Manor £153

Parkgate Rd, Mollington CH1 6NE

🖰 www.marstonhotels.com

✉ crabwallmanor@marstonhotels.com

☎ (01244) 851666 📠 (01244) 851400

"A large country house hotel with a modern annexe and excellent restaurant" – are the key attractions of this "beautiful" Marston Hotels establishment (dating from the 17th century), set in 11 acres of grounds some four miles from the city-centre. "Excellent facilities", too. / **Rooms:** 48 (of which 14 non smoking and some family rooms). **Facilities:** indoor pool; gym; spa. **Details:** meals unavailable: Sat L.

Chester Grosvenor £200

Eastgate CH1 1LT

🖰 www.chestergrosvenor.co.uk

✉ chesgrove@chesgrosvenor.co.uk

☎ (01244) 324024

"The best hotel in the North West" has a wonderful location in "the heart of the picturesque city centre". It has a grandeur which would not seem wholly out of place in Mayfair (which is perhaps no coincidence, as both are owned by the Duke of Westminster). Facilities are arguably a weak point (though a spa opened in the summer of 2003), but the food is "very good" (if, in the Michelin-starred restaurant, "overpriced"). / **Rooms:** 80 (of which all non smoking). **Facilities:** gym; spa. **Details:** meals unavailable: Sun D, Mon (Arkle restaurant).

Craxton Wood £110

Parkgate Rd, Ledsham CH66 9PB

🖰 www.macdonaldhotels.co.uk

✉ craxtonwood@macdonald-hotels.co.uk

☎ (0151) 347 4000 📠 (0151) 347 4040

With its "fine restaurant" and "lovely swimming pool", this "modern Macdonald hotel in a lovely woodland setting" (some eight miles from the city) is rated an "excellent-value" destination by most reporters (though it can seem just a fraction "soulless"). / **Rooms:** 72 (of which some non smoking and some family rooms). **Facilities:** indoor pool; gym; spa.

De Vere Carden Park £80

CH3 9QD

🖰 www.devereonline.co.uk

✉ reservations.carden@devere-hotels.com

☎ (01829) 731000 📠 (01829) 731032

Southfork comes to the Cheshire Plain, at this rambling modern hotel, set in extensive grounds. It's "OK, if you like golf" (and has quite a range of other leisure facilities), but the whole style of the place is mystifyingly "characterless" – "like an airport hotel". / **Rooms:** 192 (of which 72 non smoking and 22 family rooms). **Facilities:** indoor pool; gym; spa; golf; tennis.

Hoole Hall £98

Warrington Rd, Hoole CH2 3PD
🖥 www.corushotels.com ✉ hoolehall@corushotels.com
☎ 0870 609 6126 🖨 (01244) 320251

A useful standby ("modern, but with character"), just outside the city, and rated by most reporters as a "good-value" destination.
/ **Rooms:** *97 (of which some non smoking and some family rooms).*

Moat House £175 ☺

Trinity St CH1 2BD
🖥 www.moathousehotels.com
✉ reservations.chester@moathousehotels.com
☎ (01244) 899988 🖨 (01244) 316118

This "efficient" hotel has a "very convenient" location (if not a particularly picturesque one, over a car park), a few minutes' walk from the heart of the city. For such a central location, the leisure facilities – including a "very good swimming pool" – are of some note. The restaurant, however, is not. / **Rooms:** *160 (of which some non smoking and some family rooms).* **Facilities:** *indoor pool; gym; spa.*

Lumley Castle £145 ☺☺

Chester-le-Street DH3 4NX
🖥 www.lumleycastle.com
✉ reservations@lumleycastle.com
☎ (0191) 389 1111 🖨 (0191) 389 1881

This ancient creeper-clad castle is "a bit of a hidden gem". It attracts consistently complimentary reports for its "great" rooms ("best in the castle itself"), and for its "exceptionally good" service. / **Rooms:** *59 (of which 8 family rooms).* **Details:** *closed 24-26 Dec, 1-2 Jan.*

CHICHESTER, SUSSEX 3–4A

The Forge £110
Chilgrove PO18 9HX

🏠 www.forgehotel.com ✉ reservations@forgehotel.com
☎ (01243) 535333 🖷 (01243) 535363

This 17th-century brick and flint cottage, in an acre of garden in the Downs, has been restored to make an "informal" and "relaxed" small hotel. Its attractions include some "imaginative" accommodation, a "very good chef" and a very extensive wine list. / **Rooms:** 5 (of which all non smoking). **Details:** closed 1 wk Nov, 1 wk Feb; min age for children: 14.

Goodwood Park £138
PO18 0QB

🏠 www.marriott.com
☎ (01243) 775537 🖷 (01243) 520125

"A beautiful location" in the Goodwood Estate (and "handy for West Dean Gardens") plus "good sports facilities" helps make this hotel-cum-country club a "relaxing country weekend" destination, and it attracted quite a lot of survey comment. Otherwise, however, it's just "a bog-standard Marriott". / **Rooms:** 94 (of which some non smoking and 12 family rooms). **Facilities:** indoor pool; gym; golf; tennis.

CHIPPENHAM, WILTSHIRE 2–2C

Manor House £145
Castle Combe SN14 7HR

🏠 www.exclusivehotels.co.uk
✉ enquiries@manor-housecc.co.uk
☎ (01249) 782206 🖷 (01249) 782159

"A picturebook manor house in a picturebook village", now an 'Exclusive Hotels' property. Its "good facilities" attracted particular praise. / **Rooms:** 48 (of which all non smoking and some family rooms). **Facilities:** outdoor pool; gym; golf; tennis. **Details:** no Amex.

CHIPPING CAMPDEN, GLOUCESTERSHIRE 2–1C

Charingworth Manor £150*
Charingworth GL55 6NS

🏠 www.englishrosehotels.co.uk
✉ charingworthmanor@englishrosehotels.co.uk
☎ (01386) 593555 🖷 (01386) 593353

*Run by English Rose Hotels, this "charmingly located old manor house" (dating from the 14th century) attracted a fair amount of survey commentary and scored particularly well for atmosphere. There were numerous niggles, though, including "old-fashioned" accommodation and "hit-and-miss" service. *Prices are quoted on a DB&B basis.* / **Rooms:** 26 (of which 5 family rooms). **Facilities:** indoor pool; gym. **Details:** meals unavailable: Mon-Sat L.

Cotswold House £175

The Square GL55 6AN
🖰 www.cotswoldhouse.com
✉ reception@cotswoldhouse.com
☎ (01386) 840330

This "beautifully restored" (in contemporary style) Georgian
townhouse has a "wonderful" (if sometimes "noisy") location "in
the middle of the high street", and offers an experience "like
staying in a private house with every luxury provided". Even
supporters may find it "a bit pricey", but the accommodation is
"lovely (if a bit cramped)". / **Rooms:** 22 (of which 20 non smoking and 2
family rooms). **Facilities:** tennis. **Details:** meals unavailable: L.

The Malt House £92

Broad Campden GL55 6UU
🖰 www.malt-house.co.uk
✉ info@the-malt-house.freeserve.co.uk
☎ (01386) 840295   🖷 (01386) 841334

Those looking for a "classic Cotswold setting" might consider this
"thoughtfully luxurious" village house (complete with croquet
lawn). Accommodation is slightly variable, but the attic bedrooms
are "especially imaginative", and all reports attest to the "great"
service and "fabulous" food. / **Rooms:** 7 (of which all non smoking and 3
family rooms). **Details:** closed Christmas; meals unavailable: L, Tue-Wed D.

Three Ways £99

Mickleton GL55 6SB

🖰 www.puddingclub.com ✉ threeways@puddingclub.com
☎ (01386) 438429 📠 (01386) 438118

'The Home of the world-famous Pudding Club' (no, we hadn't heard of it either) – this "relaxing" hotel occupies a Victorian building at the heart of a "pretty" Cotswold village. It wins praise for some "exceptional" rooms (especially in the old building) named after various sticky desserts, and is approved by all reporters as a "value-for-money" destination. / **Rooms:** 41 (of which 2 family rooms).

CHIPPING, LANCASHIRE 5–1B

Gibbon Bridge £140

Green Lane PR3 2TQ

🖰 www.gibbon-bridge.co.uk
✉ reception@gibbon-bridge.co.uk
☎ (01995) 61456 📠 (01995) 61277

"A lovely country hotel on the edge of the Forest of Bowland" – over two decades, Janet Simpson has built up an "out-of-the-way" establishment with "first-class" standards, and all reports acclaim this as a "charming" destination (with "beautiful gardens"). There is even a Harden Suite (no relation). / **Rooms:** 29 (of which some family rooms). **Facilities:** gym; tennis.

CIRENCESTER, GLOUCESTERSHIRE 2–2C

Bibury Court £130

Bibury GL7 5NT

🖰 www.biburycourt.com ✉ info@biburycourt.co.uk
☎ (01285) 740337 📠 (01285) 740660

Settings don't come much more "idyllic" than the one enjoyed by this ancient manor house (dating from Tudor times), which is found "on the edge of one of the prettiest villages in England". It's "seriously comfortable", too, but even fans are inclined to note that "prices are high" – especially when the cooking is rather "rich" for some tastes, and décor and service can come as something of a "let-down". / **Rooms:** 18 (of which some non smoking and 2 family rooms). **Details:** no Amex or Switch.

CLIMPING, WEST SUSSEX 3–4A

Bailiffscourt £185

Climping St BN17 5RW

🖰 www.hshotels.co.uk ✉ bailiffscourt@hshotels.co.uk
☎ (01903) 723511 📠 (01903) 723107

This "beautiful mock-medieval hotel" is "a bit isolated", but – with its "charming" atmosphere – it's judged "the ultimate romantic retreat" by most who report on it. Its attractions were enhanced in the summer of 2003 by the addition of a spa. The occasional doubter complains of "tiny" beds and "small" rooms. / **Rooms:** 39 (of which 7 family rooms). **Facilities:** indoor pool; outdoor pool; gym; spa; tennis.

sign up for our next survey at www.hardens.com

CLITHEROE, LANCASHIRE   5–1B

Inn at Whitewell   £89
Forest of Bowland BD7 3AT
☎ (01200) 448222   🖷 (01200) 448298

"A country inn of great character, and with splendid food". Book
well ahead if you want one of the "delightful, individual" rooms at
this "gem" of a place, which overlooks the Trough of Bowland –
its "amazing" atmosphere draws a following that belies its
"obscure" location. / **Rooms:** 17 (of which 1 family room). **Details:** no Amex.

COCKERMOUTH, CUMBRIA   7–3C

Bridge   £146*
Buttermere CA13 9UZ
🖰 www.bridge-hotel.com   🖃 enquiries@bridge-hotel.com
☎ (01768) 770252   🖷 (01768) 770215
Reporters speak only in very high terms of this "chintzy" hotel
(occupying an 18th-century building), which has a "wonderful"
location in the fells. *Prices are quoted on a DB&B basis.
/ **Rooms:** 21 (of which 13 non smoking). **Details:** meals unavailable: Mon-Sat L; no
Amex.

COLEFORD, GLOUCESTERSHIRE   2–2B

Speech House   £94
GL16 7EL
🖰 www.thespeechhouse.co.uk
🖃 relax@thespeechhouse.co.uk
☎ (01594) 822607
A 17th-century hunting lodge in the heart of the Forest of Dean
(with a nice garden) provides the setting for this "welcoming" and
reasonably-priced 'Best Western'. It's decorated throughout in a
traditional, 'frilly' style. / **Rooms:** 32 (of which 5 non smoking and 5 family
rooms). **Facilities:** gym; spa; golf.

Lucknam Park   £215

SN14 8AZ
⌂ www.lucknampark.co.uk
✉ reservations@lucknampark.co.uk
☎ (01225) 742777   🖷 (01225) 743536

*Those in search of "full-on luxury" won't do much better than this "very grand, but somehow relaxing" Palladian manor house. Even many fans admit the obvious truth that the place is "rather expensive", but few seem to begrudge the cost of what they judge a "fabulous" overall experience, in which "great dining" plays no small part. / **Rooms:** 41 (of which 1 non smoking and some family rooms). **Facilities:** indoor pool; gym; spa; golf; tennis. **Details:** meals unavailable: Mon-Sat L.*

New Inn at Coln   £115

GL7 5AN
⌂ www.new-inn.co.uk   ✉ stay@new-inn.co.uk
☎ (01285) 750651   🖷 (01285) 750657

*"One of the nicest, best-run inns in England", says a fan of this ivy-covered hostelry (16th-century in origin) in a "beautiful Cotswold village". It offers "excellent" food too. / **Rooms:** 14 (of which all non smoking). **Details:** min age for children: 10.*

Norfolk Mead   £85

Church Loke NR12 7DN
⌂ www.norfolkmead.co.uk   ✉ info@norfolkmead.co.uk
☎ (01603) 737531   🖷 (01603) 737521

*This "charming" and "elegant" family-owned Georgian country house hotel (in 12 acres of gardens, with 250 yards of river frontage, and complete with its own fishing lake), inspires nothing but praise. It's a "peaceful" place, whose dining room is said by some reporters to offer "excellent" cooking (and "A1 wines"). / **Rooms:** 12 (of which all non smoking). **Facilities:** outdoor pool. **Details:** meals unavailable: L mid-week.*

Ashford Castle   €370

 www.ashford.ie   ✉ ashford@ashford.ie
☎ +353-92 46003   🖷 +353-92 46260

"One of the best hotels I've ever stayed in, and I've sampled many
all over the world" – reporters do not stint in their praise for this
imposing castle, whose history goes back seven centuries and
which stands in 350 acres of woodlands. "Full of luxuries" and
with "wonderful" staff, it attracts consistently ecstatic reports
(albeit from a small number of reporters). Activities range from a
spa to a full range of country pursuits. / **Rooms:** 85. **Facilities:** spa; golf;
tennis.

Caseys of Baltimore   €154

⌂ www.caseysofbaltimore.com
✉ info@caseysofbaltimore.com
☎ +353-28 20197   🖷 +353-28 20509

"A beautiful location, fantastic food, the friendliest service..." –
fans speak in very enthusiastic terms of this recently modernised
old inn, which houses a seafood restaurant of repute, and offers
impressive views. All this they say for "amazing value for money",
too! / **Rooms:** 14 (of which some non smoking and some family rooms).
Details: closed Dec 19-27; meals unavailable: L.

Hayfield Manor €365

Perrot Av, College Rd -
🖥 www.hayfieldmanor.ie ✉ enquiries@hayfieldmanor.ie
☎ +353-21 484 5900 📠 +353-21 431 6839

"The best service anywhere" is a theme of the (modest amount of) commentary on this neo-Georgian country house hotel, ten minutes from the Cork city centre. It is praised for its "very high standards" throughout. / **Rooms:** 88 (of which 33 non smoking and 55 family rooms). **Facilities:** indoor pool; gym; spa.

Innishannon €130

🖥 www.innishannon-hotel.ie ✉ info@innishannon-hotel.ie
☎ +353-21 477 5121 📠 +353-21 477 5609

"Delightful 'nature' views" are one of the top attractions of this pretty waterside hotel, tipped as a top "hidden-away" location. / **Rooms:** 17 (of which all non smoking and some family rooms). **Details:** no Switch.

CORSE LAWN, GLOUCESTERSHIRE   2–1B

Corse Lawn House £130

GL19 4LZ
🖥 www.corselawnhousehotel.co.uk
✉ enquiries@corselawnhouse.com
☎ (01452) 780771 📠 (01452) 780840

The style is a bit "fussy" for some tastes, but this Queen Anne building – charmingly set overlooking the village green, but with extensive gardens – is generally praised as "a good place to stay and eat". Indeed, its reputation is arguably a little stronger in the latter department. / **Rooms:** 19 (of which all non smoking and 2 family rooms). **Facilities:** outdoor pool; tennis. **Details:** closed 24-26 Dec.

Brandon Hall   £145
Main St CV8 3FW
🖱 www.macdonaldhotels.co.uk
✉ general.brandonhall@macdonald-hotels.co.uk
☎ 0870 400 8105   🖨 (024) 7654 4909

*This "sprawling" villa, in 17 acres, seven miles outside the city, is acclaimed for its "glorious location" and its "obliging staff". Even with all these advantages, though, reporters overall do not rate the charm of this Macdonald hotel particularly highly, and some find the accommodation 'average'. / **Rooms:** 60 (of which some non smoking).*

Coombe Abbey   £150
Brinklow Rd, Binley CV3 2AB
🖱 www.coombeabbey.com   ✉ callback@coombeabbey.com
☎ (02476) 450450   🖨 (02476) 635101

*This "fantastically-themed" county house hotel – where, on occasion, "staff are dressed as monks and wenches" – attracted a number of good reviews, not least for its "charming" accommodation and grounds, and its "wonderful food". (One reporter, however, just didn't 'get it' – "a vile, pretentious place, with inedible food and tenebrous lighting", he says.) / **Rooms:** 83. **Details:** meals unavailable: Mon-Sat L.*

Hilton Coventry   £118
Paradise Way, Walsgrave CV2 2ST
🖱 www.hilton.co.uk
☎ (02476) 603000   🖨 (02476) 603011

*This "typical business hotel" is located some ten miles north of the city, and benefits from "spacious rooms". It's our top tip for those doing business in a city which lacks many more handily-located destinations. / **Rooms:** 172 (of which some non smoking and some family rooms). **Facilities:** indoor pool; gym; spa.*

COWLEY, GLOUCESTERSHIRE 2–1C

Cowley Manor £205
GL53 9NL
🖰 www.cowleymanor.com 🖂 stay@cowleymanor.com
☎ (01242) 870900 🖨 (01242) 870901

Is this "the new Babington House"? Most reports certainly tend to
the view that this "modern manor house conversion" – a 19th-
century mansion set within 55 acres of woodland – has plenty of
"wow-factor". Features generating the most feedback include
"superb leisure facilities" (with a "fantastic spa") and "beautifully
designed rooms". / **Rooms:** 30 (of which 3 family rooms). **Facilities:** indoor
pool; outdoor pool; gym; spa.

CREWE, CHESHIRE 5–3B

Crewe Hall £160
Weston Rd CW1 6UZ
🖰 www.crewehall.com 🖂 info@crewehall.com
☎ (01270) 253333 🖨 (01270) 253322

Considering its accessibility (only a few minutes from either the
M6 or Crewe railway station), this "wonderfully situated"
Jacobean country house hotel – home of the Earls of Crewe until
the '20s, and for most of the subsequent period owned by the
Duchy of Lancaster – incites remarkably little feedback. In mid-
2003, however, this became a Marston hotel so changes are
afoot. / **Rooms:** 65 (of which 40 non smoking and 2 family rooms). **Facilities:**
tennis.

CRICKHOWELL, POWYS   2–1A

The Bear   £72

High St NP8 1BW

⌂ www.bearhotel.co.uk   ✉ bearhotel@aol.com
☎ (01873) 810408   🖷 (01873) 811696

This well-known ancient coaching inn has a "lovely" marketplace
location in a town set amidst the Brecon Beacons. It has quite a
reputation – not least for its "super" food and bar snacks – and
attracts a good volume of reports. There was the occasional gripe
from reporters, but its "friendly", "old-fashioned" style for the
most part won high praise as a "cosy" and "romantic" getaway.
/ **Rooms:** 34. **Details:** no Amex or Switch.

CRIEFF, PERTH & KINROSS   9–3C

Crieff Hydro   £80*

Ewanfield PH7 3LQ

⌂ www.crieffhydro.com   ✉ enquiries@crieffhydro.com
☎ (01764) 655555   🖷 (01764) 653087

"Excellent leisure and sporting facilities" – a "lovely" golf course,
for example, and a gym of some 3,000 square feet – set this
grand Scottish-Gothic palace apart. It's particularly suited to family
parties (and facilities include a children's club). *Prices are quoted
on a DB&B basis. / **Rooms:** 216 (of which some non smoking and 60 family
rooms). **Facilities:** indoor pool; outdoor pool; spa.

CRINAN, ARGYLL & BUTE   9–4B

Crinan   £260*

PA31 8SR

⌂ www.crinanhotel.com   ✉ enquiry@crinanhotel.com
☎ (01546) 830261   🖷 (01546) 830292

"Luxurious" but "unpretentious", this "welcoming" hotel enjoys a
"great location", by the edge of Loch Crinan. It has quite a
reputation for its cooking, too – borne out by most, but not quite
all, reports. *Prices are quoted on a DB&B basis. / **Rooms:** 20 (of
which 4 family rooms). **Details:** closed Christmas & New Year; meals unavailable: L;
no Amex.

CROSTHWAITE, CUMBRIA   7–4D

The Punch Bowl Inn   £60   ☺

LA8 8HR

⌂ www.punchbowl.fsnet.co.uk
✉ enquiries@punchbowl.fsnet.co.uk
☎ (01539) 568237   🖷 (01539) 568875

This "very peaceful" coaching inn has a particular name for its
"excellent food". It offers "very good value" and is hailed as "a
real gem". A repeat visitor notes that "quiet times are best", as
standards (generally "professional") may suffer when the place is
busy. / **Rooms:** 3. **Details:** closed 1 wk Jan, 1 wk May/June, 1 wk Nov, 1 wk Dec;
meals unavailable: Sun D & Mon; no Amex.

CROYDON, SURREY 3–3B

Selsdon Park £79

Addington Rd CR2 8YA
www.lemeridien.com
sales.selsdonpark@lemeridien.com
☎ (020) 8657 8811   📠 (020) 8657 3401

Hit a good day and get the right accommodation, and this "beautiful country house" overlooking a "beautiful golf course" can make a "good-value" destination (voted by one reporter as "the best hotel on London's outskirts"). Standards at this Meridien establishment are not consistent, though, and some reporters complain of accommodation which is "a let-down", and of "poor" food. "Avoid summer weekends, when the place becomes wedding-procession hell". / **Rooms:** 204 (of which some family rooms). **Facilities:** indoor pool; outdoor pool; gym; spa; golf; tennis. **Details:** meals unavailable: Sat & Sun L.

CUCKFIELD, WEST SUSSEX 3–4B

Ockenden Manor £150

Ockenden Ln RH17 5LD
www.hshotels.co.uk   ockenden@hshotels.co.uk
☎ (01444) 416111

One reporter speaks for all when he describes the "beautiful grounds and excellent food, and the "spacious, comfortable and tastefully-decorated accommodation" at this Elizabethan manor house. "Some rooms are better than others" though, with those in the main house preferred. / **Rooms:** 22 (of which 3 family rooms).

BY CUPAR, FIFE 9–3D

The Peat Inn £155 ☺☺

KY15 5LH
www.thepeatinn.co.uk   reception@thepeatinn.co.uk
☎ (01334) 840206   📠 (01334) 840530

This "inn of distinction" has had a name for its "fine cooking" for over 30 years. Its accommodation, in a new ('80s) wing with some split-level rooms, is also well rated by reporters. / **Rooms:** 8 (of which 2 family rooms). **Details:** closed 25 Dec & 1 Jan.

DARESBURY, CHESHIRE 5–2B

De Vere Daresbury Park £95

Chester Rd WA4 4BB

⌖ www.devereonline.co.uk

✉ daresburypark.salesmanager@devere-hotels.com

☎ (01925) 267331 ✆ (01925) 265615

Considering it was redeveloped very much for conferences – the location is easily accessible by motorway from Liverpool or Manchester – this "nicely designed" modern hotel is proclaimed surprisingly "good for breaks" by some reporters, thanks not least to its "friendly and helpful service". (Perhaps it's the proximity to the De Vere HQ which makes this one of the better members of that group.) / **Rooms:** 181 (of which 95 non smoking and 14 family rooms). **Facilities:** indoor pool; gym; spa. **Details:** meals unavailable: Sat L.

DARLINGTON, CO. DURHAM 8–3B

Headlam Hall £90

Headlam, Nr Gainford DL2 3HA

⌖ www.headlamhall.co.uk ✉ admin@headlamhall.co.uk

☎ (01325) 730238 ✆ (01325) 730790

"Friendly and efficient service" and a "good restaurant" are among the features praised at this family-owned country house hotel – a Jacobean building in a walled garden of four acres – to all who comment on it. It's "reasonably priced", too. / **Rooms:** 36 (of which 17 non smoking and 5 family rooms). **Facilities:** indoor pool; gym; golf; tennis.

DARTMOUTH, DEVON 1–4D

Dart Marina £114

Sandquay TQ6 9PH

⌖ www.dartmarinahotel.com

✉ general.dartmarina@macdonald-hotels.com

☎ (01803) 832580 ✆ (01803) 835040

"An excellent venue for weekending or short breaks" ("check for special deals"), this "dramatically positioned" seaside hotel (a Macdonald establishment) is generally hailed for its "decent" standards. / **Rooms:** 49 (of which 40 non smoking and 6 family rooms). **Details:** no Amex.

Royal Castle £120 😊

11 The Quay TQ6 9PS

⌖ www.royalcastle.co.uk ✉ enquiry@royalcastle.co.uk

☎ (01803) 833033 ✆ (01803) 835445

With some "great views over the Dart and marina", this "pretty hotel right on the waterfront" enjoys a "very central location". It's roundly praised by most, if not quite all reporters, particularly for its rooms. / **Rooms:** 25 (of which all non smoking and 6 family rooms). **Facilities:** golf.

sign up for our next survey at www.hardens.com

DAVENTRY, NORTHANTS   2–1D

Fawsley Hall   £130
NN11 3BA

🖰 www.fawsleyhall.com   ✉ reservations@fawsleyhall.com
☎ (01327) 892000   🖷 (01327) 892001

"Excellent in every way", this Tudor building was recently launched
as an hotel, and has made a "very promising" start as a place to
stay, thanks in no small part to "charming" and "helpful" service.
The dining room, however, can seem something of a "let down".
/ **Rooms:** 43 (of which some non smoking and 7 family rooms). **Facilities:** gym;
spa; tennis.

DEDHAM, ESSEX   3–2C

Maison Talbooth   £160
Stratford Rd C07 6HN

🖰 www.talbooth.com   ✉ maison@talbooth.co.uk
☎ (01206) 322367

An offshoot of the famous Talbooth – the Milsom family's long-
established Constable Country restaurant – this riverside Victorian
house boasts "much elegance" (in a very traditional style) and
"very individual bedrooms". Its "excellent location and ambience"
are praised by almost all reporters. / **Rooms:** 10 (of which 1 family
room). **Details:** meals unavailable: Sep-May Sun D.

DIRLETON, EAST LOTHIAN   9–4D

Open Arms   £70
EH39 5EG

🖰 http://home.clara.net/openarms/
✉ openarms@clara.co.uk
☎ (01620) 850241   🖷 (01620) 850570

This 'family-owned traditional country hotel' (the management's
description) is located in a peaceful village, and tipped for its
"open fires, view of the castle, superb friendly service and good
food". / **Rooms:** 10 (of which 1 family room). **Details:** no Mastercard.

DODDISCOMBSLEIGH, DEVON   1–3D

Nobody Inn   £70
EX6 7PS

🖰 www.nobodyinn.co.uk   ✉ info@nobodyinn.co.uk
☎ (01647) 252394   🖷 (01647) 252978

This "delightful old inn in the middle of nowhere" has a great
reputation for its food (and its "great selection of whiskies, wine
and cheese"). The rooms may be "no more than satisfactory", but
fans say "it's well worth the stay for the pleasure of staying and
eating in a such a lovely old place". Annexe accommodation is
preferred. / **Rooms:** 7. **Details:** closed 25-26 Dec, 1 Jan; meals unavailable: L;
min age for children: 14.

DORCHESTER, OXFORDSHIRE 2–2D

White Hart Inn £95
High Street OX10 7HN
✉ whitehartdorch@aol.com
☎ (01865) 340074 🖷 (01865) 341082
"A splendid weekend break location in a lovely small town" –
*that's the unanimous tenor of commentary on this 17th-century
coaching inn, which offers "good quality at a reasonable price".*
/ **Rooms:** 28 *(of which some non smoking and some family rooms).*

DORKING, SURREY 3–3A

White Horse £120
High St RH4 1BE
🖰 www.macdonaldhotels.co.uk
✉ general.whitehorsedorking@macdonaldhotels.co.uk
☎ 0870 400 8282 🖷 (01306) 887241
*"Reasonable weekend rates" help commend this "attractive" old
inn, whose "great location" is extremely handy for the capital, and
which attracted quite a lot of survey commentary. Objectively,
though, standards are of the up-and-down nature – something of
a hallmark of ownership by Macdonald Hotels.* / **Rooms:** 78 *(of which
53 non smoking and some family rooms).*

DORNOCH, SUTHERLAND 9–2C

Skibo Castle £850*
IV25 3RQ
🖰 www.carnegieclub.co.uk/skibo.html
✉ info@carnegieclubs.com
☎ (01862) 894600 🖷 (01862) 894601

*"A true taste of the high-life" or "utterly pretentious and without
charm"?* – *on limited feedback, this grand Gothic castle divides
opinion. Even the reporter who derided a "false 'club'
atmosphere" and "vulgar clientèle" conceded that its
accommodation and facilities are of the highest standard. The
hotel was sold shortly before this guide went to press, so changes
may be afoot. *Prices are quoted on a DB&B basis.* / **Rooms:** 46 *(of
which all non smoking).* **Facilities:** *indoor pool; gym; spa; golf; tennis.*

DOUGLAS, ISLE OF MAN   7–4B

Regency   £83
Queens Promenade IM2 4NN
⌂ www.iom-1.net/regency ✉ regency@iom-1.net
☎ (01624) 680680   🖷 (01624) 680690

*Like its even more businessy competitor the Sefton ((01624)
645500), this "competitively-priced" seafront hotel attracts only a
few, and slightly ambivalent reviews. So far as reporters are
concerned, however, the two establishments seem to have the
island's market sewn up. / Rooms: 45 (of which some non smoking and
some family rooms).*

DUBLIN, COUNTY DUBLIN, *ROI*   10–3D

Many of the establishments in the capital of this hospitable
country are indeed notable – but what is starkly apparent is
that, for the best chance of a successful visit, you should
steer well clear of some of the 'big names' whose age-old
reputations precede them.

Bewleys   €99
Merrion Road, Ballsbridge
⌂ www.bewleyshotels.com ✉ BB@BewleysHotels.com
☎ +353-1 668 1111   🖷 +353-1 668 1999

*"Good value for money" is the unanimous theme of commentary
on this "good 3-star hotel" in Ballsbridge, which – behind its new
Gothic façade (formerly a Masonic school) – offers "totally
refurbished accommodation". Service is "helpful", too. / Rooms: 304
(of which some non smoking and some family rooms). Details: closed Christmas; no
Switch.*

brownes townhouse   €255
22 St Stephen's Green D2
⌂ www.brownesdublin.com ✉ info@brownesdublin.com
☎ +353-1 638 3939

*"Very friendly, lots of character and great Irish breakfasts" – what
more could a weekender want from this "good-value"
establishment, in a beautiful Georgian setting that's "close to the
centre of the city". / Rooms: 11. Details: closed 24 Dec-3 Jan; meals
unavailable: no restaurant; no Switch.*

Burlington   €220
Leeson St
⌂ www.jurysdoyle.com ✉ burlington@jurysdoyle.com
☎ +353-1 660 5222   🖷 +353-1 660 8496

*To its small but loyal fan club, this "huge" Jury's establishment is
"the most Irish of Dublin's big hotels", and "consistently good for
the price". "Effervescent" and "helpful" service adds considerably
to the experience. / Rooms: 506 (of which 200 non smoking and 6 family
rooms). Facilities: gym; spa. Details: no Switch.*

Chief O'Neills   €95

Smithfield Village, Smithfield D7
✉ reservations@cheifoneills.com
☎ +353-1 817 3838

*If you like the style – "Habitatesque", as one reporter put it –
this modern hotel is "handy for the city-centre", and the modest
number of reports it incites are all positive.* / **Rooms:** *73 (of which 18
non smoking).* **Details:** *closed 24-26 Dec.*

Clarence   €300

6-8 Wellington Quay D2
🖰 www.theclarence.ie   ✉ reservations@clarence.ie
☎ +353-1 407 0800   🖳 +353-1 407 0820

*Inevitably there's "a lot of hype" surrounding this "trendy" U2-
owned hotel, but most reports find this "very classy" and
"beautifully designed" townhouse-conversion, near Temple Bar,
lives up to its billing. "Professional and charming" service was
singled out for most praise. Facilities are rather a weak spot, but
the restaurant (The Tea Rooms) is a top destination for groovy
Dublin dining, and the Sunday brunch something of an institution.*
/ **Rooms:** *50 (of which some family rooms).* **Details:** *meals unavailable: Sun L; no
Switch.*

Conrad   €215

Earlsfort Terrace
🖰 www.conraddublin.com
☎ +353-1 602 8900   🖳 +353-1 676 5424

*This "typical high-class American hotel", just around the corner
from St Stephen's Green, has recently enjoyed a major
refurbishment. Reports on it are not very numerous, but they are
consistently very favourable.* / **Rooms:** *192 (of which 120 non smoking and
some family rooms).* **Facilities:** *gym.*

The Davenport   €190

Merrion Sq -
🖰 www.ocallaghanhotels.ie
✉ davenportres@ocallaghanhotels.ie
☎ +353-1 607 3500   🖳 +353-1 661 5663

*A Victorian building that's been an hotel for just a decade, this
centrally located establishment attracts relatively modest
commentary, but all to the effect that it's a "comfortable" and
"relaxing" place, with "helpful" service.* / **Rooms:** *115 (of which some
non smoking).* **Facilities:** *gym.* **Details:** *no Switch.*

sign up for our next survey at www.hardens.com   99

Fitzwilliam €315

St Stephens Green

⌂ www.fitzwilliamhotel.com   ✉ enq@fitzwilliamhotel.com

☎ +353-1 478 7000   🖨 +353-1 478 7878

*A "fabulous" central location and some "lovely" accommodation make this modern hotel a popular place to stay (and some reporters praise the restaurant, recently taken over by star chef Kevin Thornton, as "fantastic", too). It can seem "very expensive" for what it is, though. / **Rooms:** 129 (of which some non smoking and some family rooms). **Details:** meals unavailable: - (Thorntons restaurant Mon & Sun); no Switch.*

Four Seasons €365 😊😊😊

Simmonscourt Rd, Ballsbridge

⌂ www.fourseasons.com

✉ reservations.dublin@fourseasons.com

☎ +353-1 665 4000   🖨 +353-1 665 4099

*"World-class service, plus Irish hospitality"; even those who are "not usually a fan of large corporate properties" praise this "very nice new hotel", with its "beautiful" and "elegant" accommodation, as "excellent in every way". It's located in fashionable Ballsbridge, a little way out of the city centre. / **Rooms:** 259 (of which 200 non smoking and 50 family rooms). **Facilities:** indoor pool; gym; spa. **Details:** meals unavailable: no restaurant.*

Gresham €165

23 Upper O'Connell St

⌂ www.ryan-hotels.com

☎ +353-1 874 6881   🖨 +353-1 878 7175

*This "grand old hotel" – it opened in 1817 – "still lives up to its name", say fans, and it certainly has "a great location, within easy reach of all the attractions". Equally vociferous, though, are the place's many detractors, who say it's just "a chain-style version of Fawlty Towers". A spa is being added and will open in late-2003. / **Rooms:** 288 (of which 140 non smoking). **Facilities:** gym; spa. **Details:** no Switch.*

Hilton Dublin €159

Charlemont Pl

🖰 www.dublin.hilton.com ✉ dubhc_rs@hilton.com
☎ +353-1 402 9988 📠 +353-1 402 9966

*Especially if you can get the "excellent-value short breaks"
sometimes available, this "central" chain hotel – enlivened by a
refreshing dose of "Irish charm" – is worth considering.*
/ **Rooms:** 189 (of which some non smoking and some family rooms).

Longfield €165

10 Lower Fitzwilliam St

🖰 www.longfields.ie ✉ info@longfields.ie
☎ +353-1 676 1367 📠 +353-1 676 1542

*"Two terraced houses knocked together" provide the "attractive"
Georgian setting for this "good-value" hotel, whose restaurant is of
some note.* / **Rooms:** 26. **Details:** no Switch.

Le Meridien Shelbourne €250 ☺

27 St Stephen's Green

🖰 www.shelbourne.ie ✉ shelbourneinfo@lemeridien.com
☎ +353-1 663 4500 📠 +353-1 661 6006

*This grand old dowager, "superbly located" in the city centre with
views over the green has a big name, and generates many
reports. "The charm is cracking at the seams", these days though
– even fans rarely rate it much above "average", and some
reporters just find it plain "tatty" or "sad".* / **Rooms:** 190 (of which 101
non smoking). **Facilities:** indoor pool; gym; spa. **Details:** meals unavailable: Mon-
Tue, Sat L, Sun D; no Switch.

Merrion €345

Upper Merrion St

🖰 www.merrionhotel.com ✉ info@merrionhotel.ie
☎ +353-1 603 0600 📠 +353-1 603 0700

*Fans of "Regency glory" hail this grand but "relaxed" city-centre
establishment (near the Dáil) – with its "great location and
ambience" – as "excellent all round, with the bonus of the best
restaurant, too" (in the shape of Patrick Guilbaud). It also boasts
"a great pool" among its more contemporary attractions. It's not
beyond criticism, though, and a few reporters find the
accommodation no more than "serviceable" – "stay in the front,
Georgian part".* / **Rooms:** 145 (of which some non smoking and some family
rooms). **Facilities:** indoor pool; gym; spa. **Details:** no Switch.

Morrison   €160

Ormond Quay
🖰 www.morrisonhotel.ie ✉ info@morrisonhotel.ie
☎ +353-1 887 2400 🖶 +353-1 874 4039

*With its "slick, minimalist style", this "beautifully designed", "hip"
hotel (which hides behind a Georgian façade overlooking the
Liffey) achieves consistently good reports across the board.
Attractions include a "nice" restaurant and a "pulsating" bar.*
/ **Rooms:** 90 (of which 42 non smoking and 7 family rooms). **Details:** closed 24-
26 Dec; no Switch.

31   €199   😊😊

31 Leeson Close, Lower Leeson St
🖰 www.number31.ie ✉ number31@iol.ie
☎ +353-1 676 5011 🖶 +353-1 676 2929

*"Quirky, atmospheric and individual", this "hide-away" near St
Stephen's Green – an intriguing re-design of a former mews – is
praised as "a truly remarkable hotel" by all reporters (except one,
whose experience was totally out of kilter with all others).
"Helpful" and "friendly" service, and "excellent breakfasts" are
among the most frequently highlighted plus-points.* / **Rooms:** 21 (of
which all non smoking and 1 family room). **Details:** meals unavailable: no
restaurant; no Switch; min age for children: 10.

Westbury   €265

Grafton St
🖰 www.jurys.com ✉ westbury@jurysdoyle.com
☎ +353-1 679 1122 🖶 +353-1 679 7078

*This grand hotel has an "excellent" location (in the 'Bond Street'
of Dublin) and its pleasant lounge makes a "world-class" location
for afternoon tea and the like. Service can be "very friendly", too.
More generally, however, indifferent feedback tends to support the
reporter who proclaimed the place "poor value for money".*
/ **Rooms:** 190 (of which some family rooms). **Facilities:** gym.

sign up for our next survey at www.hardens.com

Westin €230

College Green, Westmoreland St
🏠 www.westin.com
☎ +353-1 645 1000   🖨 +353-1 645 1234

A "fantastic location", opposite Trinity College, is not the least of the charms of this "chic" and "romantic" Victorian bank-conversion, run by Starwood – it is almost unanimously hailed by reporters as an "exceptional" hotel, with "great ambience and service". / **Rooms:** 162 (of which 108 non smoking and some family rooms). **Facilities:** gym. **Details:** no Switch.

DULVERTON, SOMERSET   1–2D

Ashwick House £70*

TA22 9QD
🏠 www.ashwickhouse.co.uk   ✉ ashwickhouse@talk21.com
☎ (01398) 323868

"Nothing is too much trouble for the proprietor", says the reporter who tips this "charming", small Edwardian country house hotel. *Prices are quoted on a DB&B basis.* / **Rooms:** 7 (of which 2 non smoking). **Details:** meals unavailable: Mon-Sat L; min age for children: 8.

DUNKELD, PERTH & KINROSS   9–3C

Dunkeld House £199*

Atholl Sreet PH8 0AR
🏠 www.hiltondunkeldhouse.co.uk
✉ reservations_dunkeld@hilton.com
☎ (01350) 727771   🖨 (01350) 728924

Originally a ducal summer house, this modernised country house hotel benefits from a "wonderful location" in 280 acres, overlooking the River Tay. Now run by Hilton, it offers a good range of traditional country pursuits, as well as more modern leisure facilities. "Scottish hospitality is to the fore", but there were some iffy accommodation experiences – "get a room in the old part if you can". *Prices are quoted on a DB&B basis.* / **Rooms:** 96 (of which 63 non smoking and 8 family rooms). **Facilities:** indoor pool; gym; spa; tennis.

Kinnaird £275*

Kinnaird Estate PH8 0LB
🏠 www.kinnairdestate.com   ✉ enquiry@kinnairdestate.com
☎ (01796) 482440   🖨 (01796) 482289

"When I woke up, I thought I'd died and gone to Heaven." This "superb country house hotel" – a mainly Edwardian building which was once the dower house to Blair Castle, and set in an enormous estate – is hailed as "perfect in almost every way" by the fair number of reporters who comment on it. If there is a stand-out attraction it is perhaps the "superb, personal attention, on arrival and throughout one's stay". *Prices are quoted on a DB&B basis.* / **Rooms:** 9. **Facilities:** spa; tennis. **Details:** min age for children: 12.

DUNSLEY, NORTH YORKSHIRE   8–3D

Dunsley Hall   £126
YO21 3TL
🖰 www.dunsleyhall.com   ✉ reception@dunsleyhall.com
☎ (01947) 893437   🖷 (01947) 893505
"Peacocks in the garden" set the tone at this family-run Victorian
country house, which is tipped as a *"marvellous"* place, with
"excellent" service and a *"first-class"* restaurant. / **Rooms:** 18 (of
which all non smoking and 3 family rooms). **Facilities:** indoor pool; gym; spa; golf.

DUNSTER, SOMERSET   1–2D

Luttrell Arms   £95   ☺
32-36 High Street TA24 6SG
🖰 www.luttrellarms.co.uk   ✉ info@luttrellarms.fsnet.co.uk
☎ (01643) 821555   🖷 (01643) 821587
*"An old coaching inn in the centre of an attractive small town on
the edge of Exmoor"*. It has *"plenty of 'character"* and *"oozes
charm and peace"* (…as long as you avoid *"noisy wedding
parties"* and the *"pokey little rooms at the back"*). / **Rooms:** 28 (of
which all non smoking and 3 family rooms).

DUNVEGAN, ISLE OF SKYE   9–2A

Three Chimneys   £190   ☺☺
Colbost IV55 8ZT
🖰 www.threechimneys.co.uk
✉ eatandstay@threechimneys.co.uk
☎ (01470) 511258   🖷 (01470) 511358

The *"utterly amazing"* food makes it *"well worth the long drive"*
to Shirley and Eddie Spears' famous but remote cottage (*"when
you hit the Skye Bridge, you think you're there – you're not!"*).
Gastronomy is not the only attraction, though, the rooms are *"very
spoiling"*, and the situation, overlooking the loch, is *"exceptional"*.
/ **Rooms:** 6 (of which all non smoking and 1 family room). **Details:** closed 3 wks
from mid-Jan; meals unavailable: L Oct-Apr.

DURHAM, CO. DURHAM   8–3B

Hallgarth Manor   £65
Pittington DH6 1AB
🖱 www.hallgarthmanorhotel.com
📧 Sales@HallgarthManorHotel.com
☎ (0191) 372 1188   📠 (0191) 372 1249
*"Friendly, good food, good value" – that's the invariable theme of
the commentary on this 16th-century country house hotel, set in
four acres of grounds and only three miles from the city. It seems
a better bet than anything the city itself has to offer, certainly for
leisure travellers.* / **Rooms:** 23 (of which some non smoking).

Marriott   £130
Old Elvet DH1 3JN
🖱 www.marriott.com
📧 durhamroyal.marriott@whitbread.com
☎ (0191) 386 6821   📠 (0191) 386 0704
*Originally the Royal County Hotel, this "very central"
establishment gives an initial impression quite in keeping with its
former name. Nowadays, though, it's mainly as "a decent business
hotel" that it finds favour with reporters (despite the fact that it
boasts some "excellent leisure facilities", too). Opinions divide
between those who say it's "comfortable and old fashioned" and
those who say it's "overpriced" and "mediocre".* / **Rooms:** 150 (of
which 120 non smoking and 10 family rooms). **Facilities:** indoor pool; gym; spa.

Swallow Three Tuns   £85
New Elvet DH1 3AQ
🖱 www.swallowhotels.com/durham/index.asp
📧 threetuns.sales@btinternet.com
☎ (0191) 386 4326   📠 (0191) 384 2093
*"Standing in the shadow of the Royal County (Marriott) opposite,
but a good and less formal alternative" – this "comfortable" and
"friendly" hotel attracts less commentary that its grander
neighbour, but all of it positive.* / **Rooms:** 50 (of which 40 non smoking and
6 family rooms). **Details:** meals unavailable: Sat L.

DUXFORD, CAMBRIDGESHIRE   3–1B

Duxford Lodge   £105
Ickleton Rd CB2 4RU
🖱 www.duxfordlodgehotel.co.uk   📧 duxford@btclick.com
☎ (01223) 836444   📠 (01223) 832271
*"Lovely" gardens and a restaurant (Le Paradis) which on some
(but not all) accounts is "fantastic" are the main attractions of this
small hotel in an Edwardian house. It's a "good-quality" place,
though one reporter thought its popularity with Cambridge
business folk created a rather "corporate" ambience.* / **Rooms:** 15
(of which 4 family rooms). **Details:** closed Christmas-New Year.

EASINGWOLD, NORTH YORKSHIRE   8–4C

Old Vicarage   **£60**

Market Pl YO61 3AL

🖰 www.oldvicarage-easingwold.co.uk

📧 kirman@oldvicarage-easingwold.co.uk

☎ (01347) 821015   📠 (01347) 823465

*This Georgian house is a popular B&B destination and is tipped in
particular for its "beautiful" accommodation. Complimentary use
of the local fitness centre (150 yards away) is a thoughtful 'plus'.*
/ **Rooms:** 4 (of which all non smoking). **Details:** closed Dec-Jan; meals unavailable:
no restaurant.

EAST GRINSTEAD, WEST SUSSEX   3–4B

Gravetye Manor   **£190**

Vowels Ln RH19 4LJ

🖰 www.gravetyemanor.co.uk   📧 info@gravetyemanor.co.uk

☎ (01342) 810567   📠 (01342) 810080

*"Outstanding gardens" set the scene for visitors to this "lovely"
Elizabethan manor house, buried in the Sussex countryside (and
in the ownership of the same family for over 40 years). The
accommodation is both "cosy" and "luxurious", and the well-
known, "good, if expensive", restaurant pleased most (if not quite
all) reporters.* / **Rooms:** 18. **Details:** no Amex; min age for children: 7 & babes
in arms.

EAST WITTON, NORTH YORKSHIRE   8–4B

Blue Lion Inn   **£69**

DL8 4SN

📧 bluelion@breathemail.net

☎ (01969) 624273   📠 (01969) 624189

*This "well-run and friendly country pub" has quite a name as a
gastro-destination, and attracted a good amount of survey
commentary. Some feel it's beginning "to lose it's way", however,
and reviews of the accommodation ranged all the way from
"excellent value for money" to "poor".* / **Rooms:** 12 (of which 1 family
room). **Details:** meals unavailable: L; no Amex.

EASTBOURNE, EAST SUSSEX   3–4B

The Grand   **£165**   😊😊

King Edwards Parade BN21 4EQ

🖰 www.grandeastbourne.com

📧 reservations@grandeastbourne.com

☎ (01323) 412345   📠 (01323) 412233

*For "elegance on a grand scale", the English seaside has little to
compare with this "carefully restored" but still very "comfortable"
Victorian "institution" (now under the broadly benign stewardship
of Elite hotels), which dominates the town's west end of King
Edward's Parade. The "lovely" grand dining room (The Mirabelle)
has long been a far-from-incidental attraction (even if some
reporters feel its service "could be improved").* / **Rooms:** 152 (of
which some non smoking and some family rooms). **Facilities:** indoor pool; outdoor
pool; gym; spa.

sign up for our next survey at www.hardens.com

Hydro £110
Mount Rd BN20 7HZ
🖰 www.hydrohotel.com ✉ sales@hydrohotel.com
☎ (01323) 720643 🖨 (01323) 641167
*This grand Victorian hotel retains a "very traditional" style,
perceived to be "geared to older guests" ("look for Captain
Mainwairing in the bar"). That said, reporters of all ages
consistently rated it as an all-round reliable destination. / **Rooms:** 82
(of which some non smoking and some family rooms). **Facilities:** outdoor pool; gym.
Details: no Amex.*

Lansdowne £130
King Edward's Parade BN21 4EE
🖰 www.lansdowne-hotel.co.uk
✉ reception@lansdowne-hotel.co.uk
☎ (01323) 725174 🖨 (01323) 739721
*A "comfortable" hotel which is tipped for its "excellent room
quality" (if not for the quality of its cooking). / **Rooms:** 110 (of which
25 non smoking and 7 family rooms). **Details:** meals unavailable: Mon-Fri L.*

EDINBURGH, CITY OF EDINBURGH 9–4C

Auld Reekie is not just one of the world's great cities, it's
also a great place to stay. Part of the reason for this is that
there are just quite a lot of hotels – we list over 25 (which
may be compared to some 65 in much bigger and busier
London). There therefore seems to be some sort of
equivalence between supply and demand. The main 'safety
warning' is that the old big names – and Edinburgh boasts
some very old and very big hotel names – are rarely the best
bet. Some of the smaller and more individualistic
establishments, however, really are very good indeed.

Apex City £80
61 Grassmarket EH1 2JF
🖰 www.apexhotels.co.uk ✉ city@apexhotels.co.uk
☎ (0131) 243 3456 🖨 (0131) 226 5345
*"Distinctive, but not precious", this "excellent cheap and chic new
hotel" displays the "attention to detail and high standards which
characterise the Apex group". Located below the Castle, it's
handily sited for many of the city's fine boozers. / **Rooms:** 119 (of
which 89 non smoking).*

Apex European £80
90 Haymarket Terrace EH12 5LQ
🖰 www.apexhotels.co.uk ✉ european@apexhotels.co.uk
☎ (0131) 474 3456 🖨 (0131) 474 3400
*"Not as good as the Apex City or International, but still better
than most" – one reporter neatly summarises the feedback on
this "stylish" modern hotel, near the Haymarket railway station.
Some of the rooms have "fantastic" views. / **Rooms:** 67 (of which 52
non smoking). **Facilities:** indoor pool; gym; spa. **Details:** no Mastercard.*

Apex International £80

Grassmarket EH1 2HS
🖥 www.apexhotels.co.uk
✉ international@apexhotels.co.uk
☎ (0131) 300 3456 📠 (0131) 220 5345

"Clean and modern, with friendly staff and jelly beans in the room" – what more could you want? Reporters speak only well of this *"contemporary"* establishment, with its *"above-average"* rooms and its *"fabulous Castle views"*. The prospect from the top-floor restaurant is *"breathtaking"*. / **Rooms:** 175 (of which 140 non smoking and 52 family rooms).

Balmoral £200

1 Princes St EH2 2EQ
🖥 www.roccofortehotels.com
✉ reservations@thebalmoralhotel.com
☎ 0870 460 7040 📠 (0131) 557 8740

For its many fans, this looming presence by Waverley Station – now part of the Rocco Forte empire – is *"a great traditional hotel"*, boasting *"a traditional level of service"* and *"excellent facilities"*. Even some who think it *"wonderful"*, say it's *"possibly on the slide"*, though, and to doubters it's *"trading quite heavily on its reputation"*. / **Rooms:** 188 (of which 119 non smoking). **Facilities:** indoor pool; gym; spa.

Bank £110

1 South Bridge EH1 1LL
🖥 www.festival-inns.co.uk
☎ (0131) 556 9940 📠 (0131) 558 1362

This *"party-party hotel above a very popular bar"* attracts nothing but bouquets from (younger) reporters. It has an *"excellent location"* on the Royal Mile, and is *"great for watching sport and making Antipodean friends"* – you have been warned. / **Rooms:** 9. **Details:** not suitable for children.

The Bonham £146 ☺☺

35 Drumsheugh Gdns EH3 7RN
🖥 www.thebonham.com ✉ reserve@thebonham.com
☎ (0131) 226 6050 📠 (0131) 226 6080

"A trendy townhouse hotel, in a great spot near the centre of town". Its facilities are perhaps not quite state-of-the-art, but most reporters are full of praise for its *"stylish"* and *"unstuffy"* charms. The accommodation – *"fantastic"*, *"interesting"* rooms, with *"heavenly"* beds – attracts particular praise. / **Rooms:** 48 (of which 30 non smoking).

sign up for our next survey at www.hardens.com 108

Borough £65

72-80 Causewayside EH9 IPY

🕀 www.edin-borough.co.uk

✉ borough@bookings.freeserve.co.uk

☎ (0131) 668 2255   🖷 (0131) 667 6622

An "excellent boutique-hotel in the city-centre"; it only attracts a modest level of feedback, but all confirming the place as "a haven of taste and charm", near the Castle. / **Rooms:** 9.

Bruntsfield £140

69 Bruntsfield Pl EH10 4HH

🕀 www.thebruntsfield.co.uk

✉ bruntsfield@bruntsfield.co.uk

☎ (0131) 229 1393   🖷 (0131) 229 5634

"A standard Best Western outlet" it may be, but this comfortable traditional hotel is "within a pleasant walk of the city-centre", and "is made lots better" by the "good" and "friendly" service.
/ **Rooms:** 73 (of which some non smoking and 7 family rooms). **Details:** no Amex or Switch.

Caledonian Hilton £260

Princes St EH1 2AB

🕀 www.hilton.com   ✉ ednchhirm@hilton.com

☎ (0131) 222 8888   🖷 (0131) 222 8889

Reporters who find themselves in one of "the fantastic, huge rooms with a view of the Castle" seem particularly well disposed to this grand centenarian, which comes complete with "sweeping staircases and chandeliers". "Poor" or "faded" rooms can be a problem, though, and the catering is "hit and miss". / **Rooms:** 251 (of which some non smoking and 12 family rooms). **Facilities:** indoor pool; gym; spa. **Details:** meals unavailable: Sat L Sun & Mon (The Pompadour only).

Carlton £150

North Bridge EH1 ISD

🕀 www.paramount-hotels.co.uk

✉ carlton@paramount-hotels.co.uk

☎ (0131) 472 3000   🖷 (0131) 556 2691

Some find it a touch "impersonal", but this well-equipped Old Town hotel – run by Paramount and revamped in recent times – is "comfortable" enough, and has a "great location" (near the grander Scotsman). Its "good-value, no-frills" style wins it quite a lot of votes as "an excellent city-break place to stay". / **Rooms:** 189. **Facilities:** indoor pool; gym; spa.

Channings £85

12-16 South Learmonth Gdns EH4 1EZ

🕀 www.channings.co.uk   ✉ reserve@channings.co.uk

☎ (0131) 315 2226   🖷 (0131) 332 9631

"A friendly small hotel verging on quaint " – this West End townhouse hotel wins consistent support amongst reporters, not least for its "friendly" and "helpful" service. / **Rooms:** 46 (of which 35 non smoking and 4 family rooms).

Crowne Plaza £99

80 High Street, The Royal Mile EH1 1TH
⌂ www.crowneplaza.com
✉ rescpedinburgh@allianceuk.com
☎ (0131) 557 9797 🖷 (0131) 557 9789

*"Very special service", a "very central location" and a swimming pool are principal plusses of this modern (but traditional-looking) establishment, on the Royal Mile. / **Rooms:** 238. **Facilities:** indoor pool; gym; spa. **Details:** closed Christmas.*

The George £205

19-21 George St EH2 2PB
⌂ www.edinburgh.intercontinental.com
✉ edinburgh@ichotelsgroup.com
☎ (0131) 225 1251 🖷 (0131) 226 5644

*Some find this grand old New Town hotel (part of the Intercontinental group) quite an "atmospheric" destination, and – if you get the right room, ideally in the old part – it offers some "fantastic" accommodation in a location that's very "handy for restaurants and the shops". Overall, however, reports tend to support the reporter who said that "lacklustre" standards across the board make for something of a "missed opportunity". / **Rooms:** 195 (of which 10 family rooms).*

Glenfield House £58

21 Mayfield Gdns EH9 2BX
⌂ www.glenfieldhouse.demon.co.uk
✉ mail@glenfieldhouse.demon.co.uk
☎ (0131) 667 3641 🖷 (0131) 667 9130

*"A little out of the centre, but worth it for the friendly owners and parking facilities", this boldly-decorated family-run hotel generates modest (but very consistent) feedback. / **Rooms:** 8 (of which all non smoking and 2 family rooms). **Details:** no Amex.*

Holyrood £150

Holyrood Rd EH8 8AU
⌂ www.macdonaldhotels.co.uk
✉ holyrood@macdonald-hotels.co.uk
☎ (0131) 550 4500 🖷 (0131) 550 4545

*Near the building site from which Scotland will one day be governed, this large new Macdonald hotel makes a "modern but comfortable" stand-by. It is to be hoped that the organisational standards set by the new Parliament will be better than the "chaotic" breakfasting arrangements sometimes noted here. / **Rooms:** 156 (of which some non smoking). **Facilities:** indoor pool; spa.*

sign up for our next survey at www.hardens.com

Howard £275

34 Great King St EH3 6QH
🔵 www.thehoward.com ✉ reserve@thehoward.com
☎ (0131) 315 2220 🖨 (0131) 332 9631
*"Discreet, elegant and comfortable", this Georgian townhouse in the New Town – decked out in luxurious traditional style – is especially approved for its rooms. Those who opt for the "beautiful" suites or larger doubles emerge slightly happier than those who book more modest accommodation. / **Rooms:** 18 (of which some non smoking and some family rooms).*

Ibis £50

6 Hunter Sq EH1 1QW
🔵 www.ibishotel.com ✉ H2039@accor-hotels.com
☎ (0131) 240 7000 🖨 (0131) 240 7007
*A "great location in the Old Town" helps make this "excellent" outlet of the national chain a particularly good and consistent budget recommendation. / **Rooms:** 99 (of which some non smoking and some family rooms).*

Malmaison £79

1 Tower Pl EH6 7DB
🔵 www.malmaison.com ✉ edinburgh@malmaison.com
☎ (0131) 468 5000 🖨 (0131) 468 5002
*"A good waterfront location" (a converted seaman's mission) near the bars and restaurants of the Leith dockside (and "beautiful on a summer evening") is a particular strength of this "modern and luxurious" design-hotel. It was the original of the chain, but it's a little eclipsed by its funkier siblings these days – only the rooms are consistently rated particularly highly. / **Rooms:** 101 (of which 33 non smoking and 6 family rooms). **Facilities:** gym.*

Le Meridien Edinburgh £90

18-22 Royal Terrace EH7 5AQ
🔵 www.lemeridien.com
✉ reservations.royalterrace@lemeridien.com
☎ (0131) 557 3222 🖨 (0131) 557 5334
*One reporter felt it "needs a bit of money spending on it" nowadays, but this impressive Georgian hotel achieved very consistent ratings across the board nonetheless. / **Rooms:** 108 (of which some non smoking and some family rooms). **Facilities:** indoor pool; gym; spa.*

Point £160

34 Bread St EH3 9AF
🔵 www.point-hotel.co.uk ✉ sales@point-hotel.co.uk
☎ (0131) 221 5555
*It may be still noticeably an office block conversion", but this "much-hyped", "minimalist" operation creates a lot of feedback. It's very mixed indeed, though – advocates welcome the "distinct lack of chintz" and "central location" while a sizeable band of cynics rail at "a lack of comfort and attention to detail" – "all they seem to have done is tart up the bar and lobby and stick beds in the offices". / **Rooms:** 140 (of which 70 non smoking and 10 family rooms).*

Prestonfield House £155

Priestfield Rd EH16 5UT
⌂ www.prestonfieldhouse.com
✉ info@prestonfieldhouse.com
☎ (0131) 668 3346   🖷 (0131) 668 3976

"Well worth the distance from the city-centre", this beautiful
17th-century house built up a big reputation under the ownership
of the Stevenson family. As this guide goes to press, it was
acquired by James Thomson, who plans to turn it into a 'fantastic
boutique destination hotel' – giving his management of The
Witchery, this seems far from impossible. / **Rooms:** 30 (of which 10
non smoking and 4 family rooms). **Facilities:** golf.

Rick's £118

55a Frederick St EH2 1LH
⌂ www.ricksedinburgh.co.uk   ✉ info@ricksedinburgh.co.uk
☎ (0131) 622 7800
For "real character, luxury and style", reporters are unanimous in
their praise of this "chic" and "central" restaurant-with-rooms.
The cooking is "tasty", too. / **Rooms:** 10.

Scotsman £180

20 North Bridge EH1 1YT
⌂ www.thescotsmanhotel.co.uk
✉ reservations@thescotsmanhotel.co.uk
☎ (0131) 556 5565   🖷 (0131) 652 3652
The commanding building overlooking Waverley Station that was
formerly home to the eponymous newspaper has been "very
stylishly" transformed in recent times into "a real five-star
establishment" which reporters find "hard to fault". "Very high
quality rooms", "gorgeous beds", "unobtrusive service",
"enormous breakfasts" and – last but not least – a striking,
"state-of-the-art pool" are among features which attract
particular praise. / **Rooms:** 68. **Facilities:** indoor pool; gym; spa.
Details: closed Christmas.

Sheraton Grand £130

1 Festival Sq EH3 9SR

⊕ www.sheraton.com

✉ grandedinburgh.sheraton@sheraton.com

☎ (0131) 229 9131   🖷 (0131) 229 4510

The "excellent health centre" (and in particular a "great spa"
whose "outside steam pool offers fantastic views of the city"), an
"excellent location" and "good business facilities" are particular
plusses of this imposing modern hotel, on the fringes of the city
centre. It's rather "impersonal", though. / **Rooms:** 260 (of which 56 non
smoking and 40 family rooms). **Facilities:** indoor pool; outdoor pool; gym; spa.

Travel Inn £57

1 Morrison Link EH3 8DN

⊕ www.travelinn.co.uk   ✉ edinburgh.mti@whitbread.co.uk

☎ (0131) 228 9819   🖷 (0131) 228 9836

"The usual Travel Inn-style operation, but with the bonus of great
location and a view". "If you want cheap without risking nasty",
reporters speak only well of this "basic, no-frills" establishment,
five minutes from the Haymarket railway station. / **Rooms:** 281 (of
which some non smoking and 137 family rooms).

The Witchery by the
Castle £225

Castlehill, The Royal Mile EH1 2NF

⊕ www.thewitchery.com   ✉ mail@thewitchery.com

☎ (0131) 225 5613   🖷 (0131) 220 4392

"Step into a world of velvet, dark woods, cushions and candles."
With its "magical and theatrical setting" and "fabulous" location
near the Castle, this famously Gothic establishment is the
"definitive" Aulk Reekie destination for those with romance in
mind. Though it's best-known as a restaurant, there are now six
"sumptuously furnished" suites attached – of the four added
recently, one even has it's own front door! / **Rooms:** 7 (of which all non
smoking). **Details:** closed 25-26 Dec; not suitable for children.

Great Fosters £140

Stroude Rd TW20 9UR

🖰 www.great-fosters.co.uk

✉ GreatFosters@compuserve.com

☎ (01784) 433822   📠 (01784) 472455

*Accommodation ranges from "amazing and huge" to "fairly basic", but all reporters are wowed by the "lovely" Tudor architecture and the "fabulous" gardens of this "very characterful" former royal hunting lodge. / **Rooms:** 48 (of which some non smoking and 2 family rooms). **Facilities:** outdoor pool; tennis.*

Runnymede £140

Windsor Rd TW20 0AG

🖰 www.runnymedehotel.com

✉ info@runnymedehotel.com

☎ (01784) 436171   📠 (01784) 436 340

*This "modern" hotel provides "a Thames-side location, but no character". It's "handy for Windsor", though, its rooms are "clean and comfortable", and it boasts a "good pool and spa". / **Rooms:** 180 (of which 116 non smoking and 19 family rooms). **Facilities:** indoor pool; gym; spa; tennis.*

Ynyshir Hall £120

SY20 8TA

🖰 www.ynyshir-hall.co.uk   ✉ info@ynyshir-hall.co.uk

☎ (01654) 781209   📠 (01654) 781366

*A Georgian house whose past owners include Mr Mappin (of '& Webb' fame) provides the setting for this "delightful rural retreat" (in 14 acres of gardens), which is now presided over by an artist and his wife. "Superb" cooking is one of the features which helps it attract nothing but praise from reporters – even from those who found the décor, enhanced by le patron's works, "a little OTT". / **Rooms:** 9.*

Britannia Inn £88

LA22 9HP

🖰 www.britinn.co.uk   ✉ info@britinn.co.uk

☎ (01539) 437210   📠 (01539) 437311

*"A very friendly pub with rooms in a wonderful location", in the Langdale valley. Its "cosy" ambience, as well as its "excellent beer and hearty meals", commend it to all who comment on it. / **Rooms:** 9.*

ENNIS, CO. CLARE, *ROI*   10–3B

Woodstock   €150

Shanaway Rd -
🖰 www.slh.com   ✉ woodstockhotel@slh.com
☎ +353-65 684 6600   🖨 +353-65 684 6600

*It may be "a bit remote", but this "lovely" new (2000) resort –
part of the Small Luxury Hotels of the Word consortium – is
located "in a scenic part of Western Ireland", and is tipped for its
high standards across the board. It offers many facilities – for
golfers and others.* / **Rooms:** 67 (of which 40 non smoking and 10 family
rooms). **Facilities:** indoor pool; gym; golf. **Details:** closed Christmas; no Switch.

EVERSHOT, DORSET   2–4B

Summer Lodge   £145

DT2 0JR
🖰 www.summerlodgehotel.com
✉ enquiries@summerlodgehotel.co.uk
☎ (01935) 83424   🖨 (01935) 83005

*Fans of "chintzy comfort" find much to applaud at this
"cosseting" country house hotel (set in a "quiet and beautiful"
location), whose "friendly but professional service" is one of its
strongest points. To some reporters, however, the whole formula
seems a bit "tired".* / **Rooms:** 17 (of which some family rooms).
Facilities: outdoor pool; tennis.

EVESHAM, WORCESTERSHIRE   2–1C

Evesham   £113   ☺☺

Coopers Ln WR11 1DA
🖰 www.eveshamhotel.com
✉ reception@eveshamhotel.com
☎ (01386) 765566

*"Great attention to every detail" is the hallmark which makes this
"pleasantly eccentric" and "informal" hotel "special in every way",
and it's "notably family-friendly" too. Thanks to a "very good"
restaurant – which boasts an impressive and unusual wine list –
there's plenty to interest grown-ups, too.* / **Rooms:** 40 (of which some
non smoking and some family rooms). **Facilities:** indoor pool.

---

sign up for our next survey at www.hardens.com

Riverside £98

The Parks, Offenham Rd WR11 5JP
🖰 www.broadway-cotswolds.co.uk/river.html
✉ Riversidehotel@theparksoffenham.freeserve.co.uk
☎ (01386) 446200 📠 (01386) 40021

A "beautiful setting" (the gardens, sloping down to the River Avon were part of Evesham Abbey's 15th-century deer park) and "great food" make this restaurant-with-rooms a consistently popular destination. The '20s building incorporates three 17th-century cottages. / **Rooms:** 7. **Details:** closed first 2 wks in Jan; meals unavailable: Sun D & Mon; no Amex.

EXETER, DEVON   1–3D

Barcelona £80

Magdalen St EX2 4HY
🖰 www.hotelbarcelona-uk.com
✉ info@hotelbarcelona-uk.com
☎ (01392) 281000 📠 (01392) 281001

This "rather funky hotel in a former eye hospital" (part of the hip Alias group) can seem a "strange find" in a city as square as this one. No matter, this is "a good hotel in a town with a shortage of good places to stay". Its "wacky", "retro-mix" design goes down well with most reporters, who say it offers "an all-round fantastic experience". / **Rooms:** 46 (of which 30 non smoking and 1 family room).

Combe House £146

Honiton EX14 3AD
🖰 www.thishotel.com ✉ stay@thishotel.com
☎ (01404) 540400 📠 (01404) 46004

"Idyllic surroundings" – an "amazing" estate of some 3500 acres, complete with Arabian horses and pheasants – contributes much to the charms of this "elegant", "tranquil" and "atmospheric" Elizabethan manor house, where a "warm" welcome awaits. / **Rooms:** 15 (of which 2 family rooms).

Royal Clarence £110
Cathedral Yard EX1 1HD
⌂ www.michaelcaines.com/royalclarence.html
☎ (01392) 319955
"A wonderful location overlooking the Cathedral Close" adds lustre
to this "grand old hotel". The catering – presided over from afar
by Michael Caines of Gidleigh Park – is widely thought to be "top
notch", and even some reporters who found their room a mite
"tired" thought this Corus hotel a "nice" place overall. / **Rooms:** 56
(of which 16 non smoking and some family rooms).

Southgate £116
Southernhay East EX1 1QF
⌂ www.macdonaldhotels.co.uk
✉ general.southgate@macdonald-hotels.co.uk
☎ (01392) 412812   昌 (01392) 413549
This "modern hotel within five minutes walk of quays, cathedral
and shops" is unanimously acclaimed as a "very enjoyable"
Macdonald Hotels establishment – "better than average, for a
chain". / **Rooms:** 110 (of which 60 non smoking and 6 family rooms).
Facilities: indoor pool; gym.

Travelodge £60
Moto Service Area, M5 Motorway, Sandygate EX2 7HF
⌂ www.travelodge.co.uk
☎ 0870 085 0950   昌 (01392) 410406
"As good as the Holiday Inn, and cheaper" – this motorway inn
has a "handy location" for those seeking to break a journey West.
The eating possibilities it offers, however, are not exciting.
/ **Rooms:** 102 (of which 78 non smoking).

White Hart £69 T
66 South Street EX1 1EE
⌂ www.roomattheinn.info
✉ whitehart.exeter@eldridge-pope.co.uk
☎ (01392) 279897   昌 (01392) 250159
"A good reception, good food and an olde worlde atmosphere" –
this large, 14th-century coaching inn is tipped as "an excellent
place for a city break". / **Rooms:** 55 (of which 50 non smoking and 4 family
rooms).

FALMOUTH, CORNWALL 1–4B

Budoch Vean £190*
Helford Passage, Mawnan Smith TR11 5LG
⌂ www.budockvean.co.uk   ✉ relax@budockvean.co.uk
☎ (01326) 250288   昌 (01326) 250892
"An excellent family hotel without the downside of family hotels" –
that's how one reporter sees this modern establishment, which
enjoys a "wonderful location" by the River Halford. Its wide range
of attractions scored highly, though when it came to overall charm
a couple of reports found the place "lacking". *Prices include
DB&B, as well as golf and tennis. / **Rooms:** 56. **Facilities:** indoor pool;
spa; golf; tennis. **Details:** no Amex or Switch.

Greenbank £105

Harbourside TR11 2SR
⌂ www.greenbank-hotel.com
✉ sales@greenbank-hotel.co.uk
☎ (01326) 312440   🖷 (01326) 211362

"I could have jumped out my window into the estuary" – an "exceptional position" on the harbour ensures some "stunning" views for this waterside hotel. Other aspects of the hotel are not especially remarkable, although the restaurant is "pleasant".
/ Rooms: 58 (of which 30 non smoking and 4 family rooms).

Royal Duchy £170*

Cliff Rd TR11 4NX
⌂ www.royalduchy.co.uk   ✉ info@royalduchy.co.uk
☎ (01326) 313042   🖷 (01326) 319420

*It inspires less (and slightly less positive) feedback than some of its stablemates in the generally commendable Brend hotels stable, but all reports confirm this seaside hotel is an "accommodating" destination nonetheless. *Prices are quoted on a DB&B basis.*
/ Rooms: 43 (of which some family rooms). **Facilities:** indoor pool; spa.
Details: meals unavailable: L.

St Michaels £86

Gyllyngvase Beach, Seafront TR11 4NB
✉ sales@stmichaelshotel.com
☎ (01326) 312707   🖷 (01326) 211772

"Bright, well-furnished rooms", "lovely views" and "good leisure facilities" are a combination leading to general reporter satisfaction with this long-established seaside hotel, recently extensively refurbished by the family which acquired it in 2001.
/ Rooms: 65 (of which some non smoking and some family rooms).
Facilities: indoor pool; gym; spa.

Reads £198*

Macknade Manor, Canterbury Rd ME13 8XE
⌂ www.reads.com   ✉ email@reads.com
☎ (01795) 535344   🖷 (01795) 535344

*This may be "only a restaurant-with-rooms" (albeit in an elegantly understated Georgian manor house), but it offers some "huge" and "lovely" accommodation, and is praised for offering "all-round good value" (with the best deals to be had midweek). *Prices are quoted on a DB&B basis.* **/ Rooms:** 6 (of which all non smoking).
Details: closed Christmas; no children.

FAWKHAM, KENT   3–3B

Brandshatch Place   £90
Fawkham Valley Rd DA3 8NY
🖰 www.arcadianhotels.co.uk
📧 brandshatch@arcadianhotels.co.uk
☎ (01474) 872239   📠 (01474) 879652

*Perhaps a major refurbishment – under way as we go to press –
will enable this potentially charming Georgian building in 12 acres
(now an Arcadian hotel), to achieve its potential. In the run-up,
reporters were pretty consistently of the view that it was "very
average".* / **Rooms:** 38. **Facilities:** *indoor pool; gym; tennis.*

FERRENSBY, NORTH YORKSHIRE   8–4B

General Tarleton Inn   £85
Boroughbridge Rd HG5 0PZ
🖰 www.generaltarleton.co.uk   📧 gti@generaltarleton.co.uk
☎ (01423) 340284   📠 (01423) 340288

*"Great food" is the highlight of a visit to this 18th-century
coaching inn, under the same ownership as the celebrated Angel
at Hetton. It's generally favourably commented on (though some
of the rooms can "lack charm").* / **Rooms:** *14 (of which 9 non smoking).*
Details: *meals unavailable: Mon-Sat L, Sun & Mon D.*

FINTRY, STIRLINGSHIRE   9–4C

Culcreuch Castle   £124
G63 0LW
🖰 www.culcreuch.com   📧 info@culcreuch.com
☎ (01360) 860555   📠 (01360) 860556

*Given that Scotland's oldest inhabited castle – set in a working
estate of some 1600 acres – is surprisingly handy for both of the
major cities north of the Border, it inspired surprisingly little survey
commentary. All of it was broadly complimentary, however.
Families might like to consider the Scandinavian-style chalets in
the grounds.* / **Rooms:** *14 (of which 4 family rooms).*

FISHGUARD, PEMBROKESHIRE   4–4B

Manor House   £56
11 Main St SA65 9HG
☎ (01348) 873260   📠 (01348) 873260

*"Magnificent views from the rear rooms" are one of the features
recommending this "well-run" townhouse hotel to an (older) band
of reporters. It offers "very individual" accommodation in a variety
of styles (from Victorian to Art Deco) and dependable cooking.
"The friendly owners also sell antiques on the premises."*
/ **Rooms:** *6 (of which all non smoking).* **Details:** *closed Christmas, restricted
opening Oct & Feb; meals unavailable: L; no Amex or Switch.*

Moonfleet Manor   £120*
DT3 4ED
🖰 www.luxury-family-hotels.co.uk
✉ info@moonfleetmanor.com
☎ (01305) 786948   🖷 (01305) 774395

"A decent compromise between child-friendliness and grown-up comfort" – this "old villa" (part of the Luxury Family Hotels group) has become well-known to London professional parents. It offers a crèche (the Den), a large indoor play area and enjoys a "beautiful windswept seaside location". It's decidedly "not cheap, though", the "OK" cuisine can become "repetitive", and staff can "lack attention to detail". *Prices are quoted on a DB&B basis.
/ **Rooms:** 39 (of which some non smoking and some family rooms).
Facilities: indoor pool.

The Griffin Inn   £85
TN22 3SS
🖰 www.thegriffininn.co.uk
☎ (01825) 722890   🖷 (01825) 722810

"Fantastic food, fantastic rooms" – reporters use the "F" word a lot to describe this "little gem of an inn", in "a really stunning part of Sussex". Its attractions include a "proper 'pub' atmosphere", a "jolly landlord" and "lovely beer and wine". / **Rooms:** 8 (of which all non smoking).

FLITWICK, BEDFORDSHIRE   3–2A

Flitwick Manor   £165
Church Rd MK45 1AE
🖰 www.flitwickmanor.activehotels.com
✉ info@menzies-hotels.co.uk
☎ (01525) 712242   📠 (01525) 718753

*The fact that "all rooms are in the original building" helps make this "pleasant" Georgian house an "atmospheric" destination. Facilities at this Menzies establishment are "limited" and – though there was no clear pattern – most aspects of the operation drew some sort of flak from reporters. / **Rooms:** 17 (of which 1 non smoking and 1 family room). **Facilities:** tennis. **Details:** no Switch.*

FOLLIFOOT, NORTH YORKSHIRE   5–1C

Rudding Park   £158
Rudding Park HG3 1JH
🖰 www.ruddingpark.co.uk   ✉ sales@ruddingpark.com
☎ (01423) 871350

*This "very pleasant country house hotel" – an impressive, largely 18th-century house owned by the same family for over 30 years – is a "quiet" and "efficient" place, where the service shows impressive "attention to detail". Golf is an important attraction, but by no means the only one. / **Rooms:** 50 (of which 31 non smoking and 4 family rooms). **Facilities:** golf.*

FORT WILLIAM, HIGHLAND   9–3B

Inverlochy Castle   £330
Torlundy PH33 6SN
🖰 www.inverlochycastlehotel.co.uk
✉ info@inverlochycastlehotel.com
☎ (01397) 702177

*"Very very expensive but of exceptionally high quality throughout" – this "fabulous" Baronial pile (a member of Relais & Chateaux) in the foothills of Ben Nevis has "great views", extends a "wonderful warm welcome" and offers "fabulous food". Only on the facilities front do ratings fall anything short of rapture. / **Rooms:** 17 (of which all non smoking and 10 family rooms). **Facilities:** tennis. **Details:** closed 6 Jan-12 Feb.*

Fowey Hall   £160   ☺

Hanson Drive PL23 1ET

🖰 www.luxury-family-hotels.co.uk   ✉ info@foweyhall.com
☎ (01726) 833866

"Self-styled as a family-friendly hotel", this imposing Italianate
country house – revamped not so long ago by the Luxury Family
Hotels group – boasts a "fantastic setting overlooking the Fowey
estuary", "delightful interiors" and "excellent facilities" for sprogs.
It gets an almost unanimous thumbs-up for visits en famille, and
offers cooking that's "decent, if not outstanding". / **Rooms:** 24 (of
which all non smoking and 12 family rooms). **Facilities:** indoor pool.

Marina   £134   ☺

Esplanade PL23 1HY

🖰 www.themarinahotel.co.uk
✉ marina.hotel@dial.pipex.com
☎ (01726) 833315   🖷 (01726) 832779

There's something of an 'highs and lows' aspect to some reports
on stays at this early 19th-century house by the Fowey. Many
rooms have "a pleasant verandah, overlooking the estuary",
however, and "wonderful views" made up for any other
deficiencies for most (if not quite all) reporters. / **Rooms:** 21 (of which
all non smoking and 4 family rooms).

GALMPTON, DEVON 1–4D

Maypool Park £78 ☺

Maypool TQ5 0ET
www.maypoolpark.co.uk
peacock@maypoolpark.co.uk
☎ (01803) 842442 ℻ (01803) 845782

*Surrounded by a private estate (where Agatha Christie once lived, and where her daughter still does), this small, family-run hotel consists of Victorian cottages, with views over the Dart valley. Even a reporter who thought "the décor could be improved" judged this a "good-value" destination. / **Rooms:** 10 (of which all non smoking). **Details:** closed winter; meals unavailable: L; min age for children: 10.*

GATEHOUSE OF FLEET, DUMFRIES & GALLOWAY 7–2B

Cally Palace £90* ☺☺

DG7 2DL
www.callypalace.co.uk info@callypalace.co.uk
☎ (01557) 814341 ℻ (01557) 814522

*This imposing but "lovely" country house hotel makes a "very memorable" destination and is hailed for its "tremendous" facilities (including a "fabulous" golf course). Reports on all aspects of its operation – including the restaurant – are impressively consistent. *Prices are quoted on a DB&B basis. / **Rooms:** 56 (of which some non smoking and some family rooms). **Facilities:** indoor pool; spa. **Details:** closed Jan and part of Feb.*

GATWICK AIRPORT, SURREY 3–3B

Hilton London Gatwick Airport £150 ☹

South Terminal RH6 0LL
www.hilton.co.uk
☎ (01293) 518080 ℻ (01293) 528980

*"Shabby" and "bleak", this "totally charmless" establishment may be, but it generates many reports by virtue of its "great location" for those with early-morning flights. / **Rooms:** 789 (of which some non smoking and some family rooms). **Facilities:** indoor pool; gym; spa.*

Ibis £46 ☺

London Rd, Crawley RH10 9GY
www.ibishotel.com h1889@accor-hotels.com
☎ (01293) 590300 ℻ (01293) 590310

*An establishment self-evident in its style and purpose, but noted as offering "very good value for the location" (three miles from the airport). / **Rooms:** 104 (of which 93 non smoking). **Details:** min age for children: 8.*

Langshott Manor £185

Langshott RH6 9LN
🖱 www.alexanderhotels.com
✉ admin@langshottmanor.co.uk
☎ (01293) 786680 📠 (01293) 783905

Airport hotels don't come much more charming that this 16th-century manor house, five minutes' drive from Gatwick, which is a "great" (if "corporate") venue for entertaining. Unsurprisingly, some find the place, now run by Alexander Hotels, "expensive for what you get". / **Rooms:** 22 (of which all non smoking and some family rooms).

Meridien £80

North Terminal RH6 0PH
🖱 www.lemeridien.com
✉ sales.gatwick@lemeridien-hotels.com
☎ (01293) 567 070 📠 (01293) 555037

"An efficient and comfortable airport hotel", which attracts an astoninshingly large number of recommendations as being "surprisingly elegant, of its type", and "conveniently located", too. / **Rooms:** 494 (of which 349 non smoking and 18 family rooms). **Facilities:** indoor pool; gym.

GILLINGHAM, DORSET 2–3B

Stock Hill Country House £240*

Stock Hill SP8 5NR
🖱 www.stockhillhouse.co.uk
✉ reception@stockhillhouse.co.uk
☎ (01747) 823626 📠 (01747) 825628

*This small, family-run Victorian country house hotel, set in 11 acres of wooded grounds, is tipped as a "great" and "very restful" destination. A "great" restaurant and "excellent service" attract particular praise. *Prices are quoted on a DB&B basis.* / **Rooms:** 8 (of which 1 family room). **Facilities:** tennis. **Details:** meals unavailable: Mon L; no Amex; min age for children: 7.

GLASGOW, CITY OF GLASGOW 9–4C

The number of establishments of note in Scotland's largest city is perhaps fractionally less than one might have thought, given its size, its 'City of Culture' reputation and so on. However, given the limited number, the city offers a surprisingly good range of quality hotels, at different styles and 'price-points".

Arthouse £110 😊

129 Bath St G2 2SZ
🖱 www.arthousehotel.com ✉ info@arthousehotel.com
☎ (0141) 221 6789 📠 (0141) 221 6777

This "slick Art Deco hotel" wins praise as "an excellent conversion" of former offices. "Helpful" staff contribute to an experience which offers "good value" overall. / **Rooms:** 63 (of which 33 non smoking and 17 family rooms). **Facilities:** spa.

Carlton George £99

44 West George St G2 1DH

🖰 www.carltonhotels.co.uk   ✉ george@carltonhotels.com

☎ (0141) 353 6373   🖨 (0141) 353 6263

*"Friendy", and offering "excellent" (if "slightly small") rooms, this "good-quality" modern hotel benefits from a "very central" location, next to Queen Street station. / **Rooms:** 64 (of which 32 non smoking and some family rooms). **Details:** closed 24 Dec-1 Jan.*

City Inn £89

Finnieston Quay G3 8HN

🖰 www.cityinn.com   ✉ glasgow.reservations@cityinn.com

☎ (0141) 240 1002   🖨 (0141) 248 2754

*"Modern, stylish, very friendly" – reporters speak in glowing terms of this "incredible-value" chain hotel, near the exhibition centre. / **Rooms:** 164 (of which 134 non smoking). **Facilities:** gym. **Details:** meals unavailable: L.*

Holiday Inn £90

161 West Nile St G1 2RL

🖰 www.higlasgow.com   ✉ info@higlasgow.com

☎ (0141) 352 8305   🖨 (0141) 332 7447

*A "central location" helps generate lots of reports on this "functional" city-centre hotel. The location is "noisy at weekends", though, and reports are quite mixed. / **Rooms:** 113 (of which some non smoking and some family rooms).*

Langs £110

2 Port Dundas Pl G2 2LD
🏠 www.langshotels.co.uk ✉ reservations@langshotel.co.uk
☎ (0141) 333 1500 📠 (0141) 333 5700

This new boutique hotel near the Royal Concert Hall is "an excellent example of how to make a new hotel great and still deliver good value". Reporters speak in glowing terms of the "spacious" and "well-equipped" rooms, "pleasantly mellow atmosphere", "good restaurant" and "charming and effective service. / **Rooms:** *100 (of which 25 non smoking).* **Facilities:** *gym; spa.*

Malmaison £79

278 West George St G2 4LL
🏠 www.malmaison.com ✉ glasgow@malmaison.com
☎ (0141) 572 1000 📠 (0141) 572 1002

This "friendly, no-hassle boutique hotel in the heart of Glasgow" generated twice as much feedback as anywhere else in town. Reporters generally rate it a "first-class" choice, loving its "upbeat" and "sophisticated" style. There is the occasional disappointment, though – "this is very much a city hotel", with "few" facilities and some "pokey" rooms – and its trendy basement brasserie generates mixed reviews. / **Rooms:** *72 (of which 35 non smoking and 4 family rooms).* **Facilities:** *gym.*

Marriott £99

500 Argyle St, Anderston G3 8RR
🏠 www.marriott.com
☎ (0141) 226 5577 📠 0870 400 7330

It's notably short on the charm front – this is "a standard business hotel", and pretty "dull" – but it's "convenient for shops and nightlife", and has a "nice gym and swimming pool". / **Rooms:** *300 (of which some non smoking and 18 family rooms).* **Facilities:** *indoor pool; gym; spa.*

I Devonshire Gardens £125

I Devonshire Gdns G12 0UX
🏠 www.onedevonshiregardens.com
✉ reservations@onedevonshire.com
☎ (0141) 339 2001   📠 (0141) 337 1663

"Very classy rooms" and *"keen"* staff help make this townhouse
hotel – *"leafily located"* on the West End's main drag – Glasgow's
grandest address. This status is bolstered by the presence of
super-chef Gordon Ramsay's outpost in his home town, Amaryllis
(which has introduced a more informal section to complement the
'fine dining' on which its reputation stands). The hotel's décor is
undoubtedly on the *"ostentatious"* side, though, and some find it
"twee". / **Rooms:** 38 (of which 12 non smoking and some family rooms).
Details: meals unavailable: L.

St Jude £115

190 Bath St G2 4HG
🏠 www.saintjudes.com   ✉ reservations@saintjudes.com
☎ (0141) 352 8800   📠 (0141) 352 8801

This "very modern", "small, friendly and informal" boutique hotel
in the heart of the business district has dropped 'Groucho' from
its name (though it still has ties to the famed London media club).
"Brilliant service" and a *"super-cool bar"* are among the features
which particularly appeal to reporters. / **Rooms:** 6. **Details:** closed 25-
26 Dec, 1-2 Jan; meals unavailable: Sat & Sun.

Buggy's Glencairn Inn €110

Tallow
🏠 www.lismore.com   ✉ info@buggys.com
☎ +353-58 56232   📠 +353-58 56232

This "quaint" family-run cottage is "a star" – that's the
unanimous conclusion of the small number of reporters who
commented on it, praising its *"unpretentious"* style, *"impeccable
service"* and *"good value"*. *"The good (if limited-choice) restaurant
is used by locals as much as visitors."* / **Rooms:** 4 (of which some non
smoking and some family rooms). **Details:** closed Christmas; no Amex or Switch;
min age for children: 9.

GLENDEVON, PERTH & KINROSS 9–4C

Tormaukin Inn £90

FK14 7JY

⌂ www.tormaukin.co.uk ✉ enquiries@tormaukin.co.uk
☎ (01259) 781252 🖷 (01259) 781526

*This "posh country pub" (an 18th-century building) has a charming location in the Ochil Hills, and has been "tastefully expanded" over the years. "Outstanding" cooking features in most reports. / **Rooms:** 12 (of which some family rooms). **Details:** closed one week in Jan.*

GLENFINNAN, HIGHLAND 9–3B

Glenfinnan House £90

PH37 4LT

⌂ www.lochaber.com/glenfinnanhouse
✉ macfarlane@glenfinnanhouse.dialnet.co.uk
☎ (01397) 722235 🖷 (01397) 722235

*This 18th-century pine-panelled house – still in the ownership of the family who rescued it from dereliction over 30 years ago – is tipped for its "breathtaking views over Loch Shiel" and for its "excellent" cuisine. / **Rooms:** 17 (of which 4 family rooms). **Details:** closed End Oct-Easter; meals unavailable: L; no Amex.*

GOLCAR, WEST YORKSHIRE 5–1C

Weavers Shed £65

Knowl Rd HD7 4AN

⌂ www.weaversshed.co.uk ✉ info@weaversshed.co.uk
☎ (01484) 654284

*It's "very much a restaurant-with-rooms", but "superb bedrooms are very reasonably priced" at this "comfortably stylish" establishment (which is indeed housed in row of former weavers' cottages). The food is usually "superb", too. / **Rooms:** 5 (of which all non smoking). **Details:** meals unavailable: Sat L, Sun & Mon.*

GRANGE-IN-BORROWDALE, CUMBRIA 7–3D

Borrowdale Gates Country House £125*

CA12 5UQ

⌂ www.borrowdale-gates.com
✉ hotel@borrowdale-gates.com
☎ (01768) 777204 🖷 (01768) 777254

*"Enjoyable food" and a "marvellous location" ("especially for walkers") are the twin themes of all reports on this attractive, small country house hotel, not far from Derwentwater. Reports on rooms vary from "standard and small" to "pretty" – it looks worth paying the marginal extra for 'Premier' accommodation. *Prices are quoted on a DB&B basis. / **Rooms:** 29 (of which 2 family rooms). **Details:** min age for children: 7.*

GRANGE-OVER-SANDS, CUMBRIA   7–4D

Graythwaite Manor   £100

Fernhill Rd LA11 7JE

🏠 www.graythwaitemanor.co.uk

✉ sales@graythwaitemanor.co.uk

☎ (01539) 532001   🖷 (01539) 535549

Still just as one of your editors remembers it from 30 years ago – this "old-fashioned" hotel is tipped for its "majestic views over the lawns", its "slightly formal" style, and its "good" food. The clientèle is still "somewhat elderly". / **Rooms:** 22 (of which some family rooms).

GRANTHAM, LINCOLNSHIRE   6–4A

De Vere Belton Woods   £155

Belton NG32 2LN

🏠 www.devereonline.co.uk

✉ belton.woods@devere-hotels.com

☎ (01476) 593200   🖷 (01476) 574547

"Fantastic facilities" – squash, football, sunbed, nursery, driving range – endear this "mainly golf" (and also conference) 'activities resort' to some reporters. Generally, though, complaints of "poor rooms" and "clueless" staff dragged its ratings down. / **Rooms:** 136 (of which 105 non smoking and some family rooms). **Facilities:** indoor pool; gym; golf; tennis.

GRASMERE, CUMBRIA   7–3D

Lancrigg Country House   £100   ☺☺

Easedale Rd LA22 9QN

🏠 www.lancrigg.co.uk   ✉ info@lancrigg.co.uk

☎ (01539) 435317   🖷 (01539) 435058

Even a reporter who'd "never stayed at a vegetarian hotel before" proclaimed the food here "excellent", so carnivores should not overlook this "very pleasant" all-rounder just outside the village. The building is not without interest of its own, numbering Wordsworth among those involved in its long history. / **Rooms:** 13 (of which some family rooms).

Swan   £100   ☺

Chiswick Rd LA22 9RF

🏠 www.macdonaldhotels.co.uk

✉ inquiries@macdonald-hotels.co.uk

☎ 0870 400 8132   🖷 (01539) 435741

"Slightly tired, but full of character" is how one reporter summed up this ancient inn, now a Macdonald Hotel, which is a "very friendly" place ("good with children"), with "nice rooms" and a "cosy lounge". / **Rooms:** 38 (of which some non smoking and 4 family rooms). **Details:** meals unavailable: L.

The Wordsworth £180*

Stock Ln LA22 9SW

🖰 www.grasmere-hotels.co.uk
✉ enquiries@wordsworth-grasmere.co.uk
☎ (01539) 435592　📠 (01539) 435765

A "lovely setting" – in the heart of the village, next to the churchyard in which the eponymous bard is buried – and "excellent facilities" win praise for this "well presented" hotel. On the downside, it can seem "a little overpriced", and service "though efficient, can be rather distant". *Prices are quoted on a DB&B basis. / **Rooms:** 39 (of which 2 family rooms). **Facilities:** indoor pool; gym.

GREAT MILTON, OXFORDSHIRE　　　　2–2D

Manoir aux Quat' Saisons £295

Church Rd OX44 7PD

🖰 www.manoir.com　✉ lemanoir@blanc.co.uk
☎ (01844) 278881　📠 (01844) 278847

"Charming, beautiful, totally indulgent." Raymond Blanc's "superb" 15th-century manor house set amidst "wonderful gardens" is judged "almost faultless" by reporters (and incited more reports than anywhere else). It's home, of course, to the UK's most celebrated restaurant outside the capital – but the "superlative" and "luxurious" rooms contribute almost as much to "a fantastic all-round experience". / **Rooms:** 32 (of which 1 family room).

GREAT TEW, OXFORDSHIRE　　　　2–1D

Falkland Arms £65

OX7 4DB

🖰 www.falklandarms.org.uk　✉ sjcourage@btconnect.com
☎ (01608) 683653　📠 (01608) 683656

A "friendly" ambience and "charming" rooms make this 16th-century inn, in a "beautiful" village, a "cosy" and "comfortable" destination. The cooking is acclaimed as "delicious" by some (and the result can be "crowded" conditions in the bar and restaurant). / **Rooms:** 5 (of which all non smoking). **Details:** closed 23-26 Dec, 1 Jan; meals unavailable: Sun D; min age for children: 14.

sign up for our next survey at www.hardens.com　　130

GUERNSEY, CHANNEL ISLANDS

La Grande Mare   £148
Vazon, Castel GY5 7LL
🖱 www.lgm.guernsey.net   ✉ hotellagrandemare@cwgsy.net
☎ (01481) 256576   🖳 (01481) 256532
A resort-hotel, particularly tipped for its "perfect location", by the beach, and its "fantastic health suite". / Rooms: 25. Facilities: indoor pool; gym; golf; tennis.

Hougue du Pommier   £72
Hougue du Pommier Rd
🖱 www.hotelhouguedupommier.com
✉ hotel@houguedupommier.guernsey.net
☎ (01481) 256531   🖳 (01481) 256260
This old farmhouse near a beach is universally praised by reporters as a "superb" destination with a "lovely" atmosphere (and it is a member of the French Relais du Silence consortium). Thanks to its "excellent and varied food" and its "very good value", "many guests return again and again". / Rooms: 43 (of which 4 family rooms). Facilities: outdoor pool. Details: no Amex.

GUISBOROUGH, CLEVELAND   8–3C

Gisborough Hall   £138   ☺
Whitby Ln TS14 6PT
🖱 www.gisboroughhall.com
☎ 0870 400 8191   🖳 (01287) 610844
After restoration by Macdonald Hotels, at considerable expense, this large Victorian/Edwardian country house has recently been launched as an hotel (though it still lacks the leisure and spa facilities which seem to be de rigueur for a place of this type nowadays). An early visitor tips it, however, for "the best room quality ever". / Rooms: 71 (of which 15 non smoking and 6 family rooms).

GULLANE, EAST LOTHIAN   9–4D

Greywalls   £240
Muirfield EH31 2EG
🖱 www.greywalls.co.uk   ✉ hotel@greywalls.co.uk
☎ (01620) 842144   🖳 (01620) 842241
"A superb location, so much charm and character, lots of warmth and true Scottish hospitality" – reporters find little to complain of at this fine Lutyens house (which was originally constructed as 'a small, albeit dignified holiday home overlooking Muirfield Golf Course and the Firth of Forth'). / Rooms: 23. Facilities: tennis. Details: closed Nov-Mar.

HALIFAX, WEST YORKSHIRE · 3–2B

West Lodge Park £150

Cockfosters Rd EN4 0PY
🖰 www.bealeshotels.co.uk
✉ westlodgepark@bealeshotels.co.uk
☎ (020) 8216 3900   📠 (020) 8216 3937

"A rural retreat within the M25" – this country house hotel only 12 miles from London comes complete with 35 acres of grounds and an arboretum. It was rated highly (if on the basis of a small number of reports) for its "very good" service and quality cooking. / **Rooms:** 59 (of which some non smoking and some family rooms).

HALIFAX, WEST YORKSHIRE 5–1C

Holdsworth House £114

Holdsworth Rd, Holmfield HX2 9TG
🖰 www.holdsworthhouse.co.uk
✉ info@holdsworthhouse.co.uk
☎ (01422) 240024   📠 (01422) 245174

A grand Jacobean manor house three miles out of town is the setting for this "beautiful" hotel, four decades in the ownership of the same family. Of the limited feedback it inspired, some say it offers "excellent service and wonderful food", while others are more moderate in their praise. / **Rooms:** 40 (of which 22 non smoking and 2 family rooms). **Details:** closed 22 Dec-2Jan.

HAMBLETON, RUTLAND 5–4D

Hambleton Hall £186

LE15 8TH
🖰 www.hambletonhall.com ✉ hotel@hambletonhall.com
☎ (01572) 756991   📠 (01572) 724721

A "fantastic, quiet" rural setting – overlooking Rutland Water from a peninsula – helps create an away-from-it-all atmosphere at Tim Hart's "top-drawer" country house hotel. Rooms are arguably "small" and facilities a mite "limited", but the most common assessment was that the place is "superb" – not least the famous (if "formal" and "expensive") dining room. / **Rooms:** 17 (of which 1 non smoking and 8 family rooms).

HARLECH, GWYNEDD 4–2C

Maes Y Neuadd £165

LL47 6YA
🖰 www.neuadd.com ✉ maes@neuadd.com
☎ (01766) 780200   📠 (01766) 780211

A "very good restaurant", a "stunning location" (with views of Snowdonia) and "friendly service" come together to make this charming building (parts of which date from the 14th century) an "ideal venue for a short-break escape". As you might hope, the locality offers "excellent walking and sightseeing". / **Rooms:** 16 (of which 4 family rooms).

HAROME, NORTH YORKSHIRE   8–4C

Star Inn   £90
YO62 5JE
🖰 www.thestaratharome.co.uk
☎ (01439) 770397   🖨 (01439) 771833

*This beautiful, and aptly named, thatched inn already a reputation
as one of the UK's leading gastropubs, but it just got better! "The
newly-built bedrooms in the annexe are excellent", says one
reporter – "the accommodation matches the meals", says
another. "Superb" says another. And so on… / Rooms: 11.*
Details: meals unavailable: Sun D & Mon; no Amex.

HARROGATE, NORTH YORKSHIRE   5–1C

The Boars Head   £120
Ripley Castle Estate HG3 3AY
🖰 www.boarsheadripley.co.uk
🖂 reservations@boarsheadripley.co.uk
☎ (01423) 771888   🖨 (01423) 771509

*This grand coaching inn is very much part of the local scene
(being a personal interest of the grandees who own the village just
outside the town), and it offers "lots of character" and "good
food" (in both the restaurant and the jollier bistro). In the face of
all these virtues, there are those who find the rooms a mite
"lacklustre", but the overall verdict is that this is a "good-value"
destination, nonetheless. / Rooms: 25 (of which 15 non smoking).*
Facilities: tennis. **Details:** no Amex or Switch.

Majestic   £110   ☺
Ripon Rd HG1 2HU
🖰 www.paramount-hotels.co.uk
🖂 majestic@paramount-hotels.co.uk
☎ (01423) 700300   🖨 (01423) 521332

*For fans of the "delightfully old-fashioned", this "lovely Victorian
hotel" remains quite a "favourite", and it wins praise for its
"professional" service. Perhaps inevitably, the flip-side of this is
that for some reporters this Paramount establishment is "living on
past glories", offering accommodation (and facilities) falling gently
behind the times. / Rooms: 156 (of which some non smoking and some family
rooms). Facilities: indoor pool; gym; spa; tennis.*

Nidd Hall   £140*
Nidd HG3 3BN
🖰 www.warnerholidays.co.uk
☎ (01423) 771598   🖨 (01423) 770931

*With its "splendid grounds" (of 45 acres), "great location", "very
good leisure facilities" and "full entertainment" – the Warner
hotels (*DB&B, no-kids) formula is perhaps seen at its best at this
dramatically-located, mainly Georgian country house hotel. Only
the standard of cooking ("average") holds the place back from
total approval. Note that the minimum stay is three nights.
/ Rooms: 183 (of which some non smoking). Facilities: indoor pool; gym; spa;
tennis. Details: no children.*

---

sign up for our next survey at www.hardens.com   133

HAWES, NORTH YORKSHIRE 8–4A

Stone House £84*
Sedbusk DL8 3PT
🖰 www.stonehousehotel.com ✉ daleshotel@aol.com
☎ (01969) 667571 🖷 (01969) 667720
*This "small, family-run country house hotel" is "managed with excellent attention to detail and customer requirements". Its attractions include "views over the village, good food (with a restaurant frequented by non-residents too), plus four-posters". *Prices are quoted on a DB&B basis.* / Rooms: 22 (of which all non smoking and no family rooms). Details: closed Jan; meals unavailable: L.*

HAY ON WYE, HEREFORDSHIRE 2–1A

Old Black Lion £85
Lion St HR3 5AD
🖰 www.oldblacklion.co.uk ✉ info@oldblacklion.co.uk
☎ (01497) 820841 🖷 (01497) 822960
This "charming, eccentric, olde worlde inn", parts of which date from the 13th century, is located "in the heart of this fabulous town of books". Prices may be relatively modest, but "standards are maintained". / Rooms: 10 (of which all non smoking). Details: closed 25-26 Dec; no Amex; min age for children: 5.

HAZLEWOOD, NORTH YORKSHIRE 5–1C

Hazlewood Castle £140
Paradise Ln LS24 9NJ
🖰 www.hazlewood-castle.co.uk
✉ info@hazlewood-castle.co.uk
☎ (01937) 535353 🖷 (01937) 530630

This fortified manor house dates (in parts) back to the 13th century, and it enjoys a "beautiful" parkland setting. "Amazing", "very large and luxurious" bedrooms are attested to by all reporters (as is the fact that the restaurant service can be "a let-down"). / Rooms: 21 (of which 9 family rooms).

Comfort   £99

Shepiston Ln UB3 1LP
🔆 www.comfortheathrow.com
✉ info@comfortheathrow.com
☎ (020) 8573 6162   🖷 (020) 8848 1057
Following a complete refurbishment, this is a budget tip for a "good overnight stay", as it's only two miles from the airport. / **Rooms:** 184 (of which some non smoking and 12 family rooms). **Facilities:** gym. **Details:** meals unavailable: L.

Crowne Plaza   £125

Drayton UB7 9NA
🔆 www.crowneplaza.com
✉ business.centre@ichotelsgroup.com
☎ (01895) 445555   🖷 (01895) 445122
Not quite all reporters are impressed, but – by the dire standards of airport hotels – this is a "surprisingly good" destination. / **Rooms:** 458 (of which some non smoking and 21 family room). **Facilities:** indoor pool; gym; spa; golf.

Hilton London Heathrow   £189

Terminal 4 TW6 3AF
🔆 www.hilton.co.uk
☎ (020) 8759 7755   🖷 (020) 87597579
"The only hotel actually in the airport" (in Terminal 4) – a number of reporters felt "it does its job well", but that it "takes too long to check in and out" was a repeated gripe. / **Rooms:** 395 (of which some non smoking and some family rooms). **Facilities:** indoor pool; gym; spa.

Holiday Inn   £100

Sipson Way, Bath Rd UB7 0DP
🔆 www.holiday-inn.co.uk
☎ (020) 8990 0000   🖷 (020) 8897 8659
"Very comfortable" rooms and a location that's "excellent, for the airport, make this well-known "bed-factory" a tolerable place for pre-flight kip. "Charmless" staff, however, contribute to what is otherwise a predictably "factory" experience. / **Rooms:** 230 (of which 160 non smoking and some family rooms). **Facilities:** gym.

Marriott   £149   😐

Bath Rd UB3 5AN
🔆 www.marriott.com
☎ 0870 400 7250   🖷 0870 400 7350
One of the many "functional and unexciting" possibilities in these parts, but not the worst, by any means. / **Rooms:** 390 (of which 250 non smoking and 6 family rooms). **Facilities:** indoor pool; gym; spa.

Meridien £150
Bath Rd UB7 0DU
🖰 www.lemeridien.com
✉ reservations.heathrow@lemeridien.com
☎ 0870 400 8899   🖷 (0208) 759 3421
"Well-located, clean and friendly" – this is one of the better-rated
bed-warehouses and some reporters even found their visit here
quite *"pleasant"*! / **Rooms:** *659 (of which some non smoking and some family
rooms).* **Facilities:** *indoor pool; gym; spa.*

Radisson Edwardian £99
140 Bath Rd UB3 5AW
🖰 www.radissonedwardian.com
✉ reservations@radissonedwardian.com
☎ (020) 8759 6311   🖷 (020) 8759 4559
*Some tip it as "one of the better airport hotels" – "conveniently
located" and with bags of parking – but no one pretends there
would be any other reason to seek out this large "businessmen's
hotel", where service can be "brusque".* / **Rooms:** *459 (of which some
non smoking).* **Facilities:** *gym; spa.*

Renaissance £99
Bath Rd TW6 2AQ
🖰 www.renaissancehotels.com
✉ rhi.lhrbr.sales.reservations@renaissancehotels.com
☎ (020) 8897 6363   🖷 (020) 8897 6363
*"Probably the best Heathrow hotel", say supporters. This modern
hotel – with views over the runway – is a "restful" spot, and
"convenient", too.* / **Rooms:** *649 (of which some non smoking and some family
rooms).* **Facilities:** *gym; spa.*

Sheraton Skyline £82
Bath Rd UB3 5BP
🖰 www.starwood.com/sheraton/skyline
✉ res268_skyline@sheraton.com
☎ 0871 871 8011   🖷 (020) 8750 9155
"Overall generally quite a pleasant airport hotel" – it attracts few
'raves', but less in the way of outright condemnation than some of
its peers. / **Rooms:** *350 (of which 212 non smoking and 12 family rooms).*
Facilities: *indoor pool; gym.*

HELMSLEY, NORTH YORKSHIRE 8–4C

Black Swan £77*
Market Pl YO62 5BJ
🖰 www.macdonaldhotels.co.uk
✉ blackswan@macdonald-hotels.co.uk
☎ (01439) 770466 🖨 (01439) 770174

*Reporters see "great potential" in this grand former coaching inn – part-Tudor, part-Georgian – overlooking the marketplace of a charming town. Even with all these natural advantages, though, it can feel "very much a chain hotel", with "amateurish" service contributing to the impression that – like too many Macdonald hotels – it's "overpriced, and resting on its reputation". *Prices are quoted on a DB&B basis. / **Rooms:** 45 (of which 13 non smoking and 4 family rooms).*

Feversham Arms £150
1 High Street YO62 5AG
✉ fevershamarms@hotmail.com
☎ (01439) 770766 🖨 (01439) 770346

*Total refurbishment (in 2002, which included the installation of a fitness club) has brought a high level of sophistication to this "excellent small-town hotel". It's a "very friendly" place, whose "great" accommodation is unanimously hailed by the small number of reporters who commented on it. / **Rooms:** 17. **Facilities:** outdoor pool; gym; tennis.*

HENLEY-ON-THAMES, OXFORDSHIRE 2–2D

Red Lion £145
Hart St RG9 2AR
🖰 www.redlionhenley.co.uk
✉ enquiries@redlionhenley.co.uk
☎ (01491) 572161 🖨 (01491) 410039

*No fewer than three kings are claimed to have stayed in days of yore at this "civilised", privately-owned hotel, near the town's bridge. Fans proclaim it "a character-hotel without any downside" (except, perhaps, "during regatta week"). / **Rooms:** 26 (of which 1 family room).*

HEREFORD, HEREFORDSHIRE 2–1B

Castle House £165
Castle St HR1 2NN
🖰 www.castlehse.co.uk ✉ info@castlehse.co.uk
☎ (01432) 356321 🖨 (01432) 365909

*"Very comfortable and quiet", this pleasantly contemporary hotel in a listed Georgian townhouse near the cathedral is hailed, pretty much unanimously, as "a gem". Suites, in particular, are "wonderful" and many judge the cooking at the restaurant (La Rive) as "surprisingly good", if not "superb". / **Rooms:** 15.*

Green Dragon £101

Broad St HR4 9BG

🌐 www.heritage-hotels.com

✉ general.greendragon@heritage-hotels.com

☎ 0870 400 8113   🖷 (01432) 352139

*What some see as the "main hotel" in this attractive town (a fair-sized Victorian institution run by a division of Macdonald Hotels) looks inviting from the outside, and enjoys a good location near the cathedral. Opinions divide as to whether it's "a nice hotel let down by the restaurant" or somewhere that's "tired" all-round and "needs a revamp". | **Rooms:** 83 (of which some non smoking and some family rooms).*

The Angel £120

BD23 6LT

🌐 www.angelhetton.co.uk   ✉ info@angelhetton.co.uk

☎ (01756) 730263   🖷 (01756) 730363

*It's as one of the country's original and best gastropubs that this legendary establishment in the Dales is best known. It's also tipped as a pleasant place to stay. | **Rooms:** 5 (of which all non smoking).*
Details: *closed 1 wk in Jan; meals unavailable: Mon-Sat L.*

De Vere Slaley Hall £110

NE47 0BY

🌐 www.devereonline.co.uk

✉ slaley.hall@devere-hotels.com

☎ (01434) 673350   🖷 (01434) 673152

*"Plenty to do for golfers and non-golfers" is, on all reports, the key to the attraction of this extended Edwardian manor house hotel – a "very peaceful" place to stay (even if some do find its appearance a touch "barrack-like"). That's just as well, as the local area is "without a huge number of obvious competing attractions". | **Rooms:** 139 (of which 15 non smoking and 14 family rooms).*
Facilities: *indoor pool; gym; spa.*

HINTLESHAM, SUFFOLK · 3–1C

Hintlesham Hall · £110

IP8 3NS

🖰 www.hintleshamhall.com

✉ reservations@hintleshamhall.com

☎ (01473) 652334 · 🖨 (01473) 652463

This "enduring country house" – which first came to prominence under '60s star chef Robert Carrier – remains a "very smart" (some would say "snooty") destination. It undoubtedly has an "absolutely beautiful setting", though, amidst "stunning gardens", and with many "generous and comfortable" rooms. Some reporters say the food is still "very good", too. / **Rooms:** 33 (of which some non smoking and 3 family rooms). **Facilities:** outdoor pool; gym; spa; golf; tennis. **Details:** meals unavailable: Sat L.

HINTON CHARTERHOUSE, BATH & NE SOMERSET · 2–3B

Homewood Park · £145

BA2 7TB

🖰 www.homewoodpark.com · ✉ res@homewoodpark.com

☎ (01225) 723731 · 🖨 (01225) 723820

Fans proclaim this Georgian country house, six miles from Bath, a "lovely place", with "large" bedrooms (and "the best beds ever"), and praise the "great restaurant" (which used to be blessed by the tyre men). "Below par" service, though, can contribute to the impression that the place feels "a bit run down". / **Rooms:** 19 (of which 4 non smoking and 2 family rooms). **Facilities:** outdoor pool; tennis.

HINTON, GLOUCESTERSHIRE · 2–2B

Hinton Grange · £120

Nr Dyrham SN14 8HG

🖰 www.hintongrange.co.uk · ✉ mail@hintongrange.co.uk

☎ (0117) 937 2916 · 🖨 (0117) 937 3285

Set in six acres, this "rambling and eccentric" establishment – whose buildings started off as a 15th-century farm – is a classic low-beamed cosy destination, complete with inglenook fireplace in the dining room. (You may find a log fire in your room, too – if you light it, you pay!) Facilities include a fishing lake, a 9-hole pitch and putt golf course, tennis and croquet. / **Rooms:** 19. **Facilities:** golf. **Details:** min age for children: 14.

HOAR CROSS, STAFFORDSHIRE · 5–3C

Hoar Cross Hall · £298*

Nr Yoxall DE13 8QS

🖰 www.hoarcross.co.uk · ✉ info@hoarcross.co.uk

☎ (01283) 575671 · 🖨 (01283) 575652

*Some find "total relaxation" at this country house "health farm and hotel", which wins high acclaim all round for its "wonderful facilities". Doubters, however, are not unknown – "the treatments were excellent, but the rest was disappointing." *Prices are quoted on a DB&B basis.* / **Rooms:** 85. **Facilities:** indoor pool; gym; spa; golf; tennis. **Details:** closed Christmas; min age for children: 16.

HOCKLEY HEATH, WARWICKSHIRE 5–4C

Nuthurst Grange £165

Nuthurst Grange Ln B94 5NL

🏠 www.nuthurst-grange.com ✉ info@nuthurst-grange.com

☎ (01564) 783972 📠 (01564) 783919

A "surprisingly nice" setting – and only 12 miles from
Birmingham's NEC – is just one of the features which wins praise
for this "lovely", family-owned Edwardian country house hotel.
It's a "really friendly" place, offering "excellent rooms, food and
service", and comes complete with its own helipad. / **Rooms:** 15 (of
which 5 non smoking). **Details:** closed 25-26 Dec; meals unavailable: Sat L.

HOLKHAM, NORFOLK 6–3C

Victoria £140

Park Rd NR23 1RG

🏠 www.victoriaatholkham.co.uk

✉ victoria@holkham.co.uk

☎ (01328) 711008 📠 (01328) 711009

Having received a trendy "Indian-inspired" makeover a few years
ago, this "mellow, relaxed and cosy" gastropub-with-rooms (in "a
perfect setting opposite Holkham Bay") has acquired something
of a reputation as a "chilled" Chelsea-on-Sea destination ("full of
green wellies at weekends"). It's highly praised by all reporters,
though, for its "romantic" location, its "lovely", "laid-back" staff
and its "charmingly individual" accommodation. / **Rooms:** 11 (of
which all non smoking and 2 family rooms). **Details:** no Amex.

HOLT, NORFOLK 6–3C

Blakeney £146

Blakeney NR25 7NE

🏠 www.blakeney-hotel.co.uk

✉ reception@blakeney-hotel.co.uk

☎ (01263) 740797 📠 (01263) 740795

Many reporters tend to the view that this "traditional and family-
run hotel" – "on the edge of an attractive village", and with
"lovely views of the coast" – is "very old-fashioned but also very
charming". Doubters just find the whole approach "stuck in the
'50s". / **Rooms:** 60 (of which all non smoking and some family rooms).
Facilities: indoor pool; gym. **Details:** no Amex or Switch.

Cley Mill £74

Cley-next-the-Sea NR25 7RP

🏠 www.cleymill.co.uk

☎ (01263) 740209 📠 (01263) 740209

A "wonderful old windmill", overlooking the salt marshes, provides
the setting for this very popular B&B – book well ahead, especially
at weekends and for holidays. It's tipped as a "tastefully
decorated" place, where a "help-yourself bar" and "home
cooking" are valued attractions. / **Rooms:** 8 (of which all non smoking).
Details: meals unavailable: L; no Amex.

HOOK, HAMPSHIRE   2–3D

Tylney Hall   £165
Rotherwick RG27 9AZ

🖥 www.tylneyhall.com   ✉ sales@tylneyhall.com
☎ (01256) 764881   🖨 (01256) 768141

This "wonderful", "rambling" country house has many admirers,
who vaunt its "amazing rooms", "glorious grounds", "exquisite"
food and "unobtrusive" service. However, a style which strikes
fans as "understated", can seem a little "tired" to others, and the
popularity of this Elite group property for weddings and
conferences is a turn-off for some reporters. / **Rooms:** 112 (of which 1
family room). **Facilities:** indoor pool; outdoor pool; gym; spa; tennis.

HORTON-CUM-STUDLEY, OXFORDSHIRE   2–2D

Studley Priory   £175
OX33 1AZ

🖥 www.studley-priory.co.uk
✉ reservations@studley-priory.co.uk
☎ (01865) 351203   🖨 (01865) 351613

"Picturesque" (but "pricey"), this "very comfortable country house
hotel" is hailed by most reporters for its "cosy, warm and
welcoming" atmosphere, and for its "very good food". Even some
who concede its "picturesque" attractions, though, find its overall
style rather "stale". / **Rooms:** 18 (of which some non smoking and 3 family
rooms). **Facilities:** golf; tennis. **Details:** min age for children: 12.

HOVINGHAM, NORTH YORKSHIRE   8–4C

Worsley Arms   £95
YO62 4LA

🖥 www.worsleyarms.com   ✉ worsleyarms@aol.com
☎ (01653) 628234   🖨 (01653) 628130

For "a true away-from-it-all experience", a number of reporters
recommend this "smart" and "lovely" Georgian hotel, overlooking
the village green. / **Rooms:** 20 (of which all non smoking and no family rooms).

HULL, KINGSTON UPON HULL   6–2A

Willerby Manor   £75
Well Ln Willerby HU10 6ER

🖥 www.willerbymanor.co.uk
✉ willerbymanor@bestwestern.co.uk
☎ (01482) 652616   🖨 (01482) 652616

This family-owned hotel and health club – set in attractive
gardens, a couple of miles from the city-centre – attracted a small
number of reports which praised it for being "excellent for
business", as well as for its "excellent leisure facilities". / **Rooms:** 51
(of which 49 non smoking and 1 family room). **Facilities:** indoor pool; gym; spa.
Details: meals unavailable: Sun D.

HUNGERFORD, BERKSHIRE 2–2C

Littlecote House £265*

RG17 0SS
🖱 www.warnerholidays.co.uk/hotels/littlecotehouse
✉ admin.littlecote@bourne-leisure.co.uk
☎ (01488) 682509　🖷 (01488) 682 341

"Most rooms are in a new annexe", warns one reporter, but this *"lovely"* Tudor house (where Henry VIII wooed Jane Seymour) is in *"spectacular"* countryside, and attracted a small number of generally positive reports. In classic Warner style, there are *"good leisure facilities"*, *"full entertainment is provided"*, and children are not permitted. *Prices are quoted on a DB&B basis. / **Rooms:** 193 (of which some non smoking). **Facilities:** indoor pool, spa. **Details:** no children.

HUNSTANTON, NORFOLK 6–3B

Le Strange Arms £92

Golf Course Rd PE36 6JJ
🖱 www.abacushotels.co.uk
✉ reception@lestrangearms.co.uk
☎ (01485) 534411　🖷 (01485) 534724

A *"superb"* location near the sea, and *"friendly and efficient"* service add charm to a visit to this *"stately"* and *"old-fashioned"* hotel, now part of a small local group (Abacus Hotels). / **Rooms:** 36 (of which 6 non smoking and 6 family rooms). **Details:** meals unavailable: Mon-Sat L.

HUNSTRETE, BATH & NE SOMERSET 2–2B

Hunstrete House £195

Pensford BS39 4NS
🖱 www.hunstretehouse.co.uk
✉ user@hunstretehouse.co.uk
☎ (01761) 490490　🖷 (01761) 490732

This country house hotel set in 92 acres eight miles from Bath won praise from some reporters as a *"cosy"* and *"comfortable"* retreat, offering *"well-appointed"* accommodation. There are reporters, though, who thought the service rather *"average"*, and that the establishment generally felt *"down on its luck"*. / **Rooms:** 25 (of which 14 non smoking and some family rooms). **Facilities:** outdoor pool; tennis.

HUNTINGDON, CAMBRIDGESHIRE 3–1B

Old Bridge £125

1 High St PE29 3TQ
🖱 www.huntsbridge.com　✉ oldbridge@huntsbridge.co.uk
☎ (01480) 424300　🖷 (01480) 411017

All reporters speak well of this establishment (which is 18th century in origin) – *"a riverside town centre hotel of a high standard"*. The *"top-quality"* restaurant, which boasts *"a great wine list"*, attracts particular praise. / **Rooms:** 24 (of which all non smoking).

HYTHE, KENT   3–4D

The Hythe Imperial   £152*
Princes's Parade CT21 6AE

🖥 www.marstonhotels.com

📧 hytheimperial@marstonhotels.com

☎ (01303) 267441   📠 (01303) 264610

*This "good, mid-range" establishment (part of Marston Hotels)
has a "first-class location, adjacent to a golf course, on the
seafront". It attracted much – and notably uniform –
commentary, to the effect that it's a "reasonably-priced" place,
with "friendly" staff and quite a range of facilities.
Accommodation tends to "functional", though, and the cooking
can be "basic". *Prices are quoted on a DB&B basis. / **Rooms:** 100.*
Facilities: *indoor pool; gym; spa; golf; tennis.* **Details:** *meals unavailable: Sat L.*

ILKLEY, WEST YORKSHIRE   5–1C

Rombalds   £105
West View, Wells Rd LS29 9JG

🖥 www.rombalds.co.uk

📧 reception@rombalds.demon.co.uk

☎ (01943) 603201

*"Personal" and "old-fashioned" service contributes to positive
impressions of this long-established, family-owned hotel (in a
building which began life as a rooming house in 1835). It pleased
most, but not quite all reporters. / **Rooms:** 15 (of which 8 non smoking
and 3 family rooms). **Details:** closed 27 Dec-4 Jan.*

INVERARAY, ARGYLL & BUTE   9–3B

The George   £60
Main St East PA32 8TT

🖥 www.thegeorgehotel.co.uk   📧 george.hotel@talk21.com

☎ (01499) 302111   📠 (01499) 302098

*"Tradition" is the watchword in reports on this coaching inn, some
three centuries old, which all reporters find "full of charm", but
where the accommodation is quite up-to-date. "River views"
complete a winning package. / **Rooms:** 15. **Details:** closed Christmas, 1
Jan.*

INVERNESS, HIGHLAND   9–2C

Dunain Park   £138

IV3 8JN
🖰 www.dunainparkhotel.co.uk
✉ info@dunainparkhotel.co.uk
☎ (01463) 230512   🖷 (01463) 224532

This small, family-run country house hotel – in an Italianate 19th-century building, set in extensive grounds by a river – is tipped as a "good-value" destination that's "child-friendly without being child-centric". The annexe cottage is "excellent", too. / **Rooms:** 13 (of which 4 non smoking and 6 family rooms). **Facilities:** indoor pool. **Details:** closed 2 wks in Jan.

IPSWICH, SUFFOLK   3–1D

Holiday Inn   £80

London Rd IP2 0UA
🖰 www.holiday-inn.co.uk
☎ 0870 400 9045

Yes, this is the "standardised" product, but – at least in the under-served town – it attracts a surprising volume of commentary to the effect that it offers "amazingly, a good experience". "Very good" breakfasts and "smart and spacious" bedrooms were among features singled out for praise. / **Rooms:** 110 (of which some non smoking and some family rooms). **Facilities:** indoor pool; gym; spa.

ISLES OF SCILLY

Island   £114*

Tresco TR24 0PU
🖰 www.tresco.co.uk   ✉ islandhotel@tresco.co.uk
☎ (01720) 422883   🖷 (01720) 422883

*With its "magnificent position" (complete with five acres of gardens and a private beach), this 'private island paradise' (as the hotel modestly describes itself) is indeed described as "idyllic" by reporters. "Very friendly service and high quality" are the twin themes of all commentary. *Prices are quoted on a DB&B basis.* / **Rooms:** 48 (of which all non smoking and 7 family rooms). **Facilities:** outdoor pool. **Details:** closed 5 Nov-1 Mar; no Amex.

Atlantic £215

Le Mont De La Pulente, St Brelade JE3 8HE
🖰 www.theatlantic.hotel.com ✉ atlantic@slh.com
☎ (01534) 744101 🖨 (01534) 744102

This smart family-owned hotel – part of the Small Luxury Hotels of the World consortium – occupies a clean-lined '70s building overlooking the sea, and is tipped as a good all-rounder.
/ **Rooms:** 50. **Facilities:** indoor pool; outdoor pool; gym; tennis. **Details:** closed Jan.

de France £134

St Saviour's Rd, St Helier JE1 7XP
🖰 www.defrance.co.uk ✉ enqlsr@defrance.co.uk
☎ (01534) 614100 🖨 (01534) 614999

Some do find it a touch lacking in soul – conferences are a big part of the operation – but the consensus is that this classic grand seaside hotel is a "relaxing" place with "excellent facilities". It's also "very good for families". / **Rooms:** 266 (of which some non smoking and some family rooms). **Facilities:** indoor pool; outdoor pool; gym. **Details:** closed Christmas.

L'Horizon £180

JE3 8EF
🖰 www.hotelLHorizon.com
✉ hotelhorizon@jerseymail.co.uk
☎ (01534) 743101

"I returned after 40 years, and this place is still really first-class in every respect". This "resort-type" Victorian seaside hotel boasts a "wonderful" location, "spacious" accommodation and "attentive" service, and the restaurant is "great", too. Despite the presence of extensive conference facilities, it makes "a lovely place to spend some time unwinding, overlooking the bay" – "make sure you get a sea-facing room". / **Rooms:** 106 (of which some family rooms). **Facilities:** indoor pool; gym; spa.

Longueville Manor £230

Longueville Rd, St Saviour JE2 7WF
🖰 www.longuevillemanor.com
✉ info@longuevillemanor.com
☎ (01534) 725501

"A lovely oasis." "Superb rooms" and "informal but exceptionally good" staff ("who remember who you are") win high ratings from guests at this "good all-round" Relais & Chateaux member, which occupies a manor house dating from the 13th-century. Its restaurant has the reputation as the best in the Channel Islands. / **Rooms:** 30 (of which 3 family rooms). **Facilities:** outdoor pool; tennis.

La Place £80

Route du Coin, La Haule, St Brelade JE3 8BT
🖰 www.jersey.co.uk/hotels/laplace ✉ hotlaplace@aol.com
☎ (01534) 744261 🖨 (01534) 745164

"Friendly and efficient" service helps set the tone at this hotel built around a 17th-century farmhouse, which is set in "lovely" grounds. The volume of commentary is not huge, but impressive for its across-the-board consistency. / **Rooms:** 42 (of which 21 non smoking and 4 family rooms). **Facilities:** outdoor pool.

St Brelades Bay £140

JE3 8EF
🖰 www.stbreladesbayhotel.com
✉ info@stbreladesbayhotel.com
☎ (01534) 746141 🖨 (01534) 747278

"Couldn't be better for children, but they deal with adults beautifully, too". Reporters speak only well of this "fabulous family seaside hotel" (with seven acres of gardens) on "the best beach in Jersey". "Exceptional" service is a highlight. / **Rooms:** 84 (of which 60 family rooms). **Facilities:** outdoor pool; gym; spa; tennis. **Details:** closed Oct-Apr.

sign up for our next survey at www.hardens.com 146

Edenwater House £70

Ednam TD5 7QL
⌂ www.edenwaterhouse.co.uk
✉ relax@edenwaterhouse.co.uk
☎ (01573) 224070   🖷 (01573) 226615

Jeff and Jacqui Kelly, formerly proprietors of a popular Edinburgh restaurant, now occupy this former manse. It's tipped as a destination offering "extraordinary value". / **Rooms:** 4 (of which all non smoking). **Details:** closed 2 wks in Jan; meals unavailable: L; no Amex; min age for children: 12.

Park €446 ☺

⌂ www.parkkenmare.com   ✉ info@parkenmare.com
☎ +353-64 41200   🖷 +353-64 41402

Overlooking the Ring of Kerry, the imposing Victorian house is now a "slick" and "professional" hotel, with every modern facility – in fact, even though it's privately owned, one reporter found it rather "corporate". A spa is to be opened late in 2003. / **Rooms:** 46 (of which some non smoking and some family rooms). **Facilities:** spa. **Details:** closed Nov-Mar (but open for Christmas); no Switch.

Sheen Falls €260 ☺☺

⌂ www.sheenfallslodge.ie   ✉ info@sheenfallslodge.ie
☎ +353-64 41600   🖷 +353-64 41386

"A superb view of a rushing river" distinguishes this "excellent" (Relais & Châteaux) hotel, which most reporters say makes "a great place for a long weekend break". This is the sort of place where bedrooms are "too large", where "smoked salmon is cured on site", and where the scenery is "very green". Even fans, though, can find it "expensive, for what you get". / **Rooms:** 65 (of which some non smoking and some family rooms). **Facilities:** gym; spa; tennis. **Details:** closed Jan 4- Feb 6; no Switch.

KESWICK, CUMBRIA   7–3D

Armanthwaite Hall   £140

Bassenthwaite Lake CA12 4RE
🖰 www.armathwaite-hall.com
✉ reservations@armathwaite-hall.com
☎ (01768) 776551   🖷 (01768) 776220

Part-Jacobean, part-Victorian, part-modern, this "beautiful" house in "an incredibly lovely part of the Lakes" offers the full "stately home" experience (as well as some "sensational" views). Most reporters rated it highly, but the restaurant was thought "stuffy" by one reporter, and another thought the leisure club "in need of an update". / **Rooms:** 42 (of which 10 family rooms). **Facilities:** indoor pool; gym; spa; tennis.

The Borrowdale   £140

CA12 5UY
🖰 www.theborrowdalehotel.co.uk
✉ hotel@borrowdale-gates.com
☎ (01768) 777224   🖷 (01768) 777338

Tipped for its "excellent restaurant", "nice location" and "good service", this traditional Lakeland hotel has been in the ownership of the same family for three decades. Walking and golfing breaks a speciality. / **Rooms:** 33 (of which some non smoking and some family rooms). **Facilities:** indoor pool; golf. **Details:** no Amex.

Dale Head   £164

Thirlmere CA12 4TN
🖰 www.dale-head-hall.co.uk
✉ onthelakeside@daleheadhall.info
☎ (01768) 772478   🖷 (01768) 771070

This "idyllic", family-owned hotel, occupies a building that's Elizabethan in origin, on the shore of Lake Thirlmere. "It's our favourite in the Lakes, and that includes Sharrow Bay", says one of its (small but enthusiastic) fan club, and all aspects of the operation are very well reported on. / **Rooms:** 12 (of which all non smoking and 1 family room). **Details:** closed Jan; no Amex.

Derwentwater   £110

Portinscale CA12 4DR
🖰 www.derwentwater-hotel.co.uk
✉ info@derwentwater-hotel.co.uk
☎ (01768) 772318   🖷 (01768) 775551

This very traditional, perhaps rather chintzy, Lakeland hotel is tipped by one reporter for its "wonderful service, superb food and a brilliant location". / **Rooms:** 48. **Details:** meals unavailable: Mon-Sat L.

Hilton Keswick Lodore £113

Borrowdale CA12 5UX

🏠 www.hilton.co.uk

☎ (01768) 777285   🖷 (01768) 777343

"Spectacular scenery on the doorstep", with Derwentwater nearby, helps endear this long-established hotel to most reporters, with many of them in particular commending the "outstanding" cooking and the "very personal service". For a minority of reporters, though, "top prices" are charged for rooms and facilities they rate poor-to-mediocre. / **Rooms:** 71 *(of which some family rooms).* **Facilities:** *indoor pool; outdoor pool; gym; tennis.*

The Leathes Head £118*

Borrowdale CA12 5UY

🏠 www.leatheshead.co.uk   ✉ enq@leatheshead.co.uk

☎ (01768) 777247

*A "relaxed and civilised country house atmosphere" and "great views and walks" are among the features which wins a tip for this Edwardian house as a "wonderful" destination. *Prices are quoted on a DB&B basis.* / **Rooms:** 11 *(of which all non smoking and 2 family rooms).* **Details:** *closed mid Nov-mid Feb; meals unavailable: L; no Amex; min age for children: 7.*

Swinside Lodge £150*

Grange Rd, Newlands CA12 5UE

🏠 www.swinsidelodge-hotel.co.uk

✉ info@swinsidelodge-hotel.co.uk

☎ (01768) 772948   🖷 (01768) 772948

*This "traditional", "chintzy" and "personally-run" hotel is tipped as "friendly" and "good value"; it offers "very clean, but small rooms", and "good home cooking", too. *Prices are quoted on a DB&B basis.* / **Rooms:** 7 *(of which all non smoking).* **Details:** *no Amex.*

KILKENNY, CO. KILKENNY, *ROI*   10–3C

Mount Juliet Conrad €190

Thomastown

🏠 www.mountjulietconrad.com

✉ mountjulietinfo@conradhotels.com

☎ +353 567 3000   🖷 +353 567 3019

"A first-class resort, not too far from Dublin with all the facilities you need (golf, riding, spa, gym etc) on site." This Georgian manor house offers "exceptional surroundings" in its 1500 acre estate, and (on most reports) an "excellent" restaurant, too. / **Rooms:** 58. **Facilities:** *indoor pool; gym; spa; golf; tennis.* **Details:** *no Switch.*

---

sign up for our next survey at www.hardens.com

Aghadoe Heights   €310

🖳 www.aghadoeheights.com   ✉ info@aghadoeheights.com
☎ +353-64 31766   🖶 +353-64 31345

"A stunning location and views" are among the features which
make this modern lakeside hotel "hard to fault". "Good facilities"
too, including an especially attractive swimming pool, help make
the place "a great weekend retreat". / **Rooms:** 57 (of which 33 non
smoking and some family rooms). **Facilities:** indoor pool; gym; spa; golf; tennis.
Details: closed Jan- Feb; no Switch.

Coolclogher House   €75

Mill Rd
🖳 www.coolclogherhouse.com
✉ info@coolclogherhouse.com
☎ +353-64 35996   🖶 +353-64 30933

This "wonderful luxury B&B" in an impressive Georgian country
house is tipped as an all-round admirable destination, with "huge
antique-furnished rooms", "charming" owners and "fabulous
breakfasts (served in a room with spectacular views over the park
and lake)". No restaurant, but your hosts will book you in locally.
/ **Rooms:** 4. **Details:** closed 1 Dec-31 Jan; meals unavailable: no restaurant; no
Amex or Switch; min age for children: 5.

Killarney Towers   €150

College Sq
🖳 www.odonoghue-ring-hotels.com
✉ reservations@odonoghue-ring-hotels.com
☎ +353-64 31038   🖶 +353-64 31755

"A large tourist hotel, ideal for exploring the South West". It's a
"pleasant and relaxed" establishment, the attractions of whose
"lively" bar appealed to more than one reporter. / **Rooms:** 182 (of
which some non smoking). **Facilities:** indoor pool; gym. **Details:** no Switch.

KILLORGLIN, CO. KERRY, *ROI*   10–4A

Caragh Lodge   €180
Caragh Lake
🖰 www.caraghlodge.com   ✉ caraghl@iol.ie
☎ +353-66 976 9115   🖷 +353-66 976 9316

This Victorian fishing lodge – in seven acres of gardens which include rare trees and shrubs – is tipped for its "delightful location" and its "walking possibilities" (and there's "golf nearby" too). The proprietor and staff are "charming". / **Rooms:** 15 (of which all non smoking). **Details:** closed Oct-Apr; meals unavailable: L; no Switch; min age for children: 10.

KILWINNING, AYRSHIRE   7–1B

Montgreenan Mansion House   £115
Montgreenan Estate KA13 KA13
🖰 www.montgreenanhotel.com
✉ info@montgreenanhotel.com
☎ (01294) 557733   🖷 (01294) 850 397

A "sensitively restored" neoclassical house, set in 50 acres of "beautiful" grounds. "Wonderful friendly staff" and "gorgeous food" are among the features which make it one reporter's top tip. / **Rooms:** 21 (of which some non smoking). **Facilities:** golf; tennis.

KINGS LYNN, NORFOLK   6–4B

Congham Hall   £155 ☺
Lynn Rd PE32 1AH
🖰 www.conghamhallhotel.co.uk
✉ reception@conghamhallhotel.co.uk
☎ (01485) 600250   🖷 (01485) 601191

This cream-coloured, part-Georgian house, six miles outside the town, attracts only modest commentary from reporters. It's seen as a "welcoming and comfortable" place, despite the odd concern that it's getting a touch "weary". / **Rooms:** 14 (of which all non smoking and 1 family room).

KINGSBRIDGE, DEVON   1–4D

Buckland tout Saints   £150 ☺
Goveton TQ7 2DS
🖰 www.tout-saints.co.uk   ✉ buckland@tout-saints.co.uk
☎ (01548) 853055   🖷 (01548) 856261

Reporters hail this ancient country house "in the depths of the countryside" as a "brilliant", destination ("if you can find it"), rating it highly for charm. But even fans can find it "expensive" for what it is, and the (relatively few) reports it incites (especially on the food) give a slight hint of promise unfulfilled. Weddings are big business. / **Rooms:** 12 (of which 10 non smoking and 3 family rooms).

KINGSTON BAGPUIZE, OXFORDSHIRE   2–2D

Fallowfields Country House   £150

Faringdon Rd OX13 5BH
⌂ www.fallowfields.com   ✉ stay@fallowfields.com
☎ (01865) 820416   🖨 (01865) 821275

*Set in 12 acres in the Vale of the White Horse, this "intimate" country house is tipped as a pleasantly "homely" establishment of its type. / **Rooms:** 10 (of which all non smoking). **Facilities:** spa. **Details:** closed Christmas.*

LACOCK, WILTSHIRE   2–2C

At the Sign of the Angel   £99

6 Church St SN15 2LB
⌂ www.lacock.co.uk   ✉ angel@lacock.co.uk
☎ (01249) 730230   🖨 (01249) 730527

*"Mobile phones don't work here", apparently, adding to the "quaint" charms of this 14th-century inn, in a fabulous National Trust village which offers "so much history". The food is "basic", but it's often "delicious", too. / **Rooms:** 10 (of which all non smoking and 2 family rooms). **Details:** closed Christmas; meals unavailable: Mon L.*

LANCASTER, LANCASHIRE   5–1A

Lancaster House   £99

Green Ln, Ellel LA1 4GJ
⌂ www.elh.co.uk   ✉ lancaster@elhmail.co.uk
☎ (01524) 844822

*This "modern" family hotel (plus hair & beauty salon and indoor pool) is "well located as a base for the Lake District". It's run by a small local group, English Lakes Hotels. / **Rooms:** 80 (of which 60 non smoking and 10 family rooms). **Facilities:** indoor pool; gym; spa.*

LANGAR, NOTTINGHAMSHIRE   5–3D

Langar Hall   £130

NG13 9HG
⌂ www.langarhall.com   ✉ langarhall-hotel@ndirect.co.uk
☎ (01949) 860559   🖨 (01949) 861045

*This Georgian manor house in "lovely surroundings" is proclaimed "a jewel" by its fans, and its restaurant has quite a reputation, too. "The excellent staff, maitre d' and proprietor make you feel like a long-lost friend." / **Rooms:** 10.*

LANGFORD BUDVILLE, SOMERSET   2–3A

Bindon Country House   £105
TA21 0RU

🖰 www.bindon.com   ✉ stay@bindon.com
☎ (01823) 400070   🖷 (01823) 400071

"Very good food and service" is the general theme of most reports on this "tranquil" 17th-century building, where the "huge" and "stylishly appointed" bedrooms attract particular praise.
/ **Rooms:** 12 (of which all non smoking and 2 family rooms). **Facilities:** outdoor pool.

LAVENHAM, SUFFOLK   3–1C

Angel   £75
Market Pl CO10 9QZ

🖰 www.lavenham.co.uk/angel   ✉ angellav@aol.com
☎ (01787) 247388   🖷 (01787) 248344

This hotel has stood in the main square of this "beautiful" town since 1420. It's a "friendly" place, with "good" standards (including in the restaurant). / **Rooms:** 8 (of which 1 family room). **Details:** closed 25-26 Dec.

Great House   £96
Market Pl CO10 9QZ

🖰 www.greathouse.co.uk   ✉ info@greathouse.co.uk
☎ (01787) 247431

"Wonderful Tudor bedrooms and a cheeseboard to die for" – if that's your idea of heaven, the Crépy family's grand townhouse-restaurant-with-rooms makes "an ideal romantic away-break sort of place". It's "very French" – to the point that reporters can sometimes have difficulty making themselves understood.
/ **Rooms:** 5 (of which all non smoking and 2 family rooms). **Details:** closed Jan & 2 wks in summer; meals unavailable: Sun D & Mon.

Lavenham Priory £85
Water St CO10 9RW

🏠 www.lavenhampriory.co.uk
✉ mail@lavenhampriory.co.uk
☎ (01787) 247404   🖷 (01787) 248 472

"A pretty-as-a-picture-postcard, family-run B&B." If you're looking for a place with "tons of character", you really won't do much better than this "fabulous" former priory, parts of which date from the 13th century. No dinner, but "breakfast is ample and filling". / **Rooms:** 6 (of which all non smoking). **Details:** closed Christmas; meals unavailable: no restaurant; no Amex; min age for children: 10.

Swan £180*
High Street CO10 9QA

🏠 www.macdonaldhotels.co.uk
✉ general.swanlavenham@macdonald-hotels.co.uk
☎ (01787) 247477   🖷 (01787) 248286

This "so historic and atmospheric Tudor inn" is a "charming old destination" at the centre of this beautiful old town, with some "lovely" accommodation and a dining room complete with minstrels gallery. It's a Macdonald Hotels properly, however, so occasional reports of "average" catering and iffy service come as no great surprise. *Prices are quoted on a DB&B basis.
/ **Rooms:** 51 (of which some non smoking and 3 family rooms).

LEDBURY, HEREFORDSHIRE   2–1B

Feathers £95
High Street HR8 1DS

🏠 www.feathers-ledbury.co.uk
✉ mary@feathers-ledbury.co.uk
☎ (01531) 635266   🖷 (01531) 638955

This "old market town coaching inn, but complete with swimming pool" is a "creaky but charming" destination on the main drag. It has "good-size" rooms, too. / **Rooms:** 19 (of which some family rooms). **Facilities:** indoor pool; gym; spa.

sign up for our next survey at www.hardens.com

LEEDS, WEST YORKSHIRE   5–1C

In *42 The Calls*, Leeds boasts one of the earliest and still the most successful of the boutique city hotels. It's perhaps a touch disappointing that this has not done more to inspire by imitation, as most of the city's other hotels, with the exception of the relative recent *Leeds Townhouse*, are stuck in banal 'businessmen's hotel' mode.

De Vere Oulton Hall   £80

Rothwell Ln LS26 8HN
⌂ www.devereonline.co.uk
✉ oulton.hall@devere-hotels.com
☎ (0113) 282 1000   🖷 (0113) 282 9084
Five miles outside Leeds, this "tastefully extended" (and recently renovated) country house hotel makes an "elegant" and "graceful" destination (that's "very handy" for the nearby golf course). There are "good-value short breaks" available, too.
/ **Rooms:** 152 (of which 8 non smoking and 4 family rooms). **Facilities:** indoor pool; gym; spa; golf.

De Vere Village   £98

186 Otley Rd, Headingley LS16 5PR
⌂ www.villagehotelsonline.co.uk
✉ village.leeds@village-hotels.com
☎ (0113) 278 1000   🖷 (0113) 278 1111
"Excellent leisure facilities" are the highlight at this modern hotel, just outside the city-centre (but with easy connections). Otherwise, though some reporters felt it offered a "good basic standard", rather too many judged it "mediocre". / **Rooms:** 94 (of which 61 non smoking and 4 family rooms). **Facilities:** indoor pool; gym.

42 The Calls   £170

42 The Calls LS2 7EW
⌂ www.42thecalls.co.uk   ✉ hotel@42thecalls.co.uk
☎ (0113) 244 0099   🖷 (0113) 234 4100

In a former warehouse, by a canal, this provincial pioneer of the "good-quality boutique hotel" format retains the "individual" atmosphere that's won it a huge following, and its "fantastic" accommodation and "superb" service" continue to win much praise (even though, on the facilities front, it falls rather short). The restaurant, Pool Court, is by quite a margin the most ambitious hereabouts. / **Rooms:** 41 (of which 5 family rooms).

Hilton Leeds City £106
Neville St LS1 4BX
🖰 www.hilton.co.uk
☎ (0113) 244 2000   🖷 (0113) 243 3577
"Convenient and central", and with an "OK" leisure club, this "functional" hotel attracts quite a lot of reports. Even by chain standards, though, it's pretty "grim", and "poor parking" is a recurrent complaint. / Rooms: 206 (of which some non smoking and some family rooms). Facilities: indoor pool; gym; spa.

Leeds Town House £99
Quebecs, 9 Quebecs St LS1 2HA
🖰 www.theetongroup.com
📧 resquebecs@theetongroup.com
☎ (0113) 244 8989   🖷 (0113) 244 9090
This new outpost of the Eton Town House collection of hotels is located in the impressive and central Victorian premises of the former Liberal Club. It's tipped as "excellent for business", even if the rooms, though "very comfortable", are "very brown" ("like sleeping in a box of chocolates"). Only breakfast is served ("but it's good"). / Rooms: 45 (of which some non smoking and 1 family room).

Malmaison £125
Sovereign Quay LS1 1DQ
🖰 www.malmaison.com   📧 leeds@malmaison.com
☎ (0113) 398 1000   🖷 (0113) 398 1002
"A great business choice with a refreshingly contemporary style", this "unexpectedly chic tower", in the city-centre, retains many admirers. As with some other branches of this boutique-hotel chain, however, middling ratings support those who feel it's "resting on its laurels". / Rooms: 100 (of which 29 non smoking and 4 family rooms). Facilities: gym. Details: min age for children: 12.

Marriott £121
4 Trevelyan Sq LS1 6ET
🖰 www.marriott.com
📧 salesadmin.leeds@marriotthotels.co.uk
☎ 0871 871 8011   🖷 (0113) 244 2317
Behind a period façade, this "plush, but slightly charmless" modern chain hotel offers rather "basic" accommodation, but it does "at least try to treat you as an individual". It also has a "gem" of a location, and its "excellent leisure facilities" include a "good pool". / Rooms: 244 (of which 200 non smoking and some family rooms). Facilities: indoor pool; gym; spa.

sign up for our next survey at www.hardens.com

The Queens £140

City Sq LS1 1PL

🏠 www.paramount-hotels.co.uk

✉ queens.reservations@paramounthotels.co.uk

☎ (0113) 243 1323   📠 (0113) 242 5154

The lingering fame of this '30s hotel by the railway station helps ensure that it generates a fair degree of feedback – rather too much of it to the effect that, under Meridien's direction, it had become a "parody" of a "functional" large hotel. New owners Paramount plan a major, horribly overdue, refurbishment for 2004. / **Rooms:** 199 (of which some non smoking and some family rooms).

Thorpe Park £130

1150 Century Way, Thorpe Park LS15 8ZB

🏠 www.thorpeparkhotel.co.uk

✉ thorpepark@shirehotels.co.uk

☎ (0113) 264 1000   📠 (0113) 264 1010

This "excellent business hotel" is "right on the motorway but still has easy access to the city-centre". "Very friendly staff" are a highlight, and there's an "excellent spa". / **Rooms:** 123 (of which 100 non smoking and 8 family rooms). **Facilities:** indoor pool; gym; spa. **Details:** meals unavailable: Sat & Sun L.

LETTERKENNY, CO. DONEGAL, *ROI*   10–1C

Castlegrove Country House €130

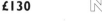

Ballymaleel

🏠 www.castlegrove.com   ✉ marytsweeney@hotmail.com

☎ +353-74 51118   📠 +353-74 51384

An "extremely charming period country house, on the banks of Lough Foyle". Family-run, it offers "atmospheric" accommodation and "superb" food, and is hailed for its "excellent value". / **Rooms:** 14 (of which 1 family room). **Details:** closed Christmas.

LEWDOWN, DEVON   1–3C

Lewtrenchard Manor £130

EX20 4PN

🏠 www.lewtrenchard.co.uk   ✉ stay@lewtrenchard.co.uk

☎ (01566) 783256   📠 (01566) 783332

Most (if not quite all) reporters found it "a truly magical experience" to visit this "very relaxing" Jacobean manor house, on account of its "beautiful, secluded setting", "old world charm" and a dining room offering some "elaborate, and technically accomplished" cooking. Post-survey, the hotel was acquired by the voracious Von Essen group, so changes may be afoot. / **Rooms:** 16 (of which 9 non smoking).

LEWES, EAST SUSSEX   3–4B

Newick Park   £165
Newick St BN8 4SB
🖰 www.newickpark.co.uk   ✉ bookings@newickpark.co.uk
☎ (01825) 723633

"In the depths of the Sussex countryside", this Georgian house is
set in 200 acres. It's "a lovely place to stay" – reports are a hymn
of praise to its "helpful" and "unobtrusive" service and its good-
quality restaurant. / **Rooms:** 16 (of which some non smoking and 3 family
rooms). **Facilities:** outdoor pool; tennis. **Details:** closed 31 Dec.

LEYBURN, NORTH YORKSHIRE   8–4B

The Sandpiper Inn   £60
Market Pl DL8
✉ hsandpiper.pp@aol.com
☎ (01969) 622206   🖶 (01969) 625367

A "clean, cottagey room above a dining pub" – that's the
proposition which wins a 'tip' for this 17th-century freehouse,
overshadowed by the village church. / **Rooms:** 2 (of which all non
smoking). **Details:** closed Mon but open Bank Holidays; no Amex; no children.

LIFTON, DEVON   1–3C

Arundell Arms   £110
Fore St PL16 0AA
☎ (01566) 784666   🖶 (01566) 784494

An "excellent" Anglo-French restaurant, and facilities for fishermen
(including a school) have long made this rather grand traditional
establishment on the River Tamar a destination of some note.
Even a reporter who acknowledged the "outstanding" food,
however, felt let down by "overpriced" accommodation.
/ **Rooms:** 28.

LIMERICK, CO. LIMERICK, *ROI*   10–3B

Jurys   €215
Ennis Rd
🖰 www.jurysdoyle.com   ✉ limerick@jurysdoyle.com
☎ +353-61 327777   🖶 (+353-61 326400

A "basic but functional hotel", recommended by some as a "well-
priced" stop for touring families. / **Rooms:** 95 (of which some non smoking
and some family rooms). **Facilities:** indoor pool. **Details:** closed Christmas.

LINCOLN, LINCOLNSHIRE   6–3A

The White Hart   £90
Bailgate LN1 3AR
🖰 www.macdonaldhotels.co.uk
✉ sales.whitehartlincoln@macdonald-hotels.co.uk
☎ (01522) 526222   🖷 (01522) 531798

If you're looking for a "suitably creaky" place full of "old world charm", this Macdonald Hotels establishment has a "good location" just by Lincoln Cathedral (complete, in some rooms, with the sound of bells from 7am), and is voted "good for business or pleasure". Even those who feel the place "could do with a bit of a make-over" seem to think the experience stacks up overall.
/ **Rooms:** 48 (of which 12 non smoking and no family rooms).

LINLITHGOW, WEST LOTHIAN   9–4C

Champany Inn   £125
EH49 7LU
🖰 www.champany.com   ✉ reception@champany.com
☎ (01506) 834532   🖷 (01506) 834302

*If you're looking for a certain style – "champagne awaits you on arrival" – the "superb" rooms adjoining this grand restaurant are tipped as a great place to stay between Edinburgh and Glasgow. Beware, though – "the room rate, and even the breakfast, is good value, but you pay for it in the evening when you order rib-eyes for two!" */ **Rooms:** 16 (of which all non smoking).

LIPHOOK, HAMPSHIRE   3–4A

Forest Mere
Health Farm   £159*
GU30 7JQ
🖰 www.healthfarms.co.uk
✉ enquiries@henlowgrange.co.uk
☎ (01428) 727722   🖷 (01428) 723501

*"Not strictly an hotel, but a health spa". It has "great facilities" and is "good for relaxation", but "the rooms and the décor could do with a revamp". *Prices are quoted on a DB&B basis.*
/ **Rooms:** 89 (of which all non smoking). **Facilities:** indoor pool; gym; spa.
Details: closed Christmas; min age for children: 16.

LIVERPOOL, MERSEYSIDE   5–2A

It is reasonable to hope that visitors in 2008 to the 'European City of Culture' will find a city with much more interesting accommodation than is the case today. Until very recently, the only recommendable establishments have been a few (surprisingly good, considering) branches of faceless chains. A couple of newcomers noted below should enliven the scene, however, and mid-2004 will see the opening of *Ropewalks* (info@aliasropewalks.com) by the commendable Alias Hotels chain.

Adelphi   £105

Ranelagh Pl L3 5UL
🖰 www.britanniahotels.com
✉ res700@britanniahotels.com
☎ (0151) 709 7200   🖷 (0151) 708 0743
This still-famous establishment – built in 1914 for the 'pre-Jet Set', en route to the New World (and with an interior reminiscent of an ocean liner) – still has a reputation in some quarters as "a top-notch classic hotel". Many reporters do comment on its "striking" architecture and "faded" grandeur, but the overwhelming impression is that it's now just a "shoddy caricature" of its former self. / **Rooms:** 402 (of which some non smoking and some family rooms). **Facilities:** indoor pool; gym.

Crowne Plaza   £109

St Nicholas Pl, Princes Dock, Pier Head L3 0AA
🖰 www.crowneplaza.com
☎ (0151) 243 8000   🖷 (0151) 243 8111
Being close to the Albert Dock, this large modern hotel attracts many reports. It has "excellent views" and a "lovely swimming pool" – otherwise it's "average". / **Rooms:** 159 (of which some non smoking and 50 family rooms). **Facilities:** indoor pool; gym; spa.

Holiday Inn Express   £55

Britannia Pavillion, Albert Dock L3 4AD
🖰 www.holiday-inn.co.uk
✉ expressbyholidayinn@cidc.co.uk
☎ (0151) 709 1133   🖷 (0151) 709 1144
Perhaps surprisingly, this is a top tip hotel in this under-served city – a chain establishment benefitting from a "fantastic location" (near the Tate and many restaurants). It's located in a converted warehouse, and some rooms have "beautiful vaulted brick ceilings" and "impressive waterfront views". / **Rooms:** 135 (of which 3 family rooms).

Hope Street   £115

40 Hope St L1 9DA
✉ sleep@hopestreethotel.co.uk
☎ (0151) 709 3000
Liverpool's first boutique hotel is set to open in late-2003, occupying a Victorian warehouse, in Venetian style, in the heart of the city. The management have high ambitions for it, including for the in-house restaurant, Pi. / **Rooms:** 48.

Ibis £46

27 Wapping L18
🖰 www.ibishotel.com   ✉ h3140@accor-hotels.com
☎ (0151) 706 9800   🖨 (0151) 706 9810
"A good, clean chain hotel overlooking Albert Dock". "For a budget hotel, I was very surprised about the quality of service", says one reporter. **/ Rooms:** *127 (of which 71 non smoking).* **Details:** *meals unavailable: L; min age for children: 8.*

Marriott £78

Speke Aerodome, Speke Rd L24 8QD
🖰 www.marriott.com
☎ (0151) 494 5000   🖨 (0151) 494 5050
This "modern chain hotel, built around the original Liverpool airport control tower and hangars" is "nicer inside than you'd think". It boasts "good facilities" nowadays, but "the Art Deco feel has been maintained". **/ Rooms:** *164 (of which some non smoking and 40 family rooms).*

Marriott £115

One Queens Sq L1 1RH
🖰 www.marriott.com
✉ liverpool.city@marriotthotels.co.uk
☎ (0151) 476 8000   🖨 (0151) 474 5000
"Well placed" near Lime Street station, this modern hotel is probably the most recommendable city-centre 'business' establishment in this under-served city, attracting good (if not rapturous) reports overall. **/ Rooms:** *146 (of which some non smoking and 49 family rooms).* **Facilities:** *indoor pool; gym.*

The Racquet Club £95 N

5 Chapel St L3 9AA
🖰 racquetclub.org.uk   ✉ info@racquetclub.org.uk
☎ (0151) 236 6676   🖨 0151 236 6870
Opened in the summer of 2003, the city's swankiest sports club (gym, squash, snooker, and so on) has bedrooms available for non-members. It is the also the new home of the popular Ziba restaurant. **/ Rooms:** *8.* **Facilities:** *indoor pool; gym; spa.* **Details:** *meals unavailable: Sat L, Sun.*

Thistle £49

Chapel St L3 9RE
🖰 www.thistlehotels.com   ✉ liverpool@Thistle.co.uk
☎ 0870 333 9137   🖨 0870 333 9237
This "bland business hotel" attracted a considerable amount of survey commentary, much of it adverse (and quite a lot of it to the effect that the "small" and "drab" rooms are "in need of modernisation"). It does have a 'plus' point — a "superb location", opposite the Royal Liver Building, with some "superb views of the Mersey". **/ Rooms:** *226 (of which 114 non smoking and 8 family rooms).* **Details:** *min age for children: 12.*

LIZARD PENINSULA, CORNWALL   1–4B

Polurrian   £102
Mullion TR12 7EN
🖰 www.polurrianhotel.com   ✉ polurotel@aol.com
☎ (01326) 240421   📠 (01326) 240083

This family-owned hotel Victorian hotel has an "excellent" cliff-top position, and is praised in particular for its "outstanding" service (especially given its relatively modest prices). / Rooms: 38.
Facilities: *indoor pool; outdoor pool; gym; spa; tennis.* **Details:** *meals unavailable: L; no Amex.*

LLANDDEINIOLEN, GWYNEDD   4–1C

Ty'n Rhos   £80
LL55 3AE
🖰 www.tynrhos.co.uk   ✉ enquiries@tynrhos.co.uk
☎ (01248) 670489   📠 (01248) 670489

"Very good food" and "wonderful views of Snowdonia or over the Menai Straights" is the gist of most reports on this former farmhouse, converted to a country house hotel. A couple of reports noted the importance of getting the 'right' room. / Rooms: 11 (of which all non smoking and no family rooms). **Details:** *closed Christmas.*

LLANDEGLA, DENBIGHSHIRE   5–3A

Bodidris Hall   £99
LL11 3AL
🖰 www.bodidrishall.com   ✉ info@bodidrishall.com
☎ 0870 729 2292   📠 (01978) 790335

Under new management from 2002, this 15th-century hall (whose origins go back over a thousand years) is tipped as "a very good hotel in a lovely setting" (of some 4000 acres), with "very good" food and service. / Rooms: 9 (of which 3 non smoking and 1 family room).

LLANDRILLO, DENBIGHSHIRE   4–2D

Tyddyn Llan   £65
LL21 0ST
🖰 www.tyddynllan.co.uk
✉ tyddynllanhotel@compuserve.com
☎ (01490) 440264   📠 (01490) 440414

A "pleasant setting" (with attractive gardens) and "considerate staff" are among the features which make this elegant and rather unusual restaurant-with-rooms a well-tipped location in an area without too many competing attractions. / Rooms: 12 (of which some non smoking and 2 family rooms). **Details:** *closed 2 wks in Jan; meals unavailable: Mon L; no Amex.*

LLANDUDNO, CONWY   4–1D

Bodsgallen Hall   £165
LL30 1RS

⌂ www.bodysgallen.com   ✉ info@bodysgallen.com
☎ (01492) 584466   🖨 (01492) 582519

For a "relaxing weekend", it's difficult to beat this "ideal" country
house (run by Historic House Hotels). Set in grounds above a
charming Victorian seaside town, it enjoys "beautiful views of
Snowdonia" and wins praise for its "wonderful" atmosphere,
"super spa" and "excellent service". Most (but not all) reports
also attest to the quality of the cooking. / **Rooms:** 19 (of which all non
smoking and 16 family rooms). **Facilities:** indoor pool; gym; spa; tennis. **Details:** no
Amex; min age for children: 8.

St Tudno   £158
Promenade LL30 2LP

⌂ www.st-tudno.co.uk   ✉ sttudnohotel@btinternet.com
☎ (01492) 874411

As comfortable a traditional venue as you will find in a seaside
town, this hotel on the promenade – family-run for over three
decades – attracts high ratings from reporters across the board.
"Very good food" and "staff who do everything they can to make
one feel at home" are among the highlights. / **Rooms:** 19 (of which 4
non smoking and 4 family rooms). **Facilities:** indoor pool.

LLANGOLLEN, DENBIGHSHIRE   5–3A

Bryn Derwen   £50
Abbey Rd LL20 8EF

⌂ www.brynderwenhotel.co.uk
✉ robert@brynderwenhotel.co.uk
☎ (01978) 860583   🖨 (01978) 861871

This "eccentric country inn", peacefully located in the Vale of
Llangollen, has built up quite a name over twenty years in the
current ownership, and is unanimously hailed as an "outstanding"
establishment of its type. / **Rooms:** 16 (of which 1 family room).
Details: meals unavailable: L (pre-booked only).

LLANWDDYN, POWYS   4–2D

Lake Vyrnwy   £120
Lake Vyrnwy SY10 0LY
🖰 www.lakevyrnwy.com   ✉ res@lakevyrnwy.com
☎ (01691) 870692   🖨 (01631) 870925

*"Fairytale views from the lakeside bedrooms and the restaurant"
are the highlight at this "very comfortable" hotel – a Victorian
building, originally built for the engineers who created the
reservoir it now overlooks. It is set in a large estate which offers
some "great walks". Service in the restaurant can sometimes
seem a touch "amateurish", but the "imaginative" cooking "has
some very high points".* / **Rooms:** *35 (of which some family rooms).*

LLANWRTYD WELLS, POWYS   4–4D

Carlton House   £65
Dolecoed Rd LD5 4RA
🖰 www.carltonrestaurant.com
✉ info@carltonrestaurant.com
☎ (01591) 610248

*"Cosy and comfortable, rather than smart" – or perhaps "fun, if
rather eccentric" – this small restaurant-with-rooms in an
attractive town can make "a marvellous weekend location"
(though kind weather helps, as there isn't much in the way of
facilities). "Very good food" is attested to by all.* / **Rooms:** *6 (of which
1 family room).* **Details:** *closed 10-30 Dec; meals unavailable: L; no Amex.*

LLYSWEN, POWYS   2–1A

Llangoed Hall   £160
LD3 0YP
🖰 www.llangoedhall.com
✉ 101543.3211@compuserve.com
☎ (01874) 754525

*For fans, this "perfect country hotel, by the Wye" (owned by the
family of the late Laura Ashley) is just an "unbeatable" location –
"charming", "relaxing", "good for walking", and with "lovely
rooms". There's a strong minority view, however, that the place is
"overpriced, and relying on its reputation", with iffy service
attracting particular criticism.* / **Rooms:** *23.* **Facilities:** *tennis.*
Details: *min age for children: 8.*

De Vere Cameron House £124

G83 8QZ

⌂ www.cameronhouse.co.uk

✉ reservations@cameronhouse.co.uk

☎ (01389) 755565   🖷 (01389) 759522

"Absolutely stunning views over the loch", "wonderful facilities" and a restaurant with quite a reputation make this "unpretentious but luxurious" restored mansion a "superb" choice, according to many of the high number of reports it generated. Not everyone is convinced, though: some say it's "overpriced", and that they "expected more". / **Rooms:** 96 (of which all non smoking and 20 family rooms). **Facilities:** indoor pool; gym; spa; golf; tennis.

Lodge on Loch Lomond £75

Luss, Alexandria G83 8PA

⌂ www.loch-lomond.co.uk   ✉ res@loch-lomond.co.uk

☎ (01436) 860201   🖷 (01436) 860203

"Amazing views" and "superb accommodation" are the theme of most commentary on this family-run waterside hotel. Half of reports, though, come hedged about with some degree of qualification, but even doubters feel the place "tries hard". / **Rooms:** 29. **Facilities:** indoor pool; gym; spa.

Talland Bay £130

Talland Bay PL13 2JB

⌂ www.tallandbayhotel.co.uk

✉ reception@tallandbay.co.uk

☎ (01503) 272667   🖷 (01503) 272940

"Beautiful gardens" and "good views" are the features which mainly inspire feedback on this "nice" and "quiet" – if fairly "basic" – seaside hotel, which occupies a building dating from the 16th century. / **Rooms:** 23 (of which some non smoking and some family rooms). **Facilities:** indoor pool.

LOUTH, LINCOLNSHIRE 6–3A

Kenwick Park £105
LN11 8NR

🖰 www.kenwick-park.co.uk
📧 enquiries@kenwick-park.co.uk
☎ (01507) 608 806 📠 (01507) 608 027
"Good facilities", including a *"first-class golf course"*, are the highlight at this Georgian-style hotel, health and leisure club, in an area of Outstanding Natural Beauty. / **Rooms:** 34 (of which 10 non smoking and some family rooms). **Facilities:** indoor pool; gym; spa; tennis.

LOWER BEEDING, WEST SUSSEX 3–4B

South Lodge £195
Brighton Rd RH13 6PS
🖰 www.exclusivehotels.co.uk
📧 enquiries@southlodgehotel.co.uk
☎ (01403) 891711 📠 (01403) 891766
This *"fabulous"* wisteria-clad Victorian house enjoys a *"beautiful"* setting in 93 acres of gardens and parkland, overlooking the Downs, and is warmly praised by all who commented on it. One fan tipped it as *"a perfect venue for a night off from the kids"*, but – given its plethora of meeting rooms and conference block – another found it *"slightly too corporate to be truly romantic"*. / **Rooms:** 39 (of which 3 family rooms). **Facilities:** gym; golf; tennis.

LOWER ODDINGTON, GLOUCESTERSHIRE 2–1C

The Fox Inn £58
GL56 0UR
🖰 www.foxinn.net 📧 info@foxinn.net
☎ (01451) 870555 📠 (01451) 870666
"A super place for a weekend à deux". This *"cosy"* inn – whose origins go back to the 11th century – attracts the very highest praise from reporters. It combines *"a beautiful setting, comfy rooms and great food"*. / **Rooms:** 3 (of which all non smoking). **Details:** closed 25 Dec; no Amex.

LOWESTOFT, SUFFOLK 6–4D

Ivy House Farm £99 ☺☺
Ivy Ln, Oulton Broad NR33 8HY
🖰 www.ivyhousefarm.co.uk 📧 admin@ivyhousefarm.co.uk
☎ (01502) 501353 📠 (01502) 501539
"A B&B with a very good restaurant attached" – this highly-rated establishment by Oulton Broad, is particularly praised for its *"large new rooms, lovely grounds and very good breakfasts"*. The adjacent barn features 'New World' cuisine, served in an 18th-century setting. / **Rooms:** 19 (of which all non smoking and 1 family room).

LUDLOW, SHROPSHIRE   5–4A

Dinham Hall   £130
By The Castle SY8 1EJ
⌂ www.dinhamhall.co.uk   ✉ info@dinhamhall.co.uk
☎ (01584) 876464   📠 (01584) 876019
"Lovely views" are one of the features distinguishing this
"unusual" 18th-century building, which boasts *"many nooks and
crannies"*. For some it makes a *"very nice"*, *"good-quality"*
destination, although there are also doubters who find its
approach *"a bit haphazard and amateurish"*. / **Rooms:** 13 *(of which
15 non smoking and 1 family room).* **Details:** *min age for children: 8.*

Feathers   £80
The Bullring SY8 1AA
⌂ www.feathersatludlow.co.uk
✉ enquiries@feathersatludlow.co.uk
☎ (01584) 875261   📠 (01584) 876030
*"The charming crooked Tudor exterior promised a quintessentially
English experience – it was, in a sense, as I left wondering if the
manager was a Mr B Fawlty."* Sadly, reports on almost all aspect
of this well-known inn (and it attracted a reasonable number of
them) were very mixed indeed. One account – of discourtesy to
an aged and disabled would-be customer – almost defies belief.
/ **Rooms:** 40 *(of which some non smoking and 2 family rooms).*

Mr Underhills   £85
Dinham Wier SY8 1EH
⌂ www.mr-underhills.co.uk
☎ (01584) 874431   📠 (01584) 874431
"Beautiful views of the River Teme" and a *"pleasant garden"* help
make this restaurant with (rather *"functional"*) rooms perhaps the
top stop-over for gastronomic pilgrims to this culinary Mecca. The
no-choice dinner menu offered here however, while *"delicious"*,
would not itself be the number one choice hereabouts. / **Rooms:** 7
(of which all non smoking). **Details:** *meals unavailable: L & Tue D; no Amex.*

LUXBOROUGH, SOMERSET   1–2D

Royal Oak   £65
Luxborough TA23 0SH
⌂ www.a1tourism.com/uk/royallux.html
✉ royaloakof.luxborough@virgin.net
☎ (01373) 640319   📠 (01984) 641561
This *"well-run"* inn in the Exmoor National Park has just the
"welcoming and comfortable atmosphere" you might hope for.
Though the establishment's ambitions are quite limited, *"every
detail is attended to"* (including quality cooking). / **Rooms:** 12 *(of
which all non smoking).*

LYNDHURST, HAMPSHIRE   2–4C

Le Poussin at Parkhill   £110
Beaulieu Rd SO43 7FZ
🖰 www.lepoussin.co.uk   ✉ sales@lepoussinatparkhill.co.uk
☎ (023) 8028 2944

*"A good location for exploring the New Forest", "cosy"
accommodation and a "stunning" location (a "secluded" Georgian
country house) are undoubted strengths of this restaurant-with-
rooms. Unfortunately, the dining room possesses an (on reporters'
estimation, undeserved) Michelin star, and service can come
encumbered with "much farcical bowing and scraping".*
/ **Rooms:** 19 (of which 3 non smoking and 1 family room). **Facilities:** outdoor pool.

MAIDENHEAD, BERKSHIRE   3–3A

Ye Olde Bell   £155   😊😊
High St, Hurley SL6 5LX
🖰 www.ramadajarvis.co.uk
✉ sales.yeoldebell@ramadajarvis.co.uk
☎ (01628) 825881

*"Lots of charm, if a bit mass-market." This "prettily-located",
"historic half-timbered village inn" (reputedly the oldest in the
country, and now run by Ramada Jarvis) still boasts a pretty
"wonderful" ambience. For a place that strikes some as being
"designed for Americans", it attracts surprisingly consistent upbeat
support from native reporters. Weekend rates are significantly
cheaper.* / **Rooms:** 46 (of which 25 non smoking and 4 family rooms).
Facilities: tennis.

MAIDSTONE, ESSEX   3–3C

Hilton Maidstone   £95
Bearsted Rd, Weavering ME14 5AA
🖰 www.hilton.co.uk
☎ (01622) 734322   🖷 (01622) 734600

*A business hotel that's "good of its type". Accommodation is the
highlight, with "excellent executive rooms" especially commended.*
/ **Rooms:** 146 (of which some family rooms). **Facilities:** indoor pool; gym; spa.

MALMESBURY, WILTSHIRE   2–2C

Old Bell   £110
Abbey Rw SN16 0AG
🖰 www.oldbellhotel.com   ✉ info@oldbell.com
☎ (01666) 822344   🖷 (01666) 825145

*This "charming" and historic Cotswold hotel (whose origins go
back to 1220) manages to represent the best of both worlds –
"old-fashioned values, but with all the mod cons". The restaurant
"tries hard", too, and children receive "excellent attention". In the
coach house, the rooms are in modern Japanese style.* / **Rooms:** 31
(of which some non smoking and some family rooms).

MALVERN WELLS, WORCESTERSHIRE 2–1B

Cottage in the Wood £99
Holywell Rd WR14 4LG
⌂ www.cottageinthewood.co.uk
✉ reception@cottageinthewood.co.uk
☎ (01684) 575859   📠 (01684) 560662
*Fans hail the "wonderful" views over the Malverns and
"exceptionally good food" at this Victorian country house hotel.
There's also a very strong minority of doubters, though, who judge
the place "very average" and "hugely overpriced". Major changes
(including the erection of a new building) were, however,
completed in the summer of 2003, so all these assessments must
be taken as rather provisional. / **Rooms:** 31 (of which some non smoking).*

MANCHESTER, GREATER MANCHESTER 5–2B

The 2002 Commonwealth Games do seem to have helped
shake up the accommodation possibilities at this great
Victorian city, long dominated by faceless and indifferent
business hotels. The scene has begun to improve notably,
though, first with the (now fading) *Malmaison*, and more
recently with the immediately-popular *Lowry* – the city's first
new grand hotel for several decades. For those not requiring
too much in the way of facilities, the top choices would
perhaps be the two boutique hotels – the recently-opened
Rossetti, or, less centrally, *11 Didsbury Park*.

Crowne Plaza £99
Peter St M60 2DS
⌂ www.crowneplaza.com
✉ sales.cpmanchester@ichotelsgroup.com
☎ (0161) 236 3333   📠 (0161) 932 4100
*For "grandeur" and "history", this vast ("a mile to the bedroom")
and "showy" Edwardian edifice – where Mr Rolls first encountered
Mr Royce – is undoubtedly the place. Conscious of its status as a
landmark, some reporters seemed to fear an 'institutional'
experience, but most (if by no means all) left reasonably
impressed by the quality of accommodation, and of customer
care. The "absence of a decent restaurant", however – neither
the swanky 'French' nor an (appalling) branch of Nico Central can
really be recommended – is undoubtedly a shame. / **Rooms:** 303 (of
which some non smoking and 42 family rooms). **Facilities:** indoor pool; gym; spa.*

11 Didsbury Park £90

11 Didsbury Pk M20 5LH

🖰 www.elevendidsburypark.com

✉ enquiries@elevendidsburypark.com

☎ (0161) 448 7711 🖶 (0161) 448 8282

This "very cool" townhouse-hotel is located a little way south west of the city-centre, in the swanky suburb of Didsbury (and benefits from proximity to a number of pleasant places to eat, including the rightly celebrated Lime Tree, tel 445 1217). Guests are made to feel "very welcome", and overall the place offers "a good package, for the price". / Rooms: 14 (of which 11 non smoking and 2 family rooms). Details: meals unavailable: no restaurant.

The Lowry £234

50 Dearmans Pl, Chapel Wharf, Salford M3 5LH

🖰 www.roccofortehotels.com

✉ enquiries@thelowryhotel.com

☎ (0161) 827 4000 🖶 (0161) 827 4001

"It's about time Manchester had somewhere like this", say fans of Rocco Forte's "ultra-modern" hotel. (Though technically in Salford, its handy location is in fact just a few minutes' walk from Deansgate.) "Clean, comfortable and contemporary", the place does strike some as a touch "clinical" or "pretentious", but its "enormous rooms and beds" win high approval (as do "good weekend rates" and a "fabulous" spa). / Rooms: 165 (of which some non smoking and some family rooms). Facilities: gym; spa.

Malmaison £79

Piccadilly M1 3AQ

🖰 www.malmaison.com ✉ manchester@malmaison.com

☎ (0161) 278 1000 🖶 (0161) 278 1002

"For true Footballers' Wives glamour" it's hard to beat the "classy and comfortable" north-western representative of this design-hotel chain – thanks to its very central (if "dreadful") location. Commentary is rather mixed, though – rooms are "well-equipped" but can be "pokey", for example, and the brasserie, while something of a 'scene', serves "forgettable" fare. / Rooms: 167 (of which 131 non smoking and 5 family rooms). Facilities: gym; spa.

Marriott £129

Hale Rd, Hale Barns WA15 8XW
🖱 www.marriott.com
☎ (0161) 904 0301 🖨 (0161) 980 1787

*In Manchester's 'stockbroker belt', this "first-class" modern
establishment is worth considering by those with no need to be in
the centre of things. It's "less soulless than one might expect", and
numbers "a good pool, and golf" amongst its amenities.*
/ **Rooms:** 142 (of which 7 family rooms). **Facilities:** indoor pool; gym; spa.

Palace £99

Oxford St M60 M60
🖱 www.lemeridien.com
☎ (0161) 288 1111 🖨 (0161) 288 2222

*"Fascinating Victorian architecture" is "incorporated as part of the
design" of this "tastefully modernised" hotel "in easy walking
distance of the centre". Room quality at this Meridien
establishment is "erratic", though, and service can be "mediocre".*
/ **Rooms:** 252.

Renaissance £80

Blackfriars St M3 2EQ
🖱 www.renaissancehotels.com/manbr
✉ rhi.manbr.sales@renaissancehotels.com
☎ (0161) 831 6000 🖨 (0161) 953 1219

*If it's 'location, location and location' you're looking for, this "bland
and functional" (but well-equipped) business hotel off Deansgate
is "great for proximity to shops and restaurants".* / **Rooms:** 204 (of
which 153 non smoking and 13 family rooms). **Facilities:** indoor pool; spa.

Rossetti £105

107 Piccadilly M1 2DB
🖱 www.aliasrossetti.com ✉ info@aliasrossetti.com
☎ (0161) 247 7744 🖨 (0161) 247 7747

*An early reporter tips this new Alias hotels outpost – in a
converted Victorian warehouse, in the gritty Northern Quarter –
as "excellent" and a "true style experience". From the brochure,
some of the accommodation really does look quite cool, and –
given the group's consistently impressive performance elsewhere –
it would be surprising if it did not become a very useful
destination.* / **Rooms:** 61 (of which 14 non smoking).

Travelodge £50

Blackfriars St M3 5AB
🖱 www.travelodge.co.uk
☎ 0870 191 1659 🖨 (0161) 839 5181

*A budget recommendation, a couple of minutes' walk from
Deansgate – "clean, comfy and cheap, and fine for an overnight
business stay".* / **Rooms:** 181 (of which 112 non smoking).

sign up for our next survey at www.hardens.com

V&A £80

Water St M3 4JQ

🖰 www.lemeridien.com

☎ (0161) 832 1188   🖷 (0161) 834 2484

This Meridien group warehouse-conversion benefits from a "very central" location, near the Granada studios. It attracts neither rave reviews nor damning critiques – from "comfortable and pleasant" through to "an average city-centre hotel, with aspirations to which it doesn't quite measure up". / **Rooms:** *158 (of which 50 non smoking and some family rooms).* **Details:** *meals unavailable: L.*

MANCHESTER AIRPORT, GREATER MANCHESTER 5–2B

Etrop Grange £85

Thorley Ln M90 4EG

🖰 www.corushotels.co.uk

📧 etropgrange@corushotels.com

☎ (0161) 499 0500   🖷 (0161) 499 0790

This "olde worlde" establishment occupies a "comfortable" Georgian house, not far from Manchester Airport. Certainly "by the standards of an airport hotel" – a description of which the management (Corus Hotels) might fairly complain! – reporters think it offers a "good" level of comfort and its restaurant is very well reputed. It can, however, seem "less special now it's owned by a chain". / **Rooms:** *64 (of which 24 non smoking and 40 family rooms).*

Radisson SAS £99

Chicago Av M90 3RA

🖰 www.radissonsas.com   📧 sales@manzq.rdsas.com

☎ (0161) 490 5000   🖷 (0161) 490 5100

"A place to stay in transit not as a destination" it may be, but this "functional" airport hotel does have the virtue of being "very convenient for the terminals, which you can walk to". Otherwise it's a "characterless" place, where the food is sometimes "shockingly bad". / **Rooms:** *360 (of which 302 non smoking and 25 family rooms).* **Facilities:** *indoor pool; gym.*

MARKINCH, FIFE   9–4C

Balbirinie House   £190
Balbirnie Park KY7 6NE
⌂ www.balbirnie.co.uk   ✉ info@balbirnie.co.uk
☎ (01592) 610066   📠 (01592) 610529

"An ideal place for complete relaxation, excellent food and elegant surroundings" – this "large, Georgian house" is set in some 400 acres, and offers suitably "spacious" accommodation. Most reports are full of praise for the "lovely" service and "outstanding" food. / **Rooms:** 30. **Facilities:** golf.

MARLOW, BUCKINGHAMSHIRE   3–3A

Compleat Angler   £170
Marlow Bridge SL7 1RG
⌂ www.macdonaldhotels.co.uk
✉ general.compleatangler@macdonald-hotel.co.uk
☎ 0870 400 8100   📠 (01628) 486388
Long-standing fame can raise "high expectations" for this – in parts ancient – hotel (and restaurant), which is celebrated for its "beautiful setting on the Thames". The reality is too often "very poor", though, and some reporters dismiss a visit to this Macdonald Hotels establishment as a "miserable, bland and depressing" experience. / **Rooms:** 64 (of which 20 non smoking and 4 family rooms). **Details:** min age for children: 12.

Danesfield House   £185
Henley Rd SL7 2EY
⌂ www.danesfieldhouse.co.uk
✉ sales@danesfieldhouse.co.uk
☎ (01628) 891010   📠 (01628) 890408
"A beautiful setting" ("just 40 minutes from London") and a "delightful spa" are among the features which make a visit to this huge 'wedding cake' of a Victorian country house an "excellent overall experience", so far as most reporters are concerned. Service "can let the place down", though, and the restaurant attracts somewhat mixed reviews. / **Rooms:** 87 (of which 3 family rooms). **Facilities:** indoor pool; gym; spa; golf; tennis.

Matfen Hall   £135

NE20 0RH
🖰 www.matfenhall   ✉ info@matfenhall.com
☎ (01661) 886500   🖷 (01661) 886055

Given that it's still owned by the original family, there seems to be more than a hint of the 'corporate' about the style of this grand, and potentially "lovely", Victorian Gothic country house hotel, not far from Newcastle. Accordingly, it's strong on facilities, with a "good-quality" golf course and, from 2004, a 'fitness, health and beauty spa'. / **Rooms:** *31 (of which 18 non smoking).* **Facilities:** *golf.* **Details:** *meals unavailable: Mon-Sat L.*

East Lodge Country
House & Restaurant   £140*   😊😊

Rowsley DE4 2EF
🖰 www.eastlodge.com   ✉ info@eastlodge.com
☎ (01629) 734474   🖷 (01629) 733949

*"Beautiful grounds" and an "outstanding location" help make this family-owned country house hotel – once an outpost of Haddon Hall, seat of the Duke of Rutland – a consistently popular survey nomination. *Prices are quoted on a DB&B basis.* / **Rooms:** *14 (of which some non smoking and some family rooms).*

sign up for our next survey at www.hardens.com   174

Riber Hall £136

Riber DE4 5JU
🖰 www.riber-hall.co.uk ✉ info@riber-hall.co.uk
☎ (01629) 582795   🖨 (01629) 580475

For pure atmosphere, this "fabulous Elizabethan manor house" is highly rated. Its "beautiful location" (on a hill above the town) and "good restaurant" make it "ideal for a relaxing break". / **Rooms:** 14 (of which 5 non smoking). **Details:** min age for children: 10.

MAWGAN PORTH, CORNWALL 1–4B

Bedruthan Steps £164* ☺

TR8 4BU
🖰 www.bedruthan.com ✉ office@bedruthan.com
☎ (01637) 860555   🖨 (01637) 860714

"A fantastic hotel for those with young children" – thanks to its *"excellent childcare and play facilities"* and its *"friendly and helpful service"*, this seaside hotel (owned by the Whittingtons for over 40 years) receives nothing but praise as a family destination, and one that's *"great value for money"*, too. *Prices are quoted on a DB&B basis.* / **Rooms:** 75 (of which all non smoking and 69 family rooms). **Facilities:** indoor pool; outdoor pool; gym; spa; tennis. **Details:** no Amex.

MIDDLESBOROUGH, NORTH YORKSHIRE 8–3C

Thistle £113

Fry St TS1 1JH
🖰 www.thistlehotels.co.uk ✉ middlesbrough@Thistle.co.uk
☎ 0870 333 9141   🖨 (01642) 232 655

Hailed by some reporters as "a good all-rounder", this "friendly" establishment, "in the heart of industrial Middlesborough", is considered "better than most in the Thistle chain". / **Rooms:** 132 (of which 70 non smoking and 12 family rooms). **Facilities:** indoor pool; gym; spa. **Details:** meals unavailable: Sat L, Sun L.

MIDHURST, WEST SUSSEX   3–4A

Angel   £110
North St GU29 9DN
✉ info@theangelmidhurst.co.uk
☎ (01730) 812421   🖷 (01730) 815982
*This "well-located" 16th-century coaching inn finds nothing but
favour with reporters, who find it a "charming" and "friendly"
place whose "lovely gardens" are a particular highlight. / Rooms: 28
(of which 2 family rooms).*

Spread Eagle   £99
South St GU29 9NH
🖳 www.hshotels.co.uk   ✉ spreadeagle@hshotels.co.uk
☎ (01730) 816911   🖷 (01730) 815668
*This "country house-style hotel" in an "interesting" town has quite
a reputation – parts of it (building was commenced in 1420)
"ooze charm" and the "cosy, luxury spa" was particularly praised.
Rooms can seem "basic", though. / Rooms: 39 (of which some non
smoking). Facilities: indoor pool; gym; spa. Details: no Amex.*

MILFORD-ON-SEA, HAMPSHIRE   2–4D

Westover Hall   £145
Park Ln SO41 0PT
🖳 www.westoverhallhotel.com
✉ info@westoverhallhotel.com
☎ (01590) 643044   🖷 (01590) 644490
*Built in 1897 to be the most luxurious building of its type on the
South Coast (for Siemens, the German industrialist), this
"outstanding" country house attracts a small but enthusiastic fan
club for its "amazing" atmosphere. Facilities include the hotel's
own hut on the beach below. / Rooms: 12 (of which all non smoking and
some family rooms). Details: min age for children: 6.*

MILNTHORPE, CUMBRIA   7–4D

Wheatsheaf   £65
Beetham LA7 7A
✉ wheatsheaf@beetham.net.com
☎ (01539) 562123   🖷 (01539) 564840
*"An old inn, recently changed hands and now the centre of village
life". It's tipped not least for its "excellent food". / Rooms: 5 (of which
all non smoking). Details: no Amex.*

MINSTER LOVELL, OXFORDSHIRE   2–2C

Mill and Old Swan   £80

OX8 5RN

🖰 www.initialstyle.co.uk

☎ (01993) 774441   🖷 (01993) 702 002

*This "beautiful" hotel in "a great riverside Cotswold setting" is run by a conference company (Initial), and, unsurprisingly, it can feel "a bit corporate". "Stay in the old building", though, and there's plenty of "olde worlde charm", and at "good-value" prices, too. / **Rooms:** 63 (of which some non smoking and some family rooms). **Facilities:** gym; spa; tennis.*

MISKIN, RHONDDA CYNON TAFF   2–2A

Miskin Manor   £126

CF72 8ND

🖰 www.miskin-manor.co.uk   🖂 info@miskin-manor.co.uk

☎ (01443) 224204   🖷 (01443) 237606

*"Pleasant and remote surroundings" make this country house hotel, some 15 miles from the Welsh capital, a "great place for a weekend getaway". Reports suggest it's a thoroughly pleasant place, without in any way being remarkable. / **Rooms:** 43 (of which some non smoking and some family rooms). **Facilities:** indoor pool; gym; spa. **Details:** meals unavailable: L.*

MOFFAT, DUMFRIES & GALLOWAY   7–1C

Beechwood Country House   £90

Harthope Pl DG10 9HX

🖰 www.beechwoodcountryhousehotel.co.uk

🖂 enquiries@beechwoodcountryhousehotel.co.uk

☎ (01683) 220210   🖷 (01683) 220889

*"A constant desire for improvement" is approvingly noted by one reporter on this modest Georgian country house hotel, which overlooks a small town. It offers a "friendly" welcome, and some reporters tip its restaurant highly. / **Rooms:** 7 (of which all non smoking and 1 family room). **Details:** closed 1 Jan-13 Feb; meals unavailable: L; no Amex.*

MOLD, FLINTSHIRE   5–2A

Soughton Hall   £120

CH7 6AB

🖰 www.soughtonhall.co.uk   🖂 info@soughtonhall.co.uk

☎ (01352) 840811   🖷 (01352) 840382

*A former episcopal palace of some grandeur, set in 150 acres and accessed down an impressive avenue of lime trees, provides the setting for this "charming" hotel. It's tipped, not least, for its "very good" dining possibilities. / **Rooms:** 15 (of which all non smoking and some family rooms). **Facilities:** tennis.*

MONKTON COMBE, BATH & NE SOMERSET 2–3B

Combe Grove Manor £110

Brassknocker Hill BA2 7HS
⌂ www.combegrovemanor.com
✉ info@combegrovemanor.com
☎ (01225) 834644 📠 (01225) 840866

A "great setting" – plus "excellent facilities" (including two swimming pools and four tennis courts) recommend this mainly Georgian country house hotel to most reporters. In other respects, though, ambiguity rules, and gripes include an annexe "with all the atmosphere of an airport motel" and a restaurant that's "not up to the location". / **Rooms:** 40 (of which 20 non smoking and 14 family rooms). **Facilities:** indoor pool; outdoor pool; gym; spa; golf; tennis.

MORETON-IN-MARSH, GLOUCESTERSHIRE 2–1C

Manor House £135 ⊤

High Street GL56 0LJ
☎ (01608) 650501 📠 (01608) 651481

This "beautiful hotel" occupies an historic building in the centre of the town. It's tipped not least for its "lovely grounds", and for the "great" nearby facilities for golf, tennis and riding. / **Rooms:** 38 (of which 8 non smoking). **Facilities:** indoor pool; spa.

MORLEY, EAST MIDLANDS 5–3C

Breadsall Priory £125

Moor Rd DE7 6DL
⌂ www.marriott.co.uk
✉ frontdesk.breadsallpriory@marriothotels.co.uk
☎ (01332) 832235 📠 (01332) 833509

A huge range of facilities, including a "marvellous" golf course (actually there are two) are among the features which win consistent applause for this "very upmarket" Marriott, which has a "wonderful location" within easy reach of the Peak District. For true charm, try for one of the dozen rooms in the (13th century) priory itself, rather than in the "warren-like" new building. / **Rooms:** 112 (of which 70 non smoking and 46 family rooms). **Facilities:** indoor pool; gym; spa; golf; tennis.

MORPETH, NORTHUMBERLAND 8–2B

Linden Hall £115

Longhorsley NE65 8XF
⌂ www.lindenhall.co.uk ✉ stay@lindenhall.co.uk
☎ (01670) 500000 📠 (01670) 500001

Lots of sporting facilities and a spa – and all included in the relatively reasonable prices – are highlights of this "lovely" country house hotel, and it's in "beautiful countryside", too. Though they are "large and well equipped", one reporter thought the rooms "a bit dated". / **Rooms:** 50 (of which 21 non smoking and 17 family rooms). **Facilities:** indoor pool; gym; spa; golf; tennis.

Longhirst Hall £71

Longhirst NE61 3LL

🖥 www.longhirst.co.uk ✉ enquiries@longhirst.co.uk
☎ (01670) 791348 🖨 (01670) 791385

The management describes this as 'an elegant period hotel with extensive leisure amenities', and it's set in 75 acres of woodlands just two miles off the A1. It's marketed strongly to the conference and training market – reports suggest it's a particularly good-value destination for those who value having sports facilities – such as two golf courses and grounds for football, cricket and hockey – easily to hand. / **Rooms:** 77 (of which some non smoking). **Facilities:** gym; spa; golf; tennis.

MORSTON, NORFOLK 6–3C

Morston Hall £190*

Main Coast Rd NR27 7AA

🖥 www.morstonhall.com ✉ reception@morstonhall.com
☎ (01263) 741041 🖨 (01263) 740419

*The "house party atmosphere" – complete with "good" food from a "no-choice" dinner menu – suits many visitors to this "relaxing", privately-owned, country house hotel. It's "nicely located", too, a couple of miles from the north Norfolk coast. *Prices are quoted on a DB&B basis.* / **Rooms:** 7 (of which some family rooms). **Details:** closed Jan; meals unavailable: Mon-Sat L.

MOULSFORD, OXFORDSHIRE 2–2D

Beetle and Wedge £175

Ferry Ln OX10 9JF

🖥 www.beetleandwedge.co.uk
✉ kate@beetleandwedge.co.uk
☎ (01491) 651381 🖨 (01491) 651376

"A gorgeous and charming location" is the special appeal of this Thames-side property. It maintains the feel of a large house rather than an hotel and – for a "romantic experience" – is one of the best destinations within easy reach of the capital. Some rooms are "small", though (and beware those "with a view of the car park"). The food is often proclaimed "very good" – perhaps rather better value in the 'Boathouse' (which is mainly a rôtisserie) than in the dining room proper. / **Rooms:** 11 (of which all non smoking and 1 family room).

Boath House   £150

Auldearn IV12 5TE
🖥 www.boath-house.com
✉ wendy@boath-house.demon.co.uk
☎ (01667) 454896

A building once (independently) described as 'the most beautiful Regency house in Scotland' provides the setting for what's tipped as an "excellent retreat", set in 20 acres and now run as an hotel by the family which rescued it from ruin. (It now boasts such up-to-date attractions as an Aveda spa.) / **Rooms:** 6 (of which all non smoking and 2 family rooms). **Facilities:** spa.

Alvaston Hall   £90

Middlewich Rd CW5 6PD
🖥 www.alvastonhall.co.uk
☎ (01270) 624341   🖨 (01270) 623395

This "typical Warners hotel" occupies a typically half-timbered Cheshire building. Offering "full entertainment" and leisure facilities (which include a 9-hole golf course), it attracts few, but consistently satisfactory, reports. / **Rooms:** 154 (of which some non smoking). **Facilities:** indoor pool; gym; spa; golf. **Details:** no Amex; no children.

Rookery Hall   £190

Worleston CW5 6DQ
🖥 www.rookeryhallhotel.com
✉ rookery@arcadianhotels.co.uk
☎ (01270) 610016   🖨 (01270) 626027

Château-style architecture distinguishes this grand Victorian house, (whose Georgian stables, in Arcadian group style, have been converted into a conference centre). It was strongly tipped by a reporter whose honeymoon night was spent here. / **Rooms:** 45 (of which 2 family rooms).

NAYLAND, SUFFOLK   3–2C

The White Hart Inn   £190
11 High St C06 4JF
⌂ www.whitehart-nayland.co.uk   ✉ nayhart@aol.com
☎ (01206) 263382   🖷 (01206) 263638
*This Constable Country coaching inn is a "nice, small place", now
owned by Michel Roux. As you might expect it boasts a "superb
restaurant", and the quality of service (from the mainly Gallic
staff) is "excellent across the board". / **Rooms:** 6 (of which all non
smoking). **Details:** closed 26 Dec-9 Jan; meals unavailable: Mon.*

NEW MILTON, HAMPSHIRE   2–4C

Chewton Glen   £290
Christchurch Rd BH25 6QS
⌂ www.chewtonglen.com
✉ reservations@chewtonglen.com
☎ (01425) 275341
*"The best in Britain, maybe the world" – reporters aren't shy in
their praise of this "magnificent" country house hotel, which offers
"unfailing standards and attention to detail" in an "idyllic" location
(near the coast, on the fringe of the New Forest). If there is a
reservation (apart from the prices, of course), it is that a small
minority judge it "a bit soulless", but the vast majority "can't fault
it" given the "total luxury and pampering", the "brilliant spa and
pool", and the "good" (if not quite world-class) cooking.
/ **Rooms:** 59. **Facilities:** indoor pool; outdoor pool; gym; spa; golf; tennis.
Details: no Switch.*

NEW ROSS, CO. WEXFORD, ROI   10–4C

Dunbrody Country
House   €200
Authurstown -
⌂ www.dunbrodyhouse.com   ✉ dunbrody@indigo.ie
☎ +353-51 389600   🖷 +353-51 389600

*A grand, family-owned Georgian country house hotel, which is
praised for its "exceptional warmth and charm". The home to the
Dunbrody Cookery School, it's also tipped for its "excellent
restaurant". / **Rooms:** 22. **Details:** closed 22-26 Dec; meals unavailable: Mon-
Sat L; no Switch.*

NEWBY BRIDGE–NEWCASTLE UPON TYNE

NEWBY BRIDGE, CUMBRIA 7–4D

Lakeside £160
LA12 8AT
🖰 www.lakesidehotel.co.uk
✉ reservations@lakesidehotel.co.uk
☎ (01539) 530001   📠 (01539) 531699
"Excellent leisure facilities and a swimming pool" and a "fantastic" location on the banks of Lake Windermere commend this grand hotel to most reporters (especially those prepared to invest in the "fantastic" higher-grade accommodation). Feedback, however, on this property (managed by De Vere), included some very mixed reports. / **Rooms:** 78 (of which 50 non smoking and 12 family rooms). **Facilities:** indoor pool; gym; spa.

NEWCASTLE UPON TYNE, TYNE & WEAR 8–2B

Newcastle vies with Cambridge for the unenviable title of Britain's Worst Major Destination for Hotels (perhaps oddly as, for restaurants, it's notably better).

Copthorne £119
The Close, Quayside NE1 3RT
🖰 www.millenniumhotels.com
✉ sales.newcastle@mill-cop.com
☎ (0191) 222 0333   📠 (0191) 230 1111
"A slightly anonymous chain hotel, but in an excellent position on the Quayside". It also boasts "good swimming pool and gym facilities", though even fans note the restaurant as no more than "moderate". / **Rooms:** 156 (of which 94 non smoking). **Facilities:** indoor pool; gym.

Gosforth Park £78
High Gosforth Park NE3 5HN
🖰 www.marriott.com
☎ (0191) 236 4111   📠 (0191) 236 8192
This "business-orientated" modern Marriott is worth knowing about for "easy access" from Newcastle (and "good parking"). Otherwise reports were rather mixed. / **Rooms:** 178 (of which 20 family rooms). **Facilities:** indoor pool; gym; spa.

Malmaison £125
104 Quayside NE1 3DX
🖰 www.malmaison.com   ✉ newcastle@malmaison.com
☎ (0191) 245 5000   📠 (0191) 245 4545
"A fantastic location on the Quayside" with "wonderful views" (of the "winking bridge") plus "stylish" and "imaginative" rooms have helped this "chic" outpost of the popular design-hotel chain to become by far the most talked-about place in town. Commentary is otherwise rather mixed, however – rather too many reporters found it "soulless", "dreary" or "overpriced", or say that it "didn't live up to expectations". / **Rooms:** 116 (of which 87 non smoking and 10 family rooms). **Facilities:** gym; spa. **Details:** min age for children: 12.

sign up for our next survey at www.hardens.com   182

Marriott £125
High Gosforth Park NE3 5HN
🖰 www.marriott.com
✉ reservations.gosforthpark@marriotthotel.com
☎ (0191) 236 4111 🖷 (0191) 236 8192

*This "efficient business hotel" may be "lacking in atmosphere",
but its "surprisingly good spa facilities" make it a destination
worth bearing in mind. A couple of reporters, though, found their
sleep disturbed by "rowdy hen parties".* / **Rooms:** 178 (of which 150
non smoking). **Facilities:** indoor pool; gym; spa; tennis.

New Northumbria £65
61-69 Osborne Rd, Jesmond NE2 2AN
✉ reservations@newnorthumbriahotel.co.uk
☎ (0191) 281 4961 🖷 (0191) 281 8588

*"Very brightly coloured rooms" help make this budget design-hotel
– a converted terrace of houses, in a residential area – a
destination not easily forgotten. It's "great for a lively weekend".*
/ **Rooms:** 40 (of which some non smoking and some family rooms).

Thistle £75
Neville St NE1 5DF
🖰 www.thistlehotels.com ✉ newcastle@Thistle.co.uk
☎ 0870 333 9141 🖷 0870 333 9242

*Some doubters say this "ex-railway hotel is run with all the skill of
Railtrack", but the majority view is remarkably consistent: that it's
"functional", "clean", "very central" and "reasonably priced", even
if it does offer "zero ambience".* / **Rooms:** 115 (of which 90 non smoking
and 2 family rooms).

Vermont £110
Castle Garth NE1 1RQ
🖰 www.vermont-hotel.com ✉ info@vermonthotel.co.uk
☎ (0191) 233 1010 🖷 (0191) 233 1234

*This "typical business hotel" has "a good location for the
Quayside", and generates quite a volume of reports. Its "gloomy"
interior, however, "lacks the charm the exterior suggests".*
/ **Rooms:** 101 (of which 50 non smoking and 7 family rooms). **Facilities:** gym.
Details: min age for children: 12.

NEWENT, GLOUCESTERSHIRE 2–1B

Three Choirs Vineyard £85
GL18 1LS
🖰 www.three-choirs-vineyards.co.uk
✉ info@three-choirs-vineyards.co.uk
☎ (01531) 890223 🖷 (01531) 890877

*'Vin de la maison' is just what it says it is in the restaurant on this
increasingly well-respected vineyard. It is accompanied by food
which can be "superb", too. There is also simple accommodation
that wins praise as a "relaxing" base for touring – with "stunning
views from the individual terraces" – but which one reporter
found too "motel-like" in style.* / **Rooms:** 8 (of which all non smoking).
Details: meals unavailable: Sun D, Mon; no Amex.

NEWMARKET, SUFFOLK   3–1B

Bedford Lodge   £145

Bury Rd CB8 7BX

🖰 www.bedfordlodgehotel.co.uk

✉ info@bedfordlodgehotel.co.uk

☎ (01638) 663175   🖷 (01638) 667391

Vaunted as "the best hotel in the area" by one reporter (and a touch "overpriced" as a result, says another), this Georgian hunting lodge has recently been the recipient of a couple of million pounds' investment. It's "very comfortable, since the refurbishment", and now boasts accommodation in contemporary style, and quite extensive fitness facilities. / **Rooms:** 55 (of which 28 non smoking and 1 family room). **Facilities:** indoor pool; gym; spa. **Details:** meals unavailable: Sat L except race days.

NEWMARKET-ON-FERGUS, CO. CLARE, *ROI*   10–3B

Dromoland Castle   €370

🖰 www.dromoland.ie   ✉ sales@dromoland.ie

☎ +353-61 368144   🖷 +353-61 363355

An enchanting (if, to some, "forbidding") Tudor castle set in 360 acres provides the "wonderful" setting for this "absolutely excellent" hotel (which comes complete with an 18-hole golf course). "Incredible" service ("friendly, and not fawning") and "delicious" cooking are among the features attracting the most particular praise. / **Rooms:** 100 (of which 8 family rooms). **Facilities:** indoor pool; gym; spa; golf; tennis. **Details:** meals unavailable: Mon-Sat L; no Switch; min age for children: 12.

NEWPORT, GWENT   2–2A

Celtic Manor Resort   £130   ☹

Coldra Woods NP18 1HQ

🖰 www.celtic-manor.com   ✉ postbox@celtic-manor.com

☎ (01633) 413000   🖷 (01633) 412910

A "large, comfortable hotel built on American lines, ideal for conferences, or golf", and with an array of "impressive leisure facilities" (including for kids). This "huge" establishment is, however, "in the middle of nowhere", and can seem pretty "soulless", and the number of reports of "poor" or "grudging" service is striking. / **Rooms:** 400 (of which 200 non smoking and 30 family rooms). **Facilities:** indoor pool; spa; golf; tennis.

sign up for our next survey at www.hardens.com

NEWTON STEWART, WIGTOWNSHIRE 7–2B

Kirroughtree House £130

DG8 6AN
 www.kirroughtreehouse.co.uk
✉ info@kirroughtreehouse.co.uk
☎ (01671) 402141   🖶 (01671) 402425

This imposing and "gracious", mainly Victorian country house is set it eight acres of grounds by the River Cress. It's tipped for its "superb accommodation and food", and as a "totally relaxing" destination. / **Rooms:** 17. **Details:** *closed 2 Jan-mid Feb; min age for children: 10.*

NORTH BERWICK, EAST LOTHIAN 9–4D

Nether Abbey £90 ☺

20 Dirleton Av EH39 4BQ
 www.netherabbey.co.uk   ✉ bookings@netherabbey.co.uk
☎ (01620) 892802   🖶 (01620) 895298

This Victorian villa is now "a good family-run hotel", offering spacious and tasteful accommodation. "Impressive" breakfasts and a "popular bar" are supporting attractions. / **Rooms:** 14.

NORTH STOKE, OXFORDSHIRE 2–2D

Springs £105 ☺☺

Wallingford Rd OX10 6BE
 www.thespringshotel.com   ✉ info@thespringshotel.com
☎ (01491) 836687   🖶 (01491) 836877

"An excellent hotel and golf course in a stunning setting" – *this half-timbered hotel (and golf club) is highly praised all round by reporters, with the possible exception that the food can be found rather "average". "Good conference facilities", too.* / **Rooms:** 31 (of which 6 non smoking and 6 family rooms). **Facilities:** *outdoor pool; golf.*

NORTHAMPTON, NORTHANTS   3–1A

Marriott   £49

Eagle Drive NN5 6XX

🖰 www.marriott.com

✉ northampton@marriotthotels.co.uk

☎ (01604) 768700   🖨 (01604) 769011

This modern hotel on the ring-road is mentioned by a couple of reporters as "very good for short business stays" – "not overpriced" and with "charming" staff. / Rooms: 120 (of which 80 non smoking and 6 family rooms). Facilities: indoor pool; gym; spa.

NORWICH, NORFOLK   6–4C

The Beeches   £81

2-6 Earlham Rd NR2 3DB

🖰 www.beeches.co.uk   ✉ reception@beeches.co.uk

☎ (01603) 621167   🖨 (01603) 620151

"Very well fitted and serviced rooms" are a theme of most commentary on this most unusual establishment, where guests are accommodated in three listed Victorian houses, located around three acres of "exceptional gardens" a few minutes from the city-centre. Prices are "reasonable", too. / Rooms: 36 (of which all non smoking). Details: min age for children: 12.

By Appointment   £95

25-29 St George's St NR3 1AB

☎ (01603) 630730   🖨 (01603) 630730

As well as "wonderful" grub, this "charming" and "quirky" townhouse restaurant-with-rooms offers "pleasant" accommodation. / Rooms: 4 (of which all non smoking). Details: closed 25-26 Dec; meals unavailable: L, Sun & Mon; no Amex; min age for children: 12.

De Vere Dunston Hall   £150

Main Rd, Dunston NR14 8PQ

🖰 www.devereonline.co.uk

✉ dhreception@devere-hotels.com

☎ (01508) 470444   🖨 (01508) 471499

"Excellent golf facilities" are the stand-out attraction at this "welcoming" Victorian (though the style is Elizabethan) country house hotel, which attracted all-round praise from reporters for its "beautiful grounds", its "welcoming" staff and its "very good" general leisure possibilities. / Rooms: 130 (of which 84 non smoking and 18 family rooms). Facilities: indoor pool; gym; spa; golf; tennis.

Maids Head   £95

Tombland NR3 1LB

🖰 www.corushotels.com/maidshead

✉ maidshead@corushotels.com

☎ 0870 609 6110   🖨 (01553) 763556

An "excellent" and "central" location – "opposite the cathedral, in the prettiest part of Norwich" – is the special feature of this "attractive" ancient 13th-century inn. / Rooms: 84 (of which some non smoking and some family rooms).

Marriott Sprowston Manor £109

Sprowston Park, Wroxham Rd NR7 8RP

⌂ www.marriott.com ✉ sprowstonmanor@whitbread.com
☎ (01603) 41087 🖷 (01603) 423911

The name says it all about this hotel, with an 18-hole golf course (and many other leisure facilities), developed around a 16th-century manor house, three miles from the city. Reports were rather mixed. / **Rooms:** 94 (of which 67 non smoking and 9 family rooms). **Facilities:** indoor pool; gym; spa; golf.

NOTTINGHAM, CITY OF NOTTINGHAM 5–3D

Citilodge £58

Wollaton St NG1 5FW

⌂ www.citilodge.co.uk ✉ mail@citilodge.co.uk
☎ (0115) 912 8000 🖷 (0115) 912 8080

The style suggests an intention to be a chain one day, but for the moment this "clean and cheerful" budget hotel is a stand-alone, and it is consistently recommended as a "good-value" destination, offering "spacious" accommodation. / **Rooms:** 90 (of which 72 non smoking and 10 family rooms). **Details:** closed 25-26 Dec.

Hart's £112

Standard Hl, Park Rw NG1 6FN

⌂ www.hartshotel.co.uk ✉ ask@hartshotel.co.uk
☎ (0115) 988 1900 🖷 (0115) 947 7600

Tim Hart is a restaurateur (Hart's Nottingham) and hotelier (Hambledon Hall) of considerable note, so it would be something of a surprise if his new design-hotel – built from scratch, and opened in the spring of 2003 – does not establish quite a reputation. / **Rooms:** 30 (of which some family rooms).

Hotel des Clos £100

Old Lenton Ln NG7 2SA

⌂ www.hoteldesclos.com ✉ info@hoteldesclos.com
☎ (0115) 986 6566 🖷 (0115) 986 0343

This "superb addition" to Nottingham occupies a "lovely", "cosy" conversion of a former farmhouse (it's a little way out of the city centre and on the banks of the Trent). Sat Bains's cooking is "beautiful" – the restaurant was one of the inaugural recipients of one of our 'Rémy Awards' for outstanding newcomers (a view subsequently endorsed by the arrival of a gong from Michelin). / **Rooms:** 9 (of which 2 non smoking). **Details:** meals unavailable: Sun & Mon; min age for children: 8.

Lace Market £109
29-31 High Pavement NG1 1HE
🖰 www.lacemarkethotel.co.uk
✉ reservations@lacemarkethotel.co.uk
☎ (0115) 852 3232   🖷 (0115) 852 3223

A "great location" and "terrific attention to detail" make this "minimalist trendy hotel" ("nicely converted" from a brace of townhouses) a very popular choice with many reporters. Even fans can find it "too expensive", though (particularly the in-house brasserie), and overall it receives occasional "disappointing" assessments. / **Rooms:** 42 (of which 3 family rooms).

Park Plaza £90
41 Maid Marian Way NG1 6GD
🖰 www.parkplazanottingham.com
✉ info@parkplazanottingham.com
☎ (0115) 947 7200   🖷 (0115) 947 7300

"Rather characterless but very good facilities and well-planned rooms" – if you value practicality over ambience, this recent arrival is worth considering. / **Rooms:** 178 (of which 126 non smoking). **Facilities:** indoor pool; gym; spa.

Travel Inn £53
Goldsmith St NG1 5LT
🖰 www.travelinn.co.uk   ✉ nottingham.nti@whitbread.com
☎ 0870 238 3314   🖷 (0115) 9081388

"Good budget accommodation", near the Theatre Royal.
/ **Rooms:** 161 (of which some non smoking). **Details:** min age for children: 15.

Nutfield Priory £135
RH1 4EL
🖰 www.nutfield-priory.com   ✉ nutbooking@aol.com
☎ (01737) 824400   🖷 (01737) 823321

"Lovely rolling hills" provide the "excellent" setting for this Victorian Gothic country house, set in 40 acres of grounds, and "very easily accessible from London". This handiness – plus its extensive leisure facilities – help account for the good number reports it attracted, but may also encourage complacency – there were some gripes about "fusty" rooms "in need of investment". / **Rooms:** 60 (of which 17 non smoking). **Facilities:** indoor pool; gym; spa. **Details:** meals unavailable: Sat L.

sign up for our next survey at www.hardens.com   188

Admiral Hornblower · £70

64 High Street LE15 6AS
www.rutnet.co.uk/customers/hornblower/admiralhornblower.htm · info@hornblowerhotel.co.uk
☎ (01572) 723004 · (01572) 722325

Built as a farmhouse in the 17th century, this is now an "atmospheric" inn in the centre of Rutland's county town. It provides spacious accommodation, often with four-posters. / **Rooms:** 10 *(of which all non smoking).*

Lord Nelsons House · £80

11 Marketplace LE15 6DT
www.nelsons-house.com
nelsonshouse@compuserve.com
☎ (01572) 723199 · (01572) 723199

The rooms which come attached to Nick's Restaurant – in a medieval timber-framed building on a corner of the marketplace – make a "charming, olde worlde, very comfortable and welcoming" place to stay. The simple cooking is also an attraction in itself. / **Rooms:** 4.

Whipper Inn · £85

The Market Pl LE15 6DT
www.brook-hotels.co.uk
whipper.inn@brook-hotels.co.uk
☎ (01572) 756971 · (01572) 757759

This "cosy" town-centre former coaching inn is tipped as "exceptional value" destination, particularly praised for its "spacious" rooms. / **Rooms:** 24 *(of which 12 non smoking and no family rooms).*

Manor House   £100*

Gallanach Rd PA34 4LS
🖱 www.manorhouseoban.com
✉ manorhouseoban@aol.com
☎ (01631) 562087   🖨 (01631) 563053

*This Georgian ducal dower house is now a "delightfully friendly and well-run hotel". Particular plusses include "terrific" bay views and a "quality" restaurant. One reporter thought the rooms "slightly small". *Prices are quoted on a DB&B basis. / **Rooms:** 11 (of which all non smoking). **Details:** closed Christmas, Jan 12-19; min age for children: 12.*

The Crown and Castle   £75   😊

IP12 2LJ
🖱 www.crownandcastle.co.uk
✉ info@crownandcastle.co.uk
☎ (01394) 450205

*This rejuvenated Victorian hotel has attracted "lots of newspaper write-ups", and consequently many reports. "Fantastic rooms and bathrooms" are indeed a great attraction (especially if, at quite a premium, you get one "with a view"). There are niggles, though – some find a grating air of "relentless self-promotion", and others complain of the "scandalous" exclusion of children from a fair proportion of the building. / **Rooms:** 18 (of which 1 family room). **Details:** closed 24-26 Dec & 4-8 Jan; meals unavailable: Sun D; no Amex.*

OSWESTRY, SHROPSHIRE   5–3A

Pen y Dyffryn   £92
Rhydycroesau SY10 7JD
🖰 www.peny.co.uk   ✉ stay@peny.co.uk
☎ (01691) 653700   🖷 (01691) 650066

This "gorgeous, small, family-owned hotel", which occupies a Georgian rectory in a "beautiful setting", just 100 yards from Wales, is an "out-of-the-way jewel" which attracts nothing but admiration from all who comment on it. "Old-fashioned personal service" is combined with thoroughly "modern" standards, making this a truly great destination for "a real country weekend". / **Rooms:** 12 (of which all non smoking and 1 family room). **Details:** closed 20 Dec-late Jan; meals unavailable: L; min age for children: 4.

OXFORD, OXFORDSHIRE   2–2D

Bear in mind that the general rule – the Big Names are rarely the best choice – applies here, but otherwise Oxford offers reasonable options at most price points.

Burlington House   £75
374 Banbury Rd OX2 7PP
🖰 www.burlington-house.co.uk
✉ stay@burlington-house.co.uk
☎ (01865) 513513   🖷 (01865) 311785

This large Victorian house, in the pleasant North Oxford suburb of Summertown, is tipped as "the best B&B in Britain" by one enthusiastic fan, offering "high levels of comfort and wonderful breakfasts". / **Rooms:** 12 (of which all non smoking). **Details:** closed Chrismas; min age for children: 12.

Hawkwell House   £95
Church Way, Iffley OX4 4DZ
🖰 www.hawkwellhouse.co.uk
✉ info@hawkwellhouse.co.uk
☎ (01865) 749988   🖷 (01865) 748525

If you don't mind being a little way from the centre, this "good overall" Iffley hotel comes quite well recommended (including on the food front). / **Rooms:** 51 (of which some non smoking). **Details:** meals unavailable: Sat L.

Holiday Inn   £125
Peartree Roundabout OX2 8JD
🖰 www.holiday-inn.co.uk
✉ reservation-oxford@ichotelsgroup.com
☎ 0870 400 9086   🖷 (01865) 888333

The odd service-hiccup aside, this "very acceptable and modern" chain establishment offers "convenience for the Park-and-Ride, and for the motorway network". "Good leisure facilities" help make it "excellent for families". / **Rooms:** 154 (of which some non smoking and some family rooms). **Facilities:** indoor pool; gym; spa.

Old Bank   £160

92-94 High Street OX1 4BN

🖰 -www.oldbank-hotel.co.uk   ✉ info@oldbank-hotel.co.uk
☎ (01865) 799599   🖨 (01865) 799598

This "gorgeous renovation of an old High Street bank" – a recent project from Jeremy Mogford, founder of the Brown's brasserie chain – offers a "refreshing" and "stylish" option in an under-served city, and reporters rate its accommodation highly. The place offers few facilities, though, and the presence of Quod (an Italian chain restaurant) doesn't seem to do a great deal for the atmosphere. / **Rooms:** *42 (of which 2 family rooms).* **Details:** *closed 24-26 Dec.*

The Old Parsonage   £133

1 Banbury Rd OX2 6NN

🖰 www.oldparsonage-hotel.co.uk
✉ info@oldparsonage-hotel.co.uk
☎ (01865) 310210   🖨 (01865) 311262

"Opulent", "charming" and "traditional", this impressive ancient townhouse boasts a wonderful location near the centre of Oxford, and is hailed by most reporters as a "very enjoyable" destination. It can sometimes seem complacent, though, and there is the occasional report of "pokey" accommodation or "bad" service. / **Rooms:** *30 (of which some family rooms).* **Details:** *closed Christmas.*

The Oxford   £120

Wolvercote Roundabout OX2 8AL

🖰 www.paramount-hotels.co.uk
✉ oxford@paramount-hotels.co.uk
☎ (01865) 489988

"A great modernisation of what was formerly a dump", this Paramount-group hotel near the ring-road receives only positive reports, for its "comfortable" (and "surprisingly quiet") rooms, and for the quality of its cooking and leisure facilities. / **Rooms:** *168.* **Facilities:** *indoor pool; gym.*

Oxford Spires   £60   ☺

Abingdon Rd OX1 4PS

🖰 www.four-pillars.co.ukspires   ✉ spires@four-pillars.co.uk
☎ (01865) 324324   🖨 (01865) 324325

"Corporate but comfortable", this establishment, a mile or so south of the city-centre, is consistently favourably reviewed as a "functional" destination. "Lovely rooms" and a "good pool" are highlights. / **Rooms:** *140 (of which 110 non smoking and 10 family rooms).* **Facilities:** *indoor pool; gym; spa.*

Randolph £140
Beaumont St OX1 2LN
🖰 www.macdonaldhotels.co.uk
☎ 0870 400 8200   🖨 (01865) 792133

The fame of this large and "traditional" Victorian hotel in the centre of the city precedes it, and it continues to generate many reports. "What the reputation is based on, I cannot imagine", says one reporter, and – like too many Macdonald hotels – it can seem "dreadfully nondescript" and "boring" nowadays ("yummy cream teas" notwithstanding). A new 40-room block is to be added in 2004. / **Rooms:** 111 (of which some non smoking and 10 family rooms).

PADSTOW, CORNWALL   1–3B

The Seafood Restaurant £105 😊😊
Riverside PL28 8BY
🖰 www.rickstein.com   ✉ reservation@rickstein.com
☎ (01841) 532700   🖨 (01841) 532942

You may "stay for the food, rather the rooms", but the "well-presented" accommodation above TV chef Rick Stein's famous eatery – mostly with water-views – wins uniform praise for being "very comfortable" and well designed. (Those on tighter budgets can stay in one of three rooms above the Café.) / **Rooms:** 13. **Details:** closed 1 May, 21-26 Dec & 31 Dec; no Amex.

St Edmund House £220 😊😊
Riverside PL28 8BY
🖰 www.rickstein.com   ✉ reservations@rickstein.com
☎ (01841) 532700   🖨 (01841) 532942

"A gorgeous room, view and setting" make this impressive modern building – in a garden behind the Seafood Restaurant – a destination that attracts uniformly high praise from reporters. / **Rooms:** 6. **Details:** closed 1 May, 21-26 Dec & 31 Dec; no Amex.

St Petroc's Hotel
& Bistro   £105

4 New St PL28 8BY

🖰 www.rickstein.com   ✉ reservations@rickstein.com
☎ (01841) 532700   🖷 (01841) 532942

"A bit small, but décor and comfort compensate" – this away-
from-the-waterfront part of the Rick Stein empire is "more
informal than the Seafood Restaurant", and makes a
"comfortable" place to stay, offering "fair value". / **Rooms:** 10.
Details: closed 1 May, 21-26 Dec & 31 Dec; no Amex.

Tregea   £84   ☺☺

16-18 High St PL28 8BB

🖰 www.tregea.co.uk   ✉ enquiries@tregea.co.uk
☎ 0871 871 2686   🖷 (01841) 533542

This "good-value small boutique hotel in the centre of town" is
hailed as a "delightful" destination. It occupies a Georgian house
that's been refurbished "in light and airy contemporary style, with
great care and attention to detail". / **Rooms:** 8 (of which all non smoking
and 4 family rooms). **Details:** closed Christmas; no restaurant; no Amex.

Treglos   £62*

Constantine Bay PL28 8JH

🖰 www.treglos-hotel.co.uk
✉ enquiries@treglos-hotel.co.uk
☎ (01841) 520727   🖷 (01841) 521163

With its "lovely indoor pool" and "smart but relaxed atmosphere"
this "old-fashioned" hotel is – according to its fans – a "great
place for a holiday by the sea". There is the odd doubter, though,
who can find its approach a touch "dated" or "inflexible". *Prices
are quoted on a DB&B basis. / **Rooms:** 42 (of which all non smoking and
some family rooms). **Facilities:** indoor pool; spa. **Details:** no Amex.

PAINSWICK, GLOUCESTERSHIRE 2–2B

Cardynham House £69
The Cross GL6 6XX
🖰 www.cardynham.co.uk ✉ info@cardynham.co.uk
☎ (01452) 814006 📠 (01452) 812321
A "luxury B&B" in a 16th-century house, whose "attractive, individually-decorated rooms" offer "lots of character and a great location" (and themes which range from 'Medieval Garden' to 'Palm Beach'). Rather remarkably, the Pool Room does indeed have its own small swimming pool. / Rooms: 9 (of which 3 family rooms). Facilities: indoor pool. Details: meals unavailable: L.

Painswick £125
Kemps Ln GL6 6YB
🖰 www.painswickhotel.com
✉ reservations@painswickhotel.com
☎ (01452) 812160 📠 (01452) 814059
This Cotswold country house in "the queen of Cotswold towns" can make a "charming" destination and its "comfortable" quarters and "welcoming" attitude helps win it a good number of recommendations. One or two reporters were less impressed, with gripes about the catering ("bland" or "a bit too ambitious") the chief area of dissatisfaction. / Rooms: 19 (of which 2 family rooms).

PAXFORD, GLOUCESTERSHIRE 2–1C

Churchill Arms £70
GL55 6XH
🖰 www.thechurchillarms.com
✉ mail@thechurchillarms.com
☎ (01386) 594000 📠 (01386) 594005
"A small county pub" with "great food and nice rooms". All reports support the view that it's "a super place for a short break or as a Cotswold touring centre". / Rooms: 4 (of which 2 family rooms). Details: no Amex.

PEASMARSH, EAST SUSSEX 3–4C

Flackley Ash £124
TN31 6YH
🖰 www.flackleyash.co.uk
✉ enquiries@flackleyashhotel.co.uk
☎ (01797) 230651 📠 (01797) 230510
Some reporters find this Georgian country house hotel an "unexpectedly charming place, with excellent food and leisure facilities", and its proximity to the lovely town of Rye (some four miles distant) help ensure a good volume of reports. Roughly half of these, however, are quite negative – usually on the basis that the interior is "dated" or "weary". / Rooms: 45 (of which 4 family rooms). Facilities: indoor pool; gym.

PEEBLES, SCOTTISH BORDERS   9–4C

Peebles Hydro   £80*

Innerleithen Rd EH45 8LX
🖰 www.peebleshotelhydro.co.uk
📧 reservations@peebleshotelhydro.co.uk
☎ (01721) 720602

The architecture may be "OTT Scottish Gothic", but most reporters are full of praise for this "big old hotel". There were one or two reports of "tired" rooms, but "amazingly polite" and "extremely helpful" staff and "all the leisure facilities you could ever want" (including an "incredible spa" and "good golf") – plus some "beautiful views" – formed the focus of most feedback. *Prices are quoted on a DB&B basis. / **Rooms:** 130 (of which some family rooms). **Facilities:** indoor pool; gym; spa; golf; tennis.*

PENISTONE, SOUTH YORKSHIRE   5–2C

Cubley Hall   £70

Mortimer Rd, Cubley S36 9DF
☎ (01226) 766086   🖨 (01226) 767335

"A lovely location on the edge of the Pennines" is just one of the features that commends this "superb" inn, which was originally a farmhouse, to all of the small number of reporters who comment on it. It's a "quaint" place, with "great service, and a warm and friendly atmosphere". The food is also consistently approved. */ **Rooms:** 12 (of which all non smoking).*

PENMAENPOOL, GWYNEDD   4–2C

George III   £98

LL40 1YD
🖰 www.george-3rd.co.uk   📧 reception@george-3rd.co.uk
☎ (01341) 422525   🖨 (01341) 423565

*This 17th-century family-run inn also includes Victorian outbuildings of the town's former railway station (a victim of Dr Beeching). It's tipped as a good place across the board, and some of the simply-furnished rooms have views over the Mawddach Estuary. / **Rooms:** 11 (of which some non smoking and some family rooms). **Details:** no Amex.*

PENRITH, CUMBRIA   7–3D

Leeming House   £87*

Watermillock CA11 0JJ
🖰 www.macdonalds-hotels.co.uk
📧 leeminghouse@macdonald-hotels.co.uk
☎ (01768) 486622   🖨 (01768) 486443

*"An excellent country house hotel in an ideal setting" – this "welcoming and eager-to-please" hotel wins (somewhat unusually for a Macdonald establishment) nothing but praise. "Lovely grounds" and a "good restaurant" are among features which find particular favour. *Prices are quoted on a DB&B basis. / **Rooms:** 40 (of which some non smoking and 10 family rooms).*

Old Church £100

Old Church Bay, Watermillock CA11 0JN

🖰 www.oldchurch.co.uk ✉ info@oldchurch.co.uk

☎ (01768) 486204

An "excellent small Regency country house hotel", whose location – on a promontory overlooking Ullswater – helps make it a strongly tipped destination. / **Rooms:** 10 (of which all non smoking). **Details:** closed Oct-Mar; meals unavailable: Sun D.

PENZANCE, CORNWALL 1–4A

Penzance Arts Club £60

Chapel House Chapel St TR18 4AQ

🖰 www.penzanceartsclub.co.uk

✉ reception@penzanceartsclub.co.uk

☎ (01736) 363761 🖨 (01736) 363761

Fans say this "eccentric" establishment – created a decade ago by a textile designer, 'to provide a congenial venue for people of like minds to meet' – offers "incredible value". It didn't please everyone, but those who liked it really liked it, praising in particular the "great" bar and "interesting" cuisine. / **Rooms:** 7 (of which 3 family rooms). **Details:** meals unavailable: Sun & Mon; no Amex.

PETERBOROUGH, CAMBRIDGESHIRE 6–4A

Orton Hall £88

The Village, Orton Longueville PE2 7DN

🖰 www.abacushotels.co.uk ✉ reception@ortonhall.co.uk

☎ (01733) 391111 🖨 (01733) 389111

This 17th-century country house hotel (owned by Abacus Hotels), has a "fabulous" setting in 20 acres of mature parkland, in a locality which offers "lots of good walks". It's somewhat let down by its restaurant, which one reporter dismisses as "a throwback to the '80s". / **Rooms:** 65 (of which some non smoking and some family rooms).

PETERHEAD, ABERDEEN 9–2D

Waterside £90

Fraserburgh Rd AB42 3BN

🖰 www.macdonaldhotels.co.uk

✉ waterside@macdonald-hotels.co.uk

☎ (01779) 471121 🖨 (01779) 470670

"Very helpful staff" are a highlight at this traditional establishment, now owned by Macdonald Hotels. / **Rooms:** 69 (of which some non smoking and some family rooms). **Facilities:** indoor pool.

PITLOCHRY, PERTH & KINROSS 9–3C

Knockendarroch House £136*

Higher Oakfield PH16 5HT
🖰 www.knockendarroch.co.uk
✉ bookings@knockendarroch.co.uk
☎ (01796) 473473 🖷 (01796) 474068

*This Victorian house – set in one-and-a-half acres almost in the centre of the town – achieved consistent recommendations for quality across the board. It runs a nightly courtesy bus to the Festival Theatre. *Prices are quoted on a DB&B basis.* / **Rooms:** 12 (of which all non smoking). **Details:** closed Nov-Feb; meals unavailable: L; no Amex; min age for children: 10.*

PLOCKTON, HIGHLAND 9–2B

Plockton Inn £64

Innes St IV52 8TW
🖰 www.plocktoninn.co.uk ✉ sales@plocktoninn.co.uk
☎ (01599) 544222 🖷 (01599) 544487

Those in search of 'Hamish MacBeth' will find many elements of his fictional environment in the attractive village where this "peaceful" and "picturesque" lochside hotel is situated. "Well-cooked local produce" adds to the attractions. / **Rooms:** 9. **Details:** closed Christmas; no Amex.*

PLUCKLEY, KENT 3–3C

Dering Arms £40

Station Rd TN27 0RR
🖰 www.deringarms.com ✉ jim@deringarms.com
☎ (01233) 840371 🖷 (01233) 840498

The "quirky" accommodation at this "friendly and characterful" inn (built as a hunting lodge) is no more than "basic, but quite nice". Fans say the food is "fabulous", though, with "superb seafood" a highlight. / **Rooms:** 3 (of which 1 family room). **Details:** closed 24-27 Dec.*

POLEGATE, EAST SUSSEX 3–4B

Crossways £80

Wilmington BN26 5SG
⌂ www.crosswayshotel.co.uk
✉ stay@crosswayshotel.co.uk
☎ (01323) 482455　📠 (01323) 487811

"So good, so personal" – that's the pretty much unanimous view
on this *"beautiful"* small country house hotel, set in a couple of
acres of gardens (and *"very handy for Glyndebourne"*). Even a
reporter who finds the accommodation rather *"tired"* says that
"staying here makes you feel good, even so". / **Rooms:** 7.
Details: *closed 24 Dec-24 Jan; meals unavailable: Sun & Mon.*

POOLE, DORSET 2–4C

The Haven £230

Banks Rd, Sandbanks BH13 7QL
⌂ www.havenhotel.co.uk　✉ sales@havenhotel.co.uk
☎ (01202) 707333　📠 (01202) 708796

All reporters comment on the *"exceptional position, overlooking
Poole harbour"* of this *"pleasant"* and *"caring"* (and family-owned)
establishment on the Sandbank peninsula (famous for offering
England's most expensive residential property outside London).
With its combination of *"traditional style and modern flair"* and its
"excellent leisure and spa facilities", this is one of the few grand
English seaside hotels which approaches the standards of the top
Continental establishments. / **Rooms:** 78. **Facilities:** *indoor pool; gym; spa.*

Mansion House £110

Thames St BH15 1JN

🖰 www.themansionhouse.co.uk/enquiries.asp

✉ jackiegodden@themansionhouse.co.uk

☎ (01202) 685666   🖷 (01202) 665709

This "wonderful-looking Georgian building" has a "pretty entrance hall" to match, and the charms of its public rooms are much commended by reporters. On the accommodation front, however, feedback is more mixed (with some reporting "tired" rooms), but the cooking is "the best in Poole". / **Rooms:** 32 (of which 6 non smoking and 2 family rooms). **Details:** meals unavailable: Sat L, Sun D.

Sandbanks £103

15 Banks Rd, Sandbanks BH13 7PS

🖰 www.sandbankshotel.co.uk

✉ reservations@sandbankshotel.co.uk

☎ (01202) 707377   🖷 (01202) 708885

Under the same ownership as the grander Haven, this "very reasonably-priced" family-hotel attracts similarly ecstatic reviews. Thanks to its "fantastic position on the beach" (with "rooms that take full advantage of the view") and its "palm trees", some reporters think a stay here is "the next best thing to a holiday in Spain". / **Rooms:** 110. **Facilities:** indoor pool; gym; spa.

Airds £224*

PA38 4DF

🖰 www.airds-hotel.com   ✉ airds@airds-hotel.com

☎ (01631) 730236   🖷 (01631) 730535

*It's early days for the new régime at this "beautiful" lochside hotel, whose "simply superb" standards have made it quite a destination. A proper assessment of the new régime will sadly have to await our next edition. *Prices are quoted on a DB&B basis.* / **Rooms:** 12 (of which all non smoking and 1 family room). **Details:** closed 5-22 Jan.

Port Charlotte £100

Main St PA48 7TU

🖰 www.portcharlottehotel.co.uk

✉ info@portcharlottehotel.co.uk

☎ (01496) 850360   🖷 (01496) 850361

This small seaside Victorian hotel is tipped as a "fantastic gem", offering "brilliant food and caring service". / **Rooms:** 10 (of which all non smoking and some family rooms). **Details:** closed Christmas; no Amex.

sign up for our next survey at www.hardens.com

PORT ISAAC, CORNWALL   1–3B

Port Gaverne   £90

PL29 3SQ

www.chychor.co.uk/hotels/port-gaverne
pghotel@telinco.co.uk
☎ (01208) 880244   🖷 (01208) 880151

*This "quaint" hotel – occupying an old inn – enjoys a "fantastic"
waterside location that has helped win it quite a reputation (and it
generated a good amount of survey commentary). It seemed to
hit a rough patch as its former owner moved towards retirement
in 2002, but the signs are that the new management are
marrying the best of the old regime – many of the "friendly" and
"welcoming" staff have been retained – with some elements of a
'new broom'.* / **Rooms:** 15 (of which all non smoking and some family rooms).
Details: no Amex.

Slipway   £72

Harbor Front PL29 3RH

www.portisaac.com   slipwayhotel@portisaac.com
☎ (01208) 880264   🖷 (01208) 880408

*This "charming, small hotel, right on the waterfront" has a history
dating back to 1527, and isn't lacking in "romantic" charm. The
restaurant specialises in fish and seafood.* / **Rooms:** 11 (of which 2
family rooms). **Details:** closed Jan.

PORTMEIRION, GWYNEDD   4–2C

Castell Deudraeth   £170

LL48 6ET

www.portmeirion-village.com
hotel@portmeirion-village.com
☎ (01766) 774400   🖷 (01766) 771331

*Reports on this "beautifully furnished", 19th-century castellated
house – refurbished in contemporary style as an hotel in 2001,
and run in tandem with the Portmeirion Hotel – are notable for
their sheer consistency. "Beds so comfy you don't want to get up"
and "fantastic food" were among the highlights.* / **Rooms:** 11 (of
which 3 family rooms). **Facilities:** outdoor pool; golf; tennis.

Portmeirion £150

LL48 6ER

🖰 www.portmeirion-village.com

✉ hotel@portmeirion.wales.com

☎ (01766) 770000 📠 (01766) 771331

A "sensational location" – in Sir Clough Williams-Ellis's "interesting and beautiful" fantasy Mediterranean village (as seen in 'The Prisoner') – is the making of this "magical" seaside hotel. The "beautifully furnished" rooms and "friendly" and "relaxed" style does not let it down, though, and the food in the dining room overlooking Cardigan Bay – if not hugely ambitious – is often "great" too. / **Rooms:** 14.

Marriott £57

North Harbour PO6 4SH

🖰 www.marriott.com

☎ (023) 9238 3151 📠 (023) 9238 8701

Apart from the fact that it's rather "remote" from the city centre – arguably no bad thing given the latter's Stalinist architecture – this is "the best-quality place hereabouts". In Marriott style, charm and food are not particular strengths. / **Rooms:** 174 (of which 130 non smoking and 77 family rooms). **Facilities:** indoor pool; gym; spa.

Shrigley Hall £160

SK10 5SB

🖰 www.paramount-hotels.co.uk

✉ shrigleyhotelreservations@paramount-hotels.co.uk

☎ (01625) 575757 📠 (01625) 573323

Expectations not quite fulfilled permeate the (good number of) reports on this Paramount group hotel. It does have "a superb setting", a golf course and a "good" range of other facilities, but some of the accommodation (especially in the annexes) is "disappointing", and service "needs work". / **Rooms:** 150 (of which some non smoking and some family rooms). **Facilities:** indoor pool; gym; spa; golf. **Details:** meals unavailable: L.

sign up for our next survey at www.hardens.com

PRESTBURY, CHESHIRE   5–2B

White House   £110

New Rd SK10 4DG
🖰 www.thewhitehouse.uk.com
✉ info@thewhitehouse.co.uk
☎ (01625) 829376   🖷 (01625) 828627

Given its location in this swankiest of Cheshire's villages it's perhaps no great surprise that this restaurant-with-rooms strikes some as having "delusions of grandeur". It's a "good-value" destination, though, with "excellent" cooking and "charming" staff. / **Rooms:** 11 (of which all non smoking). **Facilities:** gym. **Details:** closed 25-26 Dec; meals unavailable: Sun D, Mon L; min age for children: 10.

PRESTON, LANCASHIRE   5–1A

Marriott   £78

Garstang Rd, Broughton PR3 5JB
🖰 www.marriott.co.uk
✉ reservations.preston@marriotthotels.co.uk
☎ (01772) 86408   🖷 (01772) 861327

"A good comfortable, no-frills hotel, slightly out of the town". Set in 11 acres, it occupies a Victorian building, plus a more recent extension, and offers a good range of facilities. / **Rooms:** 150 (of which some non smoking and some family rooms). **Facilities:** indoor pool; gym.

PURTON, WILTSHIRE   2–2C

Pear Tree at Purton   £110

SN5 4ED
🖰 www.peartreepurton.co.uk
✉ relax@peartreepurton.co.uk
☎ (01793) 772100   🖷 (01793) 772369

"An excellent blend of efficiency and friendliness" distinguishes this large and luxuriously converted former rectory, set in seven acres on the fringe of a Saxon village. "A very high standard of cooking" is a particular attraction. / **Rooms:** 17 (of which some non smoking and 2 family rooms). **Details:** closed 26-30 Dec; meals unavailable: Sun L.

PWLLHELI, GWYNEDD 4–2C

Plas Bodegroes £80

Nefyn Rd LL53 5TH
🖱 www.bodegroes.co.uk ✉ gunna@bodegroes.co.uk
☎ (01758) 612363 🖷 (01758) 701247

A "beautiful location" in "open countryside" is just part of the
formula which wins little but praise for this small and "off-the-
beaten-track" country house hotel – an establishment decorated
in a relatively contemporary style, and which the owners prefer to
describe as a restaurant-with-rooms. Once you've arrived, you will
probably find "charming" accommodation and "friendly" service,
and excellent" dining, too. / **Rooms:** 11 (of which all non smoking).
Details: closed Sun & Mon; meals unavailable: L, Sun & Mon D; no Amex.

RAMSGILL-IN-NIDDERDALE, NORTH YORKSHIRE 8–4B

Yorke Arms £180* ☺

HG3 5RL
🖱 www.yorke-arms.co.uk ✉ enquiries@yorke-arms.co.uk
☎ (01423) 755243 🖷 (01423) 755330

Located in a "peaceful" village, this "former 17th-century shooting
lodge (now a very comfortable restaurant with rooms)" makes an
"ideal walking base", and is also handy for "shooting, fishing and
birdwatching". The kitchen – overseen by owner Frances Atkins –
is generally (if not quite unanimously) acclaimed as "superb".
*Prices are quoted on a DB&B basis. / **Rooms:** 14 (of which all non
smoking). **Details:** min age for children: 12.

READING, BERKSHIRE 2–2D

Millennium Madejski £120 ☺☺

Madejski Stadium, Junction 11, M4 RG2 0FL
🖱 www.millenniumhotels.com
✉ sales.reading@mill-cop.com
☎ (0118) 925 3500 🖷 (0118) 925 3501

Just off the M4, this establishment forming part of the rugby and
football stadium (which is also named after the modest Mr
Madejski) is unanimously hailed by reporters as a "great modern
hotel". "Trendy" fittings and a "great restaurant and leisure
facilities" are among the features which make it a good place to
visit "with, or without, children". / **Rooms:** 140 (of which 93 non smoking
and 3 family rooms). **Facilities:** indoor pool; gym; spa.

Renaissance Reading £140

Oxford Rd RG1 7RH

⌂ www.renaissancehotels.com/lhrlr

☎ (0118) 958 6222   🖶 (0118) 959 7842

There were surprisingly favourable reports overall on this modern town-centre hotel (part of a group Marriott-spin-off group), whose "well-appointed and spacious" rooms, and "efficient" and "courteous" service are generally praised. / **Rooms:** *196 (of which some non smoking and some family rooms).* **Facilities:** *indoor pool; gym; spa.*

REYNOLDSTON, SWANSEA   1–1C

Fairyhill £140 😊😊😊

SA3 1BS

⌂ www.fairyhill.net   ✉ postbox@fairyhill.net

☎ (01792) 390139   🖶 (01792) 391358

"Hidden in the outback of the Gower Peninsula", this "magical hotel" (an 18th-century house decked out in a fairly conventional style) boasts a "renowned restaurant" that many consider Wales's best. There is the occasional visitor who "expected too much" from the overall experience, but strong consensus is that this is "an absolutely fantastic place for a weekend away" (and with plenty of "pleasant walking" available, to build up an appetite). / **Rooms:** *8.* **Details:** *min age for children: 8.*

RICHMOND, SURREY   3–3A

The Petersham £160 😐

Nightingale Ln TW10 6UZ

⌂ www.petershamhotel.co.uk

✉ enq@petershamhotel.co.uk

☎ (020) 8940 7471   🖶 (020) 8939 1098

This "romantic" Victorian hotel enjoys a "beautiful location" with "lovely views" over Petersham Meadows (and to the Thames beyond). Its restaurant has something of a following locally, but reports give the impression that – despite high aspirations – overall standards are "not quite there". / **Rooms:** *61 (of which 4 family rooms).*

Richmond Hill £120

TW10 6RW

⌂ www.corushotels.co.uk/richmondhill

✉ richmondhill@corushotels.com

☎ (020) 8940 2247

A Georgian house with some pleasant views provides the setting for this "friendly and reasonably-priced" establishment, not far from Richmond's town centre. The interior of this Corus hotel, however, did strike one reporter as "a bit corporate". / **Rooms:** *137 (of which 47 non smoking and 2 family rooms).* **Facilities:** *indoor pool; gym; spa.*

RINGWOOD, HAMPSHIRE   2–4C

Burley Manor   £125

Burley BH24 4BS

⌂ www.forestdale.com   ✉ burley.manor@forestdale.com

☎ (01425) 403522   🖷 (01425) 403227

One reporter commenting on this Victorian-Baronial country house hotel on the fringes of the New Forest (part of the Forestdale group) did gripe about "complacent management", but it generally won praise for its "good accommodation", and facilities which include its own stables. / **Rooms:** 38 (of which 8 non smoking and 2 family rooms). **Facilities:** outdoor pool. **Details:** meals unavailable: Mon-Sat L.

ROADE, NORTHANTS   3–1A

Roade House   £80

16 High St NN7 2NW

⌂ www.roadehousehotel.co.uk

✉ info@roadehousehotel.co.uk

☎ (01604) 863372   🖷 (01604) 863372

Chris and Sue Kewley's "quiet, small country inn", is especially tipped for its "high quality dining in pleasant surroundings". / **Rooms:** 10 (of which all non smoking and 1 family room).

ROCK, CORNWALL   1–3B

St Enedoc   £190

PL27 6LA

⌂ www.enodoc-hotel.co.uk   ✉ enodochotel@aol.com

☎ (01208) 863394   🖷 (01208) 863970

"A plain-looking place from the outside, but beautifully stylish within" – this "fantastic boutique-style hotel" ("recently refurbished to a high standard") wins little but praise from reporters. It has a "very relaxed" ambience, with "great staff" and "superb food" (with a Thai twist). The location – on a hill with estuary-views – is "great", too. / **Rooms:** 20 (of which all non smoking and 4 family rooms). **Facilities:** outdoor pool; gym; spa. **Details:** closed Christmas (check for Jan & Feb).

ROMALDKIRK, COUNTY DURHAM 8–3B

The Rose and Crown £96
DL12 9EB
🖰 www.rose-and-crown.co.uk
✉ hotel@rose-and-crown.co.uk
☎ (01833) 650213   🖷 (01833) 650213

"Exceptional, for a pub" – this 18th-century village green coaching inn is a "beautiful" place, with "friendly and helpful" staff and offering food of "a high standard. / **Rooms:** 12 (of which all non smoking and 1 family room). **Details:** closed 24-26 Dec; no Amex; min age for children: 6.

ROSEVINE, CORNWALL 1–4B

Driftwood £150*
TR2 5EW
🖰 www.driftwoodhotel.co.uk
✉ info@driftwoodhotel.co.uk
☎ (01872) 580644   🖷 (01872) 580801

"A charming cosy seaside hotel with style" – this new venture (2002) is "worth the journey". All aspects of the operation are praised, but "great interiors", "wonderful food" and the "amazing view" from the clifftop setting are among the highlights. *Prices are quoted on a DB&B basis. / **Rooms:** 11 (of which all non smoking and 2 family rooms). **Details:** closed Jan; meals unavailable: L.

ROSSLARE, WEXFORD, ROI 10–4D

Kelly's Resort €154
🖰 www.kellys.ie   ✉ kellyhotel@iol.ie
☎ +353-53 32114   🖷 +353-53 32222

One reporter likens a stay at this well-known, fourth-generation family-owned resort hotel (which is next to five miles of beach and which, in the 'Aqua Club', now lays claim to 'Ireland's most exclusive leisure development') to "going on a cruise". Its "great style and service" win nothing but applause. / **Rooms:** 106 (of which some family rooms). **Facilities:** indoor pool; tennis. **Details:** closed early Dec - late Feb.

RYE, EAST SUSSEX   3–4C

Mermaid Inn   £160
Mermaid St TN31 7EY
⌂ www.mermaidinn.com   ✉ mermaidinnrye@btclick.com
☎ (01797) 223065   🖷 (01797) 225069

*This "totally charming hotel in the heart of Rye" – dating from the
15th century – is hailed by most reporters for its "beautiful and
comfortable rooms, lounge and bar", and its "friendly and helpful
staff". There are occasional quibbles, but it is clear that standards
are much better than your standard 'heritage' destination.*
/ **Rooms:** 31 (of which some family rooms).

SALCOMBE, DEVON   1–4D

Marine   £130*
Cliff Rd TQ8 8JH
⌂ www.bookmenzies.com
✉ marine@menzies-hotels.co.uk
☎ (01548) 844444   🖷 (01548) 843109

*As "one of the few hotels in Salcombe", this seaside establishment
may be relying rather heavily on its rarity value. Fans say it has an
"outstanding setting", a "relaxed feel" and offers "good, old-
fashioned service". The number of equivocal accounts, though,
tend to support the view of the reporter who complains that it's
"being brought downmarket", by owners Menzies hotels. *Prices
are quoted on a DB&B basis.* / **Rooms:** 53 (of which some non smoking
and some family rooms).* **Facilities:** indoor pool; spa.

The Tides Reach   £190*
South Sands TQ8 8LJ
⌂ www.tidesreach.com   ✉ enquire@tidesreach.com
☎ (01548) 843466   🖷 (01548) 843954

*Family-run for over 30 years, this "luxurious" and "peaceful" hotel
enjoys a "stunning location right by the sea", and has an
"excellent sports and leisure complex". One reporter, though, did
find it "below expectations" at the price (quoted on a *DB&B
basis). / **Rooms:** 35 (of which 6 non smoking and 3 family rooms).* **Facilities:**
indoor pool; gym; spa.* **Details:** closed Dec & Jan; meals unavailable: L; min age for
children: 8.*

SALISBURY, WILTSHIRE   2–3C

Rose and Crown   £120
Harnham Rd SP2 8JQ
⌂ www.regalhotels.co.uk/roseandcrown
✉ reservations@corushotels.com
☎ 0870 609 6163   🖷 (01722) 339816

*This "old riverside inn is full of character", and it has a "good
location" (whose "beautiful views across the river and meadows to
the Cathedral" remain broadly as immortalised by Constable).
"For atmosphere, try and stay in the old building". / **Rooms:** 28 (of
which some non smoking and some family rooms).*

SALTBURN-BY-THE-SEA, CLEVELAND 8–3C

Rushpool Hall £120

Saltburn Ln TS12 1HD

☎ (01287) 624111   🖷 (01287) 625255

This "charming Victorian Gothic pile on the North Sea coast" is a "chintzy" and "welcoming" hotel nowadays. "Super sea-views" figure in most reports. / **Rooms:** *20.* **Details:** *meals unavailable: L.*

SAUNTON, DEVON 1–2C

Saunton Sands £73

EX33 1LQ

🖰 www.sauntonsands.co.uk

✉ sauntonsands@btinternet.com

☎ (01271) 890212   🖷 (01271) 890145

"Good for a seaside family holiday" – that's the unanimous tenor of reports on this large Brend group resort hotel, whose attractions include an adjacent golf course. There's an extensive range of supervised activities for the kids (including magicians, face-painting, water fun days and football). / **Rooms:** *72 (of which some family rooms).* **Facilities:** *indoor pool; outdoor pool; gym; spa; tennis.*

SEAHAM, COUNTY DURHAM 8–2B

Seaham Hall £175 😊😊

Lord Byron's Walk SR7 7AG

🖰 www.seaham-hall.com   ✉ reservations@seaham-hall.com

☎ (0191) 516 1400   🖷 (0191) 516 1410

This "wonderful new hotel" in a "beautiful old house" boasts "very chic modern facilities" and "excellently-appointed rooms" – "huge", and with "heavenly bathrooms", they are among the survey's best-rated. Chef John Connel's eclectic cooking is "lovely" too – the dining room won one of our 'Rémy' awards (for rising stars) in 2003. There is the odd gripe about the location, but the "luxurious oriental spa" soothes most concerns. / **Rooms:** *19 (of which all non smoking).* **Facilities:** *indoor pool; gym; spa.*

SEAHOUSES, NORTHUMBERLAND 8–1B

The Olde Ship £92

Main Street NE68 7RD

🖰 www.seahouses.co.uk   ✉ theoldeship@seahouses.co.uk

☎ (01665) 720200   🖷 (01665) 721383

This nautically-themed ancient inn above the small fishing harbour generally produced good feedback – particularly from those who stay in "the fantastic new rooms with sea views". / **Rooms:** *18.* **Details:** *closed Dec-Jan; meals unavailable: L & bank holidays; no Amex; min age for children: 10.*

SEAVIEW, ISLE OF WIGHT   2–4D

Priory Bay   £90
Priory Drive PO35 5BU
🖰 www.priorybay.co.uk ✉ reception@priorybay.co.uk
☎ (01983) 613146 🖨 (01983) 616539
"A great location overlooking the Solent" (with a private, if "boring", beach) has won quite a following for this country house hotel whose "medieval charm" makes it, for its fans, a "true gem". There were too many reporters, though, who encountered "a very disappointing experience all round" – reasons varied, but a "couldn't-care-less" management attitude was a repeated criticism. / **Rooms:** 18 (of which 2 family rooms). **Facilities:** outdoor pool; golf; tennis.

Seaview   £70
High St PO34 5EX
🖰 www.seaviewhotel.co.uk
✉ reception@seaviewhotel.co.uk
☎ (01983) 612711
This is a "beautifully managed small hotel", on most accounts with notably "friendly" service, and it is home to one of the best-known dining rooms on the island. Rooms although "quaint", can seem rather "small" to some reporters and one complains that the place is "advertised as a family hotel, but seemed more suitable for older folk". / **Rooms:** 16 (of which some non smoking and some family rooms). **Details:** closed Christmas.

SHEFFIELD, SOUTH YORKSHIRE   5–2C

Marriott   £94
Kenwood Rd S7 1NQ
🖰 www.marriott.com
☎ (0114) 250 5615 🖨 (0114) 255 4744
The "attractive setting" – in 12 acres of garden, three miles from the city-centre – can come as a "pleasant surprise" to first-time visitors to this hotel based around a Victorian house, whose accommodation is generally approved. / **Rooms:** 114 (of which 20 non smoking and 4 family rooms). **Facilities:** indoor pool; gym; spa. **Details:** min age for children: 12.

Novotel   £106
Arundel Gate S1 2PR
🖰 www.novotel.com ✉ H1348-GM@accor-hotels.com
☎ (0114) 278 1781 🖨 (0114) 278 7744
"Reasonably priced, large rooms in the heart of Sheffield" are the particular strength of this city hotel. It's a "value for money" destination, which can be "excellent for business travel". / **Rooms:** 144 (of which some non smoking and some family rooms). **Facilities:** indoor pool; gym.

SHELLEY, WEST YORKSHIRE   5–2C

Three Acres   £75

Roydhouse HD8 8LR

🖐 3acres.com   ✉ 3acres@globalnet.co.uk
☎ (01484) 602606   🖨 (01484) 608411

This coaching inn near the Emley Moor TV transmitter may offer accommodation that's a mite "variable", but it makes "an excellent HQ for walking the moors". The food, in gastropub style, is often "brilliant", so the place often gets "very busy". / **Rooms:** 20 (of which 1 family room). **Details:** closed 25 Dec & 1 Jan; meals unavailable: Sat L.

SHEPTON MALLET, SOMERSET   2–3B

Charlton House   £155

Charlton Rd BA4 4PR

🖐 www.charltonhouse.com
✉ enquiry@charltonhouse.com
☎ (01749) 342008   🖨 (01749) 346362

"Open fires, friendly and attentive staff and great food – this is the perfect place for a cosy winter break." One reporter sums up the many reports on this "very romantic and comfortable" manor house establishment. That it's decked out using the full range of Mulberry fabrics and furnishings is explained by the fact that its owners founded the brand. Spring 2004 sees the opening of a spa, as well as some new accommodation. / **Rooms:** 17 (of which 2 family rooms). **Facilities:** spa.

SHREWSBURY, SHROPSHIRE   5–3A

Lion   £99

Wyle Cop SY1 1UJ

🖐 www.corushotels.com/thelion
✉ reservations@corushotels.com
☎ 0870 609 6167   🖨 (01743) 352744

Set "in the heart of Shrewsbury", this "lovely" coaching inn is "full of character". "Exceptionally helpful service" contributes to a favourable overall impression of an establishment which seems to wear its corporate (Corus Hotels) ownership lightly. / **Rooms:** 59 (of which 30 non smoking and 3 family rooms).

Rowton Castle   £84

Halfway House SY5 9EP

🖐 www.rowtoncastle.com   ✉ post@rowtoncastle.com
☎ (01743) 884044   🖨 (01743) 884949

A "magical atmosphere" and "value for money" are the themes of reports on this 17th-century castle, which has a "great setting" in 17 acres of gardens five miles west of the town. "Gargantuan" breakfasts win particular approval. / **Rooms:** 19 (of which some family rooms). **Details:** closed Christmas.

SHURDINGTON, GLOUCESTERSHIRE   2–1C

The Greenway   £150
GL51 4UG

⌂ www.the-greenway.co.uk   ✉ greenway@btconnect.com
☎ (01242) 862352   🖨 (01242) 862780

*This Elizabethan manor house – an hotel for more than half a
century – is a "tranquil" haven with some very "romantic" views.
As you might perhaps expect, state-of-the-art facilities are not a
highlight, but – with the exception of occasional quibbles regarding
the restaurant – the place attracts nothing but positive reviews.*
/ **Rooms:** 21 (of which 10 non smoking and 10 family rooms).

SIDMOUTH, DEVON   1–3D

The Belmont   £150
The Esplanade EX10 8JQ

⌂ www.brendhotels.com
✉ reservations@belmont-hotel.co.uk
☎ (01395) 512555   🖨 (01395) 579101

*"Consistently high standards of food, service and accommodation"
are attested to by all reporters on this early 19th-century hotel,
which is part of a commendable West Country group (Brend
Hotels). It has a "wonderful position overlooking the sea".*
/ **Rooms:** 50 (of which 6 family rooms).

Victoria   £210*
The Esplanade EX10 8RY

⌂ www.victoriahotel.co.uk   ✉ info@victoriahotel.co.uk
☎ (01395) 512651   🖨 (01395) 579 154

*Even a reporter who found "most guests at least 20 years older
than us" reported "an excellent time" at this "old-style", but
"efficiently-run" Victorian seaside hotel, in five acres of gardens at
the end of the esplanade. "Great views", "attentive" service and
"good food, considering the numbers catered for" make for
consistently positive (though thinly spread) reports on this
establishment, which forms part of the Brend group. *Prices are
quoted on a DB&B basis.* / **Rooms:** 62 (of which some family rooms).
Facilities: indoor pool; outdoor pool; gym; spa; golf; tennis.

SKIRLING, LANARKSHIRE   9–4C

Skirling House   £80
ML12 6HD

⌂ www.skirlinghouse.com   ✉ enquiries@skirlinghouse.com
☎ (01899) 860274   🖨 (01899) 860255

*This country house may be avowedly 'simple' in style, but it's
tipped as an all-round success, offering "impressive" attention to
detail, "delightful" service and "excellent" food.* / **Rooms:** 5 (of which
1 family room). **Facilities:** tennis. **Details:** closed Jan-Feb; meals unavailable: L; no
Amex.

---

sign up for our next survey at www.hardens.com

SLEAT, ISLE OF SKYE   9–2A

Kinloch Lodge   £170*
IV43 8QY
🖱 www.kinloch-lodge.co.uk   ✉ kinloch@dial.pipex.com
☎ (01471) 833333   📠 (01471) 833277
'Godfrey Lord Macdonald of Macdonald and his wife Claire
Macdonald of Macdonald' preside over this small hotel in a
former hunting lodge. A "breathtaking location" and "fantastic
food" – Lady M is a sort of toffs' celebrity chef – are acclaimed
by some reporters, but some do find the set-up surprisingly
"basic". (In fact, the 'New House' – built in 1998, some 50 yards
away – seems to be the preferred place to stay, though it has the
obvious downside of "having to run to the main house for dinner,
in the usual Skye weather".) *Prices are quoted on a DB&B basis.
/ **Rooms:** 14 (of which all non smoking and some family rooms). **Details:** closed
Dec-Feb; meals unavailable: L.

SNEEM, CO. KERRY, ROI   10–4A

Parknasilla   €180
🖱 www.parknasillahotel.com   ✉ res@parknasilla-gsh.com
☎ +353-64 45122   📠 +353-64 45323
Reporters all speak in pretty much identical glowing terms of this
"grand old hotel" – a large Victorian pile whose key attractions
include "an outstanding location beside the sea", "beautiful
grounds" (of some 300 acres), "very friendly and helpful" service
and a "top-class restaurant". / **Rooms:** 84 (of which some non smoking
and some family rooms). **Facilities:** indoor pool; spa; golf; tennis. **Details:** meals
unavailable: L.

SONNING-ON-THAMES, BERKSHIRE   2–2D

The French Horn   £130
RG4 6TN
🖱 www.thefrenchhorn.co.uk
✉ thefrenchhorn@compuserve.com
☎ (0118) 969 2204   📠 (01189) 442210
If you're looking for a traditional restaurant-with-rooms on the
banks of the Thames, then this "charming and comfortable" (if
"dated") destination fits the bill. It offers "spacious" rooms, and
has a well-established reputation for "good, but very expensive"
Gallic dining. / **Rooms:** 21.

SOUTHAMPTON, HAMPSHIRE   2–3D

De Vere Grand Harbour   £120
West Quay Rd SO15 1AG
🖰 www.devereonline.co.uk
✉ grandharbour@devere-hotels.com
☎ (023) 8063 3033   🖨 (023) 8063 3066

*Fans of this "big functional hotel" praise its "good waterside
views" and "convenient location" and say it "looks great
illuminated at night". It does have it's critics, though, who –
describing its style as "modern-5-star-pretentious" – find it simply
"depressing". / Rooms: 172 (of which 116 non smoking and 9 family rooms).
Facilities: indoor pool; gym; spa.*

SOUTHWOLD, SUFFOLK   3–1D

The Crown   £110
High Street IP18 6DP
🖰 www.adnams.co.uk   ✉ crown.hotel@adnams.co.uk
☎ (01502) 722275   🖨 (01505) 727263

*"Cramped" quarters are a bugbear for some visitors to this
"relaxing", "very busy" and "family-friendly" inn. However, its
"splendid food and wine" – the latter courtesy of ownership by
Adnams' brewery – are justly of considerable repute. / Rooms: 14
(of which all non smoking and 3 family rooms). Details: no Amex.*

The Swan   £120
The Market Pl IP18 6EG
🖰 www.adnams.co.uk   ✉ swan.hotel@adnams.co.uk
☎ (01502) 722186   🖨 (01502) 724800

*"A wonderful lounge, very comfy chairs and afternoon tea" – if
that's your idea of heaven, this famously "old-fashioned and
genteel" establishment overlooking the marketplace, and owned
by Adnams the brewery, is probably for you. Some reporters,
though, feel that service has become more "haphazard" in recent
times, and the food "is better at the Crown". / Rooms: 42. Details: no
Amex.*

ST ALBANS, HERTFORDSHIRE   3–2A

Sopwell House   £158
Cottonmill Ln AL1 2HQ
🖰 www.sopwellhouse.co.uk
✉ reservations@sopwellhouse.co.uk
☎ (01727) 864477   🖨 (01727) 844741

*Supporters find this converted Georgian manor house (once home
to Lord Mountbatten) a "good all-round country house hotel" – a
"relaxing" place, with "comfortable" rooms and "excellent" leisure
facilities. This style of this De Vere establishment strikes some as
rather "Footballers' Wives", though, and it can seem "expensive"
for what it is. / Rooms: 128. Facilities: indoor pool.*

St Michaels Manor £170

Fishpool St AL3 4RY
🖳 www.stmichaelsmanor.com
✉ smmanor@globalnet.co.uk
☎ (01727) 864444   🖨 (01727) 848909

"An outstandingly charming and relaxed atmosphere" and "very accommodating staff" are features which make this 16th-century house – with five acres of garden, and a lake – an "excellent" destination for all of the (relatively few) reporters who comment on it. / **Rooms:** 22 (of which 3 non smoking and 1 family room).

ST ANDREWS, FIFE   9–3D

Old Course £225

Old Station Rd KY16 9HX
🖳 www.oldcoursehotel.co.uk
✉ reservations@oldcoursehotel.co.uk
☎ (01334) 475906   🖨 (01334) 477668

This "large, swish hotel" – run by an international group – strikes some people as the sort of place "where rich Americans would feel at home". It's "the place to stay for golf", and reporters agree it offers "all one would expect of an expensive hotel" – a "magical" setting, "great spa" "super food" and "luxurious rooms". / **Rooms:** 134 (of which 21 non smoking and 10 family rooms).
Facilities: indoor pool; gym; spa; golf.

St Andrews Bay £85

KY16 8PN

🖰 www.standrewsbay.com ✉ info@standrewsbay.com

☎ (01334) 837000 📠 (01334) 471115

*The American owners of this five-star complex certainly don't undersell it – 'an international standard of service and meticulous attention to detail in the comfort and convenience of a modern world-class resort shrouded in the history of the Home of Golf'. Reports do confirm its "amazing facilities" – which help make it "a very good place for families" – but, as you might expect, it's not found particularly characterful. / **Rooms:** 209 (of which 187 non smoking and 18 family rooms). **Facilities:** indoor pool; gym; spa; golf.*

ST AUSTELL, CORNWALL 1–4B

Carlyon Bay £178

PL25 3RD

🖰 www.carlyonbay.com ✉ info@carlyonbay.com

☎ (01726) 812304 📠 (01726) 814938

*"Easy access to the Eden Project" and "very good leisure facilities" (including a golf course) are among the best features of this "well-appointed" (and recently extended) hotel (part of the West Country's Brend group). Winter breaks, especially, offer "good value". / **Rooms:** 86 (of which some non smoking and 8 family rooms). **Facilities:** indoor pool; outdoor pool; spa; golf; tennis.*

ST DAVID'S, PEMBROKESHIRE 4–4A

Warpool Court £146 ☺

SA62 6BN

🖰 www.warpoolcourthotel.com

✉ warpool@enterprise.net

☎ (01437) 720300 📠 (01437) 720676

*A reputation as an "exceptional" culinary destination is (mainly) upheld by reports on this privately-owned hotel, whose tranquil situation on the Pembrokeshire coast gives some rooms spectacular views. Its "nice grounds" offer a good range of leisure facilities. / **Rooms:** 25 (of which 3 family rooms). **Facilities:** indoor pool; gym; tennis.*

ST IVES, CORNWALL 1–4A

Porthminster £136

TR26 2BN

🖰 www.porthminster-hotel.co.uk

✉ reception@porthminster-hotel.co.uk

☎ (01736) 795221 📠 (01736) 797043

*"A lovely, if old-fashioned, hotel overlooking the fabulous Porthminster Beach." A "very relaxing" establishment, its sub-tropical gardens have direct access to the sand, and it's notable for the consistency of the (relatively few) reports it inspires. Make sure you get a sea-side room, though – these are the ones which have the "fantastic views". / **Rooms:** 43 (of which some family rooms). **Facilities:** indoor pool; outdoor pool; gym; spa. **Details:** closed 2 wks in Jan.*

Tregenna Castle £156

St Ives TR26 2DE

🖰 www.tregenna-castle.co.uk

✉ tregenna-castle@demon.co.uk

☎ (01736) 795254 🖷 (01736) 796066

It strikes some as rather "busy and impersonal", but if you're looking for a good-value West Country leisure destination, this castellated hotel – in a wonderful position overlooking St Ives (and complete with its own golf course) – is worth bearing in mind. / **Rooms:** 84 (of which 7 family rooms). **Facilities:** indoor pool; outdoor pool; gym; spa; golf; tennis. **Details:** meals unavailable: L.

ST KEYNE, CORNWALL 1–3C

The Well House £115

PL14 4RN

🖰 www.wellhouse.co.uk ✉ enquiries@thewellhouse.co.uk

☎ (01579) 342001 🖷 (01579) 343891

"I'd go back any time" – a pretty typical report on this small Victorian country house hotel in the Looe Valley (and half an hour from the Eden Project), lauded for its "relaxing and stylish, but informal" atmosphere and its "excellent food and service". Children are accommodated "without fuss, but without diluting the adult atmosphere". / **Rooms:** 9 (of which 3 non smoking and 1 family room). **Facilities:** outdoor pool; tennis. **Details:** closed 2 wks in Jan; no Amex.

ST MARGARET'S AT CLIFFE, KENT 3–3D

Wallett's Court Country House £90

West Cliffe CT15 6EW

🖰 www.wallettscourt.com ✉ stay@wallettscourt.com

☎ (01304) 852424 🖷 (01304) 853430

Whether or not you make use of the "great spa", this "lovely", "old-fashioned", family-run country house hotel makes "a good place for a relaxing night before setting off for the ferry at Dover, four miles away". On most accounts, the cooking is "wonderful", too (though its high prices have come in for some criticism in recent years). / **Rooms:** 16 (of which 2 family rooms). **Facilities:** indoor pool; gym; spa; golf; tennis. **Details:** closed 24-26 Dec; meals unavailable: Mon L.

ST MAWES, CORNWALL   1–4B

Idle Rocks   £128

Harbourside TR2 5AN

⌂ www.idlerocks.co.uk   ✉ reception@idlerocks.co.uk

☎ 0800 243020   🖷 (01326) 270062

*An "idyllic" waterside location and "surprisingly good food" are themes which crop up in almost all reports concerning this "unassuming" hotel on the harbour. It generated an impressive volume of commentary. / **Rooms:** 27 (of which some non smoking and some family rooms).*

Tresanton   £245

27 Lower Castle Rd TR2 5DR

⌂ www.tresanton.com   ✉ info@tresanton.com

☎ (01326) 270055   🖷 (01326) 270053

*"What a PR machine they have, but it all turns out to be true!" – Olga Polizzi (née Forte) has quickly acquired a very high profile for this "wonderful away-from-it-all location", which most reporters agree "sets new standards" for Britain's seaside hotels. "A perfect location overlooking the bay", "lovely comfortable rooms" and "good" (if not remarkable) cooking are factors which combine to create many positive reporters. Downsides? – some rooms are "very small", and occasionally "off-hand" service can contribute to an atmosphere some find a touch "cliquey". / **Rooms:** 26 (of which 2 family rooms). **Details:** no Amex or Switch.*

STADDLEBRIDGE, NORTH YORKSHIRE   8–4C

McCoys   £100

DL6 3JB

⌂ www.mccoysatthetontine.co.uk

✉ enquiries@mccoysatthetontine.co.uk

☎ (01609) 882671   🖷 (01609) 882660

*"Great food and eccentric style" evoke nothing but praise for this long-established restaurant-with-room, which serves "good" dinners and "the best breakfasts". Being "just off the A19" makes it a boon for travellers. ("Thank heavens for double-glazing", too!) / **Rooms:** 6. **Details:** closed 25-26 Dec, 1 Jan.*

STADHAMPTON, OXFORDSHIRE   2–2D

Crazy Bear   £120

Bear Ln OX44 7UR

⌂ www.crazybearhotel.co.uk

✉ sales@crazybearhotel.co.uk

☎ (01865) 890714   🖷 (01865) 890714

*"Outrageously kinky décor" – "zebra-patterned carpets", and so on – helps win a warm reception from a relatively youthful fan club for this "vibrant", "outlandishly converted" pub (which incorporates a Thai restaurant and a British brasserie). Service seems the weakest link. / **Rooms:** 5 (of which 4 family rooms).*

STAMFORD, LINCOLNSHIRE   6–4A

The George   £105
St Martins PE9 2LB

🖰 www.georgehotelofstamford.com.
✉ reservations@georgehotelofstamford.com
☎ (01780) 750750   🖷 (01780) 750701

"A favourite that's full of character" – reporters applaud this
famous coaching inn at the heart of a gem of a Georgian town
(just off the A1) as a *"great British tradition"*. The *"lovely"* (but
not inexpensive) dining room makes a good spot for a traditional
blow-out (and in summer you can dine in the courtyard). There is
the odd complaint of *"noisy"* rooms. / **Rooms:** 47 (of which some non
smoking and some family rooms).

STANLEY, PERTH & KINROSS   9–3C

Ballathie House   £150
Kinclaven PH1 4QN

🖰 www.ballathiehousehotel.com
✉ email@ballathiehousehotel.com
☎ (01250) 883268   🖷 (01250) 883396

"Excellent fishing and shooting" are among the attractions which
set the tone at this *"relaxing"* country house hotel (which is
17th-century in origin and overlooks the River Tay). It's an
"efficiently-run" place, too, with *"great"* food to nourish guests
after a hard day's sport. / **Rooms:** 42.

STAPLEFORD, LEICESTERSHIRE   5–3D

Stapleford Park   £233
LE14 2EF

🖰 www.stapleford.co.uk   ✉ f&b@stapleford.co.uk
☎ (01572) 787522   🖷 (01572) 787651

"Marvellous service" and *"extremely comfortable rooms"* are two
features which particularly commend this *"totally luxurious"*
country house hotel to almost all reporters, and it boasts a *"great
spa"*, too. The cooking is no particular attraction, though, and –
though the décor is incredibly *"plush"* – the 'charm-factor' seems
to be good rather than outstanding. / **Rooms:** 52. **Facilities:** indoor pool;
gym; spa; golf; tennis.

STOCKBRIDGE, HAMPSHIRE 2–3D

Fifehead Manor £130

Middle Wallop SO20 8EG
☎ (01264) 781565   🖷 (01264) 781400

*This ancient (16th-century) house is a "small and intimate"
establishment, but a number of reports on it contain an element
of promise unfulfilled. Still, prices are reasonable, the cooking can
be "good" and fans proclaim this an "ideal place for escaping
from city life".* / **Rooms:** 17 (of which 3 family rooms).

STOCKCROSS, BERKSHIRE 2–2D

Vineyard £269

RG20 8JU
⌂ www.the-vineyard.co.uk   🖂 general@the-vineyard.co.uk
☎ (01635) 528770   🖷 (01635) 528398

*"A lack of personality" – bizarrely, as the place is entirely the
product of one man's dream (Sir Peter Michael) – is the theme of
many reports on this "chic" but "shiny" California-style restaurant-
with-rooms. Service is often "accommodating', though, and the
cooking – whose high aspirations are intermittently realised – is
twinned with an "unbelievable wine list".* / **Rooms:** 31 (of which all non
smoking). **Facilities:** indoor pool; gym; spa; golf.

STOCKPORT, GREATER MANCHESTER 5–2B

Hilton Moorside £120

Mudhurst Ln, Higher Disley SK12 2AP
⌂ www.hilton.co.uk
☎ (01663) 764151   🖷 (01663) 762794

*Hilton and "idyllic location" may not normally go together like a
horse and carriage, but this "comfortable" modern hotel is the
exception that proves the rule. It has a "great leisure club", too.*
/ **Rooms:** 98 (of which some non smoking and some family rooms).

STOKE POGES, BUCKINGHAMSHIRE 3–3A

Stoke Park £270

Park Rd SL2 4PG
⌂ www.stokepark.com   🖂 reception@stokeparkclub.com
☎ (01753) 717171

*Most reporters find this "very luxurious" and "very well equipped"
country club an "exquisite" place that's "perfect for a romantic
get-away". The restaurant is not a particular strong-point,
however, but the place's real downside is the obvious one –
"golfers everywhere".* / **Rooms:** 21 (of which some non smoking and some
family rooms). **Facilities:** indoor pool; gym; spa; golf; tennis.

STON EASTON, SOMERSET   2–3B

Ston Easton Park   £185

BA3 4DF

⌂ www.stoneaston.co.uk   ✉ admin@stoneaston.co.uk
☎ (01761) 241631   🖴 (01761) 241377

This "beautiful" Palladian house – in a "superb setting" (created
by famed 18th-century landscape gardner Humphrey Repton)
that now comes complete with helipad – is "elegantly furnished",
and makes an ideal place for indulging in plutocratic fantasies.
The dining room does nothing to let it down. / **Rooms:** 23 (of which all
non smoking and 6 family rooms). **Facilities:** tennis.

STONOR, OXFORDSHIRE   2–2D

Stonor Arms   £150

RG9 6HE

⌂ www.mystonor.com   ✉ info@mystonor.com
☎ (01491) 638866   🖴 (01491) 638863

This "friendly", privately-owned country hotel – in a pretty village
that's handy for Henley – is a "comfortable" place, ideal "for a
weekend away". / **Rooms:** 11 (of which some non smoking).

STOW ON THE WOLD, GLOUCESTERSHIRE   2–1C

Grapevine   £130

Sheep St GL54 1AU

⌂ www.vines.co.uk   ✉ enquiries@vines.co.uk
☎ (01451) 830344   🖴 (01451) 832278

This 17th-century hotel at the heart of this Cotswold market town
was rated as a good all-rounder by most reporters. It changed
hands during 2003, so changes may be afoot. / **Rooms:** 22 (of which
all non smoking and 8 family rooms).

STRAFFAN, CO. KILDARE, ROI   10–3D

Barberstown Castle   €220

⌂ www.barberstowncastle.ie   ✉ castleir@iol.ie
☎ +353-1 628 8157   🖴 +353-1 627 7027

This "historic" castle (evolved periodically since the 13th century)
is now an "excellent country house hotel". Reports are not
numerous, but they all speak in terms of "old-fashioned and
discreet service" (and "excellent food", too). / **Rooms:** 22 (of which
some non smoking). **Details:** no Switch.

K Club €395

🖰 www.kclub.ie   ✉ hotel@kclub.ie
☎ +353-1 601 7200   🖨 +353-1 601 7299

"Excellent hospitality and superb food" are the hallmarks of almost all reports on this *"fabulous country house hotel"*, which some reporters hail as *"probably the best five-star establishment in the British Isles"*. Small niggles include a beauty centre that can seem *"poorish"*, relatively speaking, and also *"members getting given priority over guests for the golf course"*. / **Rooms:** 69 (of which some family rooms). **Facilities:** indoor pool; gym; spa; golf.

STRATFORD UPON AVON, WARWICKSHIRE   2–1C

Alveston Manor £145

Clopton Bridge CV37 7HP
🖰 www.macdonaldhotels.co.uk
✉ sales.alvestonmanor@macdonaldhotels.co.uk
☎ 0870 400 8181   🖨 (01789) 414095

Under the same ownership as the Shakespeare (Macdonald Hotels), this traditional hotel based around a Tudor townhouse similarly offers a location that's "close to the centre". Reports here are rather more mixed, though, making it the less obvious choice of the two. / **Rooms:** 113 (of which 39 non smoking and some family rooms).

Ettington Park £150

Alderminster CV37 8BU
🖰 www.ettingtonpark.co.uk
✉ ettington@arcadianhotels.co.uk
☎ (01789) 450123   🖨 (01789) 450472

This Gothic mansion, set in 40 acres of gardens and parkland some six miles from the town, "may look haunted", but it is in fact generally held to be a "cosy and relaxing" destination, consistently winning favourable ratings for its charming ambience. / **Rooms:** 48 (of which 7 family rooms). **Facilities:** indoor pool. **Details:** meals unavailable: Mon-Sat L.

Falcon   £119

Chapel St CV37 6HA
⌂ www.corushotel.com   ✉ reservations@corushotel.com
☎ (01789) 279953   🖷 (01789) 414260

"A fine location in the centre of the town" is the particular plus of this 16th-century inn (which, remarkably, boasts *"a large car park"*). The *"old and very attractive"* rooms in the *"charming original section"* attract special praise – beware the rather *"anonymous"* new rooms, though and the rather *"ordinary"* restaurant of this Corus Hotels establishment. / **Rooms:** 84 *(of which some non smoking and some family rooms).*

Grosvenor   £110

12-14 Warwick Rd CV37 6YT
⌂ www.groshotelstratford.co.uk
✉ info@groshotelstratford.co.uk
☎ (01789) 269213   🖷 (01789) 266087

Admittedly some do find its location a touch "noisy", but this Georgian hotel comes extremely well (if not copiously) reported on for its *"lovely"* accommodation and *"nice"* food. / **Rooms:** 66 *(of which some non smoking and some family rooms).*

Shakespeare   £128

Chapel St CV37 6ER
⌂ www.macdonaldhotels.co.uk
✉ info@shakespearehotel.net
☎ 0870 400 8182   🖷 (01789) 415411

An *"excellent location"* (and *"its own car-park"*, too) makes this early 17th-century hotel a very *"convenient"* destination for theatre-goers, and one with *"lots of character"*. Service can be *"variable"*, but overall this is one of the better establishments in the Macdonald Hotels stable. / **Rooms:** 73 *(of which some non smoking and some family rooms).*

Stratford Manor   £165*   ☺

Warwick Rd CV37 0PY
⌂ www.marstonhotels.co.uk
✉ stratfordmanor@marstonhotels.com
☎ (01789) 739307   🖷 (01789) 731131

Some three miles from the town centre, this modern establishment, set in 21 acres of grounds, offers – as Marston Hotels usually do – some *"very good"* facilities. Despite a *"friendly"* welcome from staff, though, some reporters did find the style of the place a bit *"drab"*. *Prices are quoted on a DB&B basis. / **Rooms:** 104 *(of which some non smoking and some family rooms).*
Details: *meals unavailable: Mon-Sat L.*

Stratford Victoria   £90

Arden St CV37 6QQ
🖰 www.marstonhotels.com
✉ stratfordvictoria@marstonhotels.com
☎ (01789) 271000   🖨 (01789) 271001

*The neo-Victorian styling of this "modern" hotel, within walking
distance of the theatre, may perhaps grate on some visitors, but
this is an "efficient" establishment, of which reporters speak only
well. Unusually for a Marston hotel, facilities are on the
lightweight side. / **Rooms:** 102 (of which some non smoking and some family
rooms). **Facilities:** gym; spa.*

The Welcombe   £185

Warwick Rd CV37 0NR
🖰 www.welcombe.co.uk   ✉ sales@welcombe.co.uk
☎ (01789) 295252   🖨 (01789) 414666

*This 'Fine Individual Hotel' – well, that's what the group's called,
anyway – is a "pleasant" establishment, occupying a grand
Victorian house in a "great setting" of 150 acres, just outside the
town. An "excellent golf course" is a key attraction – sometimes
indifferent standards in the restaurant less so. / **Rooms:** 64.
Details: meals unavailable: Mon-Fri L.*

STUCKTON, HAMPSHIRE   2–3C

Three Lions   £65

Stuckton Rd SP6 2HF
🖰 www.thethreelionsrestaurant.co.uk
✉ thethreelionsrestaurant@btinternet.com
☎ (01425) 652489   🖨 (01425) 656144

*"Very welcoming hosts" and an "excellent restaurant" are key to
the success of this small, family-run establishment, converted from
a pub. Some reporters find it a "romantic" destination, and
facilities include a hot tub in the garden. / **Rooms:** 4 (of which all non
smoking). **Details:** closed end of January; meals unavailable: Sun D, Mon; no Amex.*

STURMINSTER NEWTON, DORSET   2–3B

Plumber Manor   £100
DT10 2AF

🖰 www.plumbermanor.com   ✉ book@plumbermanor.com

☎ (01258) 472507   🖷 (01258) 473370

"A good location and good food" – the restaurant is a mainstay of
the operation – commend this Jacobean country house hotel. It's
been owned and run by the same family for nearly three decades
(so one must assume that they've been doing something right),
but service that "tries too hard" takes the edge off the experience
for some reporters. / **Rooms:** 16 (of which all non smoking and 2 family
rooms). **Facilities:** tennis. **Details:** closed Feb; meals unavailable: Mon-Sat L.

SUTTON COLDFIELD, WEST MIDLANDS   5–4C

Moor Hall   £140
Moor Hall Drive, Four Oaks B75 6LN

🖰 www.moorhallhotel.co.uk   ✉ mail@moorhallhotel.co.uk

☎ (0121) 308 3751   🖷 (0121) 308 8974

This *"good country hotel"*, over 40 years in the same family
ownership, doesn't attract a huge amount of commentary, but it's
all positive. A *"superb location"* (in charming gardens, and
reasonably handy for the NEC, for example, about 15 miles
away) and *"excellent leisure facilities"* are features singled out for
praise. / **Rooms:** 82 (of which 53 non smoking and 5 family rooms).
Facilities: indoor pool; gym; spa.

New Hall   £107
Walmley Rd B76 1QX

🖰 www.newhallhotel.net

✉ reservations.newhall@thistle.co.uk

☎ (0121) 378 2442   🖷 (0121) 378 4637

This *"delightfully moated"* building claims to be the oldest manor
house in England still 'occupied' today, and its "traditional" virtues
make it a popular destination from nearby Brum. "It doesn't feel
like a chain hotel" (remarkably, as it's owned by Thistle), but there
is undoubtedly a hint of the "average" about some reports – no
'disasters', though, and this is certainly a useful place to know
about in an area with few competitors. / **Rooms:** 60 (of which some non
smoking and 3 family rooms). **Facilities:** indoor pool; gym; spa; golf; tennis.

SWAFFHAM, NORFOLK   6–4C

Stratton's   £100
4 Ash Close PE37 7NH

🖰 www.strattons-hotel.co.uk/   ✉ enquiries@strattons.co.uk

☎ (01760) 723845   🖷 (01760) 720458

"Luxurious" rooms help create a *"romantic setting"* at this slightly
quirky (and vaguely eco-friendly) establishment, which occupies a
Queen Anne villa just a minute's walk from the marketplace of
this charming town. Its restaurant – with an emphasis on organic
and local produce – is also an attraction. / **Rooms:** 8 (of which all non
smoking and some family rooms). **Details:** closed Christmas; meals unavailable: Sun.

SWANSEA, SWANSEA   1–1D

Marriott   £109

Maritime Quarter SA1 3SS
🖰 www.marriott.com
☎ (01792) 642020   🖨 (01792) 650345

"A good business hotel in a good location" (in a city-centre
marina). It's a "comfortable" place, and all reports acclaim its
"solid" performance. / **Rooms:** 122 (of which some non smoking and 24
family rooms). **Facilities:** indoor pool; gym; spa.

Patrick's   £95

638 Mumbles Rd SA3 4EA
🖰 www.patricks-restaurant.co.uk
☎ (01792) 360199   🖨 (01792) 369926

Tipped for its "fantastic food", this lively bistro has long been one
of the restaurants of most note in these parts. Its "great,
individual rooms" (with views over the Mumbles seafront) are also
well worth knowing about. / **Rooms:** 8 (of which all non smoking and some
family rooms). **Details:** closed Sep; meals unavailable: Sun D.

TAIN, HIGHLAND   9–2C

Glenmorangie House   £150

Cadboll, Fearn IV20 1XP
🖰 www.glenmorangie.com   🖃 relax@glenmorangieplc.co.uk
☎ (01862) 871671   🖨 (01862) 894371

"Excellent food and service" – and copious tots of the amber
nectar – make this "country house-style" establishment (run by
the eponymous distillery) an ideal location for a sybaritic retreat,
in the 'Glen of Tranquillity'. Service is "helpful, and very friendly",
too. / **Rooms:** 9. **Details:** min age for children: 12.

TALYBONT ON USK, BRECON, POWYS   2–1A

Usk Inn   £100*

Station Rd LD3 7JE
🖰 www.uskinn.com   🖃 stay@uskinn.co.uk
☎ (01874) 676251   🖨 (01874) 676392

This "very pleasant" village inn has a "great location". It's tipped
for its "very friendly and helpful" service, and its "great" cooking.
*Prices are quoted on a DB&B basis. / **Rooms:** 11 (of which all non
smoking and 1 family room). **Details:** closed Christmas.

TAPLOW, BERKSHIRE   3–3A

Cliveden House   £250

Berry HI SL6 0JF

🖰 www.clivedenhouse.co.uk   ✉ info@clivedenhouse.co.uk

☎ (01628) 668561   🖷 (01628) 661837

"Gosford Park-style" living doesn't come much better than at this "amazing" Italianate palazzo, which has a "fabulous" location at the heart of the Astors' former estate (now National Trust), by the Thames. Its "smart but pretentious" style doesn't suit everyone, but if you want to feel "like ancien-régime royalty" – most reporters do, it seems – this is just the place. / **Rooms:** 39 (of which some family rooms). **Facilities:** indoor pool; outdoor pool; gym; spa; tennis.

TARPORLEY, CHESHIRE   5–2B

Nunsmere Hall   £250*

Tarporley Rd, Oakmere CW8 2ES

🖰 www.nunsmere.co.uk   ✉ reservations@nunsmere.co.uk

☎ (01606) 889100   🖷 (01606) 889055

*This "quiet" Edwardian country house hotel has a "wonderful woodland setting" surrounded by a lake, the management is "hands on" and the accommodation includes some "great suites". With one reporter – who still rated the rooms and service highly – it still struck the wrong note: "phoney and expensive, like all these country house hotels". *Prices are quoted on a DB&B basis.* / **Rooms:** 36 (of which some non smoking and some family rooms).

Willington Hall   £110

Willington CW6 0NB

🖰 www.willingtonhall.co.uk

✉ enquiries@willingtonhall.co.uk

☎ (01829) 752231   🖷 (01829) 752596

"Magnificent views" are tipped as a special attraction of this small, family-run hotel, in a early 19th-century country house standing in some 30 acres of grounds. / **Rooms:** 10 (of which 2 family rooms). **Details:** closed 25-27 Dec; meals unavailable: Sun D.

TAUNTON, SOMERSET   2–3A

The Castle   £165

Castle Grn TA1 1NF
🖰 www.the-castle-hotel.com
✉ reception@the-castle-hotel.com
☎ (01823) 272671

"Personalised" service is a particular strength of this grand and "very well-run" traditional hotel, that's been in the ownership of the Chapman family for half a century now. Situated by the town's Norman castle, it's right in the centre of things (with some rooms rather "noisy" as a result). A "good" restaurant – which came to particular fame when Gary Rhodes was at the stoves – has long been a feature, though it's arguably a touch "expensive" for what it is nowadays. / **Rooms:** 44 (of which 36 non smoking and 2 family rooms).

TAYNUILT, ARGYLL & BUTE   9–3B

Ardanaiseig   £82

Kilchrenan PA35 1HE
🖰 www.ardanaiseig.com   ✉ info@ardanaiseig.com
☎ (01866) 833333   🖷 (01866) 833 222

A "simply stunning location", by Loch Awe, is not the least of the attractions of this "fadedly luxurious" country house hotel – its style may strike the occasional reporter as rather "eccentric", but the cooking is, by all accounts, "wonderful". / **Rooms:** 16 (of which some non smoking and some family rooms). **Details:** closed Jan.

TEFFONT EVIAS, WILTSHIRE   2–3C

Howards House   £145

SP3 5RJ
🖰 www.howardshousehotel.com
✉ enq@howardshousehotel.com
☎ (01722) 716392   🖷 (01722) 716820

This converted 17th-century house in a "very pretty village" is universally praised as "the archetypal, small, family-run hotel" which makes "a delightful destination for a weekend away". It has a "beautiful location", a "nice garden" and "friendly service", and offers "very good food". / **Rooms:** 9 (of which some family rooms). **Details:** closed Christmas.

TENBY, PEMBROKESHIRE   4–4B

Penally Abbey   £126

Penally SA70 7PY
🖰 www.penally-abbey.com
✉ penally.abbey@btinternet.com
☎ (01834) 843033   🖷 (01834) 844714

Reports are not numerous, but are consistently positive about this "very pleasant" and "welcoming" country house hotel, standing in five acres of gardens and woodlands, overlooking Tenby golf course and Carmarthen Bay. For families, "easy beach access" is a particular plus. / **Rooms:** 12 (of which some family rooms). **Facilities:** indoor pool.

TETBURY, GLOUCESTERSHIRE 2–2B

Calcot Manor £180
GL8 8YJ

⌂ www.calcotmanor.co.uk
✉ reception@calcotmanor.co.uk
☎ (01666) 890391   🖷 (01666) 890394

*This "nicely situated" country house hotel – some three miles
west of Tetbury – is "very good for families" (with "excellent
children's facilities"), but adults can also benefit from its "beautiful
location", its "very friendly and professional' service and its
"decent" dining possibilities. The place's all-round appeal was
enhanced in the summer of 2003 by the addition of a spa.*
/ **Rooms:** 28 (of which 10 family rooms). **Facilities:** indoor pool; outdoor pool; gym;
spa; tennis.

Close £100
Long St GL8 8AQ

⌂ www.theclosehotel.co.uk   ✉ 6429@greeneking.co.uk
☎ (01666) 502272   🖷 (01666) 504401

*This townhouse hotel, not far from the market square, can make
a "very pleasant choice". A tip from one reporter: "room quality
varies – it's worth paying the supplement for the luxury rooms
overlooking the closed garden".* / **Rooms:** 15 (of which all non smoking).

Snooty Fox £97
Market Pl GL8 8DD

⌂ www.snooty-fox.co.uk   ✉ res@snooty-fox.co.uk
☎ (01666) 502436   🖷 (01666) 503479

*"A comfortable place for a night if you're antique-hunting in
Tetbury", this "romantic" inn comes complete with an appropriate
dose of "olde-worlde charm".* / **Rooms:** 12 (of which 10 non smoking).

THAME, OXFORDSHIRE 2–2D

Old Trout £85
29-30 Lower High St OX9 2AA

⌂ www.theoldtrouthotel.co.uk
✉ info@theoldtrouthotel.co.uk
☎ (01844) 212146   🖷 (01844) 212614

*This stylishly-furnished 16th-century inn, in the heart of this
market town, is a "very characterful" destination, with "beautiful"
rooms. Some find dining here "pricey", but it's often thought to be
"excellent" too.* / **Rooms:** 7 (of which all non smoking).

Oxford Belfry £130

Milton Common OX9 2JW
⌂ www.marstonhotels.com
✉ oxfordbelfry@marstonhotels.co.uk
☎ (01844) 279381   🖶 (01844) 279624

This modern hotel, set around a brace of courtyards, is unusual in the extent to which it inspires completely contradictory reactions. Fans proclaim it a "delightful" place with "huge" rooms and "excellent food", whereas for doubters it's just "uninspiring" and "tacky". As is usual at Marston hotels, facilities, here including all-weather tennis courts, are something of a strength. / Rooms: 130 (of which 78 non smoking and some family rooms). Facilities: indoor pool; gym; tennis.

THIRSK, NORTH YORKSHIRE 8–4C

Crab Manor £150

Asenby Y07 3QL
⌂ www.crabandlobster.co.uk
✉ reservations@crabandlobster.co.uk
☎ (01845) 577286   🖶 (01845) 577109

Some say the rooms are "a little over-staged" (each themed around a grand hotel of note), but this "eccentric" establishment comes complete with "lots of charm", and a "beautiful setting", too. Its restaurant, which trades as the Crab & Lobster, has a big reputation, which most reporters say is deserved. / Rooms: 12. Facilities: golf.

THORNBURY, GLOUCESTERSHIRE 2–2B

Thornbury Castle £140

Castle St BS35 1HH
⌂ www.vonessenhotels.com
✉ info@thornburycastle.co.uk
☎ (01454) 281182   🖶 (01454) 416188

Those in search of Olde England need look no further than this "historic" and "extremely romantic" castle (once home to royalty, and now part of the very grand Von Essen group). It comes complete with "roaring fires" and "four-posters" – plans for a pool and spa are afoot. / Rooms: 25.

sign up for our next survey at www.hardens.com

TORQUAY, DEVON   1–3D

Imperial   £170*
Park Hill Rd TQ1 2DG
⌂ www.paramount-hotels.co.uk
✉ imperialtorquay@paramount-hotels.co.uk
☎ (01803) 294301   📠 (01803) 298293

*"Could be Nice's Baie des Anges", says one reporter extolling the
"stunning" views (from the main restaurant, and from many of
rooms) offered by this "comfortable" and "old-world" grande
dame of the English Riviera. "Lovely" accommodation (where you
awake to "the sound of waves from the sea below") and the
"helpful" staff help make this establishment probably the
strongest member of the Paramount group. *Prices are quoted on
a DB&B basis. / **Rooms:** 153. **Facilities:** indoor pool; outdoor pool; gym;
tennis.*

TROON, SOUTH AYRSHIRE   9–4B

Highgrove House   £175*
Old Loans Rd KA10 7HL
⌂ www.costley-hotels.co.uk
✉ highgrove@costleyhotels.co.uk
☎ (01292) 312511

*A couple of miles outside the town, this "chintzy" and "intimate"
hotel – part of a small local group, Costley Hotels – boasts fine
coastal views. It's tipped for its "very good and well sourced"
cooking (though even the reporter nominating it warns that the
dishes are "a tad cheffy"). *Prices are quoted on a DB&B basis.
/ **Rooms:** 40 (of which all non smoking).*

Marine   £130
Crosbie Rd KA10 6HE
⌂ www.paramount-hotels.co.uk
✉ marine@paramount-hotels.co.uk
☎ (01292) 314444   📠 (01292) 316922

*"Very friendly" staff are tipped as a key attraction of this Victorian
hotel, now a Paramount property. It overlooks the Royal course, so
"popularity with golfers" comes with the territory. / **Rooms:** 74 (of
which 5 family rooms). **Facilities:** indoor pool; gym; spa.*

TRURO, CORNWALL   1–4B

Hundred House   £148*
Ruan Highlanes TR2 5JR
⌂ www.hundredhousehotel.co.uk
✉ clarke@hundredhousehotel.co.uk
☎ (01872) 501336   📠 (01872) 501151

*This "olde worlde" "country house hotel and public house", dating
from the late 18th-century, is located in "superb countryside". It
has "many interesting features" and quite a high 'profile' as a
destination of character. *Prices are quoted on a DB&B basis.
/ **Rooms:** 10 (of which all non smoking). **Details:** closed Nov-Feb; meals
unavailable: Sun L; min age for children: 12.*

Lugger £80

Portloe TR2 5RD

🖰 www.luggerhotel.com   📠 emailoffice@luggerhotel.com
☎ (01872) 501322   🖷 (01872) 501691

"A good blend of 'cool' and comfort" wins praise for this recently renovated but "understated" old building (which was originally a 17th-century inn, but which has had a number of uses over the years). It benefits from an "amazing location" overlooking the harbour, and the food is "imaginative" too – best consumed "on the tiny terrace, watching the waves crashing in the tiny bay". Four new rooms were added in the summer of 2003. / Rooms: 21.
Facilities: *spa.* **Details:** *closed 2 wks in Jan; min age for children: 12.*

TUNBRIDGE WELLS, KENT   3–4B

Hotel du Vin and Bistro £89

Crescent Rd TN1 2LY

🖰 www.hotelduvin.com
📠 info@tunbridgewells.hotelduvin.com
☎ (01892) 526455   🖷 (01892) 512044

"Wonderful rooms" (with "great linen") are a stand-out attraction at this "friendly" and "elegant" outpost of the UK's best large boutique-hotel chain. It occupies an "interesting" grade II listed building, and maintains the formula of "wine-themed decoration", with a "buzzy restaurant" and an "exceptional" wine list.
/ Rooms: 36 (of which some non smoking).

Spa £115

Mount Ephraim TN4 8XJ

🖰 www.spahotel.co.uk   📠 reservations@spahotel.co.uk
☎ (01892) 520331   🖷 (01872) 510575

Reports on the elegant Georgian country outpost of the family which owns London's eponymous Goring Hotel do not achieve nearly the same consistency as its metropolitan twin. It does benefit from 14 acres of gardens, though and there are some "very nice" rooms. / Rooms: 69 (of which some family rooms).
Facilities: *indoor pool; gym; spa; tennis.*

TURNBERRY, SOUTH AYRSHIRE   7–1A

The Westin Turnberry Resort £150

The Westin KA26 9LT

🏠 www.westin.com/turnberry   ✉ turnberry@westin.com

☎ (01655) 331000   🖨 (01655) 331706

"A stunning hotel, overlooking the Irish Sea", where most reporters speak of "outstanding" experiences. "Wonderful views" are a special highlight as are the "fabulous golf, spa, and sports facilities" (including guaranteed tee times on two Open Championship golf courses) and, on most accounts, "fabulous food". All this, plus reports of service for whom "nothing is too much trouble", and a "child-friendly" attitude, too! / **Rooms:** 221 (of which 25 non smoking and 85 family rooms). **Facilities:** indoor pool; gym; spa; golf; tennis. **Details:** closed Christmas.

TYNEMOUTH, TYNE & WEAR   8–2B

Grand £84

Grand Parade NE30 4ER

🏠 www.grand-hotel.demon.co.uk

✉ info@grand-hotel.demon.co.uk

☎ (0191) 293 6666   🖨 (0191) 293 6665

This "lovely old Victorian hotel" has "lots of character" and – with its "wonderful seafront location" – it's found "romantic" by some reporters. It offers "great views", "good food" and "good value". Across the road, there's "a good beach". / **Rooms:** 45 (of which some non smoking and some family rooms). **Details:** meals unavailable: Sun D.

UCKFIELD, EAST SUSSEX   3–4B

Buxted Park £135

Buxted TN22 4AY

🏠 www.arcadianhotels.co.uk   ✉ bph@arcadianhotels.co.uk

☎ (01825) 732711   🖨 (01825) 732770

Set in 312 acres of charming countryside, complete with fallow deer, this Georgian mansion is marketed as 'everything a country house should be'. Perhaps its owner, Arcadian, might consider a bit of an investment programme? – service can be iffy and practically all reporters felt they need to "spend some money on the rooms!" / **Rooms:** 44 (of which some non smoking).

ULLSWATER, CUMBRIA   7–3D

Inn on the Lake £96

CA11 0PE

🏠 www.innonthelakeullswater.co.uk

✉ info@innonthelakeullswater.co.uk

☎ (01768) 482444   🖨 (01768) 482303

This long-established hotel has a "prime position", with a lake frontage onto Ullswater and impressive views of the fells. Reports, however, are rather up-and-down. / **Rooms:** 46 (of which some non smoking and some family rooms). **Facilities:** gym; spa; golf. **Details:** meals unavailable: Sun L.

sign up for our next survey at www.hardens.com

Sharrow Bay £320*

CA10 2LZ

🖰 www.sharrow-bay.com ✉ enquiries@sharrow-bay.com

☎ (01768) 486301 📠 (01768) 486349

This "stunningly-located" country house hotel (established by Francis Coulson and Brian Sack in 1948, and often cited as the original country house hotel), remains a living memorial to their dream. As ever, "the only criticism would be that the food is sometimes a little too rich and the antiques a touch too rococo", but for its (fairly mature) market, this remains a "supremely comfortable" and "friendly" destination and "a wonderful place to relax". *Prices are quoted on a DB&B basis. / Rooms: 26. Details: closed Mid Dec-end of Feb; min age for children: 13.

ULVERSTON, CUMBRIA   7–4D

Bay Horse £165*

Canal Foot LA12 9EL

🖰 www.thebayhorsehotel.co.uk

✉ reservations@thebayhorsehotel.co.uk

☎ (01229) 583972

This long-established and traditionally-styed restaurant-with-rooms – the price is quoted on a *DB&B basis – has a "lovely" setting, with panoramic views of the Leven estuary. All aspects of the operation show "good attention to detail", and service is particularly praised. / Rooms: 9. Details: min age for children: 12.

UPPER SLAUGHTER, GLOUCESTERSHIRE   2–1C

Lords of the Manor £155 ☺

GL54 2JD

🖰 www.lordsofthemanor.com

✉ lordsofthemanor@btinternet.com

☎ (01451) 820243 📠 (01451) 820696

A "beautiful setting" in a story book Cotswold village contributes much to the "romantic" charms of this "beautifully appointed" country house hotel. A prime attraction has long been its gastronomic reputation (though a new chef took over during the survey year, making an assessment of the current régime rather problematic). Facilities are limited, and critics can find the place "expensive for what it is". / Rooms: 27.

UPPINGHAM, RUTLAND   5–4D

The Lake Isle £70

16 High Street East LE15 9PZ

🖰 www.lakeislehotel.com ✉ info@lakeislehotel.com

☎ (01572) 822951 📠 (01572) 824400

"Comfortable accommodation" and "very welcoming staff" make this small hotel (almost a restaurant-with-rooms) a tipped location in this attractive small town. The cooking has a strong reputation locally. / Rooms: 13 (of which some non smoking and 2 family rooms). Details: meals unavailable: Mon L.

UPTON ST LEONARDS, GLOUCESTERSHIRE 2–1B

Hatton Court £100
Upton Hill GL4 8DE
🖰 www.hatton-hotels.co.uk ✉ res@hatton-court.co.uk
☎ (01452) 617412 🖷 (01452) 612945
With occasional misgivings, reporters are generally pretty 'up' on this "charming" traditional hotel, which enjoys dramatic views across to the Malvern Hills. / **Rooms:** 45 (of which 10 non smoking). **Facilities:** gym.

VENTNOR, ISLE OF WIGHT 2–4D

Hillside £54
Mitchell Av PO38 1DR
🖰 www.wight-hotels.co.uk/hillside.html
✉ hillside@wight-hotels.co.uk
☎ (01983) 852271 🖷 (01983) 855310
A small family-run hotel that's tipped as a "very friendly and helpful" destination, with a "delightful" setting and "excellent food". / **Rooms:** 11 (of which all non smoking and 1 family room). **Details:** no Amex; min age for children: 5.

Royal £115
Belgrave Rd PO38 1JJ
🖰 www.royalhoteliow.co.uk ✉ royalhotel@zetnet.co.uk
☎ (01983) 852186 🖷 (01983) 855395

"Consistently outstanding food and service" help win nothing but positive reviews for this "beautiful" and "welcoming" seaside hotel. Building started in 1832, though, and some of the accommodation is rather "quirky". / **Rooms:** 55 (of which all non smoking and 7 family rooms). **Facilities:** outdoor pool. **Details:** closed 1st 2wks in Jan; meals unavailable: Mon-Sat L.

VERYAN, CORNWALL   1–4B

The Nare   £160

Carne Beach TR2 5PF
⌂ www.narehotel.co.uk   ✉ office@narehotel.co.uk
☎ (01872) 501111   🖨 (01872) 501856

"An outstanding hotel, with an even more outstanding view" – this
"unpretentious" '20s establishment in an "idyllic" position
overlooking the beach wins the highest praise. Reporters – noting
its "every comfort", "superb" service and commendable food –
say it is "a marvellous family holiday hotel", even though the
average age of guests can seem "rather high". / **Rooms:** 39 (of which
4 family rooms). **Facilities:** indoor pool; outdoor pool; gym; spa; tennis. **Details:** no
Amex or Switch.

VIRGINSTOW, DEVON   1–3C

Percy's   £230*

Coombeshead Estate EX21 5EA
⌂ www.percys.co.uk   ✉ info@percys.co.uk
☎ (01409) 211236   🖨 (01409) 211460
"Very good for an undisturbed and relaxing holiday" – this
"delightful small hotel", set in 130 acres, promises a child-free,
smoke-free environment. Food is a feature both in the restaurant
(*prices are quoted on a DB&B basis) and in the recently-
launched chefs' academy. / **Rooms:** 8 (of which all non smoking).
Details: min age for children: 12.

WAKEFIELD, WEST YORKSHIRE   5–1C

Waterton Park   £130

Walton Hall, Walton WF2 6PW
⌂ www.watertonparkhotel.co.uk
✉ watertonpark@bestwestern.co.uk
☎ (01924) 257911   🖨 (01924) 240082
"An excellent location for a wedding or romantic weekend" – this
"beautiful" hotel, reached by footbridge, has "a beautiful setting
on an island in the middle of a lake". Back on the mainland, there
are extensive modern leisure facilities, and a golf course.
/ **Rooms:** 61 (of which 20 non smoking and 4 family rooms). **Facilities:** indoor
pool; gym; spa; golf.

WARE, HERTFORDSHIRE   3–2B

Hanbury Manor   £138
SG12 0SD
⌂ www.marriott.com
☎ 0870 400 7222   🖷 0870 400 7322
*This famous country house hotel, now a prestige property in the Marriott portfolio, gathers a fair amount of support as an "expensive but nice" destination. For a lot of reporters, though, it's just "too much of a money-making operation to have any real charm", and reports on the service (and the cooking) are less consistent than one might hope. / **Rooms:** 161 (of which 45 non smoking and 10 family rooms). **Facilities:** indoor pool; spa; golf.*

WAREHAM, DORSET   2–4C

Priory   £165
Church Grn BH20 4ND
⌂ www.theprioryhotel.co.uk
✉ reception@theprioryhotel.co.uk
☎ (01929) 551666   🖷 (01929) 554519

*They claim a 1000-year history of hospitality at this "characterful" hotel (in a former priory), which is "delightfully situated" in "beautiful gardens" on the bank of the River Frome. The establishment is generally hailed as a "good all-rounder" – with the "very romantic rooms in the boathouse" winning a particular thumbs-up. / **Rooms:** 18. **Details:** no Amex; min age for children: 8.*

WARMINSTER, WILTSHIRE   2–3B

Bishopstrow House   £160
BA12 9HH
⌂ www.bishopstrow.co.uk   ✉ enquiries@bishopstrow.co.uk
☎ (01985) 212312   🖷 (01985) 216769
*"Great facilities" – including two pools, and a "cool" spa – help make this "classic country house hotel" a popular destination, and for most reporters, it retains an air "of unhurried hospitality" (including to kids). It doesn't please everyone, though, with too many complaints in particular of "variable" (or even plain "poor") accommodation. / **Rooms:** 32 (of which 2 family rooms). **Facilities:** indoor pool; outdoor pool; gym; spa; tennis.*

Sportsman's Arms   £90

HG3 5PP

✉ sportsmans@wath-in-nidderdale.com

☎ (01423) 711306   🖷 (01423) 712524

"A fantastic location and a consistent standard of cooking" have made this Dales inn – under the same husband-and-wife ownership for a quarter of a century – a destination of some renown. It is – on all accounts – "a wonderful place". / **Rooms:** 11 (of which all non smoking). **Details:** closed Christmas; no Amex or Switch.

Crown   £55

The Buttlands NR23 1EX

🖱 www.thecrownhotelwells.co.uk

✉ reception@thecrownhotel.co.uk

☎ (01328) 710209   🖷 (01328) 711432

"They've "successfully updated without losing the plot", say fans of the relaunch of this former coaching inn ("on the outskirts of the town, by a green"), who praise "attractive modern décor" and "excellent food" (the new patron was formerly head chef of the Crown at Southwold). There are critics, though, who tend to find a "lack of charm". / **Rooms:** 11 (of which 2 family rooms). **Details:** no Amex.

Weston Manor   £121

Weston on the Green OX25 3QL

🖱 www.westonmanor.co.uk

✉ reception@westonmanor.co.uk

☎ (01869) 350621   🖷 (01869) 350901

"A bit tired, but loads of character" – that's the pretty much unanimous tone of commentary on this "beautifully-located" country house. Its focus on conferences and weddings, however, led one reporter to describe it as a "function-hotel". / **Rooms:** 35 (of which 2 family rooms). **Facilities:** outdoor pool.

WESTPORT, CO. MAYO, *ROI*   10–2B

Knockranny   €230

Knockranny
🖱 www.khh.ie   ✉ info@khh.ie
☎ +353-98 28600   🖨 +353-98 28611

*A "very nice" place, with "wonderful" service, "gorgeous" views
over the town and a "relaxed atmosphere" – that's the tenor of
feedback on this privately-owned, modern hotel, purpose-built in a
Victorian style. "Good all-in deals, if you stay for two nights or
more" are especially recommended.* / **Rooms:** 54 (of which 4 non
smoking).

WHITBY, NORTH YORKSHIRE   8–3D

The White Horse
& Griffin   £58

Church St YO22 4BH
🖱 www.whitehorseandgriffin.co.uk
✉ info@whitehorseandgriffin.co.uk
☎ (01947) 604857
*For its fans, this "lovely old coaching inn" (17th century) has been
"saved from dereliction but not at the expensive of character",
and its "lovely ambience" is hailed by most reporters. The cooking
can be an attraction in itself.* / **Rooms:** 20 (of which all non smoking and 2
family rooms). **Details:** no Amex.

WHITEBROOK, MONMOUTHSHIRE 2–2B

Crown £90

NP25 4TX
🖰 www.crownatwhitebrook.co.uk
✉ crown@whitebrook.demon.co.uk
☎ (01600) 860254 🖷 (01600) 860607

It's as an "excellent restaurant" that this "remote" Wye Valley
establishment, is best-known. It also provides rooms, however, and
the staff offer a "warm welcome". / **Rooms:** 10 (of which all non
smoking). **Details:** closed Christmas & New Year; meals unavailable: Mon L; min
age for children: 12.

WHITSTABLE, KENT 3–3C

Continental £75

29 Beach Walk CT5 2BP
🖰 www.hotelcontinental.co.uk
✉ reservations@hotelcontinental.co.uk
☎ (01227) 280280 🖷 (01227) 280257

This "trendy" Art Deco hotel is associated with the Whitstable
Oyster Fishery and has become a fashionable destination for
visitors from the Smoke. It offers some "excellent sea views", but
some rooms are "very small". / **Rooms:** 23 (of which all non smoking and
3 family rooms).

WILMINGTON, KENT   3–3B

Rowhill Grange   £125
DA2 7QH
🖰 www.alexanderhotels.co.uk
✉ admin@rowhillgrange.com
☎ (01322) 615136   🖷 (01322) 615137

*The "excellent spa and beauty facilities" are – almost all
reporters agree – the particular attraction of this "nice" part-
thatched country house hotel, handily located for the metropolis.
Its accommodation is also well rated, though support for other
aspects of the operation (part of a local chain of 'character'
establishments called Alexander Hotels) was slightly up-and-down.
/ Rooms: 38. Facilities: gym; spa.*

WIMBORNE MINSTER, DORSET   2–4C

Beechleas   £79
17 Poole Rd BH21 1QA
🖰 www.beechleas.com   ✉ information@beechleas.com
☎ (01202) 841684   🖷 (01202) 849344

*This "immaculate" small hotel occupies a very attractive town-
centre Georgian house (and coach house). The location can make
some rooms "noisy", but otherwise the reports, though modest in
number, are a hymn of praise to its "well-appointed"
accommodation and "excellent" restaurant. / Rooms: 9 (of which all
non smoking and 2 family rooms). Details: closed Christmas; meals unavailable: L.*

WINCANTON, SOMERSET   2–3B

Holbrook House   £135
BA9 8BS
🖰 www.holbrookhouse.co.uk
✉ reception@holbrookhouse.co.uk
☎ (01963) 32377   🖷 (01963) 32681

*A paucity of feedback may have prevented this family-owned
Georgian country house hotel (which has extensive spa facilities),
from receiving from us quite the degree of recognition it may
deserve. (One reporter voted in "the nicest hotel I have ever
stayed in".) / Rooms: 21 (of which some non smoking and some family rooms).
Facilities: indoor pool; outdoor pool; gym; spa.*

WINCHCOMBE, GLOUCESTERSHIRE   2–1C

Wesley House   £75
High St GL54 5LJ
🖰 www.wesleyhouse.co.uk
✉ enquiries@wesleyhouse.co.uk
☎ (01242) 602366

*Most reporters speak only well of this half-timbered 15th-century
Cotswold inn – a "magical" place, where "interesting and good-
value" cooking contributes to a high level of overall contentment.
/ Rooms: 6. Details: meals unavailable: Sun D.*

Hotel du Vin and Bistro £105

Southgate St SO23 9EF
🖰 www.hotelduvin.com
📧 info@winchesterhotelduvin.com
☎ (01962) 841414   📠 (01962) 842458

"Bags of charm" and a "great relaxed feel" are the cornerstone to the appeal of this "lovely country house property in town" – the original of this increasingly well-known boutique chain. The rooms are "beautifully set out", there's a cute courtyard, and the centrepiece is the bistro, roundly praised for its "terrific atmosphere and wonderful staff" (plus, of course, an "amazing" wine list). / **Rooms:** 23 (of which some non smoking and some family rooms).

Lainston House £155

Sparsholt SO21 2LT
🖰 www.exclusivehotels.co.uk
📧 enquiries@lainstonhouse.com
☎ (01962) 863588   📠 (01962) 776672

"Fantastic bedrooms" ("ask for one in the main building") are a highlight at this "peaceful' and "immaculate" William & Mary country house hotel (now an 'Exclusive Hotels' property), which generated a high volume of survey commentary. Most reports are to the effect that it's "a beautiful place in a wonderful location" – even for some fans, though, the restaurant is "far too expensive for its quality". / **Rooms:** 50 (of which 4 family rooms). **Facilities:** gym; tennis.

Wykeham Arms £90

75 Kingsgate St SO23 9PE
🖰 www.georgegirl.co.uk
📧 doreen@wykehamarms.fsnet.co.uk
☎ (01962) 853834   📠 (01962) 854411

"Full of charm, and very close to the cathedral", this "charmingly gentrified pub" in the heart of the city has long had a name for its "great atmosphere and its delicious food" (and perhaps more particularly its wine list). "Everything about the place is perfect, including the price", says one of its many supporters. / **Rooms:** 14 (of which all non smoking). **Details:** closed Christmas; min age for children: 14.

Gilpin Lodge Country House   £170

Crook Rd LA23 3NE
 www.gilpin-lodge.co.uk   ☞ hotel@gilpinlodge.com
☎ (01539) 488818   🖨 (01539) 488058

For "real pampering", reporters find it difficult to beat this "stylish" and "comfortable" Edwardian house in 20 acres, which offers, on almost all reports, a "simply superb" experience. "Very attentive and friendly" service and the "outstanding" restaurant are among the highlights (with "excellent" breakfasts given a particular thumbs-up). / **Rooms:** 14 (of which all non smoking). **Details:** min age for children: 7.

Holbeck Ghyll   £200*

Holbeck Ln LA23 1LU
 www.holbeckghyll.com   ☞ stay@holbeckghyll.com
☎ (01539) 432375   🖨 (01539) 434743

This "charming, quiet country house hotel" (originally a hunting lodge), where many rooms have "views over the lake", is unanimously hailed by reporters as "utterly stupendous". Feedback is so consistent it's almost invidious to single out individual aspects for praise, but "fantastic" service and a truly "excellent" restaurant (prices are quoted *DB&B) are key factors in making the place "ideal for a relaxing break in beautiful countryside". / **Rooms:** 21 (of which 6 non smoking and 3 family rooms). **Facilities:** gym; spa; tennis.

Low Wood   £146

LA23 1LP
🖱 www.elh.co.uk/hotels/lowwood
✉ owwood@elhmail.co.uk
☎ (01539) 433338   🖨 (01539) 434072

"Very good facilities" – including a gym and swimming pool that's popular with the locals, too – distinguish this "charming, old-fashioned" hotel, by the lakeside road. For character and a view, older rooms are preferred – the small rooms in the new annexe are quieter. / **Rooms:** 111 (of which some non smoking and some family rooms). **Facilities:** indoor pool; gym.

Samling   £145

Ambleside Rd LA23 1LR
🖱 www.thesamling.com   ✉ info@thesamling.com
☎ (01539) 431922   🖨 (01539) 430400

"An escape-from-reality experience", offering "peace, tranquility, everything". It only started out as an hotel in 2002, but this "beautifully-located" hillside venture ('emphatically not a country house hotel', according to the website) wins the highest praise from those reporters who have truffled it out. "It's really luxurious, and the food is wonderful". / **Rooms:** 10. **Details:** meals unavailable: L.

WINDSOR, WINDSOR & MAIDENHEAD   3–3A

Castle   £118

High Street SL4 1LJ
🖱 www.macdonaldhotels.co.uk
✉ castle@macdonald-hotels.co.uk
☎ 0870 400 8300   🖨 (01753) 830244

This "time-warp" Macdonald hotel is cherished by some reporters for its "amazingly ungroovy décor", its "nice cocktail bar" and its "fantastic position" by the (other) Windsor Castle. Even fans, though, can come to the unsurprising conclusion that "it's a bit overpriced, due to its location". / **Rooms:** 111 (of which 49 non smoking and 10 family rooms).

Oakley Court   £184

Windsor Rd SL4 5UR
🖱 www.moathousehotels.com
✉ reservations.oakleycourt@moathousehotels.com
☎ (01753) 609988   🖨 (01628) 637011

"A pretty setting on the Thames" and "wonderful grounds" distinguish this – potentially at least – "superb" Edwardian hotel, which in particular makes an "excellent" summer destination. (There are one or two reports, however, which suggest that standards at this Moat House establishment "could use a bit more professionalism".) / **Rooms:** 118 (of which 53 non smoking and 15 family rooms). **Facilities:** indoor pool; gym; spa; golf; tennis.

Sir Christopher Wren's House £150

Thames St SL4 1PX
🖰 www.sirchristopherwren.co.uk
✉ info@grandheritage.demon.co.uk
☎ (01753) 861354 🖶 (01753) 860172

*Once the home of the architect, this "romantic" hotel is an attractive place on the corner of Eton Bridge, with some "lovely" accommodation – the "fantastic four-poster room, overlooking the river" is particularly praised. / **Rooms:** 92 (of which some non smoking and some family rooms).*

WINTERINGHAM, NORTH LINCOLNSHIRE 5–1D

Winteringham Fields £115

DN15 9PF
🖰 www.winteringhamfields.com ✉ wintfields@aol.com
☎ (01724) 733096 🖶 (01724) 733898

*Annie and Germain Schwab have mercifully reversed their decision to close this "fantastic restaurant-with-rooms" (which was the best place to eat in the UK, according to our 2003 restaurant survey). Housed in a 16th-century manor-house, it boasts little in the way of 'facilities', but is still hailed as "a great place to stay".
/ **Rooms:** 10 (of which all non smoking). **Details:** meals unavailable: Sun & Mon.*

WISHAW, WARWICKSHIRE 5–4C

De Vere Belfry £189

B76 9PR
🖰 www.devereonline.co.uk ✉ enquiries@thebelfry.com
☎ 0870 900 0066 🖶 (01675) 470256

*Although this "pseudo-luxurious" golf, conference and leisure hotel – the flagship of the De Vere group – attracted a good deal of survey commentary, it could be summarised in five words: "OK, if you like golf". Otherwise there was a good deal of opinion to the effect that it "lacks atmosphere" and "is a bit disappointing".
/ **Rooms:** 324 (of which 100 non smoking and 20 family rooms). **Facilities:** indoor pool; gym; spa; golf; tennis.*

WITNEY, OXFORDSHIRE 2–2C

Witney £54

7 Church Green OX28 4AZ
🖰 www.thewitneyhotel.co.uk
✉ reservation@thewitneyhotel.co.uk
☎ (01993) 702137 🖶 (01993) 705337

*This family-owned establishment has a "lovely location on a picturesque green". It's tipped for its "charmingly decorated rooms, with excellent facilities" and for its "great breakfasts".
/ **Rooms:** 10.*

WOODBRIDGE, SUFFOLK   3–1D

Seckford Hall   £120

IP13 6NU

🖱 www.seckford.co.uk   ✉ reception@seckford.co.uk

☎ (01394) 385678

"Well appointed, interesting, comfortable" – this country house hotel (under the same ownership for half a century) occupies a "fantastic" Tudor building, and comes generally well-recommended, especially "for a weekend break, with golf and so on". The occasional doubter, while agreeing that the place "looks wonderful", judges overall standards "unexceptional". / **Rooms:** 32. **Facilities:** indoor pool; gym; spa; golf. **Details:** closed 25 Dec; meals unavailable: Mon L.

WOODSTOCK, OXFORDSHIRE   2–1D

Feathers   £225

Market St OX20 1SX

🖱 www.feathers.co.uk   ✉ enquiries@feathers.co.uk

☎ (01993) 812291   🖨 (01993) 813158

"An amazing location near Blenheim" – practically by the gates of the estate – is part of the appeal that has won much fame for this "lovely 'character' hotel", whose "friendly and caring" service is often applauded. Many view the restaurant as an attraction in itself, and a "lovely courtyard for drinking and simple meals" is a feature. Some rooms are "small", though and even some fans note that the place is "not cheap". / **Rooms:** 20 (of which 1 non smoking and 2 family rooms).

WOOLACOMBE, DEVON   1–2C

Watersmeet   £83*

Mortehoe EX34 7EB

🖱 www.watersmeethotel.co.uk

✉ info@watersmeethotel.co.uk

☎ (01271) 870333   🖨 (01271) 870890

*A grand Edwardian residence in an "excellent" location, right on the beach, provides the setting for this "lovely" seaside hotel – all rooms have views. It's notable for the consistently positive reports it attracts (including on the food front). *Prices are quoted on a DB&B basis.* / **Rooms:** 23 (of which no non smoking and 3 family rooms). **Facilities:** indoor pool; outdoor pool; tennis. **Details:** closed Jan.

WORCESTER, WORCESTERSHIRE   2–1B

Elms   £140

Abberley WR6 6AT

🖱 www.theelmshotel.com   ✉ elmshotel@ukonline.co.uk

☎ (01299) 896666   🖨 (01299) 896804

The modest name doesn't really prepare you for the grandeur of this imposing Queen Anne house (which was designed by an assistant to Christopher Wren). Part of the Small Luxury Hotels consortium, it's tipped as a "comfortable, high-class country house hotel". / **Rooms:** 21 (of which some non smoking and 1 family room). **Facilities:** tennis.

WOTTON-UNDER-EDGE, GLOUCESTERSHIRE   2–2B

Tortworth Court   £172

Tortworth GL12 8HH

🖥 www.four-pillars.co.uk   ✉ tortworth@four-pillars.co.uk

☎ (01454) 263000   🖨 (01454) 263001

*A neo-Gothic Victorian mansion formed the starting point of this large Cotswold establishment which boasts ample leisure and conference facilities. Part of the Four Pillars chain, it's tipped by one reporter as a "wonderful" destination. / **Rooms:** 189 (of which some non smoking and some family rooms). **Facilities:** indoor pool; gym. **Details:** closed Christmas.*

WYCH CROSS, EAST SUSSEX   3–4B

Ashdown Park   £165

RH18 5JR

🖥 www.ashdownpark.com

✉ reception@ashdownpark.com

☎ (01342) 824988   🖨 (01342) 826206

*"A great setting" – in a couple of hundred acres of gardens and woodland in the Ashdown Forest, and including an 18-hole golf course – contributes much to the charm of this "luxurious and well-appointed" Victorian country house hotel. On the downside, the style of this Elite group property is somewhat "businessy", and service can be rather "slow". / **Rooms:** 107 (of which some family rooms). **Facilities:** golf.*

YARM, STOCKTON ON TEES   8–3C

Crathorne Hall   £103

Crathorne TS15 0AR

🖥 www.arcadianhotels.co.uk   ✉ chh@arcadianhotels.co.uk

☎ (01642) 700398   🖨 (01642) 700814

*This "impressive" country house (apparently England's largest such legacy from Edwardian times) is nowadays a "very high-quality hotel" (run by Arcadian Hotels) whose "lovely" position and "extensive" grounds help make it a "charming" and "relaxing" destination. "Welcoming" staff are a particular plus, and the "superb, if expensive" dining room also has quite a name. There are extensive conference facilities. / **Rooms:** 37 (of which some non smoking and 2 family rooms).*

Judges at Kirklevington Hall   £159

Kirklevington TS15 9LW

🖥 www.judgeshotel.co.uk   ✉ enquiries@judgeshotel.co.uk

☎ (01642) 789000   🖨 (01642) 787692

*This "beautiful" Victorian country house (used in former years as judges' lodgings) enjoys a "lovely" setting in 22 acres of "well-tended" gardens", and offers some "superb" accommodation. Service is "friendly and welcoming" and the restaurant generally well received. / **Rooms:** 21 (of which 4 family rooms). **Facilities:** gym.*

YATTENDON, BERKSHIRE   2–2D

Royal Oak   £130
The Square RG18 0UG
🖱 www.corushotels.com   ✉ royaloak@corushotels.com
☎ (01635) 201325   🖷 (01635) 201926
Though only a dozen miles from Reading, this famous old inn is at the heart of a village "in the middle of beautiful countryside", and wins praise for its "elegant" accommodation and often "very pleasant" service. Some reporters, though, say it misses its potential and "could use updating". / Rooms: 5.

YORK, CITY OF YORK   5–1D

The Grange   £130   ☺
1 Clifton YO30 6AA
🖱 www.grangehotel.co.uk   ✉ info@grangehotel.co.uk
☎ (01904) 6447   🖷 (01904) 612453
"Georgian charm" helped win recommendations for this "friendly" and "relaxed" establishment, whose attractions include "individually decorated rooms", "a bistro serving good, reasonably priced food" and "good weekend deals". / Rooms: 30 (of which 5 family rooms).

Lady Anne Middleton's   £90   ☺
Skeldergate YO1 6DS
🖱 www.ladyannes.co.uk   ✉ bookings@ladyannes.co.uk
☎ 0800 169 9793   🖷 (01904) 613043
A jumble of interesting historic buildings and a courtyard garden provides the setting for this "pleasant" hotel, which is particularly handily located for the tourist attractions of the city. / Rooms: 52 (of which some non smoking and some family rooms). Facilities: gym.

Middlethorpe Hall   £160
Bishopthorpe Rd YO23 2GB
🖱 www.middlethorpe.com   ✉ info@middlethorpe.com
☎ (01904) 641241
"Fantastic" accommodation is part of the formula which wins some very high praise for this superbly located country house, in a 200-acre estate right on the fringe of the city. Even fans of this 'Historic House Hotels' establishment are prone to noting how "expensive" it is, though, and a vociferous minority decries it as "really overpriced, and very stuffy". / Rooms: 30 (of which 4 non smoking). Facilities: indoor pool; gym; spa. Details: min age for children: 8.

Moat House £150

North St YO1 1JF
⌂ www.moathousehotels.com
✉ revyrk@queensmoat.co.uk
☎ (01904) 459988   🖷 (01904) 641793

*"A good central location, overlooking the Minster" – and enhanced by "views over the river" – makes this a "typical conference hotel", but it's of some interest in a city without a huge number of competing attractions. / **Rooms:** 200 (of which some non smoking and some family rooms). **Facilities:** gym; spa.*

Monk Bar £135

St Morris Rd, Monkbar YO31 7JA
⌂ www.monkbarhotel.co.uk   ✉ sales@monkbarhotel.co.uk
☎ (01904) 638086   🖷 (01904) 629195

*A handy location "just outside the walls", is the highlight of this modern (but traditionally-styled) member of the Best Western consortium. In such an historic city, however, the lack of much in the way of true character is all the more striking, and some do find it "a little overpriced". / **Rooms:** 99 (of which some non smoking).*

UK MAPS

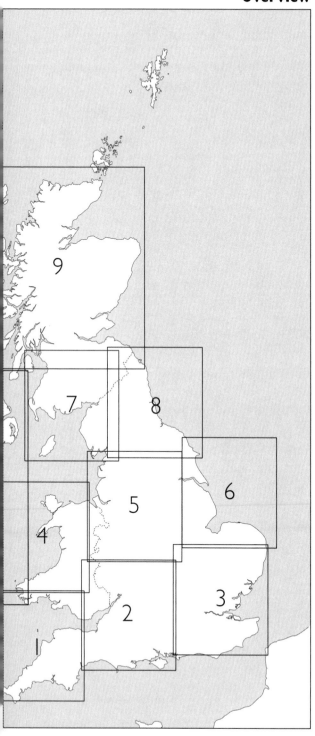

Map I

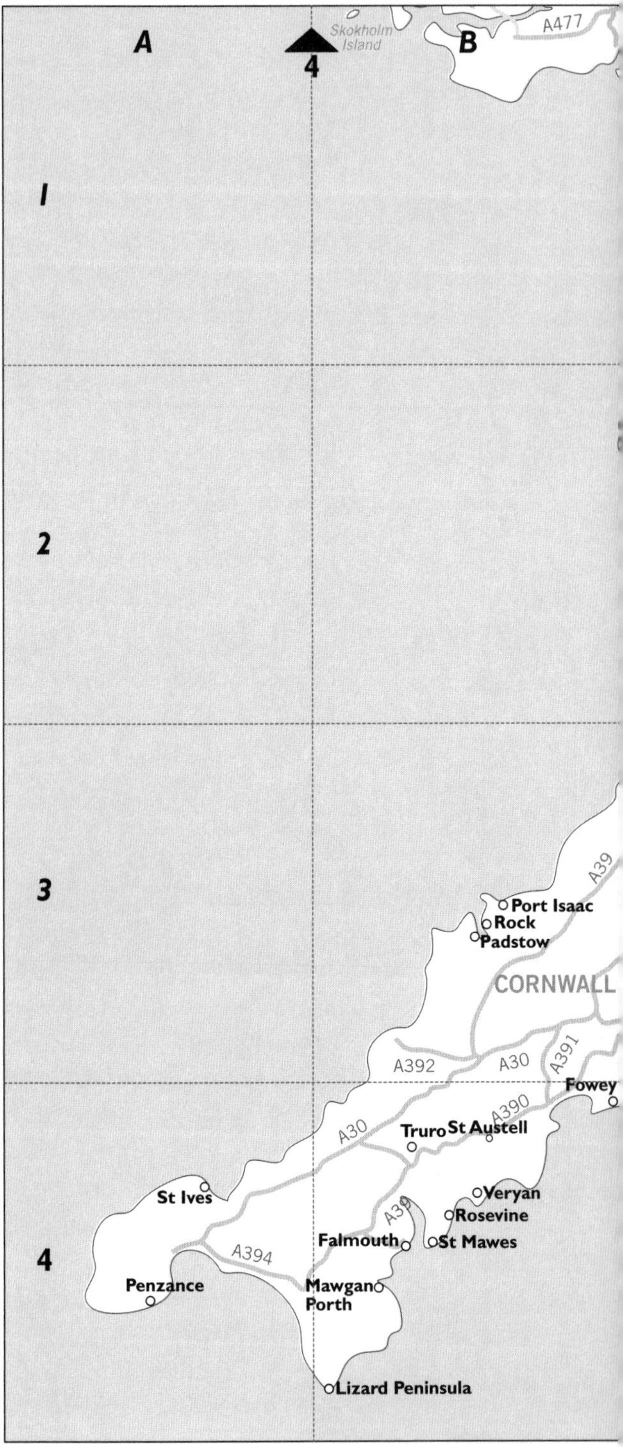

A   B

4   Skokholm
     Island

I

A477

2

3   Port Isaac
     Rock
     Padstow

     CORNWALL

     A39

     A392   A30   A391

     A30   A390   Fowey

     Truro St Austell

     St Ives   Veryan
            A39   Rosevine
     Falmouth   St Mawes

4   A394

     Penzance   Mawgan
            Porth

     Lizard Peninsula

Map I

C

D

Caldey
Island

NEATH
AND
PORT TALBOT

A465

RHONDDA
CYNON
TAFF

▲4

SWANSEA

○ Swansea

Reynoldston ○

M4

BRIDGEND

Brynmenyn ○

VALE OF
GLAMORGAN

Lundy

○ **Woolacombe**

A361

A39

Exmoor

A39

Dunster ○

Luxborough ○

○ **Saunton**

Dulverton ○

A396

○ **Barnstaple**

A361

A39

A388

A386

A3072

DEVON

A377

2 ▶

M5

○ **Virginstow**

Exeter ○

Lewdon ○

A30

Chagford ○

Doddiscombesleigh

A388

A395

○ **Lifton**

A80

A376

Dartmoor

Sidmouth ○

A388

Bodmin
Moor

A38

A390

A386

Ashburton ○

A38

Torquay ○

A38

○ **St Keyne**

○ **Looe**

Dartmouth ○

A379

A379

Kingsbridge

Bigbury on Sea

Galmpton ○ ○ **Salcombe**

Map 2

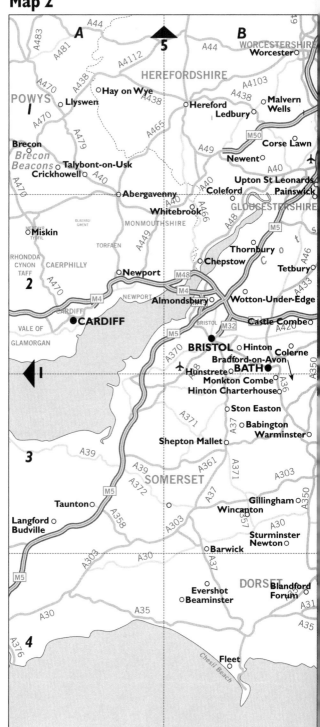

Map 2

Map 3

A427

A A605 **B**

A6116

▲
6

CAMBRIDGESHIRE

A43 A14 A45 A14

o Huntingdon

NORTHAMPTONSHIRE

Newmarket o

A45

1 A6 A428 A14

oNorthampton CAMBRIDGE ●

A428 A1198 A11

M1

Roade ●

Duxford o A307

BEDFORDSHIRE A1 A505

A421

A507

o Flitwick

BUCKINGHAM- A5 M1 A1(M) HERTFORDSHIRE A120 ✈

SHIRE

A602 A10

2 oAylesbury

o Ware M11

A413

Amersham

oSt Albans

M10 M25

oChandler's Cross

M40 ◄ M1 A400 oHadley Wood M11

2

Marlow o Hayes LONDON ● A12 A13 M25

Taplow o oStoke Poges A41 ✈

Bray o Maidenhead

Windsor o A329(M) Heathrow ✈ A4 o Richmond Wilmington o

Egham Croydon o A20 Fawkham o M25

3 o Bracknell A232 M20

Bagshot o M26

A331 A23 A22 A26

SURREY M25 M25

Dorking o Nutfield o A21

A25 M23 A22

A31 Gatwick ✈ Tunbridge Wells o

Airport East A26

Grinstead A267

A3 A264 Wych Cross o

Lower o

Liphook o A272 Beeding o Cuckfield o Fletching

A29 Uckfield o

4 WEST SUSSEX A24 A272 E. SUSSEX

o Midhurst o Amberley A23 South

A27 o Lewes

Chichester o Arundel A27 Downs Polegate o

o Bosham Climping o BRIGHTON ●

Eastbourne o

Map 3

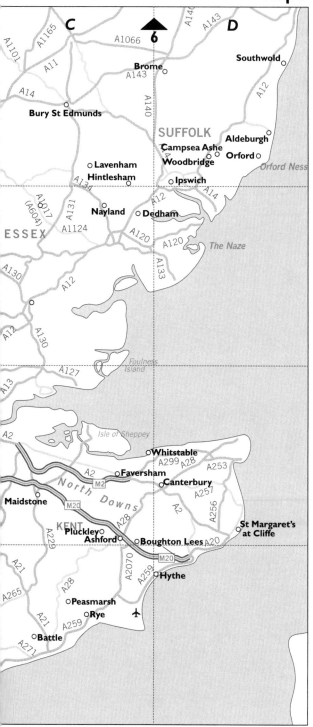

Map 4

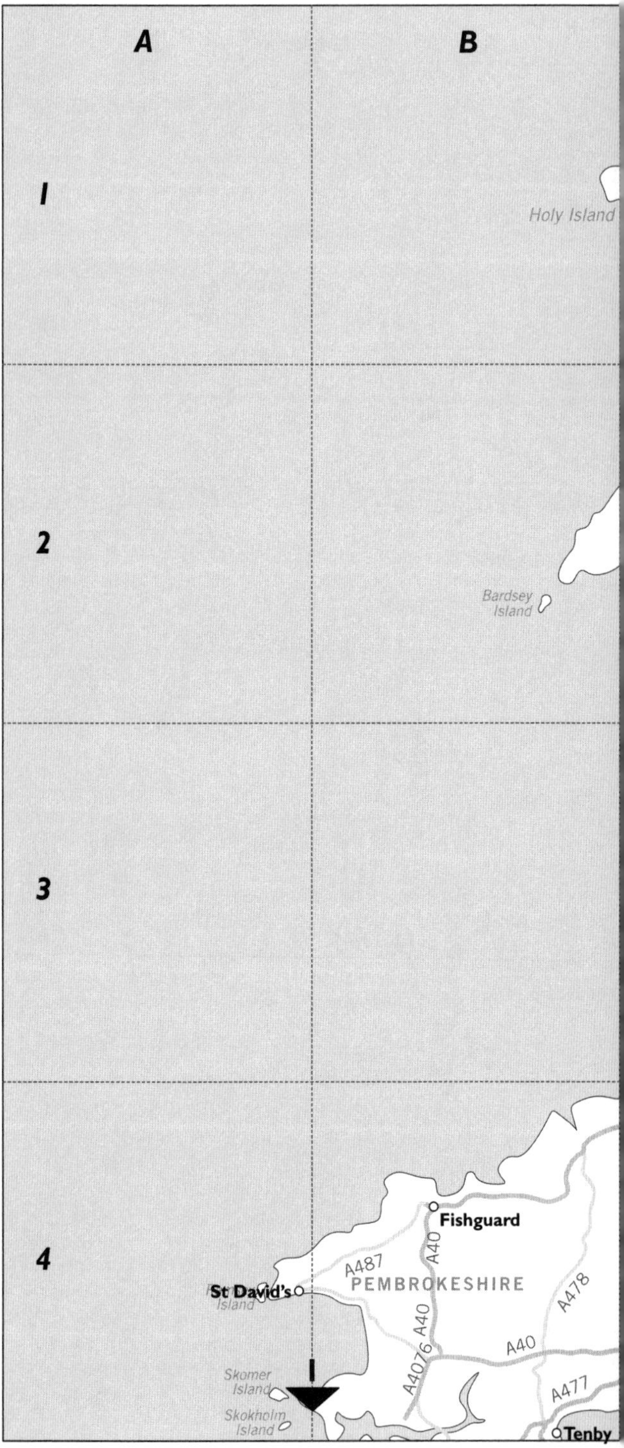

	A	**B**
1		Holy Island
2		Bardsey Island
3		
4	St David's, St David's Island, Skomer Island, Skokholm Island	Fishguard, A487, A40, PEMBROKESHIRE, A4076, A40, A478, A40, A477, Tenby

Map 4

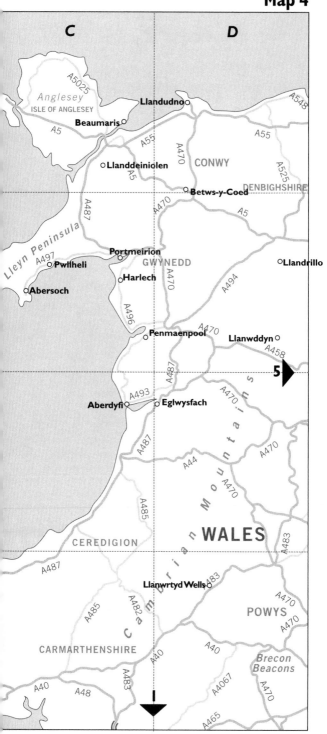

Map 5

A
B

Lancaster ○

M6
8

Hetton ○

LANCASHIRE

A6068

Chipping ○

Clitheroe ●

A6

A59

Blackburn ●

1 **Blackpool** ○

A585

M55

A6

M65

A646

Preston ○

A59

A58

M6

M62

M61

M66

A570

A59

Aughton ○

M58

Bolton ●

A58

M6

MANCHESTER ●

MERSEYSIDE

M62

M67

LIVERPOOL ●

M62

Stockport ○

A57

Daresbury ○

Birch Vale ○

2

M53

A556

Manchester Airport

Pott Shrigley ○

A548

M56

Prestbury ○

A537

CHESHIRE

A49

Buxton ●

FLINTSHIRE

M6

A50

A54

Chester ○

4 **Mold** ○

A51

Tarporley ●

A523

A494

A55

A41

A534

Llandegla ○

A483

Crewe ●

Nantwich ○

A525

A49

WREXHAM

A525

STAFFORDSHIRE

3 **Llangollen** ○

A5

A53

A51

Oswestry ○

A5

A495

A49

A53

A41

A518

M6

A34

A483

A5

Albrighton ○

A442

Shrewsbury ○ A5

M54

A458

SHROPSHIRE

A458

A49

A483

A489

A442

A458

M5

4

Ludlow ○

A49

2

A456

Chaddesley Corbett ○

A488

A449

M5

Map 5

Map 6

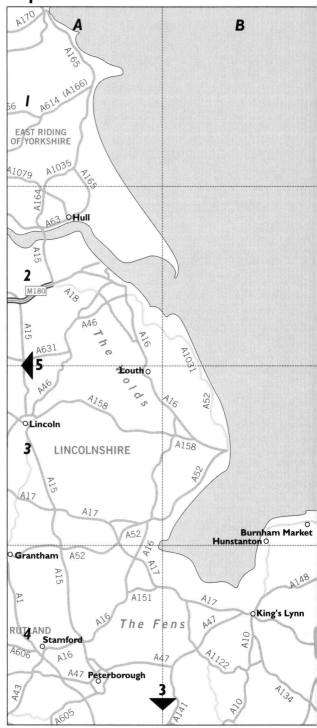

Map 6

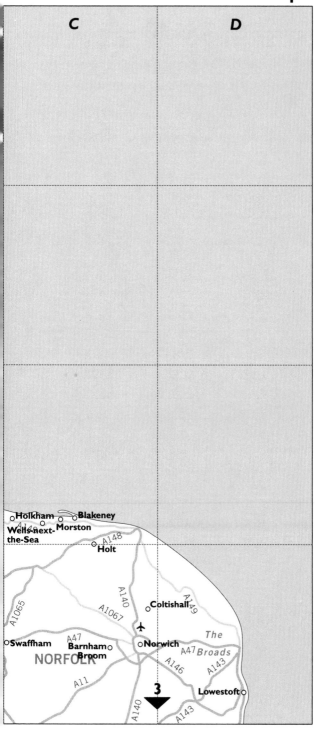

Map 7

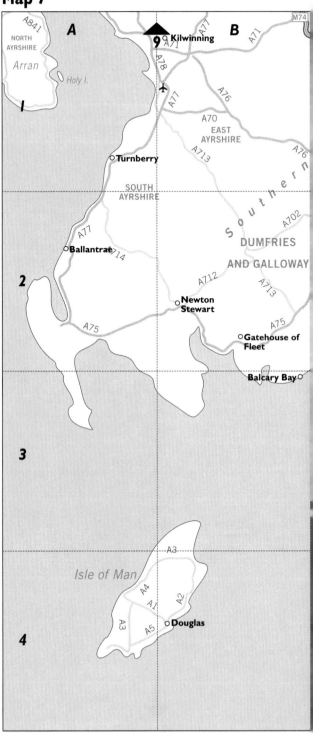

Map 7

Map 8

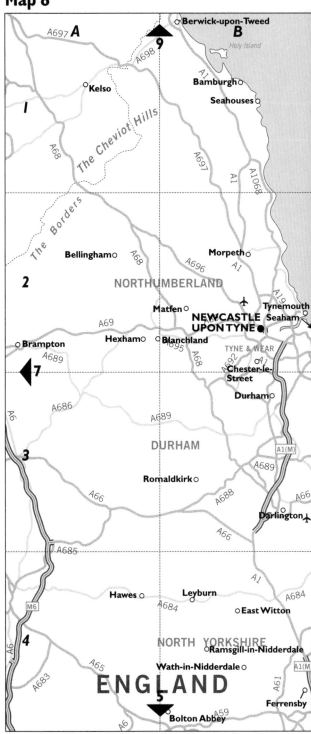

A
A697

B
Berwick-upon-Tweed

Holy Island

A698

9

1

○ Kelso

A68

The Cheviot Hills

Bamburgh ○

Seahouses ○

A697

A1

A1068

The Borders

Bellingham ○

A68

A696

Morpeth ○

A1

A19

2

NORTHUMBERLAND

Matfen ○

NEWCASTLE UPON TYNE ●

Tynemouth

Seaham

A69

Hexham ○

○ **Blanchland**

A695

A68

TYNE & WEAR

A192

A1

○ **Brampton**

A689

7

A686

A689

Chester-le-Street

Durham ○

A6

3

DURHAM

A1(M)

Romaldkirk ○

A689

A66

A688

A66

Darlington ✈

A66

A685

A1

Hawes ○

Leyburn

A684

A6

M6

A684

○ **East Witton**

4

NORTH YORKSHIRE

○ **Ramsgill-in-Nidderdale**

A1(M)

A65

Wath-in-Nidderdale ○

A61

A683

ENGLAND

5

A459

Ferrensby

A6

Bolton Abbey

Map 8

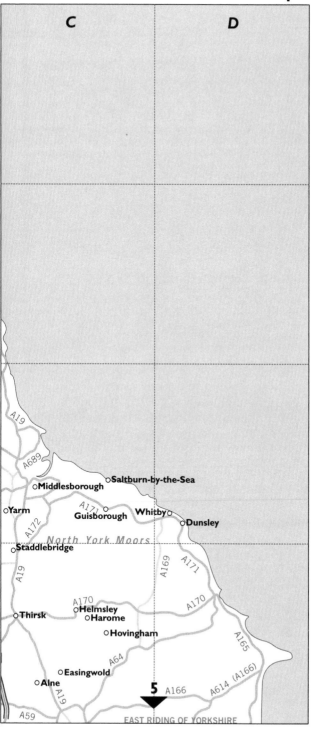

C

D

A19

A689

Middlesborough

Saltburn-by-the-Sea

Yarm

A171
Guisborough

Whitby

A172

Dunsley

North York Moors

Staddlebridge

A19

A169

A171

A170
Helmsley
Harome

A170

Thirsk

Hovingham

A165

A64

Easingwold

Alne

A19

5 A166

A614 (A166)

EAST RIDING OF YORKSHIRE

Map 9

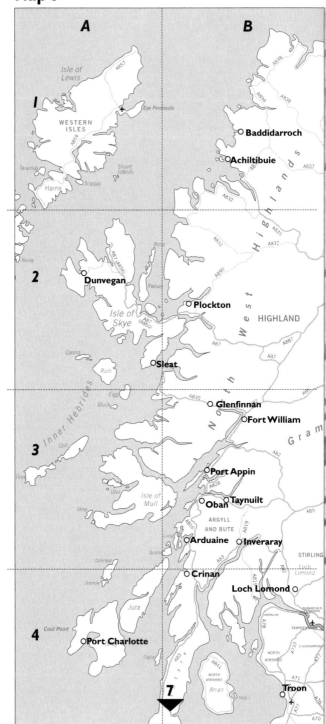

A **B**

1

Isle of Lewis
A857

WESTERN ISLES

A859

Eye Peninsula

Taransay

Shiant Islands

Scalpay

Harris

A838

A894

A835

○ **Baddidarroch**

s

○**Achiltibuie**

A837

d

n

a

l

h

g

i

H

A832

2

Rhum

Isle of Skye

A87 (A850)

A890

A832

A836

A832

A852

t

s

e

W

○ **Dunvegan**

Raasay

Rona

○ **Plockton**

A87

HIGHLAND

A87

Canna

Rum

A87 (A850)

○**Sleat**

A87

3

Inner Hebrides

Coll

Tiree

Eigg

Muck

Ulva

Iona

Isle of Mull

A830

○ **Glenfinnan**

h

t

r

o

N

○**Fort William**

G r a m

A82

○**Port Appin**

A828

○ **Oban**

○**Taynuilt**

A85

ARGYLL AND BUTE

A819

A816

○**Arduaine**

○ **Inveraray**

A83

STIRLING

Colonsay

Scarba

4

Oronsay

Jura

Coul Point

○ **Crinan**

A816

Loch Lomond ○

Loch Lomond

A811

A82

A83

DUMBARTON R.

A814

INVERCLYDE

RENFREWSHIRE

A78

A737

E. RENFREWSHIRE

A841

NORTH AYRSHIRE

NORTH AYRSHIRE

A71

○**Port Charlotte**

Gigha

Arran

Holy I.

7

Troon
○

A77

A70

A71

Map 9

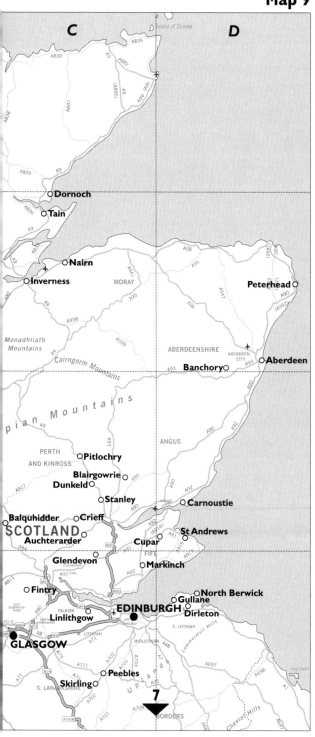

C

D

Island of Stroma

Dornoch

Tain

Nairn

Inverness

MORAY

Monadhliath
Mountains

Cairngorm Mountains

Peterhead

ABERDEENSHIRE

ABERDEEN
CITY

Banchory

Aberdeen

pian Mountains

ANGUS

PERTH
AND KINROSS

Pitlochry

Blairgowrie

Dunkeld

Stanley

Carnoustie

Balquhidder

Crieff

SCOTLAND

Auchterarder

Cupar

St Andrews

Glendevon

FIFE

Markinch

Fintry

FALKIRK

Linlithgow

EDINBURGH

Gullane

North Berwick

Dirleton

W. LOTHIAN

E. LOTHIAN

Lammermuir Hills

GLASGOW

CITY OF
GLASGOW

MIDLOTHIAN

Peebles

Skirling

S. LANARKSHIRE

7

Uplands

BORDERS

Cheviot Hills

Holy Island

Map 10

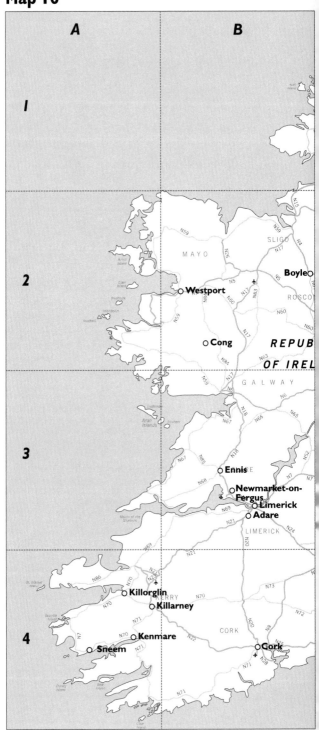

Map 10

LONDON

WHICH PART OF TOWN TO STAY IN?

Considering London is so large, and initially baffling for first-time visitors, the obvious areas to stay are surprisingly limited, and relatively short to describe.

Most traditional top-end hotels tend to be gathered together around the western borders of the West End (the business and shopping heart of London): in Mayfair and St James's (the areas to the north and south of Piccadilly), and in Knightsbridge and Belgravia.

The larger medium-price hotels tend to be to the eastern side of the West End, particularly around Bloomsbury and Covent Garden (and hence particularly convenient for the theatres).

Pleasant boutique hotels are usually located in the leafier inner western suburbs, such as Chelsea, South Kensington, Kensington, Notting Hill and Maida Vale.

The City of London (the Financial District, in US parlance) – to the east of central London – has not for the past century been considered a natural hotel location. This is slowly changing, but a weekend visitor may still feel rather isolated there from the buzz of the capital generally.

In style and appeal, the hotels of London fall, appropriately enough, somewhere between those of New York and Paris.

The hotels which attracted most survey commentary were as follows:

1. Savoy
2. The Sanderson
3. The Dorchester
4. St Martin's
5. Claridge's
6. The Berkeley
7. The Ritz
8. 1 Aldwych
9. The Lanesborough
10. The Landmark

The grip which the Savoy Group maintains on London's top hotels – with Claridge's and the Berkeley, it accounts for three of the top ten names – is impressive. Perhaps even more striking, however, has been the quick-fire success of New York design-hotelier Ian Schrager, who can claim two of the top five names (the Sanderson and St Martins).

Best Hotels

Judging on the overall ratings awarded by reporters, five hotels clearly emerged as The Best in London. They were, in order, as follows:

The Milestone
The Lanesborough
1 Aldwych
The Carlton Tower
The Mandarin Oriental

It is rather sad that none of the (now American-owned) Savoy Group hotels makes it into this list, nor such other great traditional names as the Dorchester, the Grosvenor House or the Ritz.

The Best Rooms

Three of the 'Best Hotel' names also crop up in the top five for Best Rooms:

The Milestone
The Lanesborough
The Carlton Tower
The Landmark
The Royal Garden

Charm

When it comes to charm, it's notable that the smaller establishments have the edge.

The Milestone
Brown's
Blake's
The Lanesborough
1 Aldwych

The largest establishment in the list, Brown's, has only 118 rooms.

Best on a Budget

London is an infamously poor budget hotel destination, but more reasonably-priced survey successes included:

Blooms
The Basil Street
The Bonington
The Colonnade
Dolphin Square
The Gore
Goring
Kingsway Hall
My Hotel
Portobello
Rookery
Rubens

Athenaeum £199

116 Piccadilly W1   2—3B

🖰 www.athenaeumhotel.com
✉ info@athenaeumhotel.com
☎ (020) 7499 3464   🖷 (020) 7493 1860

Reporters speak only well of this "good and reliable" modern hotel, whose central location (with some rooms overlooking Green Park) and "excellent" service make it a natural for business. Even fans can sometimes find it "expensive" for what it is, though – "it's worth checking for deals". / **Rooms:** 157 (of which 90 non smoking and 40 family rooms). **Facilities:** gym; spa.

Basil Street £240

8 Basil St SW3   2—3A

🖰 www.thebasil.com   ✉ info@thebasil.com
☎ (020) 7581 3311   🖷 (020) 7581 3693

That it attracts "no executives or reps" plays a big part in creating the "very pleasant Victorian atmosphere" of this "cosy" family-owned hotel, a couple of minutes' walk from Harrods. Those looking for state-of-the-art plumbing and plasma-screen TVs, should look elsewhere, but many reporters find that "long-serving staff who remember your name" provide more than adequate compensation. The dining room, in particular, boasts much traditional charm. / **Rooms:** 80 (of which 60 non smoking and 4 family rooms).

The Berkeley £438

Wilton Pl SW1   2—3A

🖰 www.the-berkeley.co.uk   ✉ info@the-berkeley.co.uk
☎ (020) 7235 6000   🖷 (020) 7235 4330

Most reporters praise the "understated" charms of this "comfortable", "conservative" Savoy Group hotel in Belgravia – built in the early '70s and significantly revamped in recent years. Highlights include an "excellent" location, a "first-class" spa and the fashionable Blue Bar. On the downside, some rooms are "very small", prices are high (though good 'phone' deals are reported), and charging guests to use the swimming pool (even a rare rooftop one) does seem a bit petty. Mid-2003 saw the opening of no fewer than two new Gordon Ramsay restaurants – the very serious Pétrus (with chef Marcus Wareing) and the 'NYC-style' Boxwood Café. / **Rooms:** 214 (of which 40 non smoking and some family rooms). **Facilities:** indoor pool; outdoor pool; gym; spa.

Blakes £255

33 Roland Gdns SW7   1—3B

🖰 www.blakeshotels.com   ✉ blakes@easynet.co.uk
☎ (020) 7370 6701   🖷 (020) 7373 0442

This "eclectic", "opulent" datedly glamorous South Kensington design-hotel – often cited as the original of the concept worldwide – is famed for being "very romantic, in a decadent sort of way". Most reporters find it continues to live up to its reputation, though a fair number of doubters complain of "lackadaisical" service and the lack of facilities. The basement dining room is as famous for its prices as it is for its seductive atmosphere. / **Rooms:** 52 (of which 2 family rooms). **Facilities:** gym.

Blooms £195

7 Montague St WC1 2—1C
🖰 www.grangehotels.com ✉ blooms@grangehotels.com
☎ (020) 7323 1717

A Georgian terrace adjacent to the British Museum provides the setting for this "very comfortable" townhouse hotel (which offers a "great breakfast" to start the day). Rooms can be "small" but are also "well-appointed". A reporter who found the place "expensive" tipped checking out the "various deals" available (especially at weekends). / **Rooms:** 26 (of which 13 non smoking).

Bonnington £159

92 Southampton Row WC1 2—1D
🖰 www.bonnington.com ✉ sales@bonnington.com
☎ (020) 7242 2828 🖨 (020) 7831 9170

"Unexceptional, but prices are good by central London standards" – this "well-positioned" Edwardian hotel, in Bloomsbury, attracts consistent reviews as a "good-value" destination. "Rooms at the back are quieter." / **Rooms:** 247. **Facilities:** gym. **Details:** meals unavailable: L; no Amex or Switch.

Browns £376 [N]

Albemarle St W1 2—2B
🖰 www.roccofortehotels.com/browns.html
✉ reservations.brownshotel@rfhotels.com
☎ (020) 7493 6020 🖨 (020) 7493 9381

In the summer of 2003, this "charming", traditional establishment – which has occupied a jumbled but interesting site in a row of former Mayfair townhouses since the early 19th century – was acquired by Rocco Forte, who has big plans for it. We do hope he doesn't try to 'improve' its restaurant, 1837, which is increasingly establishing itself as one of the best traditionally grand Gallic dining rooms in town. / **Rooms:** 118 (of which 15 family rooms). **Facilities:** gym.

Cannizaro House £134

Westside Wimbledon Common SW19   1—4B

www.thistlehotels.co.uk

CannizaroHouse@Thistle.co.uk

☎ 0870 333 9124   🖷 0870 333 9224

"Potentially a first class country house hotel, only 20 minutes from Harrods, so it's a shame that standards have been allowed to drop to such a low level" – though its "beautiful" gardens and "lovely" location (adjoining Wimbledon Common) help win it some praise, there is too much criticism from reporters of the "tired" and "fusty" standards of this Thistle Hotel. / **Rooms:** 45 (of which some non smoking). **Facilities:** café/restaurant.

Carlton Tower £382

2 Cadogan Pl SW1   2—4A

www.carltontower.com   📧 contact@carltontower.com

☎ (020) 7235 1234   🖷 (020) 7235 9129

This modern Knightsbridge tower may look a bit anonymous, but inside this is a "top-marks-all-round" grand hotel, in fairly traditional style. "Good-sized rooms" (some, unusually for London, with elevated views) and a "fabulous" top-floor fitness-centre (with pool) are particular attractions. In-house dining facilities include the Rib Room, and an elegant Italian restaurant, Grissini – both solid, but rather pricey. / **Rooms:** 220 (of which 60 non smoking). **Facilities:** indoor pool; gym; spa.

Chancery Court
(Renaissance London) £215

252 High Holborn WC1   2—1D

www.marriott.com

📧 sales.chancerycourt@renaissancehotels.com

☎ (020) 7829 9888   🖷 (020) 7829 9889

This vast Edwardian building – originally the headquarters of Pearl Assurance – can seem rather imposing. Reporters, though, rather warm to its grand architecture and the "wonderful", "understated" design of its refurbished interior. A location "convenient for both the West End and the City" make it an ideal location (perhaps most obviously for those on business), while other attractions include "helpful and friendly staff" and the better-than-average QC restaurant. / **Rooms:** 356 (of which 213 non smoking and 56 family rooms). **Facilities:** gym; spa.

Charlotte Street £259

15 Charlotte St W1 2—1C
⌂ www.firmdalehotels.com ✉ charlotte@firmdale.com
☎ (020) 7806 2000 🖷 (020) 7806 2002

"Living up to its cool address", this *"modern but comfortable"* boutique hotel (recently converted from a warehouse, in ever more trendy Fitzrovia) is praised by most reporters as a *"sexy"* destination which offers an *"all-round very good experience"*. There were one or two complaints, though, of *"dismissive"* service. / **Rooms:** 52 (of which some non smoking). **Facilities:** gym.

Chesterfield £275 😊

35 Charles St W1 2—3B
⌂ www.chesterfieldmayfair.com ✉ bookch@rchmail.com
☎ (020) 7491 2622 🖷 (020) 7491 4793

In the heart of Mayfair, this *"small and elegant"* traditional-style hotel – which has a particularly pleasant cocktail bar – makes a *"discreet"* and *"convenient"* destination. / **Rooms:** 110.

Churchill £329

30 Portman Square W1 2—2A
⌂ www.london-churchill.intercontinental.com
✉ churchill@interconti.com
☎ (020) 7486 5800 🖷 (020) 7486 1255

The lobby may be *"very busy"*, but this large hotel not far from emergingly-trendy Marylebone High Street is quite a *"tranquil"* place to spend a night, though the rather *"functional"* style suits business better than pleasure. Book ahead if you want a table in the semi-detached restaurant, Locanda Locatelli – it's been one of the biggest dining hits in the capital of recent years, and prime-time reservations are hard to come by. / **Rooms:** 445 (of which 122 non smoking and 63 family rooms). **Facilities:** gym; tennis.

Claridges £457

Brook St W1 2—2B
⌂ www.the-savoy-group.com/claridges
✉ info@claridges.co.uk
☎ (020) 7629 8860 🖷 (020) 7499 2210

"A stylish Art Deco vibe" helps distinguish the grandest of Mayfair's hotels, which has been the subject of an ongoing improvement programme in recent years. *"Incredible attention to detail"* and *"impeccable service"* are singled out for particular praise from reporters (while the biggest of the occasional gripes is the *"oddly poor general facilities"*). The dining room has been taken over in recent times as Gordon Ramsay's number two restaurant, but its standards fall well short of those at his Chelsea original. / **Rooms:** 204 (of which 234 non smoking and 70 family rooms). **Facilities:** gym; spa.

The Colonnade
Townhouse £173

2 Warrington Cres W9   1—2B

🖰 www.theetongroup.com

✉ res_colonnade@theetongroup.com

☎ (020) 7286 1052   🖷 (020) 7286 1057

Two Victorian houses in charming Little Venice (one of them, as it happens, the birthplace of the man who invented the WWII 'Enigma' machine) provide the setting for this townhouse hotel. Reports, though few in number, all speak in terms of "beautiful" rooms and "impeccable" service. / **Rooms:** 43 (of which 21 non smoking and 2 family rooms).

Connaught £481

Carlos Pl W1   2—2B

🖰 www.the-connaught.co.uk   ✉ info@the-connaught.co.uk

☎ (020) 7499 7070   🖷 (020) 7495 3262

The Savoy Group's ongoing attempts to rejuvenate the charms of this Mayfair hotel – long (and justly) famed for its "gentlemen's club" environment, and exceptional service – seem, so far as reporters are concerned, to be proceeding reasonably smoothly. Those who used to like it precisely because it was not like other hotels, however, cannot but be a little disappointed by the modernisation (which have included the closure of the famous ancien régime restaurant, which is now run in contemporary style by a protégée of Gordon Ramsay). / **Rooms:** 92 (of which all non smoking and 2 family rooms). **Facilities:** gym. **Details:** min age for children: 12.

Conrad £330

Chelsea Harbour SW10   1—3B
🖰 www.conradhotels.com
✉ londoninfo@conradhotels.com
☎ (020) 7823 3000   🖨 (020) 7351 6525

"Large balconies" overlooking a Thames-side marina impart an out-of-town air to this modern suite-hotel, on the outermost fringes of Chelsea – appropriately enough as the place is some 15 minutes from the West End by cab and with no convenient tube. "Excellent rooms" are a highlight, but the corporate style of the establishment itself strikes some as decidedly "unatmospheric". / **Rooms:** 160 (of which 88 non smoking). **Facilities:** indoor pool; gym.

Covent Garden £288

10 Monmouth St WC2   2—2C
🖰 www.firmdale.com   ✉ covent@firmdale.com
☎ (020) 7806 1000   🖨 (020) 7806 1100

"Superb staff, a good location, beautifully designed rooms, a neat bar and good bistro" – reporters express little but praise for this "stylish" hotel in the heart of Theatreland, which is decorated in a way that manages to be both modern and traditional. Visiting media folk will be pleased to find a luxurious 53-seat cinema, with state-of-the-art AV facilities. / **Rooms:** 58 (of which some non smoking and 6 family rooms). **Facilities:** gym.

Dolphin Square £185

Chichester St SW1   2—4C

🖰 www.dolphinsquarehotel.co.uk

✉ reservations@dolphinsquarehotel.co.uk

☎ (020) 7834 3800   📠 (020) 7798 8735

Some consider it "impersonal", but if you're looking for "lots of space and a pool", this apartment-hotel incorporated into a vast '30s block – with its "fantastic" (handy but quiet) Pimlico location – is unanimously hailed as a "good-value" destination. / **Rooms:** 165 *(of which some non smoking and 3 family rooms).* **Facilities:** *indoor pool; spa; tennis.*

Dorchester £370

53 Park Ln W1   2—3A

🖰 www.dorchesterhotel.com

✉ reservations@dorchesterhotel.com

☎ (020) 7629 8888   📠 (020) 7409 0114

Given its exalted prices and reputation, reports on this grand '30s Mayfair landmark fall short of a truly ringing endorsement. Yes, for most reporters it is a "lovely, elegant" place with "real olde world charm and service to match", but – in all aspects of its operations – the consensus is that it's good rather than great. As we go to press, however, a lavish refurbishment programme reaches its conclusion, so efforts are clearly ongoing. / **Rooms:** 250 *(of which some non smoking and some family rooms).* **Facilities:** *gym; spa.* **Details:** *meals unavailable: Sun (Oriental restaurant).*

Draycott £259

22-26 Cadogan Gdns SW3   2—4A

🖰 www.draycotthotel.com

✉ reservations@draycotthotel.com

☎ (020) 7730 6466   📠 (020) 7730 0236

"Good-size rooms" and "helpful staff" are among the virtues of this "very traditional" townhouse hotel near Sloane Square, which number "excellent breakfasts" and a garden amongst its attractions. Formerly the Cliveden Town House, it assumed its new name in June 2003 – in spite of a change of ownership, the 'formula' does not seem set to change radically. / **Rooms:** 35 *(of which 6 family rooms).*

11 Cadogan Gardens £215

11 Cadogan Gardens SW3   2—4A

🏠 www.number-eleven.co.uk

✉ reservations@number-eleven.co.uk

☎ (020) 7730 7000   🖷 (020) 7730 5217

"This quaint little hotel is tucked away in a lovely garden square between Harrods and Sloane Square". Occupying four stately Victorian townhouses, it's not the place if you're looking for state-of-the-art facilities, but it has plenty of "charm", and breakfast – in the library – is a "sumptuous" affair. "You can use the garden", too. / **Rooms:** 59 (of which 5 family rooms). **Facilities:** gym.

51 Buckingham Gate £370

51 Buckingham Gate SW1   2—4B

🏠 www.51-buckinghamgate.com

✉ reservation@51-buckinghamgate.co.uk

☎ (020) 7769 7766   🖷 (020) 7233 5014

Semi-detached from the larger (and very Edwardian) Crowne Plaza London St James, this townhouse-style hotel offers surprisingly "modern rooms and furnishings". It's rated a "very comfortable and cosy" place to stay, in a quiet courtyard just a few minutes' walk from Buckingham Palace. / **Rooms:** 82 (of which 25 non smoking and 40 family rooms). **Facilities:** gym; spa.

41 £230

41 Buckingham Palace Rd SW1   2—4B

🏠 www.41hotel.com   ✉ book41@rchmail.com

☎ (020) 7300 0041   🖷 (020) 7300 0141

"Friendly and helpful" staff are a strength of this odd-but-interesting boutique hotel operation near Buckingham Palace, run by the estimable Red Carnation group. The former all-in (food, phones, cleaning, and so on) tariff has now been replaced with a more conventional B&B basis. / **Rooms:** 20 (of which some family rooms).

Four Seasons £405

Hamilton Pl, Park Ln W1   2—3A

⌂ www.fourseasons.com   ✉ fsh.london@fourseasons.com
☎ (020) 7499 0888   🖷 (020) 7493 1895

*This '70s block in Mayfair offers a "peaceful" haven and wins
high praise from many for its "superb" service and "very
comfortable" beds. Aficionados of the Four Seasons group,
though, feel "it's not up to the standards of this chain" and that it
"needs updating".* / **Rooms:** 220 (of which 112 non smoking and 28 family
rooms). **Facilities:** gym.

The Franklin £223 ☺☺

28 Egerton Gdns SW3   1—3B
⌂ www.franklinhotel.co.uk
✉ bookings@franklinhotel.co.uk
☎ (020) 7584 5533   🖷 (020) 7584 5449

*A Knightsbridge townhouse hotel, in traditional style, overlooking
private gardens. It offers "an oasis of quiet and elegant luxury",
and, of course, proximity to some of London's best shopping.*
/ **Rooms:** 47 (of which 30 non smoking and 5 family rooms). **Details:** no Switch.

Gore £165 ☺☺

190 Queen's Gate SW7   1—3B
⌂ www.gorehotel.co.uk   ✉ reservations@gorehotel.co.uk
☎ (020) 7584 6601   🖷 (020) 7589 8127

*Rooms are on the "small" side but this "idiosyncratic" (or even
"eccentric") South Kensington townhouse hotel has its fans, and
some say it's "ideal for a romantic weekend". For Proms-goers,
and the like, a location only two minutes from the Albert Hall is a
further plus. Another is the atmospheric late-night bar.* / **Rooms:** 53
(of which 15 non smoking).

Goring £195

15 Beeston Pl SW1   2—4B

🖰 www.goringhotel.co.uk   ✉ reception@goringhotel.co.uk
☎ (020) 7396 9000   🖨 (020) 7834 4393

"Exceptional old-fashioned service" ("which really tries to go the extra mile") is the special forte of this "outstanding" and "wonderfully comfortable" Edwardian hotel, near Victoria station. It shows "how to run a proper hotel" according to its (older) fan club, and derives much of its special charm from being one of the handful of family-owned quality establishments in town. The bar is "a great meeting point", too, and the restaurant the epitome of tradition. / **Rooms:** 74 (of which some non smoking and some family rooms).

Grange City £260

8-10 Cooper's Row EC3   1—2C

🖰 www.grangehotels.com   ✉ city@grangehotels.com
☎ (020) 7863 3700   🖨 (020) 7863 3701

"Fabulous views over the Tower of London and Tower Bridge", rooms of a "very high standard" (with 2 queen-size beds in Executive accommodation) and "helpful" service are already winning strong support for this (inevitably businessy) 12-floor newcomer, by Fenchurch Street station. / **Rooms:** 247 (of which some non smoking). **Facilities:** indoor pool; gym; spa.

Great Eastern £310 ☺

Liverpool St EC2   1—2C

🖰 www.great-eastern-hotel.co.uk
✉ reservations@great-eastern-hotel.co.uk
☎ (020) 7618 5000   🖨 (020) 7618 5011

"Excellent, well-equipped" bedrooms are acclaimed as the star attraction at Conran's designer conversion of this former railway hotel by Liverpool Street, helping make the place a good base for visiting financial types. Thereafter, views diverge – what some reporters see as a "modern classic" others find too "functional", and both the restaurants and the overall charm level are indifferently rated. Leisure visitors should be aware that the place "rather closes down at weekends". / **Rooms:** 267 (of which 112 non smoking and 28 family rooms). **Facilities:** gym.

Grosvenor House £470 ☹

Park Lane W1   2—2A

🖰 www.lemeridien.com
☎ (020) 499 6363   🖨 (020) 7629 9337

"Bland", "expensive" and "trading on past glories" – this large and famous Mayfair hotel is, in many reporters' estimation, "in need of a total revamp". Its Great Room – with its vast unpillared space (originally constructed as an ice-rink) – remains the key West End rendezvous for the largest business get-togethers. / **Rooms:** 448. **Facilities:** indoor pool; gym; spa.

Halkin £359
5 Halkin St SW1   2—3A
🖰 www.halkin.co.uk   ✉ res@halkin.co.uk
☎ (020) 7333 1000   🖷 (020) 7333 1100

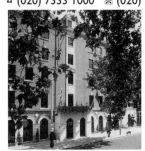

Most reporters find this small Belgravia hotel a "first-class" establishment, offering "very stylish" contemporary surroundings and "wonderful and luxurious" rooms. The service is generally highly rated too (although there is a disgruntled minority put off by a "smug" and "pretentious" attitude). Nahm, the Michelin-starred Thai-fusion restaurant, offers a love-it-or-hate-it experience. / **Rooms:** 41 *(of which 14 family rooms).* **Details:** *meals unavailable: Sat & Sun L.*

Hazlitt's £240
6 Frith St W1   2—2C
🖰 www.hazlittshotel.com   ✉ reservations@hazlitts.co.uk
☎ (020) 7434 1771   🖷 (020) 7439 1524

"A lovely alternative to the flash Schrager-type establishments", this "understated" hotel converted from Georgian townhouses enjoys a "great location" near Soho Square. "Great décor" too, with some rooms coming complete with four-posters. / **Rooms:** 23 *(of which 6 non smoking and 2 family rooms).* **Details:** *meals unavailable: no restaurant.*

Hempel £275
31-35 Craven Hill Gdns W2   1—2B
🖰 www.the-hempel.co.uk   ✉ hotel@the-hempel.co.uk
☎ (020) 7298 9000   🖷 (020) 7402 4666

"Aesthetically pleasing if you like minimalist-chic", this design-hotel – with, for example, a reception area which is "totally white" – is hailed as "serene" and "timeless" by some reporters. The contingent which holds that "the PR is better than the reality" is vociferous, though – critics just find the place "stark" and "characterless" and service that can be "slow" and "inattentive" does nothing to fill this void. The trendy basement restaurant, I Thai, was relaunched in the summer of 2003. / **Rooms:** 41 *(of which some non smoking and 5 family rooms).*

Hilton on Park Lane £265

22 Park Lane W1   2—3A
⌂ www.london-parklane.hilton.com
☎ (020) 7493 8000   ≣ (020) 7208 4142

"Stay on the executive floor, and make use of the executive
lounge", and this rather "unatmospheric" 28-floor Mayfair
landmark has its attractions, though reports are rather
inconsistent. The top-floor restaurant (and cocktail bar), Windows
on the World, is most notable for its inflated prices – the younger-
scene, ground-floor Zeta bar is more popular with reporters.
/ **Rooms:** 450. **Facilities:** gym.

Kingsway Hall £165

Great Queen St WC2   2—2D
⌂ www.kingswayhall.co.uk   ✉ enquiries@kingswayhall.co.uk
☎ (020) 7309 0909   ≣ (020) 7309 9696

The style is pretty corporate, but "good consistent quality" is
winning a following for this "nice, modern hotel", in Covent
Garden. / **Rooms:** 170 (of which some non smoking and some family rooms).
Facilities: gym; spa. **Details:** closed Christmas.

Knightsbridge £205

10 Beaufort Gdns SW3   2—4A
⌂ www.firmdalehotels.com   ✉ knightsbridge@firmdale.com
☎ (020) 7584 6300   ≣ (020) 7584 6355

Though this revamped Knightsbridge hotel was relaunched after
our survey closed, we list it on the basis of the warm reception
which reporters gave all other Firmdale properties (such as the
Covent Garden). It aims to offer the traditional virtues of a
townhouse hotel, but in a contemporary style. / **Rooms:** 44.

The Landmark £265

222 Marylebone Rd NW1 2—1A
🖰 www.landmarklondon.co.uk
✉ reservations@thelandmark.co.uk
☎ (020) 7631 8000   🖷 (020) 7631 8080

"Huge rooms" are a special plus at this truly Victorian-scale
Marylebone hotel, which was revamped by the eponymous
international group a few years ago. Some find the place has a
"wonderful atmosphere" – especially in the Winter Garden
created by glazing over a vast internal courtyard – but there's a
large dissident faction who find the ambience "bland". Reports on
service are similarly inconsistent. / *Rooms:* 299 (of which some non
smoking and 33 family rooms). *Facilities:* indoor pool; gym; spa.

Lanesborough £464

1 Lanesborough Pl SW1 2—3A
🖰 www.lanesborough.com   ✉ info@lanesborough.com
☎ (020) 7259 5599   🖷 (020) 7259 5606
With its "timeless" appeal, this landmark 18th-century building
overlooking Hyde Park Corner (originally a hospital, and now
refurbished in Empire style) is "quite simply the best hotel in
London" (of the larger sort). "Beautiful" rooms, a "great" butler
service and the "best hotel bar in the world" are all amenities
which commend it, and even those who complain the place is "so
grand it's almost a parody of itself" concede that it has a "lovely"
feel. The restaurant has never lived up to the standards of the rest
of the operation. / *Rooms:* 95 (of which 30 non smoking and 10 family
rooms). *Facilities:* gym.

Langham Hilton £219

Portland Pl W1 2—1B
🖰 www.hilton.co.uk   ✉ langham@hilton.com
☎ (020) 7636 1000   🖷 (020) 7323 2340
"We had a great time, more due to the health spa than the
hotel" – a sadly characteristic report on this palatial
establishment north of Oxford Circus, which attracts too many
reports to the effect that, unless you place a lot of weight on the
facilities, it's "way overpriced for what it is". / *Rooms:* 429 (of which
some non smoking and some family rooms). *Facilities:* indoor pool; gym; spa.

The Leonard £259

2—2A

15 Seymour St W1

🖰 www.theleonard.com ✉ the.leonard@dial.pipex.com

☎ (020) 7935 2010 📠 (020) 7935 6700

"Vast and very well furnished" rooms are one of the attractions which make this *"friendly"* townhouse hotel near Portman Square *"a wonderful city retreat"*. There's no restaurant, but the management prides itself on the guidance given to guests about places to eat. / **Rooms:** 44 (of which 3 family rooms). **Facilities:** gym. **Details:** no restaurant.

Mandarin Oriental £358

2—3A

66 Knightsbridge SW1

🖰 www.mandarinoriental.com ✉ molon-info@mohg.com

☎ (020) 7235 2000 📠 (020) 7235 2001

This towering late-Victorian edifice was until recently known as the Hyde Park (over which many of its rooms, and the restaurant, have views). New owners *"have imported all the charm of the famed Hong Kong Oriental"*, and – with its *"hyper-comfortable"* accommodation, *"brilliant"* service and an *"amazing"* spa – this is now, for some, *"by far the best of the grand London hotels"*. The restaurant, Foliage, has quite a reputation in its own right, and there's a *"great bar"*. / **Rooms:** 200 (of which 93 non smoking and 55 family rooms). **Facilities:** gym; spa.

Melia White House £218 ☺

2—1B

Albany St NW1

✉ melia.white.house@solmelia.com

☎ (020) 7391 3000 📠 (020) 7388 0091

Most reporters speak in positive terms of this Deco-ish hotel near Regent's Park, which was refurbished in 2002. It's perhaps best-suited to longer-term visitors, as *"good-quality"* accommodation is by far its strongest feature. / **Rooms:** 582 (of which some non smoking and some family rooms). **Facilities:** gym.

Meridien Piccadilly £335

21 Piccadilly W1   2—2B

🖱 www.lemeridien.com

✉ impiccres@lemeridien-hotels.com

☎ (020) 7734 8000   🖷 (020) 7437 3574

"A great hotel for theatre, sightseeing etc", say fans of this grand hotel near Piccadilly Circus – a "brilliant location" for those who want to be truly in the thick of things. It's perhaps not the most atmospheric establishment, but its most of its rooms are "large and high-ceilinged". / **Rooms:** 266 (of which some non smoking and some family rooms). **Facilities:** indoor pool; gym; spa.

Metropolitan £275

19 Old Park Ln W1   2—3A

🖱 www.metropolitan.co.uk   ✉ res@metropolitan.co.uk

☎ (020) 7447 1000   🖷 (020) 7447 1100

This "hip hotel" in Mayfair has shot particularly to fame as the home of Nobu (the restaurant which many still find "fantastic", book ahead) and of the mega-hyped Met Bar. The rooms get an OK assessment from reporters, but overall there's a strong feeling among some that the hotel is "overhyped" and "overpriced", with "poor" and "superior" service a particular irritant. / **Rooms:** 150 (of which 111 non smoking and 27 family rooms). **Facilities:** gym; spa. **Details:** meals unavailable: Sat & Sun L.

The Milestone £305

1 Kensington Ct W8   1—3B

🖱 www.milestonehotel.com   ✉ bookms@rchmail.com

☎ (020) 7917 1000   🖷 (020) 7917 1010

"Fabulous in every way possible", this "wonderful" red-brick hotel opposite Kensington Gardens is generally hailed as being "well beyond expectations" by reporters. Those seeking plush Baronial style – but with all mod cons, and within an easy cab's hop to the West End – will find it hard to do better elsewhere. / **Rooms:** 57 (of which 22 non smoking and 3 family rooms). **Facilities:** gym.

My Hotel £182

11-13 Bayley St WC1   2—1C

⌂ www.myhotels.com   ✉ guest-services@myhotels.co.uk

☎ (020) 7667 6000   🖷 (020) 7667 6001

Fans proclaim this small design-hotel just off Tottenham Court Road (allegedly conceived with the principles of Feng Shui in mind) a "hidden gem" with "bags of style". Even some of its supporters, though, think it "tries a tad too hard to be trendy". (It now has a quietly-located Chelsea sibling, tel (020) 7225 7500). / **Rooms:** 78 (of which some non smoking and some family rooms). **Facilities:** gym.

One Aldwych £370

One Alwych WC2   2—2D

⌂ www.onealdwych.com

✉ reservations@onealdwych.com

☎ (020) 7300 1000   🖷 (020) 7300 1001

"Chic and contemporary, without going over the top"; this Covent Garden-fringe design-hotel pulls off a too-rare double-act – "it combines minimalist style with charm". "Exceptionally willing service", a "great bar" (with "awesome cocktails") and a "lovely pool" are among the plusses which have established it as by far the best modern hotel in the West End. There are two commendable restaurants: the basement and businessy Axis, and Mezzanine, which, as the name suggests, boasts a view of the bar and lobby. / **Rooms:** 105 (of which 60 non smoking). **Facilities:** indoor pool; gym; spa.

The Pelham £211

15 Cromwell Pl SW7   1—3B

⌂ www.firmdale.com   ✉ pelham@firmdale.com

☎ (020) 7589 8288   🖷 (020) 7584 8444

If you're looking for "English style" (by the bucket-load), it's hard to beat this small but particularly handily-located South Kensington hotel, where "traditional hospitality" is a strength. / **Rooms:** 51 (of which 3 family rooms). **Details:** meals unavailable: Sat L.

Portobello £160

1—2B

22 Stanley Gdns W11
🖰 www.portobello-hotel.co.uk
✉ info@portobello-hotel.co.uk
☎ (020) 7727 2777   📠 (020) 7792 9641

*"Very unusual, and good fun"; those in search of a "romantic"
retreat find this "charmingly located" and somewhat Bohemian
Notting Hill boutique townhouse hotel "a real treat". It's been
going for over thirty years and has long been a popular
destination for rock stars in search of a degree of seclusion.*
/ **Rooms:** *24.* **Details:** *closed Christmas & New Year; meals unavailable: no
restaurant.*

Rembrandt £215

1—3B

11 Thurloe Pl SW7
🖰 www.sarova.com   ✉ rembrandt@sarova.co.uk
☎ (020) 7589 8100   📠 (020) 7225 3476

*"Efficient, welcoming, professional, relaxed" – this "old-fashioned"
hotel makes a handy destination (for families too), thanks to its
"convenient" location between the South Kensington museums
and Harrods. Some reporters do find it a touch "dated".*
/ **Rooms:** *195 (of which some non smoking and some family rooms).*

Ritz £305

2—3B

150 Piccadilly W1
🖰 www.theritzlondon.com   ✉ enquire@theritzlondon.com
☎ (020) 7493 8181   📠 (020) 7493 2687

*This "special" Edwardian hotel overlooking Green Park has "the
best location in London", say its supporters, and a walk through
its Louis XVI-style salons can create an impression little short of
"spectacular". Rather like the Savoy and the Dorchester, though, a
notable proportion of reporters just find the place "jaded", and
"relying on its reputation".* / **Rooms:** *133 (of which 27 non smoking and 37
family rooms).* **Facilities:** *gym.*

Rookery £165

Peters Ln, Cowcross St EC1 1—2C
🖱 www.rookeryhotel.com ✉ reservations@rookery.co.uk
☎ (020) 7336 0931 🖨 (020) 7336 0932

Looking for "disgraceful decadence"? – this "quiet" and
"characterful" small hotel in Clerkenwell (under the same
ownership as The Gore and Hazlitts) offers "luxurious"
surroundings which most reporters proclaim "a delight".
/ **Rooms:** 33 (of which 15 non smoking).

Royal Garden £359

2-24 Kensington High St W8 1—3B
🖱 www.royalgardenhotel.co.uk
✉ sales@royalgardenhotel.co.uk
☎ (020) 7937 8000 🖨 (020) 7361 1991

"Excellent rooms" and "wonderful views" – including from the
10th-floor restaurant (which can offer "marvellous" cooking, at
least by hotel standards) – are among the features which
distinguish this "well-run" modern establishment, by Kensington
Gardens. If there is a reservation, it's that the 'feel' of the place –
a tower block originally constructed in the '70s, but substantially
refurbished in recent years – is a touch anonymous. / **Rooms:** 396
(of which 229 non smoking and 19 family rooms). **Facilities:** gym; spa.

Rubens £140

39 Buckingham Palace Rd SW1   2—4B

🖰 www.rubenshotel.com ✉ bookrb@rchmail.com
☎ (020) 7834 6600   📠 (020) 7233 6037

"Comfortable" and *"in a good location"* (overlooking the
Buckingham Palace mews) this is one of the best 'superior-tourist'
hotels in town. Some find the décor *"a bit twee"* – *"that's why it
appeals to us visitors!"* – but otherwise most reporters say they
had a *"lovely"* stay at this Red Carnation hotel, thanks in no small
part to the *"competent and friendly"* service. / **Rooms:** 172.

Sanderson £250

50 Berners St W1   2—1B

🖰 www.ianschragerhotels.com
✉ sanderson@ianschragerhotels.com
☎ (020) 7300 1400   📠 (020) 7300 1401

"Innovative, slick and kitsch", Ian Schrager's design-hotel north of
Oxford Street has been a big PR success and continues to attract
a *"trendy, happy crowd"*, for whom its wacky Philippe Starck
design makes it *"a space-age oasis of comfort"*. Almost half of
reporters, however, tend to the view that the place *"lacks charm"*,
or that *"the overall package is weak for such an expensive place"*
(with *"low-quality service"* a particular bugbear). Spoon+, its Alain
Ducasse-branded restaurant, has become a byword for expensive
pretentiousness in some circles – the adjoining Long Bar is a
greater attraction. / **Rooms:** 150 (of which 70 non smoking and 16 family
rooms). **Facilities:** gym; spa. **Details:** no Switch.

Savoy £394

Strand WC2   2—2D

🖰 www.the-savoy.com ✉ info@the-savoy.co.uk
☎ (020) 7950 5492   📠 (020) 7950 5482

For its fans, this *"grand old lady"*, by the Thames offers
"consistently good" results, and those who hanker for a *"bygone
age"* proclaim it as having *"the priceless gift of making guests feel
comfortable, welcome and important"*. The location – *"convenient
for the theatre, shops and a walk along the Embankment after
breakfast"* (and handy for the City, too) – is also a huge plus.
Standards can be *"patchy"*, though, and – for roughly a quarter of
reporters – the place *"needs more updating"*. The famous Grill
Room was indeed relaunched in the summer of 2003, under the
supervision of Gordon Ramsay protégé Marcus Wareing.
/ **Rooms:** 263 (of which some non smoking and some family rooms).
Facilities: indoor pool; gym; spa.

Sherlock Holmes £241

108 Baker St W1
2—1A

🖰 www.sherlockholmeshotel.com
✉ info@sherlockholmeshotel.com
☎ (020) 7958 5222   🖷 (020) 7958 5223

Having received a surprisingly convincing "trendy boutique" makeover, this revivified establishment in re-emerging Marylebone is praised by early reporters for its "tasteful modern rooms", its "great bar" and "good gym". The restaurant is a more than incidental attraction. / **Rooms:** 119 (of which 59 non smoking and some family rooms). **Facilities:** gym.

Sofitel St James £323

6 Waterloo Pl SW1
2—3C

🖰 www.sofitel.com   ✉ h3144@accor-hotels.com
☎ (020) 7747 2200   🖷 (020) 7747 2210

"Sharp and modern without being cold", this newly-opened hotel has a very central location in an imposing Edwardian building, very near Trafalgar Square. Attractions include "amazing plumbing", and a brasserie which serves "decent" food – its ambience is perhaps more suited to business than pleasure. / **Rooms:** 186 (of which 90 non smoking and 15 family rooms). **Facilities:** gym; spa.

St Martins £292

St Martin's Ln WC2
2—2C

🖰 www.ianschragerhotels.com
✉ sml@ianschragerhotels.com
☎ (020) 7300 5500   🖷 (020) 7300 5501

Fans proclaim this made-over Theatreland office block a "hip hotel par excellence" and – like all Ian Schrager's places – it remains a darling of the fashion and media crowds. But while the initial impression may be "spectacular" and some think the accommodation is "awesome", others think the rooms are "tiny" ("cheap shoeboxes, dressed up as Armani") and service "arrogant". Needless to say, the main restaurant, Asia de Cuba, is very expensive for what it is. / **Rooms:** 204 (of which some non smoking). **Facilities:** gym.

Stafford   £282

16-18 St James's Pl SW1   2—3B
ⓓ www.thestaffordhotel.co.uk
✉ info@thestaffordhotel.co.uk
☎ (020) 7493 0111   🖷 (020) 7493 7121

This "excellent little hide-away" is furnished in grand traditional style, It has a super location (just off Piccadilly, but in a cute warren of St James's lanes) and "wonderful" service, too. Features include its "romantic" courtyard rooms, and the American Bar, which has "loads of personality". / **Rooms:** 81 *(of which some family rooms).* **Details:** *meals unavailable: Sat L.*

Threadneedles   £155

5 Threadneedle St EC2   1—2C
ⓓ www.theetoncollection.com
✉ res_threadneedles@etontownhouse.com
☎ (020) 7657 8080   🖷 (020) 7657 8100

This "boutique hotel with minimalist décor, excellent service and great attention to detail" is all the more worth knowing about for offering the rare chance to stay in the heart of the Square Mile. It only opened in 2002, but its "luxurious and calming atmosphere" has already attracted a number of admirers. Facilities include an impressively designed restaurant, Bonds. / **Rooms:** 70 *(of which all non smoking and 6 family rooms).* **Facilities:** *spa.* **Details:** *min age for children: 5.*

Travel Inn   £80

Belvedere Rd SE1   2—3D
ⓓ www.travelinn.co.uk
✉ london.county.hall.mti@whitbread.com
☎ 0870 238 3300   🖷 (020) 7902 1619

The County Hall branch of this budget chain (there are many others in town) does have some "odd-shaped" rooms, but – being just over the bridges from Parliament and Covent Garden– it's also incredibly convenient for sightseers and theatre-goers. / **Rooms:** 313 *(of which 50 non smoking and some family rooms).* **Details:** *meals unavailable: L; no Amex.*

Victoria Park Plaza   £200

2—4B

239 Vauxhall Bridge Rd SW1
🖱 www.parkplazahotel.co.uk
✉ vppres@parkplazahotels.co.uk
☎ (020) 7769 9999   📠 (020) 7769 9998

This brand-new establishment by Victoria Station has all the charm of an airport hotel, but its "bright and airy" accommodation and its "great location for business and leisure" have already won it a surprisingly large following among reporters. The food can be "terrible" (but there are quite a few reasonable cheap restaurants nearby, and some pricier places a few minutes away in Belgravia). / **Rooms:** *299 (of which 150 non smoking and 6 family rooms).* **Facilities:** *gym.*

Westbury Mayfair   £282

2—2B

Bond St W1
🖱 www.westbury-london.co.uk
✉ sales@westburymayfair.com
☎ (020) 7629 7755   📠 (020) 7495 1163

It may look a bit dowdy, but – for shopaholics (and even those who are not) – it's difficult to beat the "excellent location" of this "rather '60s" establishment, bang in the middle of Bond Street. Otherwise, however, reports (which are many) are constant only in their inconstancy – if you get a 'deal' though (they "always" have them, apparently) and "ask for a quiet room at the rear", this is a destination well worth considering. / **Rooms:** *247 (of which some non smoking and 30 family rooms).* **Facilities:** *gym.*

LONDON MAPS

MAP I – LONDON OVERVIEW

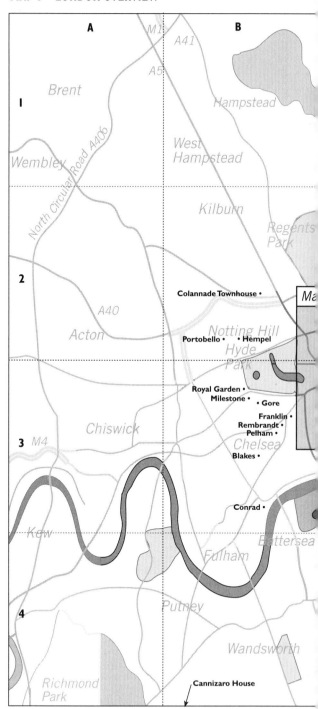

MAP I – LONDON OVERVIEW

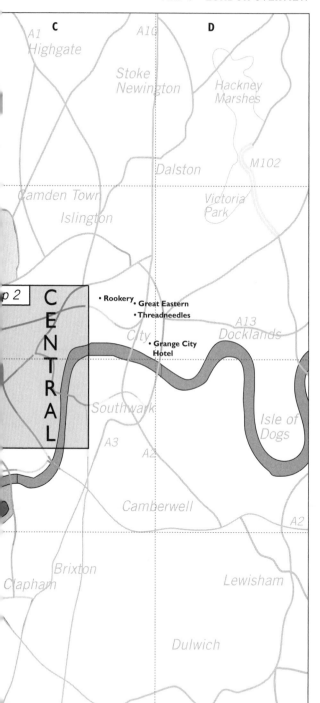

C

A1
Highgate

A10

D

Stoke
Newington

Hackney
Marshes

Dalston

M102

Camden Town

Victoria
Park

Islington

p 2

C
E
N
T
R
A
L

• Rookery
• Great Eastern
• Threadneedles

A13
Docklands

City

• Grange City
Hotel

Southwark

Isle of
Dogs

A3

A2

Camberwell

A2

Brixton

Lewisham

Clapham

Dulwich

MAP 2 – WEST END

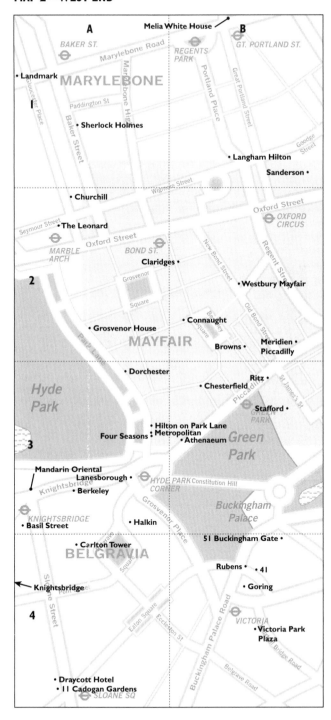

A   Melia White House   **B**

BAKER ST.   *REGENTS PARK*   *GT. PORTLAND ST.*

Marylebone Road

• Landmark

MARYLEBONE

Paddington St

Marylebone High St

• Sherlock Holmes

• Langham Hilton

Sanderson •

Wigmore Street

• Churchill

Oxford Street

OXFORD CIRCUS

Seymour Street

• The Leonard

MARBLE ARCH

Oxford Street

BOND ST.

New Bond Street

Regent Street

2

Claridges •

Grosvenor

• Westbury Mayfair

Square

• Connaught

Old Bond St

• Grosvenor House

MAYFAIR

Browns •

Meridien •
Piccadilly

• Dorchester

Ritz •

• Chesterfield

Piccadilly

St James's St.

Stafford •

Hyde Park

• Hilton on Park Lane

GREEN PARK

Four Seasons : Metropolitan

3

• Athenaeum

Green Park

Mandarin Oriental

Lanesborough •

• Berkeley

Knightsbridge

HYDE PARK CORNER

Constitution Hill

Buckingham Palace

Grosvenor Place

KNIGHTSBRIDGE

• Basil Street

• Halkin

• Carlton Tower

BELGRAVIA

51 Buckingham Gate •

Rubens •

• 41

← Knightsbridge

• Goring

Sloane Street

4

Eaton Square

Eccleston St

Buckingham Palace Road

VICTORIA

• Victoria Park Plaza

Bridge Road

Belgrave Road

• Draycott Hotel

• 11 Cadogan Gardens

SLOANE SQ.

MAP 2 – WEST END

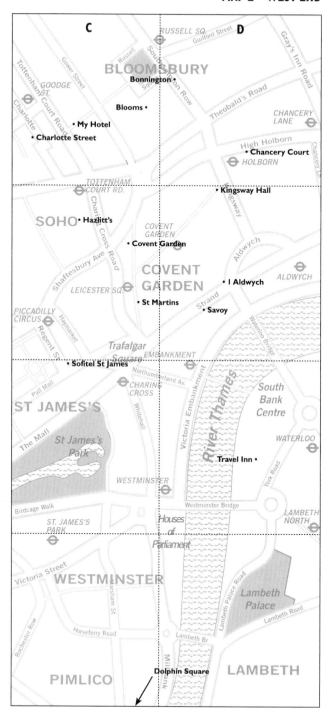

NEW YORK

WHICH PART OF TOWN TO STAY IN?

Midtown

Midtown – Manhattan's central business district – is a good place for a typical first-time visitor to stay. It is within walking distance of many quintessential Big Apple attractions: Times Square and Broadway; the shopping section of Fifth Avenue; all the major department stores; many of the best more 'traditional' restaurants; and Central Park. Over on the less fashionable west side, there are many large hotels: with the obvious exception of Ian Schrager's design-hotels, they tend to large and anonymous places you're likely to find yourself in if you go on a package. Midtown hotels included in this guide are:

Algonquin
The Benjamin
Box Tree
Bryant Park
Elysee
Essex House
Fitzpatrick
Flatotel International
Four Seasons
Hudson
Metropolitan
Millennium Broadway
Morgans
New York Palace
Paramount
Parker Meridien
Peninsula
Plaza
Ritz Carlton
Roger Smith
Roger Williams
Royalton
The Sherry-Netherland
Sofitel
St Regis
Swissotel
W – 541 Lexington Av
W – 1567 Broadway
W – 120 East 39th St
Waldorf Astoria
Warwick

The Upper East Side

For those in search of quiet and refinement, the swanky Upper East Side (the area to the east of Central Park) has many de luxe hotels, usually in a style characterised locally as 'European'. This area also houses many of the major visual arts and cultural attractions.

Hotels included:

Carlyle
Lowell
The Mark
Melrose
Pierre
Plaza Athénée
Stanhope

The Upper West Side

On the other side of Central Park, the traditionally less
fashionable, but more relaxed, Upper West Side – which,
apart from the Lincoln Center, boasts few obvious visitor
attractions – is relatively thinly provided with hotels:

Empire
Trump International

Downtown

Definitions of Downtown – the home of 'Manhattan cool' –
vary a bit, although no one would put it uptown of 34th
street. The prime visitor (and shopping) area downtown is
now SoHo, but it remains relatively thinly provided with
hotels. The hipper (but quite desolate) TriBeCa (triangle
below Canal Street) has only one establishment on any scale.

Hotels included:

Carlton Arms
Gershwin
Holiday Inn
Mercer
60 Thompson
SoHo Grand
Tribeca Grand
W – 201 Park Av South

The Financial District ('Wall Street')

Day-tripping to the Statue of Liberty aside, it is difficult to
see why anyone without business in this area would stay
here. Those who need to stay for business, however, have an
improving range of hotels in what has traditionally been a
poor area for accommodation.

Just one recommendation:

Marriott Financial Centre

SURVEY RESULTS

The "city that never sleeps" doesn't sound a great place to find a satisfactory hotel room! In a city where many hotels are exceptionally large by European standards, and almost all are very 'commercial', it is indeed quite hard to find accommodation that is clean, quiet, comfortable and spacious – certainly at any reasonable cost. The situation, however, is far from hopeless.

The hotels which reporters mentioned most in the survey were as follows:

1. Hudson

2. SoHo Grand

3. Waldorf Astoria

4. W Hotels

5. Four Seasons

6. Paramount

7. Plaza

8. Essex House

9. New York Palace

10. Royalton

The most immediately striking feature of this list is the extraordinary success which Ian Schrager – once, half of the legendary Studio 54 disco partnership – has created. His hotels, which have become a byword for a certain type of contemporary chic, account for no fewer than three of the names in the list (the Hudson, the Paramount and the Royalton). Objectively speaking, however, none of these establishments is especially well regarded by reporters.

NB: the caveats about prices on p6 most particularly apply to New York. All prices are indicative: some hotels have indicated that 'peak' rates can be up to two to three times low-season rates so there really is no subsitute for checking the rates applicable at the time of your intended stay.

The Best Hotels, and the Best Rooms too

Five hotels clearly emerged as The Best in New York. Judging on the overall ratings awarded by reporters, they were, in order, as follows:

Pierre
The Mark
Four Seasons
St Regis
New York Palace

Exactly the same names appear if it's the best rooms you're after (but this time with the more modern establishments, the Four Seasons and the Palace, rising to the top of the list).

Most Charm

Even when it comes to charm, four of the same five names come up again, but with the great downtown success of recent years (the SoHo Grand) easing out the businesslike Palace:

Pierre
St Regis
The Mark
SoHo Grand
Four Seasons

Best on a Budget

As in London, there is little doubt that those seeking pleasant accommodation on a budget will have to compromise to some extent. The best of the less expensive places identified by the survey were:

The Fitzpatrick Manhattan
Millennium Broadway
Gershwin
Metropolitan
Roger Smith
Roger Williams
Swissotel
Tribeca Grand
W hotels
Warwick

Indeed, if there was a 'surprise success' from the survey, it was the W Hotels, which are well worth considering whether or not you're on a limited budget.

Algonquin $179

59 West 44th St, NY 10036
🖥 www.thealgonquinhotel.com
☎ +1 212 840 6800   📠 +1 212 944 1419

Famed for its '20s literary associations (Dorothy Parker and the Round Table), this Midtown centenarian is a copper-bottomed Manhattan institution (in a very central Midtown location), and duly inspires commentary such as "charming or outdated, depending on your point of view". New management (from 2002) may perhaps change all that. / **Rooms:** *174 (of which some non smoking).* **Details:** *no Switch.*

The Benjamin $420

125 East 50th St, NY 10022
🖥 www.thebenjamin.com   ✉ info@affinia.com
☎ +1 212 320 8002   📠 +1 212 465 3697

"A reasonably-priced suite hotel (by New York standards)", this impressively revamped 1927 building offers "reasonably spacious" accommodation in a "great" Midtown location (near the Waldorf Astoria). To ensure your best night's sleep, the 'pillow concierge' will advise on no fewer than ten possibilities on offer. / **Rooms:** *209.* **Facilities:** *gym; spa.* **Details:** *no Switch.*

Box Tree $272

250 East 49th St, NY 10017
✉ frontdesk@theboxtree.com
☎ +1 212 758 8320   📠 +1 212 308 3899

Two 18th-century townhouses in Turtle Bay (a rather intriguing Midtown enclave) provides the setting for this "elegant" and "opulent" establishment. If your vision of New York is curling up in a four-poster in front of a roaring fire, this may well be just the place for you. / **Details:** *no Switch.*

Bryant Park $255

40 West 40th St, NY 10018
🖥 www.bryantparkhotel.com
☎ +1 212 869 0100   📠 +1 212 869 4446

Overlooking the eponymous Midtown park (behind the Public Library), this trendily retro new hotel (founded in 2001, in the American Radiator building of 1924) has already attracted a small fan club among reporters. "Large rooms" are a particular plus. / **Rooms:** *128 (of which some non smoking).* **Details:** *no Switch.*

Carlton Arms $100   ☺

160 East 25th St, NY 10010
🖥 www.carltonarms.com   ✉ arthotel@aol.com
☎ +1 212 684 8337

Affectionately described by one reporter as "a Bohemian dump", this "friendly" artified townhouse near Gramercy Park – where all rooms have their own theme, ranging from Versailles to sadomasochism – is the place to choose if you want to live inside a funky bite of the Big Apple. It's not, however, a place for the faint-hearted. / **Rooms:** *52.* **Details:** *no Amex or Switch.*

Carlyle $495

35 East 76th St, NY 10021

🖰 www.thecarlyle.com   ✉ thecarlyle@rosewoodhotels.com

☎ +1 212 744 1600   🖷 +1 212 717 4682

Long famed for its "elegance" and "aristocratic charm", this genteel grande dame (1929) of the Upper East Side maintains a strong following, not least thanks to its "great location" (especially for art-lovers, with the Metropolitan, Frick, Whitney and Guggenheim all an easy walk away). "Faultless" service was also praised, but – for a minority of reporters – the place had got "tired" and was "living on its reputation" in its last days under private ownership. "I hope that changing hands will mean a big revamp", says one reporter, and there are signs that Rosewood are wielding their new broom with some vigour – the restaurant was relaunched in mid-2003, for example, to some acclaim.
/ **Rooms:** 180 (of which 10 non smoking and some family rooms). **Facilities:** gym.
Details: no Switch.

Elysee $325

60 East 54th St, NY 10022

🖰 www.elyseehotel.com

☎ +1 212 753 1066   🖷 +1 212 980 9278

The name does not lie – European-style "charm" is the keynote of this "elegant" and "very friendly" Midtowner, whose "small" rooms offer a cosy "home away from home" feel. The basement Monkey Bar – a watering hole since the '30s – attracts at least one vote as "the best in NYC" (but, as we go to press, news reaches us that it's now doubling up as a steakhouse). / **Rooms:** 101
(of which some non smoking and some family rooms). **Details:** meals unavailable:
Sat & Sun.

Empire $137   😐

44 West 63rd St, NY 10023

🖰 www.empirehotel.com

✉ reservations@empirehotel.com

☎ +1 212 265 7400   🖷 +1 212 315 0349

Slightly off the tourist-beaten track, this slab-like Upper West Sider is "ideally located for the Lincoln Center" and within very easy reach of Central Park. Note that standard rooms can be "small" or "scruffy" – "I paid the small premium for a superior room, and it was worth it 20 times over". / **Rooms:** 381. **Details:** no
restaurant; no Switch.

sign up for our next survey at www.hardens.com

Essex House $226

160 Central Park South, NY 10019
🖰 www.essexhouse.com.   ✉ email@essexhouse.com
☎ +1 212 247 0300   🖨 +1 212 315 1839

"Incredible views of Central Park" contribute much to the undoubted "authenticity" of this swanky Midtown Art Deco landmark. Commentary, though, is often tempered by ambiguity: "good value, but service has deteriorated since being acquired by Westin", "great rooms, but terrible bathrooms", "efficient but stuffy", and so on. All, agree, however, that the beds are "heavenly". The main restaurant – run by Alain Ducasse – is the most expensive in town. / **Rooms:** 605 (of which some non smoking and some family rooms). **Facilities:** gym; spa.

Fitzpatrick $259

687 Lexington Av, NY 10022
🖰 www.fitzpatrickhotels.com
✉ reservations@fitzpatrickhotels.com
☎ +1 212 355 0100   🖨 +1 212 308 5166

This "small, comfortable Irish-owned hotel" is a pleasantly dated Midtown spot almost all of whose staff seem to hail from the Emerald Isle. Junior Suites – often available at a modest premium – "are better than standard small rooms". (A more modern sibling establishment near Grand Central – tel + 1 212 351 6800 – is also touted as "a nice boutique hotel"). / **Rooms:** 143 (of which 118 non smoking and some family rooms). **Facilities:** outdoor pool; gym.

Flatotel International $189

135 West 52nd St, NY 10019
🖰 www.flatotel-Intl.com
☎ +1 212 887 9400   🖨 +1 212 887 9442

"Not fancy, but a large room" – if you're looking for "good amenities" and "an excellent location", this impressive Midtown building has quite a lot to recommend it. Many reservations are of course for extended periods, but you can book by the night. / **Rooms:** 282 (of which 270 non smoking and 10 family rooms).

Four Seasons $475

57 East 57th St, NY 10022
🖰 www.fourseasons.com
☎ +1 212 758 5700   🖨 +1 212 758 5711

"A great New York experience in a perfect location" – "massively expensive, but really worth it". Reporters have barely a bad word to say about this "classic" (in the best Gothamite style) Midtown representative of the top-end international chain. With its "very big" rooms (some higher ones with "fantastic views of Central Park") and "wonderful" service, its forte is as a "great business hotel", but – if money is no object – it's also tipped as being "very good for a break". **Rooms:** 368 (of which some non smoking and some family rooms). **Facilities:** gym; spa. **Details:** no Switch.

Gershwin $114
7 East 27th St, NY 10016
🖰 www.gershwinhotel.com
✉ reservations@gershwinhotel.com
☎ +1 212 545 8000   📠 +1 212 684 5546

"A fantastic location, just a few blocks from the Empire State Building" commends this "wacky" hotel – where you might just find a Warhol in your room – to younger-at-heart reporters. Even one unimpressed by the housekeeping conceded: "it's cheap and brilliantly situated, and does weekend deals". / **Rooms:** 133 (of which 120 non smoking and 6 family rooms). **Details:** no Switch.

Holiday Inn $202
138 Lafayette St, NY 10013
🖰 www.holidayinn.nyc.com   ✉ info@holidayinn-nyc.com
☎ +1 212 966 8898   📠 +1 212 966 3933

No, they don't get rated highly for charm, but – objectively speaking – reporters speak well of the Big Apple outposts of this you-know-what-you're-getting chain. A couple of the hotels are of particular note – the Downtown branch, listed, is 'a good value', as the Americans say, and one of the still few places to stay around SoHo. Wall Street (15 Gold St, NY 10038, tel + 1 212 323 7700) is similarly worth knowing about if you want to stay in the heart of the Financial District. / **Rooms:** 227 (of which 185 non smoking and 45 family rooms). **Details:** no Switch.

Hudson $145
356 West 58th St, NY 10019
🖰 www.ianschragerhotels.com
✉ hudson@ianschragerhotels.com
☎ +1 212 554 6000   📠 +1 212 554 6511

"Uncomfortable" rooms – "large enough for a small gnome without luggage" – disenchant many visitors to Ian Schrager's enormous budget design-hotel near Times Square. If you can overlook this rather basic reservation, however, this is a "very cool" place whose "so-hip-it-hurts" vibe can make a visit a "top-notch" experience. "Fantastic" public spaces are a particular plus – "the bar alone makes a stay here worthwhile", says one reporter, and the roof terrace is likened to "a Mediterranean haven". / **Rooms:** 820 (of which some non smoking and some family rooms). **Facilities:** gym. **Details:** no Switch.

Lowell $413

28 East 63rd St, NY 10021
🖱 www.lowellhotel.com ✉ reservations@lowellhotel.com
☎ +1 212 838 1400 🖨 +1 212 319 4230

"As luxurious as the 'big names' but small enough for personal service", this Upper East Sider – handily located for Midtown, too – was opened in 1927 as a residential hotel. Its 17 floors never have more than six bedrooms apiece, putting the whole operation on a "personal" scale. / **Rooms:** *70 (of which 10 family rooms).* **Facilities:** *gym.* **Details:** *no Switch.*

The Mark $575

25 East 77th St, NY 10021
🖱 www.mandarinoriental.com
✉ tmnyc-reservations@mohg.com
☎ +1 212 744 4300 🖨 +1 212 744 2749

Reporters speak nothing but good of this "smart and swanky" (but quite "low-key") Mandarin Oriental establishment, in a quiet part of the Upper East Side. Its "very personal" service and "the best location for the Museum Mile" are especially commended, as are its "good business facilities" (which include the self-explanatory Wall Street Shuttle). / **Rooms:** *180 (of which some non smoking and some family rooms).* **Facilities:** *gym.*

Marriott Financial Center $300

85 West St, NY 10006
🖱 www.marriotthotels.com
☎ +1 212 385 4900 🖨 +1 212 227 8136

"Fantastic rooms, with views over the Hudson" help make this large new chain hotel a useful tip for visitors who need to stay around the Financial District. / **Rooms:** *499 (of which 300 non smoking and some family rooms).* **Facilities:** *indoor pool; gym.*

sign up for our next survey at www.hardens.com

Melrose $239

140 East 63rd St, NY 10021

🖰 www.melrosehotel.com   ✉ jvelez@melrosehotel.com
☎ +1 212 838 5700   🖶 +1 212 888 4271

The establishment formerly known as the Barbizon has a "great" Upper East Side location, especially for those wanting to shop at Bloomies or in the fashion stores of Madison Avenue. It can seem "fairly characterless", but, for at least one reporter, a "best-ever" gym offered some recompense – at 34,000 square feet, and occupying four floors, it does indeed sound pretty impressive. / **Rooms:** 306 (of which some non smoking and some family rooms). **Details:** no Switch.

Mercer $395

147 Mercer St, NY 10012

🖰 www.mercerhotel.com
✉ reservations@mercerhotel.com
☎ +1 212 966 6060   🖶 +1 212 965 3838

"High chic in the heart of SoHo" (with a location better than that of the nearby SoHo Grand) wins fans for this "glamorous", "downtown haven", with its "ultra-chic lobby bar". There are others, though, who feel the place badly "needs a reality-check", citing "bland" rooms and exceptionally "snooty" staff. / **Rooms:** 75 (of which some family rooms). **Details:** no Switch.

Metropolitan $139

569 Lexington Av, NY 10022

🖰 www.metropolitanhotelnyc.com
✉ metropolitanhotelnyc@loewshotels.com
☎ +1 212 752 7000   🖶 +1 212 758 6311

If you're looking for a combination of a "very good location" (just behind the Waldorf Astoria) with "reasonable prices", you won't do much better than this "otherwise unexceptional" Midtowner. Unsurprisingly, though, given the prices, rooms in this vaguely modernistic establishment can be "teeny tiny" (and "make sure you are not close to the lifts"). / **Rooms:** 722 (of which some non smoking and some family rooms). **Facilities:** spa. **Details:** no Switch.

Millennium Broadway $200

145 West 44th St, NY 10036

🖰 www.millenniumbroadway.com
✉ broadway@mhrmail.com
☎ +1 212 768 4400   🖶 +1 212 768 0847

"An ideal city-break hotel right in the middle of the Theater District." Reports about this "modern, efficient, clean and comfortable" establishment are impressively consistent for a place on this enormous scale. The only real complaint, unsurprisingly, is that it's "a little impersonal". / **Rooms:** 761 (of which 638 non smoking). **Details:** no Switch.

Morgans $225

237 Madison Av, NY 10016
🖥 www.morganshotel.com
📧 morgans@ianschragerhotels.com
☎ +1 212 686 0300 🖨 +1 212 779 8352

*It's a lot less famous than its restaurant (Asia da Cuba, where guests take breakfast) nowadays, but this Murray Hill spot is of historical interest as Ian Schrager's first foray into the hotel business (1984). The accommodation is arguably rather "dull", but this is a discreet establishment in a handy location, convenient for both up- and downtown. / **Rooms:** 113 (of which 77 non smoking and 1 family room). **Details:** no Switch.*

New York Palace $450

455 Madison Av, NY 10022
🖥 www.newyorkpalace.com 📧 info@nypalace.com
☎ +1 212 888 7000 🖨 +1 212 303 6000

*The external appearance may be rather odd – a tower block erupting from a Beaux-Arts townhouse – but reporters are consistently of the view that this "lavish" establishment is a "reliable" and "under-rated" destination. "Huge rooms" ("in a world of designer broom cupboards") win it particular support, especially from business travellers. In Le Cirque 2000, the hotel houses (albeit in a new incarnation) one of the city's longest-running restaurant success-stories. / **Rooms:** 896. **Facilities:** gym; spa. **Details:** no Switch.*

Paramount $155 😐

235 West 46th St, NY 10036
🖥 www.ianschragerhotels.com
📧 paramount@ianschragerhotels.com
☎ +1 212 764 5500 🖨 +1 212 575 4892

*"Starck by design, and stark by nature", this "hip younger-scene hotel" in the Theater District gets a very mixed press. On the plus side, "good design, a good location and a good bar" combine to make it "a fun place to hang out" (and "relatively cheap", too). On the downside some bedrooms are "unbelievably minute", and the "ludicrous techno-beat" to which the lobby resounds can contribute to an atmosphere some find "a little forbidding". / **Rooms:** 594 (of which 200 non smoking and 25 family rooms). **Facilities:** indoor pool; gym; spa. **Details:** no Switch.*

Parker Meridien $322

118 West 57th St, NY 10019

🏠 www.lemeridien.com

✉ reservations@parkermeridien.com

☎ +1 212 245 5000   🖨 +1 212 307 1776

As "one of only a few hotels in New York with a rooftop swimming pool", not to mention a "great gym and a 43rd floor running track, it's perhaps no surprise that facilities are the highest rated feature of this large Midtown fixture. One reporter warns that "rooms down the bottom are quite dark and unremarkable – so ask for one higher up or pay the extra for an upgrade".
/ **Rooms:** 731 (of which 450 non smoking and 84 family rooms). **Facilities:** indoor pool; gym; spa. **Details:** no Switch.

Peninsula $449

700 Fifth Av, NY 10019

🏠 www.fasttrack.newyork.peninsula.com

✉ pny@peninsula.com

☎ +1 212 956 2888   🖨 +1 212 903 3949

"The location couldn't be better" (on a prominent corner in Midtown), and for grandeur, it's difficult to beat this grand Beaux-Arts building – now part of the eponymous international hotel group. Commentary is, however, unusually mixed. Fans vaunt a "truly pampering" experience ("all the way down to the TV by the bath") with a "fantastic" location, "a great in-house pool and gym" and a "happening rooftop bar". Doubters, however, are strident, noting that a combination of "tiny" rooms ("all of which seem to have a view of a vent, or noisy Fifth Avenue") and "tip-hungry staff" made their visit "underwhelming in the extreme".
/ **Rooms:** 339 (of which some non smoking and some family rooms). **Details:** no Switch.

Pierre $425

Fifth Av (61st St), NY 10021

🏠 www.fourseasons.com/pierre

☎ +1 212 838 8000   🖨 +1 212 940 8109

"Old-world style" ("very New Yorkish of the 1960s") helps win glowing commentary for this top-drawer Upper Eastsider, right by Central Park (and within a very easy stroll of Midtown). Just occasionally, the approach can seem "fussy and impersonal", but for many reporters this Four Seasons establishment remains simply "the best hotel in town". / **Rooms:** 202 (of which some non smoking and some family rooms). **Facilities:** gym. **Details:** no Switch.

Plaza $259   ☹

768 Fifth Av, NY 10019
🖰 www.lhw.com/plazanyc   ✉ newyork@fairmont.com
☎ +1 212 759 3000   🖷 +1 212 759 3167

For "faded glamour" and "a New York feeling", fans say you just "can't beat" this ultra-famous landmark – a dominant presence on the corner of Central Park, and a bit-player in so many movies. However, many reporters find the place "resting on its past reputation" nowadays with accusations of "gloomy" rooms ("even those with a view!"), "out-of-date" bathrooms, "poor housekeeping" and even, in one case, "a reception so poor we cancelled". / **Rooms:** 745. **Facilities:** gym; spa.

Plaza Athénée $373   ☺

37 East 64th St, NY 10021
🖰 www.lhw.com/atheneenyc   ✉ res@plaza-athenee.com
☎ +1 212 734 9100   🖷 +1 212 772 0958

"A very good hotel with excellent service and strong focus on guest satisfaction" – reporters speak only well of this "pleasant", rather 'European', establishment, where the "quiet" and "comfortable" accommodation is particularly approved. Midtown is just a stroll away, too. / **Rooms:** 152 (of which some non smoking and some family rooms). **Facilities:** gym. **Details:** no Switch.

Ritz Carlton $398   ☺

2 West St, NY 10004
🖰 www.ritzcarlton.com
☎ +1 212 344 0800   🖷 +1 212 344 3801

"Great rooms" (among the best in the city) and "service that's trying very hard" make this new waterside hotel a top downtown destination. Note, though – the feel of this skyscraper in an area without much in the way of street-life is very "corporate-hotel". / **Rooms:** 298 (of which some non smoking and some family rooms). **Facilities:** gym; spa. **Details:** no Switch.

sign up for our next survey at www.hardens.com

Roger Smith $169

501 Lexington Av, NY 10017

🖰 www.rogersmith.com   ✉ reservations@rogersmith.com
☎ +1 212 755 1400   🖨 +1 212 758 4061

*This "arty" boutique hotel – "the décor is getting a little tired but offers lots of character" – offers "functional" accommodation, but it's "reasonably priced" for somewhere in the handy heart of Midtown. / **Rooms:** 130 (of which some non smoking and some family rooms). **Details:** no Switch.*

Roger Williams $179

131 Madison Av, NY 10016

🖰 www.rogerwilliamshotel.com
✉ rw-reservations@rogerwilliamshotel.com
☎ +1 212 448 7000   🖨 +1 212 448 7007

*"Small rooms, but comfortable and great value" – reporters speak only well of this "modern" and elegant Murray Hill establishment, which fans say is "perfect for business or leisure". / **Rooms:** 187 (of which 18 non smoking). **Facilities:** gym. **Details:** no Switch.*

Royalton $334

😐

44 West 44th St, NY 10036

🖰 www.ianschragerhotels.com
✉ royalton@ianschragerhotels.com
☎ +1 212 869 4400   🖨 +1 212 869 8965

*It's been around so long (well, since 1988) that it's perhaps no surprise that Ian Schrager's "lively" Starck-designed Midtown hotel strikes some as "hip but not happening" nowadays, and offering accommodation that's "showing its age". For its fan club, though, it's still "always fun" (with the "great bar" in the lobby attracting particular support). The restaurant, 44, is a legendary power scene for Manhattan media types. / **Rooms:** 800 (of which some non smoking and some family rooms). **Facilities:** gym. **Details:** no Switch.*

The Sherry-Netherland $425

☺

781 Fifth Av (59th St), NY 10022

🖰 www.sherrynetherland.com
☎ +1 212 355 2800   🖨 +1 212 319 4306

*Perhaps it's the small scale of operations which accounts for the surprisingly limited volume of commentary on this sumptuously fitted out grand hotel (1927), just across Fifth Avenue from the Plaza. All reports, however, confirm that "excellent" service is a highlight. / **Rooms:** 60 (of which some non smoking and some family rooms). **Facilities:** gym. **Details:** no Switch.*

60 Thompson $229

60 Thompson St, NY 10012
🖰 www.60thompson.com   ✉ info@60thompson.com
☎ +1 212 431 0400   🖨 +1 212 431 0200

If you want to stay in SoHo, there's still not a great deal of choice, so the "great" location of this undoubtedly "cool" design-hotel is a major attraction. It's "not as stylish as the SoHo Grand", though, and its "popularity with the locals" can be something of a handicap – "beware of noise in the evening when the reception turns into a bar". / **Rooms:** 98 (of which 78 non smoking and 24 family rooms). **Details:** no Switch.

Sofitel $250

45 West 44th St, NY 10036
🖰 www.sofitel.com   ✉ h2185@accor-hotels.com
☎ +1 212 354 8844   🖨 +1 212 354 2480

A "stunning building" – part of the ongoing redevelopment of Times Square and its environs – provides the setting for this new 30-floor Gallic outpost, which an early reporter tips as one to watch. / **Rooms:** 398 (of which 350 non smoking). **Facilities:** gym. **Details:** no Switch.

SoHo Grand $399

310 W Broadway, NY 10013
🖰 www.sohogrand.com   ✉ reservations@sohogrand.com
☎ +1 212 965 3000   🖨 +1 212 965 3200

The first major hotel to open downtown in over a century has been a huge success with British visitors since its launch in 1996. The reporter who finds it "very funky, if not especially comfortable" speaks for many – the charms of its "chic" lobby, "fab" bar and "great" SoHo-fringe location being somewhat offset by "shoe-box-sized" accommodation and service which (just sometimes) comes "with attitude". / **Rooms:** 366 (of which 258 non smoking). **Facilities:** gym. **Details:** no Switch.

St Regis $610

2 East 55th St, NY 10022
🖰 www.stregis.com   ✉ stregisny.res@stregis.com
☎ +1 212 753 4500   🖨 +1 212 787 3447

"A short stroll from Tiffany's", this "lovely" hotel occupies an impressive building that's positively ancient by Midtown standards (1904 – two years before London's Ritz, and in a style not so very different). The reports it attracts are notable for their across-the-board upbeat consistency. (L'Espinasse, formerly the city's longest-established grand hotel dining room, closed its doors in the spring of 2003.) / **Rooms:** 315 (of which some non smoking and some family rooms). **Facilities:** gym; spa. **Details:** no Switch.

Stanhope $259

995 Fifth Av, NY 10028
🖰 www.stanhopepark.hyatt.com
☎ +1 212 774 1234 🖨 +1 212 517 0088

This small Hyatt hotel has the perfect Upper East Side location for culture-vultures, bang opposite the Metropolitan Museum. It attracted only modest, but enthusiastic, survey support, especially for its "perfect" service. Accommodation floors were refurbished during 2003. / **Rooms:** 185 (of which some non smoking and some family rooms). **Facilities:** gym. **Details:** no Switch.

Swissotel $225

440 Park Av, NY 10022
🖰 www.swissotel-newyork.com
📧 emailus.newyork@swissotel.com
☎ +1 212 421 0900 🖨 +1 212 371 4190

This large and "very efficient" Midtowner is "the perfect business hotel", says one reporter whose regular NYC home it is. "Good value", says another, who praises its "ideal shopping location". It's perhaps surprising that it didn't gather more survey support — perhaps it's because even the fan first cited above admits the place is slightly "charmless"? / **Rooms:** 495 (of which some non smoking and some family rooms). **Details:** no Switch.

Tribeca Grand $259

2 Av of the Americas, NY 10013
🖰 www.tribecagrand.com
📧 publicrelations@tribecagrand.com
☎ +1 212 519 6600 🖨 +1 212 519 6700

Perhaps because the area is not so obviously inviting, the trendy Tribeca sibling to the (not so distant) SoHo Grand has never attracted anything like the same following (and it can seem "quiet", certainly in comparison). Perhaps they just have to try harder here, as reporters (though much less numerous) speak nothing but praise for its "chic" but "fun" ambience, and its "solicitous" service. / **Rooms:** 203. **Facilities:** gym. **Details:** no Switch.

Trump International $600

1 Central Park West, NY 10023
🖰 www.trumpintl.com ✉ reservations@trumpintl.com
☎ +1 212 299 1000   📠 +1 212 299 1150

Those in search of a "quality business hotel" (and certainly one on the West Side) could do very much worse than The Donald's "superb" Central Park-side tower. Its practical attractions include "a first-class pool and workout area", and the fact that "all rooms have kitchenettes". Readers filled with horror by this last observation will be consoled by the presence of Jean Georges (Vongerichten) – an "exquisite" restaurant, usually rated among the best in town. / **Rooms:** 167 (of which all non smoking). **Facilities:** indoor pool; gym; spa. **Details:** no Switch.

W New York Hotel $225

🖰 www.whotels.com
541 Lexington Av, NY 10022
☎ +1 212 755 1200   📠 +1 212 319 8344
1567 Broadway, NY 10036
☎ +1 212 930 7400   📠 +1 212 930 7500
201 Park Av South, NY 10003
☎ +1 212 253 9119   📠 +1 212 253 9229
120 East 39th St, NY 10016
☎ +1 212 686 1600   📠 +1 212 779 7822

Ian Schrager may be the man whose name has become synonymous with design-hotels, but this competing collection of "cool", "chic" and "funky" Starwood-group properties consistently received higher ratings from reporters. Rooms vary from "tiny" to "very large", but beds are "exceptionally comfortable", and staff attitude is a real plus – they "seem to like working here, and actually help". As is typical at such places, the bars are a particular attraction (though the presence of "too many beautiful people" seems to be an ever-present risk). As to choosing which W might be for you, it's really down to geography: the "Blade Runner views" from the Times Square hotel are particularly praised; Lexington Avenue is the 'plain vanilla' Midtown choice; The Court, in Murray Hill, is the quiet and intimate option; and Union Square has the advantage of being one of the relatively few recommendable establishments downtown.

Waldorf Astoria $299

301 Park Av, NY 10022
🖱 www.hilton.com
☎ +1 212 355 3000   🖷 +1 570 450 1588

It's difficult not to be initially wowed by the fame and grandeur of this "quintessential" Midtown landmark, which is "where the President always stays when he's in town", and which has a big business following. Such is the scale of the operation, though, it's inevitable that some find staying here an "anonymous" experience, and after the "glorious" Art Deco reception rooms, the "variable" quality of the accommodation at this Hilton property can come as quite a let-down. / **Rooms:** 1245 *(of which some non smoking).* **Details:** *no Switch.*

Warwick $180

65 West 54th St, NY 10019
🖱 www.warwickhotels.com
☎ +1 212 247 2700   🖷 +1 212 489 3926

Cary Grant lived for 12 years in a suite at this hotel – built by Randolph Hearst for his celebrity chums in 1927. For today's travellers, it still offers a "first-rate" Midtown location" (near the Rockerfeller Center), and is consistently approved as a "reliable" choice. / **Rooms:** 425 *(of which some non smoking).* **Facilities:** *gym.* **Details:** *no Switch.*

PARIS

WHICH PART OF TOWN TO STAY IN?

Paris is small by London or New York standards, with a density of underground stations greater than either. From a practical point of view, location is therefore less of an issue than in the other two cities.

The main division in Paris is between the more businesslike and traditionally residential Right Bank (where most of the grander hotels are found) and the 'intellectual' Left Bank. Subdivison may be made according to 'arrondissements' – the 20 administrative areas into which the city has long been divided.

The Right Bank
1st, 2nd, 3rd, 4th

The old heart of Paris around the Ile de la Cité (Notre Dame), the Louvre and the Palais-Royal (and nowadays the home of a number of the grandest palace-hotels). The 4th arondissement comprises Le Marais – a former aristocratic stronghold, which has emerged in recent years as the trendiest part of central Paris. Hotels listed:

du Bourg Tibourg
Costes
Jeu de Paume
Louvre
Meurice
Molière
Pavillon de la Reine
Ritz
Thérèse

8th, 17th

Straddling the Champs-Elysées for its full length, the 8th is the ritziest of the arrondissements, and home to many of the grandest hotels. The 17th is its quieter, more residential extension to the north. Hotels listed:

George V
Balzac
Le Bristol
Crillon
Grand Hommes
Hyatt Regency
Lancaster
Monna Lisa
Napoléon
Plaza Athénée
Prince de Galles
Rond Point des Champs-Elysées
Royal Monceau
Trémoille
de Vigny

9th, 10th

North-central Paris. A mixed area extending all the way from the (very grand) Opéra to the (sleazy) Pigalle. It includes the (very busy) Gare du Nord, handy for the Eurostar. Hotels listed:

Ambassador
du Nord
Scribe

11th, 12th, 19th, 20th

To the east of the city, the 'Paris des commerçants' – interesting and vibrant in part, but not of particular interest to the general visitor (though the 11th is developing an 'alternative' reputation). Indeed, the survey generated no suggestions in these unfashionable quartiers!

16th

The home of the BCBG (Bons Chics Bon Genres), where grand Parisians still often choose to live. Hotels listed:

Pergolese
Raphael
La Villa Maillot

18th

Montmartre, the site of the Sacré-Coeur and once the rallying point of the Impressionists. Besieged by tourists, but still very romantic. Hotels listed:

Le Bouquet de Montmartre
Villa Royale

The Left Bank
5th, 6th, 7th

Students, the literary world, academia… and some of the most fashionable shops in Paris. The 7th, home of the Eiffel Tower, is rather grand and governmental. Hotels listed:

L'Abbaye
Bel Ami
L'Hôtel
Lutetia
Notre Dame
Relais Christine
Relais St Germain
Verneuil

13th, 14th, 15th

The outer (or, in the case of the 15th, less accessible) Left Bank arrondissments. Still pleasant, but mainly of interest as an economical choice, or for relative quiet. Only one listing:

Hilton

SURVEY RESULTS

It was apparent from the survey that, perhaps unsurprisngly, smaller hotels in major cities tend to be more highly rated than larger ones. This is to the particular benefit of the hotels of the City of Light, many of whose largest central hotels would be almost 'boutique' by NYC standards. The city also benefits from a reputation as a sybaritic destination – not least with rich 'anglos' – which goes back over two centuries

The hotels which reporters mentioned most in the survey were as follows:

1. Costes

2. George V

3. Crillon

4. Le Bristol

5. Meurice

6. Prince de Galles

7. Ritz

8. Royal Monceau

9. Bel Ami

10. Lancaster

Grand traditional hotels completely dominate the list, accounting, paradoxically, for all but the first slot.

The Best Hotels
Six hotels (there was a tie for fifth place) emerged as The Best in Paris. Judging on the overall ratings awarded by reporters, they were, in order, as follows:

George V
de Vigny
Lutetia
Plaza Athénée
Raphael
Hyatt Regency

The Best Rooms
Three of the same names crop up in the list of the top five for best rooms:

Hyatt Regency
George V
Raphael
Lancaster
de Vigny

Charm

When it comes to charm, it's notable that the smaller establishments have the edge.

de Vigny
Raphael
Lutetia
Pavillion de la Reine
Lancaster

Best on a Budget

Paris is undoubtedly the best of the world cities for travellers on a budget. More modestly priced hotels which emerged with particular credit included:

L'Abbaye
du Bourg Tibourg
Monna Lisa
Jeu de Paume
Molière
Thérèse
Verneuil

See also Libertel

The large number of cheaper establishments in Paris can lead to a low density of reports on individual hotels. Our coverage of cheaper establishments is therefore less than we would like, and we particularly invite recommendations of budget hotels for inclusion in future editions.

L' Abbaye €190
10 rue Cassette (6th)
🖰 www.hotel-abbaye.com ✉ hotel.abbaye@wanadoo.fr
☎ +33 1 45 44 38 11   🖷 +33 1 45 48 07 86

Is this "the best small hotel in Paris"? Fans of this "very quiet and friendly" establishment in the heart of the Left Bank – between Saint-Germain des Prés and St Sulpice – certainly think so. It's generally seen as a "good-value" destination, but – if you're minded to push the boat out a bit – the "rooftop suite with its own little garden" comes highly recommended. / **Rooms:** 44 (of which some family rooms). **Details:** meals unavailable: no restaurant; no Switch.

Ambassador €360
16 boulevard Haussmann (9th)
🖰 www.hotelambassador-paris.com
✉ ambass@concorde-hotels.com
☎ +33 1 44 83 40 40   🖷 +33 1 42 46 19 84

"A very good central location" (especially convenient for the old Opéra and the major department stores) and "very pleasant public areas" are among the features which commend this grand Concorde Hotels establishment to most reporters. It was refurbished in 2002, and the general view is that it's "more attractive that most chain hotels", and "every comfort" ("including a full English breakfast") is catered for. / **Rooms:** 297 (of which 106 non smoking and 120 family rooms). **Details:** meals unavailable: Sat L & Sun; no Switch.

Balzac €425
6 rue Balzac (8th)
🖰 www.hotelbalzac.com ✉ reservation@hotelbalzac.com
☎ +33 1 44 35 18 00   🖷 +33 1 44 35 18 05

Some find it a touch on the "faded" side nowadays, but perhaps that's just how an hotel in a former aristocratic townhouse – not far from the Arc de Triomphe – ought to feel. It's "friendly" and "nicely kept", though, and rooms vary "from average to exceptional". The "very good restaurant" is presided over by Pierre Gagnaire. / **Rooms:** 70 (of which 10 non smoking and 9 family rooms).

Bel Ami €280

7-11 rue St. Benoît (6th)
🖥 www.hotel-bel-ami.com ✉ contact@hotel-bel-ami.com
☎ +33 1 42 61 53 53   🖨 +33 1 49 27 09 33

*A classic Rive Gauche location ("next to the Deux Magots") has
inspired quite a few reporters to visit this "very stylish" new hotel.
After the "impressive lobby", however, the "small rooms" can
come as something of a let-down, and the overall verdict is that
the place is "so cool, it's really rather cold".* / **Rooms:** 115 (of which 5
family rooms). **Details:** meals unavailable: no restaurant; no Switch.

Le Bouquet
de Montmartre €138

1 rue Durantin (18th)
🖥 www.paris-montmartre-hotel.com
✉ bouquet.montmartre@club-internet.fr
☎ +33 1 46 06 87 54   🖨 +33 1 46 06 09 09

*"A lively, characterful location" is the special strength of this
"tasteful" value-destination, not far from the Sacré-Coeur.*
/ **Rooms:** 36. **Details:** no Switch.

du Bourg Tibourg €200

19 rue du Bourg-Tibourg (4th)
🖥 www.hoteldubourgtibourg.com
✉ hotel.du.bourg.tibourg@wanadoo.fr
☎ +33 1 42 78 47 39   🖨 +33 1 40 29 07 00

*Costes' little sister is a small Marais townhouse recently made
over in a 'cosy' Moroccan-influenced style by leading designer
Jacques Garcia. Facilities are few – this is really just a superior
B&B – but you do get the feeling that you have your own little
place in the heart of one of the trendiest quarters of Paris. All-in-
all "good value for money."* / **Rooms:** 30. **Details:** meals unavailable: no
restaurant.

Le Bristol   €583

112 rue du Fauborg St Honoré (8th)
🖱 www.hotel-bristol.com   ✉ resa@hotel-bristol.com
☎ +33 1 53 43 43 25   🖨 +33 1 53 43 43 26

"Magnifique" – this "indulgent" and "classy" '20s legend, near the Elysée Palace, remains "the gold standard of hotels" for many reporters. At these sort of prices, expectations are of course very high, but "huge" rooms and the "delightful" garden are among the features which – for most reporters – make this a place which "lives up to its fantastic reputation". / **Rooms:** 175.
Details: no Switch.

Costes   €400

239 rue St-Honoré (1st)
☎ +33 1 42 44 50 00   🖨 +33 1 42 44 50 01

Paris's design-hotel par excellence – the "sexy and happening" flagship for the celebrated Costes brothers – excited more commentary from reporters than anywhere else in town. It was, however, deeply mixed. Fans praise the fabulous location (just off the Place Vendôme), the "indulgent" and "luxurious" décor, the "amazing" pool, and the "fantastic atmosphere in the restaurant and the bar". Doubters (about a third of those reporting) decry it as a "disco/restaurant-with-rooms", and complain of "dark" and "shoebox-sized" accommodation and "snooty" and "unhelpful" service – "unless being seen with the pop/media crowd is the main objective, the place is greatly overpriced". / **Rooms:** 83 (of which all non smoking and some family rooms). **Facilities:** indoor pool; gym; spa.
Details: no Switch.

Crillon   €480

10 pl. de la Concorde (8th)
🖱 www.crillon.com   ✉ crillon@crillon.paris.com
☎ +33 1 44 71 15 00   🖨 +33 1 44 71 15 02

"A great location, and worth the expense" – that's the majority view on this 'grand palais' on one of the world's greatest squares. Accordingly, its style ("white-tie waiters at breakfast", for instance) strikes some reporters as "frighteningly grand". The level of dissatisfaction, however, is higher than one would expect at these exalted price-levels – "some very small rooms" are a bugbear, and service strikes some as plain "sniffy". / **Rooms:** 147 (of which some non smoking and some family rooms). **Facilities:** gym; spa.

George V €670

31 av. George V (8th)
🖰 www.fourseasons.com
✉ reservation.paris@fourseasons.com
☎ +33 I 49 52 70 00 🖷 +33 I 49 52 70 I0

"The best grand hotel in Paris" (and, according to our survey, London and New York too) is hailed as "virtually faultless" by reporters, who say that for "grand international luxury" it can't be beaten. Praise is fulsome for the "opulently extravagant" recent refurbishment by the Four Seasons group which has restored this famed '20s institution in the heart of the swankiest part of the 8th arrondissement to its former glory. Its restaurant, Le Cinq, was recently awarded its third Michelin star. Even the flower arrangements – "the best in the world" – shock and awe.
/ **Rooms:** *245 (of which some non smoking and some family rooms).*
Facilities: *indoor pool; gym; spa.* **Details:** *no Switch.*

Grand Hommes €I68

I7 pl. du Pantheon (I7th)
🖰 www.hoteldesgrandshommes.com
✉ reservation@hoteldesgrandshommes.com
☎ +33 I 46 34 I9 60 🖷 +33 I 43 26 67 32

Tipped as "nice, quiet and romantic" – and offering "good rates", too – this "quaint" hotel is right by the Panthéon. If you can, "get a room with a balcony". / **Rooms:** *3I (of which some family rooms).*

Hilton €380

I8 av. de Suffren (I5th)
🖰 www.paris.hilton.com ✉ sales_paris@hilton.com
☎ +33 I 44 38 56 00 🖷 +33 I 44 38 56 0I

It undoubtedly has "great view of the Eiffel Tower", but – except for this obvious tourist-appeal – some find the location of this modern hotel on the Left Bank rather "inconvenient". "Kind" service, however, is a particular compensation. Note that Business Rooms offer much more space than 'Deluxe' ones, at relatively modest extra cost. / **Rooms:** *46I (of which some non smoking and some family rooms).*

L'Hôtel €272

I3 rue des Beaux Arts (6th)
🖰 www.l-hotel.com ✉ reservation@l-hotel.com
☎ +33 I 44 4I 99 00 🖷 +33 I 43 25 64 8I

'Calme et luxe au coeur de la Rive Gauche' – that's the motto of this "chic and comfortable" establishment, and most reporters find it amply justified. Rooms are named after famous folk (one of whom, Oscar Wilde, died on the premises), perhaps contributing to a minority view that the hotel's style is a touch "pretentious". The "great swimming pool in the cellar" – capacity, two – is a rare amenity in an hotel of this type. / **Rooms:** *20.* **Facilities:** *indoor pool; spa.* **Details:** *meals unavailable: Sun & Mon; no Switch; min age for children: I2.*

Hyatt Regency   €530   ☺☺

24 boulevard Malesherbes (8th)
🖰 www.paris.hyatt.com   ✉ madeleine@paris.hyatt.com
☎ +33 1 55 27 12 34   🖨 +33 1 55 27 12 35

This "luxurious", "small, discreet and modern" hotel attracts (as
you might hope in this price-bracket) little but bouquets from
reporters, with "a pretty lounge" and "gorgeous bathrooms"
singled out for praise. It has a "good location", too, near the
Madeleine and the shopping temptations of the rue du Faubourg
St-Honoré. / **Rooms:** 86 (of which 46 non smoking and 10 family rooms).
Facilities: gym; spa. **Details:** no Switch.

Jeu de Paume   €147   ☺

54 rue St-Louis-en-l'Ile (4th)
🖰 www.jeudepaumehotel.com
✉ info@jeudepaumehotel.com
☎ +33 1 43 26 14 18   🖨 +33 1 40 46 02 76

"A delightful hotel, though the rooms are very small". Reporters
find "lots of personality" in this "very romantic" establishment,
located in a 17th-century building originally created as a tennis
court. Its location, on the Ile St-Louis, is exceptionally quiet, too.
/ **Rooms:** 28 (of which 4 family rooms). **Facilities:** gym; spa. **Details:** closed 1 wk
mid-Aug; no Switch.

Lancaster   €438

7 rue de Berri (8th)

🖱 www.hotel-lancaster.fr   ✉ pippoana@hotel-lancaster.fr

☎ +33 I 40 76 40 00   📠 +33 I 40 76 40 00

*Good overall assessments – you'd hope for at these sorts of prices
– conceal some misgivings about this "lovely boutique hotel", just
north of the Champs-Elysées. A converted 19th-century
townhouse, it's undoubtedly "chic" and "convenient", but even
fans can find the accommodation a touch "variable" – "make
sure you get a room overlooking the courtyard" – and there is the
odd report of "upkeep not as good as you might expect".*
/ **Rooms:** *60 (of which some family rooms).* **Facilities:** *café/restaurant; gym; spa.*
Details: *no Switch.*

Libertel

🖱 www.libertel-hotels.com

*This "great chain" has many properties that make "an excellent
budget choice for a short break", and we include it as a safety net
for those (not infrequent) occasions when Paris is 'complet'. There
are in fact over 45 such hotels around the city, which trade under
the names Libertel ("tourist class"), as well as Libertel Tradition
and, for the best properties, Libertel Grande Tradition. They claim
that all their hotels 'offer you outstanding comfort, a warm and
cosy atmosphere and truly personalised hospitality and service' –
remarkably, reporters are unanimous in their praise and seem
broadly to agree. Check the website for details.*

Louvre   €311

I pl. André Malraux (1st)

🖱 www.hoteldulouvre.com

✉ hoteldulouvre@hoteldulouvre.com

☎ +33 I 44 58 38 38   📠 +33 I 44 58 38 01

*This grand-looking Concorde-group hotel – between the Palais
Royal and the eponymous gallery – has the benefit of being "in
the heart of tourist Paris". Perhaps not wholly coincidentally, the
rooms can be "tiny" (if "comfortable"), and "not cheap" for what
they are.* / **Rooms:** *177 (of which 70 non smoking and 30 family rooms).*
Facilities: *café/restaurant; gym.* **Details:** *no Switch; min age for children: 12.*

Lutetia   €380

45 boulevard Raspail (6th)
🖱 www.lutetia-paris.com   ✉ lutetia-paris@lutetia-paris.com
☎ +33 1 49 54 46 46   🖨 +33 1 49 54 46 00

"A long history" distinguishes this palatial Left Bank building of
1907, and current standards at this Concorde Hotels
establishment do nothing to let it down. Room service "on silver
platters", bathrooms which offer "total luxury" and an "amazing"
bar are among the features which win enthusiastic reports
(though, considering the place's apparent attractions, they are
surprisingly few). / **Rooms:** 230 (of which 30 non smoking and 23 family
rooms). **Facilities:** café/restaurant; gym.

Meurice   €720

228 rue de Rivoli (1st)
🖱 www.meuricehotel.com
✉ reservations@meuricehotel.com
☎ +33 1 44 58 10 10   🖨 +33 1 44 58 10 15

"Beautiful" and "elegant" (after a major renovation in recent
times), this "very French" palace benefits from "a great location
by the Tuilleries". Owned by the Sultan of Brunei, the hotel is – on
almost all reports – "exquisite and refined". The only real
reservation is that – with a dining room which takes its theme
from Versailles, for example – it can seem "a little OTT".
/ **Rooms:** 160 (of which some non smoking and some family rooms).
Facilities: gym; spa.

Molière   €145

21 rue Molière (1st)
🖥 www.hotels-unis.com   ✉ moliere@worldnet.fr
☎ +33 1 42 96 22 01   🖷 +33 1 42 60 48 68

"A charming, friendly small hotel beautifully situated near the Palais Royal" – "not trendy, but quiet" and offering "discreet service" and "good rooms". / Rooms: 32 (of which some non smoking). **Details:** *meals unavailable: L, D; no Switch.*

Monna Lisa   €235

97 rue de la Boetie (8th)
🖥 www.hotelmonnalisa.com
✉ contact@hotelmonnalisa.com
☎ +33 1 56 43 38 38   🖷 +33 1 45 62 39 90

"Trendy but not too expensive" (by the standards of this part of town), this "small style-hotel" – where each room comes decorated with an enlarged section of La Giocanda – is universally praised by reporters. Rooms, if "small", are "smart and comfortable", and the Italian owners are "charming". Caffè Ristretto, the restaurant, attracts similarly high praise. / Rooms: 22 (of which some non smoking and some family rooms). **Details:** *no Switch.*

Napoléon   €260

40 av. de Friedland (8th)
🖥 www.hotelnapoleonparis.com
✉ napoleon@hotenapoleonparis.com
☎ +33 1 56 68 43 21   🖷 +33 1 47 66 82 33

The decoration can seem a bit "stuffy" – in the style the place's name suggests – but the few who comment speak only well of the "large bedrooms" and "pleasant staff" at this "beautiful" establishment, just a couple of minutes' walk from the Etoile. / Rooms: 101 (of which some non smoking and some family rooms). **Details:** *meals unavailable: D; no Switch.*

du Nord   €68

37 rue de St-Quentin (10th)
🖥 www.nordhotel.com   ✉ nordhotel@wanadoo.fr
☎ +33 1 45 26 43 40   🖷 +33 1 42 82 90 23

"A good-value hotel across the road from the Gare du Nord" – for Eurostar travellers, its attractions are self-evident. / Rooms: 46 (of which 12 non smoking and 12 family rooms). **Details:** *no Switch.*

Notre Dame   €100   🅃

1 quai St-Michel (5th)
🖥 www.paris-hotel-notredame.com
✉ hotel.lenotredame@libertysurf.fr
☎ +33 1 43 54 20 43   🖷 +33 1 43 26 61 75

"Looking like a Paris hotel should look", this "simple" but "charming" establishment lives up to its image, and is tipped, not least, for its "splendid views of the Seine and Notre Dame". / Rooms: 26 (of which 3 family rooms). **Details:** *meals unavailable: no restaurant; no Switch.*

Pavillon de la Reine €365

28 pl. des Vosges (3rd)
🖰 www.pavillon-de-la-reine.com
✉ contact@pavillon-de-la-reine.com
☎ +33 1 40 29 19 19   🖷 +33 1 40 29 19 20

"It has the best location in Paris", say fans of this "romantic" establishment on the "stunning" place des Vosges. Some rooms are "tiny", but reporters find consolation in the "gorgeous" lounge (with honesty-bar) and a "beautiful" courtyard. / Rooms: 55.
Details: no Switch.

Pergolese €230

3 rue Pergolese (16th)
🖰 www.hotelpergolese.com   ✉ hotel@pergolese.com
☎ +33 1 53 64 04 04   🖷 +33 1 53 64 04 40

"For what it is", this "chic but basic hotel", near the Porte Maillot, is "very good". You get "good furniture and bathrooms, but space is limited". / Rooms: 40 (of which 7 non smoking and 10 family rooms).
Details: no Switch.

Plaza Athénée €614

25 av. Montaigne (8th)
🖰 www.plaza-athenee-paris.com
✉ reservation@plaza-athenee-paris.com
☎ +33 1 53 67 66 65   🖷 +33 1 53 67 66 61

*This is "one of the last great hotels of the world", say some reporters, who particularly praise the "impeccable" service at this great Dorchester Group establishment in the heart of the 8th arrondissement. Its ratings are high, but the relatively limited feedback it incites tends to support the reporter who finds it "luxurious, but not quite as outstanding as the George V", nearby.
/ Rooms: 188 (of which some non smoking and some family rooms).*
Facilities: café/restaurant; gym. **Details:** no Switch.

Prince de Galles   €370

33 av. Georges V (8th)
🖰 www.luxurycollection.com
✉ hotel_prince_de_galles@sheraton.com
☎ +33 1 53 23 77 77   🖷 +33 1 53 23 78 78

This "understated" Art Deco palais de luxe "has retained its style and Gallic elegance", and its restaurant (Le Jardin) is especially praised by a number of reporters as "very good, and (almost) a bargain" – perhaps that's because it lacks the Michelin star which is practically de rigueur in this part of town! Overall, however, rather middle-of-the-road ratings support those who think that this Starwood property "could be better". / **Rooms:** 168 (of which 70 non smoking and some family rooms). **Facilities:** café/restaurant; gym.

Raphael   €438

🙂🙂

17 av. Kléber (16th)
🖰 www.raphael-hotel.com
✉ reservation@raphael-hotel.com
☎ +33 1 53 64 32 00   🖷 +33 1 53 64 32 01

"A gem amongst Parisian hotels, utterly charming and impeccably discreet" – reporters speak only in terms of rapture about this "exquisite" establishment near the Etoile, where the décor is "like an elegant private club, with beautiful antique furniture and works of art", and where staff are "superb". / **Rooms:** 85 (of which some non smoking and some family rooms). **Facilities:** spa. **Details:** no Switch.

Relais Christine   €375

3 rue Christine (6th)
🖰 www.relais-christine.com
✉ contact@relais-christine.com
☎ +33 1 40 51 60 80   🖷 +33 1 40 51 60 81

As you might expect, this hotel in an "ancient monastery" on "a quiet side-street", just off St Germain" strikes some as "quite staid". Fortunately, it's also "extremely charming", and has a "great courtyard setting" (with "a small garden!"). / **Rooms:** 51 (of which 8 family rooms). **Facilities:** gym; spa. **Details:** meals unavailable: no restaurant; no Switch.

Relais St Germain   €275

9 carrefour de l'Odéon (6th)

🖰 www.hotel-rsg.com

☎ +33 1 43 29 12 05   🖷 +33 1 46 33 45 30

"Tucked in behind the church of St Sulpice", in the heart of the Left Bank, this "very pleasant" small hotel offers "a peaceful oasis", and makes "a great base for exploring Paris". / **Rooms:** 22 (of which some family rooms). **Details:** no Switch.

Renaissance   €239

60 Jardin de Valmy, La Défense

🖰 www.renaissancehotels.com

✉ rhi.parld.sales.mgr@renaissancehotels.com

☎ +33 1 41 97 50 50   🖷 +33 1 41 97 51 51

A reporter who found himself staying in this modern hotel by the Grande Arche de la Défense "by accident" found himself favourably impressed, and another confirms that its "large" rooms come at "good prices". / **Rooms:** 327 (of which some non smoking and some family rooms). **Facilities:** indoor pool; outdoor pool; gym; spa. **Details:** no Switch.

Ritz   €590

15 pl. Vendôme (1st)

🖰 www.ritzparis.com   ✉ resa@ritzparis.com

☎ +33 1 43 16 30 30   🖷 +33 1 43 16 31 78

Mohamed al Fayed's "opulent" palace-hotel enjoys a superb location in the Place Vendôme. Most (if not quite all) reporters find that — with its "er, Ritzy" charm, and its extensive leisure facilities (including squash courts and a cookery school) — it "lives up to its reputation". / **Rooms:** 162. **Facilities:** café/restaurant; indoor pool; gym; spa. **Details:** no Switch.

Rond Point des
Champs Elysees   €130

10 rue de Ponthieu (8th)

🖰 www.hotelrondpoint.com

☎ +33 1 53 89 14 14   🖷 +33 1 45 63 19 75

This pleasant tourist hotel is judged "a reliable standby", and it has "a great location, just off the Champs-Elysées". / **Rooms:** 41 (of which some non smoking and some family rooms). **Details:** meals unavailable: no restaurant; no Switch.

Royal Monceau €476

37 av. Hoche (8th)
🖰 www.royalmonceau.com
✉ royalmonceau@jetmultimedia.fr
☎ +33 1 42 99 88 00   📠 +33 1 42 99 89 90

Having quite a 'name', this '20s palace inspired a lot of feedback from reporters, but – considering the prices – it was far too mixed to make it a safe recommendation. Some do still consider it a "classic", but for others it's "a grand hotel needing a serious revamp", with the rooms generally identified as the weakest link. / **Rooms:** 201 *(of which some non smoking and some family rooms).* **Facilities:** *indoor pool; gym.* **Details:** *no Switch.*

Scribe €430

1 rue Scribe (9th)
🖰 www.sofitel.com   ✉ hotelscribe@wanadoo.fr
☎ +33 1 44 71 24 24   📠 +33 1 42 65 39 97

This "grand hotel near the (old) Opéra" maintains its place in the affections of some reporters (especially for its "great coffee shop"). "Rooms differ widely", though ("even within the same category"). / **Rooms:** 217 *(of which some non smoking and some family rooms).* **Details:** *no Switch.*

Sofitel

🖰 www.sofitel.com
As you'd expect, the modern properties which bear this well-known Accor-group brand can seem rather "anonymous". Objectively, though, the various outlets generate impressively consistent reports, and are well worth considering if more interesting options are booked up – check the website for details.

Thérèse €125

5-7 rue Thérèse (1st)
🖰 www.hoteltherese.com   ✉ hoteltherese@wanadoo.fr
☎ +33 1 42 96 10 01   📠 +33 1 42 96 15 22

"Personal service", "reasonable prices" and "modern" (and quite artistic) décor commend this recently-refurbished small hotel, near the Palais Royal, to most reporters. Cheaper rooms are modest in scale. / **Rooms:** 43 *(of which all non smoking).* **Details:** *no Switch.*

La Trémoille   €339

14 rue de la Trémoille (8th)
⌂ www.hotel-tremoille.com
✉ reservation@hotel-tremoille.com
☎ +33 1 56 52 14 00   🖶 +33 1 40 70 01 08

"A good position in the Golden Triangle" (the swanky heart of the
8th arrondissement) *is just one of the strengths of this* *"quiet"*
and *"classy"* *establishment, voted a* *"good-value destination in a
top-end part of town"*. *Recently refurbished by the same owners
as Leeds's 42 The Calls and Edinburgh's Scotsman, it's quite a
"funky and refreshing venue"* (at least by local standards). *The
restaurant, Senso, is run by Monsieur Conran.* / **Rooms:** 93 (of which
some family rooms).

Verneuil   €140   ☺☺

8 rue de Verneuil (7th)
⌂ www.hotelverneuil.com   ✉ hotelverneuil@wanadoo.fr
☎ +33 1 42 60 82 14   🖶 +33 1 42 61 40 38

*This "small" and "intimate" townhouse "gem" ("don't tell
anyone") is praised by all reporters for its "character and views".
It's also the only recommendation which cropped up in the thinly
commented-on* (grandly residential) *7th arrondissement, near the
Musée d'Orsay.* / **Rooms:** 26. **Details:** meals unavailable: no restaurant; no
Switch.

de Vigny €395

9-11 rue Balzac (8th)
🖥 www.hoteldevigny.com
✉ reservation@hoteldevigny.com
☎ +33 1 42 99 80 80   🖨 +33 1 42 99 80 40

"Just off the Champs-Elysées", this "charming boutique establishment" – oddly, the only Relais & Château hotel in the City of Light – offers "a rare, warm and welcoming Parisian experience". The 'style anglais' rooms (Nina Campbell) are "beautifully furnished", too. / **Rooms:** 37 (of which 11 family rooms). **Details:** no Switch.

La Villa Maillot €360

143 av. de Malakoff (16th)
🖥 www.lavillamaillot.fr   ✉ resa@lavillamaillot.fr
☎ +33 1 53 64 52 52   🖨 +33 1 45 00 60 61

"Beautiful rooms" and "friendly" service are among the highlights at this architecturally odd building (with Art Deco flourishes), which comes complete with a small courtyard. It's in the fashionable 16th arrondissement, but, given proximity to the Porte Maillot, it's location is arguably no more than "OK". / **Rooms:** 42 (of which some non smoking and some family rooms). **Facilities:** spa. **Details:** meals unavailable: no restaurant; no Switch.

Villa Royale €210

2 rue Duperré (18th)
✉ royale@leshotelsdeparis.com
☎ +33 1 55 31 78 78   🖨 +33 1 55 31 78 70

"Amazing décor" – think 'boudoir', writ large – wins a tip for this somewhat bizarre establishment, located among the peep shows of the Pigalle. / **Rooms:** 31 (of which some non smoking).

ALPHABETICAL INDEX

ALPHABETICAL INDEX

sign up for our next survey at www.hardens.com   348

ALPHABETICAL INDEX